THE WORLD OF BOB DYLAN

Bob Dylan has helped transform music, literature, pop culture, and even politics. *The World of Bob Dylan* chronicles a lifetime of creative invention that has made a global impact. Leading rock and pop critics and music scholars address themes and topics central to Dylan's life and work: the Blues, his religious faith, Civil Rights, gender, race, and American and World literature. Incorporating a rich array of new archival material from never-before-accessed archives, *The World of Bob Dylan* offers a comprehensive, uniquely informed, and wholly fresh account of the songwriter, artist, filmmaker, and Nobel Laureate, whose unique voice has permanently reshaped our cultural landscape.

SEAN LATHAM is the Pauline McFarlin Walter Professor of English at the University of Tulsa where he serves as director of the Institute for Bob Dylan Studies.

THE WORLD OF BOB DYLAN

EDITED BY

SEAN LATHAM

CAMBRIDGE
UNIVERSITY PRESS

CAMBRIDGE
UNIVERSITY PRESS

University Printing House, Cambridge CB2 8BS, United Kingdom

One Liberty Plaza, 20th Floor, New York, NY 10006, USA

477 Williamstown Road, Port Melbourne, VIC 3207, Australia

314–321, 3rd Floor, Plot 3, Splendor Forum, Jasola District Centre, New Delhi – 110025, India

79 Anson Road, #06–04/06, Singapore 079906

Cambridge University Press is part of the University of Cambridge.

It furthers the University's mission by disseminating knowledge in the pursuit of education, learning, and research at the highest international levels of excellence.

www.cambridge.org
Information on this title: www.cambridge.org/9781108499514
DOI: 10.1017/9781108583398

© Cambridge University Press 2021

First published 2021

Printed in the United Kingdom by TJ Books Limited, Padstow Cornwall

A catalogue record for this publication is available from the British Library.

ISBN 978-1-108-49951-4 Hardback

Cambridge University Press has no responsibility for the persistence or accuracy of URLs for external or third-party internet websites referred to in this publication and does not guarantee that any content on such websites is, or will remain, accurate or appropriate.

Contents

Contributors

STEVEN BELLETTO is Professor of English at Lafayette College. He is author of *The Beats: A Literary History* (2020) and *No Accident, Comrade: Chance and Design in Cold War American Narratives* (2012). He is also editor of *American Literature in Transition, 1950–1960* (2018), *The Cambridge Companion to the Beats* (2017), and co-editor of *Neocolonial Fictions of the Global Cold War* (2019), and *American Literature and Culture in an Age of Cold War: A Critical Reassessment* (2012). He is an editor of the journal *Contemporary Literature*.

DAMIAN A. CARPENTER is the author of *Lead Belly, Woody Guthrie, Bob Dylan and American Folk Outlaw Performance* (2017). Some of his other critical and creative Dylan-related publications appear in *The Life, Music and Thought of Woody Guthrie: A Critical Appraisal* (2011), *Visiting Bob: Poems Inspired by the Life and Music of Bob Dylan* (2018), and *Polyvocal Bob Dylan: Music, Performance, Literature* (2019).

RONALD D. COHEN is Emeritus Professor of History at Indiana University Northwest. He is the author or co-author/co-editor of numerous folk music books, including *Rainbow Quest* (2002), *Woody Guthrie: Writing America's Songs* (2012), *Roots of the Revival* (2014), *Folk City: New York and the American Folk Music Revival* (2015), *Depression Folk* (2016), and *Selling Folk Music: An Illustrated History* (2018).

MARK A. DAVIDSON is Archives Director of the American Song Archives in Tulsa, Oklahoma, which includes The Bob Dylan Archive® and the Woody Guthrie Archive, as well as numerous smaller collections. Mark earned his PhD in musicology from UC Santa Cruz in 2015. His dissertation, "Recording the Nation: Folk Music and the Government in Roosevelt's New Deal, 1936–1941" focused on government-sponsored folk music collecting during the Great Depression. Mark earned his MSIS in information studies at UT Austin in 2014, with a focus on academic librarianship, music archiving, and audio preservation. He has worked for the *Journal of the Society for American Music* since 2008, and is currently the journal's editorial associate.

KEVIN DETTMAR is W.M. Keck Professor of English and Director of the Humanities Studio at Pomona College. He is the editor of *The Cambridge Companion to Bob Dylan*; his cultural criticism has appeared in the *New Yorker, Atlantic, New York Times, Los Angeles Times, Chronicle of Higher Education*, and other publications.

FLORENCE DORE is Professor of American literature at the University of North Carolina, Chapel Hill and a founding member of the board at the TU Institute for Bob Dylan Studies. She has written on the blues, censorship, and literary formalism, and her book *Novel Sounds: Southern Fiction in the Age of Rock and Roll* was published by Columbia University Press in 2018. Florence is also a rock musician finishing her second album. Her first release, *Perfect City* was signed to Slewfoot Records in 2001, and her song "Christmas" was recorded by the Posies for the 1994 Geffen release *Just Say Noel.*

LEIGH H. EDWARDS is Professor of English at Florida State University. She is the author of *Dolly Parton, Gender, and Country Music* (2018), *Johnny Cash and the Paradox of American Identity* (2009), and *The Triumph of Reality TV: The Revolution in American Television* (2013). She focuses on intersections of gender and race in popular music, television, and new media. Her work has appeared in *Feminist Media Studies, The Journal of Popular Culture, Journal of Popular Television, Film & History, Narrative, FLOW*, and the *Journal of Popular Music Studies*. She is on the advisory board of the Institute for Bob Dylan Studies.

JAMES F. ENGLISH is the John Welsh Centennial Professor of English at the University of Pennsylvania, where he is also founding faculty director of the Price Lab for Digital Humanities. He has published books on modernist and contemporary British literature, the history and future of the discipline of literary studies, and the sociology of literary and cultural value. *The Economy of Prestige*, a study of cultural prizes and awards, was named Best Academic Book of 2005 by *New York* magazine. Current projects include a history of rating and ranking systems in literature and the arts, and a volume of essays on literature and human flourishing, co-edited with Heather Love.

RAPHAEL FALCO is Professor of English at the University of Maryland, Baltimore County, where he held the 2012–2013 Lipitz Professorship of the Arts, Humanities, and Social Sciences. He is a co-editor of the *Dylan Review* and Book Review Editor of *Soundings: An Interdisciplinary Journal*. Among his recent books are *Cultural Genealogy and Early Modern Myth* (2016) and *Charisma and Myth* (2010). His articles have appeared in a range of journals including *Diacritics, English Literary Renaissance, Modern Philology, Shakespeare Studies, Criticism*, and *Max Weber Studies*, and he is the author of the forthcoming book *Dylan and Imitation: Originality on Trial*.

WILL KAUFMAN is Professor of American Literature and Culture at the University of Central Lancashire, England. He is the author of *The Civil War in American Culture* (2006), *American Culture in the 1970s* (2009), *Woody Guthrie, American Radical* (2011), *Woody Guthrie's Modern World Blues* (2017), and *Mapping Woody Guthrie* (2019). He is co-author, with Ronald D. Cohen, of *Singing for Peace: Antiwar Songs in American History* (2015).

MICHAEL J. KRAMER is an Assistant Professor in the Department of History at SUNY Brockport. He is the author of *The Republic of Rock: Music and Citizenship in the Sixties Counterculture* (2013) and is at work on a book, *This Machine Kills Fascists*, about technology and tradition in the US folk music movement as well as a digital public history project about the Berkeley Folk Music Festival and folk music on the West Coast (bfmf. net). He writes about the arts, culture, history, politics, and other topics for the *New York Times, Washington Post, Salon*, and on his blog, *Culture Rover* (culturerover.net).

SEAN LATHAM is the Pauline McFarlin Walter Professor of English and Comparative Literature at the University of Tulsa where he serves as Director of the Institute for Bob Dylan Studies. He is the author or editor of ten books on modern literature and culture including *Am I a Snob?* (2003), *The Art of Scandal* (2009), and (with Gayle Rogers) *Modernism: Evolution of an Idea* (2015).

ANDREW MCCARRON is a teacher and writer born and raised in the Hudson River Valley. He holds a PhD in psychology and chairs the Religion, Philosophy & Ethics Department at Trinity School in Manhattan. His books include *Mysterium*, a poetry collection (2011), *Three New York Poets: Charles North, Tony Towle & Paul Violi*, a collection of critical biographies (2016), *Light Come Shining: The Transformations of Bob Dylan*, a study of the Nobel Laureate's religious identities (2017), and *The Ballad of Sara and Thor: A Novella* (2017). In addition to teaching and writing, Andrew also serves on the ethics committee at New York Presbyterian Hospital in Manhattan.

ANNE-MARIE MAI is Professor of Literature at University of Southern Denmark, a member of the Danish Academy, and the winner of the Søren Gyldendal Literature Prize. Her research areas include literary historiography, literary archives, the history of Nordic literature, the European and American Beat generation, Bob Dylan studies, and narrative medicine. She is the author of *Bob Dylan. The Poet* (2018) and *Danish Literature of the 20th and Early 21st Century* (2016), and editor of *New Approaches to Bob Dylan* (2020).

GREIL MARCUS is the author of *The Old Weird America: The World of Bob Dylan's Basement Tapes* (1997, 2011), *Like a Rolling Stone* (2005, and adapted theatrically by the Comédie Française in 2017), and *Bob Dylan by Greil Marcus* (2010). With Werner Sollors he is the editor of *A New Literary History of America* (2009). He was born in San Francisco and lives in Oakland. His copy of *The Freewheelin' Bob Dylan*, which he bought at the Stanford Shopping Center in 1963, has the wrong songs on it.

ANDREW MUIR is a freelance writer and teacher of English Literature and Language. Current commitments include teaching at the Leys School, Cambridge, UK and delivering a variety of Shakespeare talks at conferences and conventions and on literature and drama courses. His publications include two books on Bob Dylan as a live performer, *Razor's Edge* (2001) and *One More Night* (21013), plus a study of Dylan's lyrics, *Troubadour* (2003), and an examination of historical and contemporary outdoor Shakespeare performances, *Shakespeare in Cambridge* (2015). His latest book came out in 2019 and was entitled *Bob Dylan and William Shakespeare: The True Performing of It*.

KEITH NEGUS is Professor of Musicology at Goldsmiths, University of London. He entered higher education after a few years playing keyboards and guitar in a range of bands. He completed a PhD study of the music industry, and taught at the universities of Leicester and Puerto Rico before joining Goldsmiths. He is the author of *Producing Pop* (1992), *Music Genres and Corporate Cultures* (1999), and *Bob Dylan* (2008) and was a member of the team that researched and wrote the influential *Doing Cultural Studies: The Story of the Sony Walkman* (1997). He collaborated with Pete Astor (The Loft, Weather Prophets) in writing and producing "Love Repeats"/ "Alpha November" (2015) as the Fairlight Myth.

LISA O'NEILL-SANDERS is Professor and Chair of Philosophy at Saint Peter's University where she regularly teaches a course on Bob Dylan and philosophy. She has published numerous articles on Dylan and lectures publicly on the philosophical intersections in Dylan's art. She is the founding editor of the *Dylan Review* (www.dylanreview.org), a scholarly journal devoted to investigating the works of Bob Dylan.

ANN POWERS is NPR Music's critic and correspondent. Her books include *Good Booty: Love and Sex, Black and White, Body and Soul in American Music* (2017), *Weird Like Us: My Bohemian America* (2000), and (with the artist) Tori Amos: *Piece by Piece* (2005). She is the co-editor, with Evelyn McDonnell, of *Rock She Wrote: Women Write about Rock, Rap, and Pop* (1995), the first published anthology of women music writers. In 2017 she founded Turning the Tables, an ongoing NPR initiative re-centering the popular music canon on marginalized, underestimated, and forgotten voices. She lives in Nashville with her family.

DEVON POWERS is Associate Professor of Advertising at Temple University. She is the author of *On Trend: The Business of Forecasting the Future* (2019), *Writing the Record: The* Village Voice *and the Birth of Rock Criticism* (2013), and co-editor of *Blowing Up the Brand: Critical Perspectives on Promotional Culture* (2010). Her research explores historical and contemporary consumer culture and the dynamics of cultural intermediation, circulation, and promotion. Her work has appeared in *Journal of Consumer Culture, New Media & Society,* and *Critical Studies in Media and Communication,* among other publications.

KIM RUEHL is a writer, editor, and folk music advocate based in Asheville, North Carolina. She was an editor of *No Depression* – the roots music journal – for nearly a decade, bringing it back to print in 2015 and ending her run there as editor-in-chief. Her writing about American folk and roots music has also been published by NPR Music, *Billboard,* and *Seattle Weekly,* and she is the author of *A Singing Army: Zilphia Horton and the Highlander Folk School* (2021).

DAVID R. SHUMWAY is Professor of English, and Literary and Cultural Studies, and is the founding Director of the Humanities Center at Carnegie Mellon University. He is also founder and co-director of the Pittsburgh Humanities Festival. His most recent book is *Rock Star: The Making of Musical Icons from Elvis to Springsteen* (2014). He has published numerous articles on popular music, including contributions to *The Cambridge Companion to Bob Dylan* and *The Cambridge Companion to the Singer-*

Songwriter. Some of his other books include *Michel Foucault* (1989), *Modern Love: Romance, Intimacy, and the Marriage Crisis* (2003), and *John Sayles* (2012).

LARRY STARR is Professor Emeritus of American Music Studies at the University of Washington, Seattle. He remains active as a speaker for the Seattle Symphony and local educational organizations. He is the author of books on American composers Charles Ives, Aaron Copland, and George Gershwin, and is co-author (with Christopher Waterman) of the textbook *American Popular Music: From Minstrelsy to MP3*, a sixth edition of which is forthcoming. He is now completing work on a new book, *Listening to Bob Dylan*.

GAYLE WALD is Professor of American Studies at George Washington University. She is author of *Shout, Sister, Shout! The Untold Story of Rock-and-Roll Trailblazer Sister Rosetta Tharpe* (2007), as well as *It's Been Beautiful: Soul! and Black Power TV* (2015), and *Crossing the Line: Racial Passing in U.S. Literature and Culture* (2000). Her piece "Women Do Dylan: The Aesthetics and Politics of Dylan Covers," co-authored with Daphne Brooks, appears in the collection *Highway 61 Revisited: Bob Dylan's Road from Minnesota to the World* (2009). Her current project is centered on the renowned children's musician and educator Ella Jenkins.

IRA WELLS is Academic Programs Director at Victoria College in the University of Toronto. His writing has appeared in *Popular Music and Society*, *American Quarterly*, *The Guardian*, *New Republic*, *Los Angeles Review of Books*, and elsewhere. He is currently at work on a biography of the film director Norman Jewison.

ELLIOT R. WOLFSON is a Fellow of the American Academy of Arts and Sciences, the American Society for the Study of Religion, and the American Academy of Jewish Research, and is the Marsha and Jay Glazer Endowed Chair in Jewish Studies and Distinguished Professor of Religion at University of California, Santa Barbara. He is the author of several award-winning monographs and hundreds of scholarly essays. His most recent publications include *The Duplicity of Philosophy's Shadow: Heidegger, Nazism and the Jewish Other* (2018) and *Heidegger and Kabbalah: Hidden Gnosis and the Path of Poiesis* (2019). He is also a poet and a painter.

Acknowledgments

This book is the first published project to emerge from the Institute for Bob Dylan Studies at the University of Tulsa, a broadly interdisciplinary organization dedicated to exploring the work, context, and legacy of the Nobel-winning songwriter. For their support in launching this initiative, we are deeply grateful to the University of Tulsa, the Bob Dylan Archive®, the Bob Dylan Center, the George Kaiser Family Foundation, Neil and Sharon Zimmerman, and the Chapman Trusts. Thanks to their ongoing support, we anticipate this being only the first of many such scholarly projects that will emerge from the Institute in the coming years.

We also want to thank Layne Farmen, Annie Paige, and Nathan Blue, the graduate student assistants at the Institute who did everything from organizing contact lists to proofing pages, tracking sources, compiling the bibliography, and preparing the index. Their patient efforts have made this book stronger, tighter, and better. We also owe a real debt to the Institute's assistant director, Tara Aveilhe, who both helped with the book and took on other tasks so that we could keep on keepin' on with our editorial work. And finally, we want to thank Ray Ryan at Cambridge University Press, a dedicated Dylanologist himself who helped conceive this sprawling project, gave us its title, and patiently supported us as it took shape.

Introduction: Time to Say Goodbye Again

Sean Latham

Is there any writer or performer more haunting – and more haunted – than Bob Dylan? We recognize his songs, his vision, his inventiveness, his poetry, and especially his distinctive voice nearly everywhere: in music and film, popular culture and politics, global protest movements and intimate moments of self-reflection. As he now turns eighty, it's a shock to realize that, for most us, Dylan has always been there, singing, touring, laughing, snarling, and sometimes even hawking whiskey and underwear. Like the members of the Nobel committee that awarded him the world's most important cultural prize, we know he is a vastly influential artist. But which Dylan is it? The folk-singing activist who shared the stage with Dr. King at the March on Washington? The rocker in Ray Bans and a leather jacket who faced down hostile crowds by ordering his band to "play it fucking loud?" Is it the country boy who went to Nashville and befriended Johnny Cash? Or the Beat-inspired hipster who took to the road with a ramshackle medicine show? The Christian convert? The brilliant curator of folk and blues? The Sinatra-inspired crooner? Or the weary old man who's "standin' in the doorway cryin'?"

Just as we grapple with these many Dylans, so too we can see him as an artist who built a career around wrestling with strong spirits from the past. When he reached New York City in 1961, he was already a young man possessed: walking, talking, and singing like Woody Guthrie – a revenant from another world. He had even half-invented a fake history for himself by lifting bits and pieces from the pages of *Bound for Glory*, Guthrie's semi-fictional account of his life in the Dust Bowl. Not long after Dylan's arrival, however, it became clear that this was not some youthful journey to freedom, but an Odyssean trip into the underworld. When he passed through the iron gates of Greystone Psychiatric Hospital to seek out his idol, Dylan instead discovered a frail man suffering Huntington's chorea who was too palsied to talk or sing. The young man later claimed there had been some spark of recognition, but if so, it would have been hard to discern and Dylan was haunted enough by what he had seen to try to exorcise this ghost. His first original composition, "Song to Woody" (1962), after all, concludes with desperate hope that he might escape such a world and such a fate – that he would be spared this kind of "hard travelin'."

That song helped lay Woody to rest in Dylan's imagination – and thus free him from the often icy grip of the folk music world that clutched at him throughout the early 1960s. He instead set out to explore and then invent the larger, richer, and stranger world this volume seeks to describe. The twenty-seven essays gathered here each offer a different way of understanding the depth, complexity, and legacy of Dylan's music, while at the same time setting out an entirely new agenda for writing, research, and invention. Although written by experts and scholars, they are designed to be accessible both to long-time fans and those who are curious about how and why this musician has become such a singular figure. The chapters are simply titled and concisely written so that readers can make their way through the book with only their own curiosity as a guide, jumping perhaps from rock music, to the counterculture, to the Nobel Prize. But the book can also be read in order as it moves outward from Dylan's life then into his music, influence, fame, and legacy. The first section is largely biographical and aims to provide a general introduction to a remarkable story that leads from a small town in Minnesota through New York and out into the world. This is followed by a series of chapters that each look closely at the many different genres of music from which Dylan drew inspiration and which his own work helped to reshape. As the Nobel Prize committee realized, however, Dylan is far more than a musician and his lyrics are now part of a vast historical and cultural web that stretches into the deep past and around the world. The authors in Part III thus offer some sense of how Dylan's work intersects with literature, theatre, religion, and the visual arts, while those in Part IV look at the extraordinary way his art has shaped our politics and even our idea of justice. The book then ends with a series of chapters that step back to consider Dylan's legacy, including a closing piece by the director of the Bob Dylan Archive®.

This book is occasioned, in part, by the extraordinary riches of those archives. Purchased by the George Kaiser Family Foundation and resting now in Tulsa, Oklahoma alongside the lifetime works of Woody Guthrie, the Dylan collection contains some 100,000 objects, including notebooks, session tapes, photographs, letters, and page after page after page of lyrics. They spill out everywhere: some neatly typed and others hastily scrawled on advertisements or worked out in tiny handwriting on pocket notebooks. On these pages, we see evidence of a restlessly creative mind, one deeply engaged with all the complexity and confusion of being human in a messy, ever-changing world.

One of the things that makes Dylan's work so extraordinary, in fact, is precisely our inability to slot it neatly into categories, genres, or cultural histories. In his songs, the civil rights movement can somehow cross with the work of obscure Confederate poets, while the electric energy of rock melds with the plaintive honesty of folk and the smooth sophistication of the American Songbook. The world of Bob Dylan is defined by such fault lines. It is an art of thresholds and doorways, of arrivals and departures, full of restless farewells and the fear that he might stay just a day too long. There always seems to be another world that calls to him, tugging him Gatsby-like into the past or propelling him into a future the rest of us didn't quite see coming.

In "Song to Woody," Dylan learned to live with the past so that it might possess but never overpower him. He then built an astonishing career around a relentless series of similar farewells: first to Guthrie, then to his folk audience on a steamy Newport evening, to rock fans in a Nashville studio, to his devout Christian believers with an album called *Infidels* (1983), and – more recently – to the very idea of himself as a singer-songwriter in five long LPs packed with crooning covers. Again and again, Dylan uses his albums to imagine and even enact the end of one musical world in order to clear the way for another. Some of his most astonishing albums – *Highway 61 Revisited* (1965), *John Wesley Harding* (1967), *Blood on the Tracks* (1975), "*Love and Theft*" (2001) – might even be seen as murder ballads: attempts to kill off a public persona that had become burdensome, even dangerous. Such deaths, however, create entire musical and imaginative worlds that we critics, musicians, scholars, and fans continue to explore. Meanwhile, Dylan himself slips away, refusing once again to be entombed in vinyl.

In order to introduce this volume, I want to compare two of his most powerful farewells as a way of demonstrating his ability to both make and shatter imaginative worlds. The first is his infamous envoi to the folk world, which we can date not to that distant Newport evening when he plugged in his sunburst Stratocaster, but instead to "Restless Farewell" – the song and poem that he hurriedly added to *Times They Are A-Changin'* in 1963. The second is one of his more recent gestures of farewell: the 14-minute epic recounting of the *Titanic* disaster that appeared in 2012 on *Tempest*. Although he has disavowed any allusion to Shakespeare in the album's title, it's impossible not to hear the voice of the old wizard now exhausted by decades of "rough magic."[1]

The first of these farewells is now an integral part of Dylan's myth. In November 1963, just on the eve of his Carnegie Hall concert, *Newsweek* published a two-column note buried in its arts and culture section titled "I Am My Words." Dylan, his manager, and his PR team all expected this to be a major profile, on par with the recent *Time* profile of Joan Baez that had occupied the cover, a photo spread, and a dozen pages in the magazine. Instead, it was a short exposé that deftly revealed the truth about Dylan's past: that he was a middle-class kid from Hibbing and not a latter-day hobo poet. More troublingly, it wrongly suggested that his landmark hit, "Blowin' in the Wind," had been cribbed from a kid in New Jersey. Dylan was furious and the article became a kind of wound – one that still ached, as we'll see, some fifty years later. At the time, an angry Dylan first refused to talk to the press before beginning what became a lifelong attack on every erstwhile journalist or interviewer who tried to get a quote from him or gain some insight into his music.

Shortly after the Carnegie Hall concert, he returned to Columbia's New York studios and added an additional track titled "Restless Farewell" to an album that otherwise contained his most politically activist songs – the kind of music that led Pete Seeger to champion his work and that still makes critics and historians alike insist (despite Dylan's many protestations) that he is the voice of the 1960s. Derived from a Scottish folk tune, this last-minute addition aims directly at the folk world from which these songs grew as well as at the many writers, critics, and editors who had sought to shape and therefore constrain him. His lyrics are soaked in the imagery of martyrdom, and by the song's end, he envisions himself facing what seems to be defeat, an effect heightened by the tune's derivation from a ballad tradition that romanticizes doomed rebellions: "I'll make my stand," he proclaims, "And remain as I am / And bid farewell and not give a damn."

This heroic declaration of independence, however, is complicated by the lines just before it. Plainly invoking the *Newsweek* article, he describes the dirt and dust of gossip that cover him, before imagining an arrow in flight: "if the arrow is straight / And the point is slick / It can pierce through dust no matter how thick." Crucially, we cannot tell if Dylan himself has loosed this missile. If so, then it becomes a metaphor for his art and the underlying truths that cannot be obscured by gossip or the press. Alternatively, or maybe simultaneously, Dylan imagines himself as the martyred Saint Sebastian, in

---

[1] William Shakespeare, *The Tempest*, V, i.

which case that arrow is the truth about his own past, punching through the false stories he has told in order to land fatally in his own breast. The restless farewell thus does not come from a troubadour heading once more for the road (as is in the original Scottish tune), but instead marks the death of the Guthrie-esque persona that Dylan had fashioned. This Dylan had to be killed to make way for a new world, created by an artist who has learned to not give a damn.

In addition to penning "Restless Farewell," Dylan also added the ominously titled poem "11 Outlined Epitaphs" to the album – heightening the sense that the song may be laying to rest some older version of himself. One of the sections directly invokes the *Newsweek* interview and the larger mechanisms of fame it represented to him:

> I don't like t' be stuck in print
> starin' out at cavity minds
> who gobble chocolate candy bars
> quite content an' satisfied.[2]

He then adopts a clever rhetorical trick that he will return to consistently throughout his career, suggesting that what he says and sings only makes sense within the moment and context of performance itself. Reporters and fans, he writes,

> have no way of knowin'
> that I
> 'expose' myself
> every time I step out
> on the stage.

There is no deeper meaning behind the lyrics, these lines suggest, no other way of understanding the man or the music than in the moment of the performance itself. In performance, at least, the world of Bob Dylan shrinks for a moment to encompass only the singer and his audience.

Such is his hope anyway, but this is a strategy doomed to failure since the past cannot be so easily banished. The boos and slow claps – first at Newport in 1965 and then on the 1966 tour – demanded the revenant return. This refusal to accept Dylan's various farewells and the accompanying demand that he thus freeze one of his many worlds in amber has plagued him throughout his career. And so he has to keep saying goodbye, keep trying to exorcise the spirits that might otherwise overwhelm him.

---

[2] Bob Dylan, "11 Outlined Epitaphs," reprinted in Bob Dylan, *Writings and Drawings* (New York: Knopf, 1973), p. 107.

His attempts to escape, however, are never fully successful and one of his most recent farewells offers a glimpse of a man still struggling with the past, but now determined to live amid the cascade of imaginative worlds he has left in his long and winding wake.

A Sinking Feeling

In 2012, Dylan released *Tempest*, his thirty-fifth studio album. Shortly afterward, he sat down for an interview with *Rolling Stone*'s Mikal Gilmore, who starts the conversation by trying to goad the singer into admitting that his fame essentially rests on those early albums from the 1960s. Not surprisingly, Dylan reacts pugnaciously. He resorts first to his old claim that his words and songs have meaning only in the moment of utterance. When Gilmore presses him to at least explain what he meant when he told an audience that "It looks like things are gonna change now" just after Obama's election, Dylan insists that "whatever was said, it was said for people in that hall for that night."[3] He seems, in other words, to be managing the ghosts the same way he did in 1963 – by insisting that the old songs, indeed entire performances, die the moment the house lights come up.

Near the end of the interview, however, things take a turn as one of Dylan's oldest ghosts suddenly materializes. Gilmore asks about the humorous moment when a young New Jersey cop arrested the musical superstar while he was out looking for Bruce Springsteen's house. Dylan playfully relates the story and the whole thing feels a bit Guthrie-esque; after all, here's an international celebrity, who started his career pretending to be a drifter, now planted in the back of a squad car on suspicion of vagrancy. But things take an abrupt turn. The problem, Dylan tells Gilmore, is that he cannot ever be mistaken for someone else, that someone always sees through his act and gives him away. "That's the side of people I see," he snarls. "People like to betray people . . . . They want to be the one to do it . . . . I've experienced that. A lot."[4]

Gilmore hits a nerve here and when he next asks about Dylan's unacknowledged borrowing from Civil War poet Henry Timrod on "*Love and Theft*" (2001), the songwriter returns unexpectedly to that now ancient *Newsweek* article: "People have tried to stop me every inch of the way," he bitterly complains.

---

[3] Mikal Gilmore, "Bob Dylan Unleashed," *Rolling Stone*, September 27, 2012.   [4] Ibid.

They've always had bad stuff to say about me. *Newsweek* magazine lit the fuse way back when. *Newsweek* printed that some kid from New Jersey wrote "Blowin' in the Wind" and it wasn't me at all. And when that didn't fly, people accused me of stealing the melody from a 16th-century Protestant hymn. And when that didn't work, they said they made a mistake and it was really an old Negro spiritual.[5]

Can those two narrow, yellowing columns in *Newsweek* still be haunting him all these years later? His outlined epitaphs, the lines of "Restless Farewell," the insistence that the songs live only in the moment, and his various attempts to bid us farewell appear not to have worked after all. Dylan's many revenants still roam through his imagination and he admits that they cannot be forgotten, ignored, or exorcised. Fifty years on, it turns out, he still does give a damn.

And this brings us to the title track for *Tempest*, itself another kind of farewell, fashioned by a man in the crowded company of ghosts. This haunted song rambles through fourteen minutes of sounds, images, and characters from the past, all presided over by an enigmatic watchman who nightly dreams their doom. Like his other sprawling epics – such as the eleven-minute "Sad Eyed Lady of the Lowlands" from *Blonde on Blonde* (1966)or its reprise, the sixteen-minute "Highlands" from *Time Out of Mind* (1997) – this one too is built around a looping musical structure that could seemingly go on forever. It differs in one key way from those earlier songs, however: it tells the story of the *Titanic* and thus a tragic, predestined ending awaits from the moment it begins. In those earlier songs, length fills time as the singer waits for something to happen. In "Tempest," however, it delays the inevitable moment of death's victory.

The song's forty-five four-line stanzas unfurl without a chorus over an up-tempo waltz that belies the descriptions of terror, death, and violence woven through the lyrics. Dylan wrote the song amid the frenzy of *Titanic* mania that marked the centenary of the maritime disaster and it jumbles together a disparate collection of fictional and historical source material. As is so often the case in Dylan's late songs, "Tempest" is also laden with literary and musical references that reflect the writer's deep yet wildly disparate reading. It first quotes the Carter Family's 1956 song about the disaster – itself one of the very last singles released by country music's most influential group.[6] Dylan also invokes Shakespeare's final play – even though he limply tried to deny it, saying the Bard's work was called *The Tempest*, while his was merely "Tempest." This is the play in which

---

[5] Ibid.   [6] The Carter Family, "The Titanic," Acme, 1956.

Shakespeare uses the character Prospero to bid farewell to his audience on the shores of the last fantastical world he fashioned.

Most of the songs recorded for *Tempest* made it quickly into Dylan's concert sets and many of them, such as "Pay in Blood" and "Early Roman Kings," have become immediate favorites performed at nearly every live show.[7] The title track, however, like "Restless Farewell," joins a handful of recorded songs that Dylan has almost never played live. The 1963 song has only been performed twice – once just after he recorded it and then again at Frank Sinatra's eightieth birthday party. And it has been covered only rarely – itself another oddity for a Dylan song.[8] If we can indeed read it as Dylan's attempt to bid the folk world an angry goodbye, then this makes sense. The jabs it lands, after all, only sting when he can deliver them directly, then turn and walk away. "Tempest," however, has never been covered – indeed, has never been performed in public at all. There are, of course, sound technical reasons for this, since just remembering all those verses would be daunting. Still, if it is something like a final farewell, then it makes sense that he has no interest in performing it live – no interest in saying goodbye more than once. Like the sinking of the *Titanic*, this particular ending is both fated and final: death will come to silence his voice and give the lie to the idea of a "never ending tour."[9]

But is this really the end? Like "Restless Farewell" some five decades earlier, "Tempest" too is beset by a crucial ambiguity. In the original Carter Family tune, the disaster unfolds after a careless watchman falls asleep. In Dylan's version, however, the watchman becomes a double for the song-writer, who invents this catastrophe. "The watchman, he lay dreaming," Dylan sings, "He dreamed the Titanic was sinking / And he tried to tell someone." The song becomes that telling, each new verse an act of both creation and destruction as Dylan engages in a fury of invention. Just as it's unclear in "Restless Farewell" if Dylan is firing the arrow of truth or is instead felled by it, so too in "Tempest" we cannot tell if Dylan the watchman sinks with the ship or instead presides over its destruction. At one point, the watchman sits at forty-five degrees, seemingly poised to slip beneath the waves, but in the final verse he's safe and simply dreaming

---

[7] According to bobdylan.com, "Early Roman Kings" has been performed 498 times since November 7, 2012 and "Pay in Blood" 477 times.

[8] Curiously, those covers have only been performed by people who have been relatively close to Dylan at various points in his career, including Joan Baez (on *Baez Sings Dylan* – Vanguard, 2006), Mark Knopfler (on the 2012 tribute album, *Chimes of Freedom: The Songs of Bob Dylan Honoring 50 Years of Amnesty International*), and Liam Clancy (*Clancy, O'Connell & Clancy* – Helvic, 1997).

[9] This is the popular name fans and critics have given to Dylan's rigorous touring and performance schedule since 1988.

again "of all the things that can be." So maybe this isn't the final farewell it appears to be.

After complaining to Gilmore in that *Rolling Stone* interview about constantly being betrayed, Dylan summons his old familiar snarl. "Fuck 'em," he concludes, "I'll see them all in their graves."[10] That's not the voice of resignation or of a latter-day Prospero content to drown his book and break his staff. Instead, it's the credo of an artist who has learned to live with his ghosts. Where "Restless Farewell" mixes martyrdom with a desire to destroy a restrictive public persona, "Tempest" seemingly accepts, even welcomes, the many worlds Dylan has made for himself and for generations of listeners. Unlike Shakespeare's *Tempest*, which concludes with Prospero's gentle plea that the audience "let your indulgence set me free," Dylan's song ends on a braver, if more bitter note.[11] Its cascade of verses might be an attempt to literally clear the decks of his mind, but through it all, the figure of the watchman endures, a double for Dylan himself who also returns to the dream-like space of the stage night after night. Up there, he is surrounded by the ghosts of his many other selves – both those that stalk him and the ones that each new audience brings with them. As that sudden explosion of anger about a 50-year-old *Newsweek* article suggests, he has decided *not* to make peace with the past, but neither does he hope to escape it. Instead, he faces down the ghosts that might crowd him out, content to wrestle with them – and with us – through one more performance. Like the watchman, he may well see them into their graves, but the songs will summon them again in a potentially endless loop. "Fuck 'em" he says as he takes the stage – it's time to say goodbye again: an act of farewell that clears the way yet again for another of Dylan's many worlds.

[10] Gilmore, "Bob Dylan Unleashed."   [11] William Shakespeare, *The Tempest*, V, i.

PART I

Creative Life

CHAPTER I

A Chronology of Bob Dylan's Life

Kevin Dettmar and Sean Latham

1941   Robert Allen Zimmerman, son of Abram and Beatrice ("Beatty"), born May 24 in Duluth, Minnesota.

1948   Abram relocates the Zimmerman family to Hibbing, Minnesota where Robert Allen spends the rest of his childhood.

1959   After playing in high school rock bands, he moves to Minneapolis and enrolls at the University of Minnesota. Hearing Odetta in a record store, he trades his electric guitar for an acoustic to begin performing folk music.

1960   Becomes involved in local folk scene, playing the Dinkytown area of Minneapolis. Adopts and performs under the name Bob Dylan (a nod to the Welsh poet, Dylan Thomas); legally changes name two years later.

1961   Moves to New York where he seeks out his ailing idol, Woody Guthrie. Begins performing regularly at folk clubs and coffee houses in Greenwich Village. Becomes romantically involved with the 17-year-old Suze Rotolo, whose political and artistic commitments make a profound impression on Dylan; the relationship survives many rough patches until the summer of 1964. His September show at Gerde's Folk City was reviewed favorably by Robert Shelton in the *New York Times*; signed to a record deal with Columbia by John Hammond.

1962   First album, *Bob Dylan*, featuring two original songs, "Talkin' New York" and "Song to Woody," and covers of traditional folk material, released. Sells only 5,000 copies. Dylan referred to as "Hammond's Folly."

This chronology was created by Kevin Dettmar in 2009 and published in *The Cambridge Companion to Bob Dylan*; updated by Sean Latham, 2020.

1963   In January appears in *Madhouse on Castle Street* (BBC TV play), now lost. Releases *The Freewheelin' Bob Dylan* in May; contains mostly originals ("Blowin' in the Wind," "Masters of War," and "A Hard Rain's A-Gonna Fall") with two covers ("Corrina, Corrina" and "Honey, Just Allow Me One More Chance"). Refuses to play the *Ed Sullivan Show* after an attempt to censor his set list. Joan Baez invites Dylan to tour with her; they become romantically involved. Performs at the March on Washington for Jobs and Freedom in August.

1964   *The Times They Are A-Changin'* released. Meets the Beatles at Kennedy Airport in New York; reportedly introduces the group to marijuana. *Another Side of Bob Dylan* appears, marking the beginnings of his turn from the folk genre.

1965   Dylan gives "Mr. Tambourine Man" to Roger McGuinn; it becomes a major hit for the Byrds. Ends relationship with Baez; marries Sara Lowndes (sometimes spelt "Lownds"). Releases *Bringing It All Back Home* in March; the album has a decidedly different sound from the previous folk recordings, featuring heavy electric arrangements alongside some acoustic tracks. Dylan is booed when he performs an electric set at the Newport Folk Festival. Releases the all-electric *Highway 61 Revisited* with the definitive single "Like a Rolling Stone" in August. Hires backing band the Hawks (later the Band) featuring Robbie Robertson and Levon Helm for tour supporting the album.

1966   Records *Blonde on Blonde* in Nashville. Embarks on a world tour where he performs split sets at every stop, first performing solo on acoustic guitar and harmonica, then, backed by the Hawks, delivering a high-voltage electric set. In July, mysteriously crashes his Triumph 55 motorcycle outside Woodstock, NY. Dylan begins to withdraw from public performing and recording.

1967   While recovering, records several sessions with the Hawks in their nearby Woodstock basement (which become the first widely distributed bootlegs); sessions later released by Columbia as *The Basement Tapes* (1975). In October and November records *John Wesley Harding* in Nashville.

1968   In January, appears for the first time in public since his crash, performing three songs at the Woody Guthrie Memorial Concert.

1969   Releases an all-country album, *Nashville Skyline*. Appears on the first episode of Johnny Cash's television show in May, performing three songs with the host. Headlines the Isle of Wight festival in

England in August, having rejected offers to perform at the Woodstock Music Festival.

1970   *Self Portrait*, an album comprising mostly covers, is released and poorly received. *New Morning* released to more favorable reviews. On June 9, receives honorary doctorate in music from Princeton University.

1971   Performs at ex-Beatle George Harrison's benefit concert for Bangladesh. The single "George Jackson" is his only studio release of the year. Conducts recording sessions with Allen Ginsberg (still unreleased).

1972   Worked on Sam Peckinpah's film *Pat Garrett and Billy the Kid*, providing the songs (released on the 1973 soundtrack album) and acting as "Alias."

1973   Records *Planet Waves* (released in January 1974) with the Band, and begins rehearsing for a supporting tour after leaving Columbia for the Asylum label.

1974   The Bob Dylan and the Band tour recorded and released as *Before the Flood*. Begins recording *Blood on the Tracks* (1975) in September, once again on the Columbia label.

1975   Visits boxer Rubin "Hurricane" Carter in prison and pens "Hurricane," a single depicting the fighter's wrongful conviction in a triple-murder case in Paterson, NJ. Embarks on Rolling Thunder Revue tour, featuring T-Bone Burnett, "Ramblin'" Jack Elliott, Allen Ginsberg, Roger McGuinn, Joni Mitchell, and Joan Baez.

1976   As the Rolling Thunder Revue continues, Dylan releases *Desire* featuring collaborations with playwright Jacques Levy. It is his last number 1 album for thirty years. Appears at the Band's farewell concert, documented by Martin Scorsese (*The Last Waltz*).

1978   Releases *Street Legal*. Marriage to Sara ends in divorce. *Renaldo and Clara*, a four-hour film directed by Dylan, using concert footage of the Rolling Thunder Revue and starring himself alongside Joan Baez, is released to poor reviews.

1979   From January to April, participates in Bible study classes at the Vineyard School of Discipleship in Reseda, CA. Releases gospel-inspired *Slow Train Coming*, winning the Grammy for "Best Male Vocalist" for the song "Gotta Serve Somebody."

1980   Second "born again" album released: *Saved*. Tours, reviving songs from a number of his 1960s recordings.

1981 *Shot of Love* released, featuring both Christian-influenced and secular material.

1982 Travels to Israel; it is rumored that he rejects his born-again Christian status.

1983 Releases *Infidels* to critical acclaim.

1984 Appears in March on *Late Night with David Letterman*, backed by a punk band, performing three songs. *Real Live* samples the subsequent European tour.

1985 Releases *Empire Burlesque* and *Biograph* box set. Performs to poor reception at Live Aid backed by Keith Richards and Ronnie Wood; performs to higher acclaim at Farm Aid, backed by Tom Petty and the Heartbreakers.

1986 Tours with Tom Petty and the Heartbreakers. *Knocked Out Loaded* released. Secretly marries backup singer, Carol Dennis (they divorce in 1992).

1987 Embarks on summer tour with the Grateful Dead (sampled on *Dylan and the Dead*, 1988), to mostly poor reviews. Has successful tour of the Middle East and Europe with Petty.

1988 *Down in the Groove* poorly received. *Hearts of Fire* film and soundtrack both released. Records with supergroup the Traveling Wilburys alongside George Harrison, Tom Petty, Roy Orbison, and ELO founder Jeff Lynne. Inducted into the Rock & Roll Hall of Fame, introduced by Bruce Springsteen. Begins "The Never Ending Tour" (and has continued touring to present).

1989 Records and releases the well-received *Oh Mercy* with producer Daniel Lanois. Accompanied by "Political World" music video on MTV.

1990 Reunites with the Wilburys (*sans* the deceased Orbison) for a second album: *The Traveling Wilburys Vol. 3*. Releases *Under the Red Sky* with contributions from George Harrison, Slash, Stevie Ray Vaughn, and Elton John. Named a *Commandeur dans l'Ordre des Arts et des Lettres*, France's highest cultural honor.

1991 Receives lifetime achievement award at the Grammy Awards ceremony; performs "Masters of War" in protest at the first US Iraq invasion on the show. *The Bootleg Series Vol. 1–3* releases a number of previously discarded but now praised Dylan recordings.

1992 *Good as I Been to You* released; features acoustic versions of old folk tunes.

1993 *World Gone Wrong*, an acoustic blues album, released.

1994   Appears at the twenty-fifth anniversary Woodstock '94 Festival. Performs on MTV's *Unplugged*, releasing a live album of acoustic versions of some of his electric classics.

1997   In January, reteams with Lanois to record *Time Out of Mind*. Before the album's scheduled spring release, suffers a near-fatal heart infection, pericarditis. Recovers to begin touring by midsummer; performs for Pope John Paul II in the fall. *Time Out of Mind* released in September, peaking at number 10 on the Billboard charts, his highest position in twenty years. In December, President Clinton presents Dylan with a Kennedy Center Lifetime Achievement Award.

1998   Wins first "Album of the Year" Grammy for *Time Out of Mind*. Tours the USA in the fall with Van Morrison and Joni Mitchell. The legendary 1966 *"Royal Albert Hall" Concert* released by Columbia.

1999   Tours with Paul Simon.

2001   Single "Things Have Changed," written for the film *Wonder Boys* (2000) wins a Grammy, a Golden Globe, and an Academy Award for best song. The Oscar statue tours with Dylan atop an amplifier as he performs. Releases *"Love and Theft"* in September to high critical praise.

2003   Pens "Cross the Green Mountain" for the film *Gods and Generals*. Releases his own film (in collaboration with Larry Charles) *Masked & Anonymous* to poor reviews.

2004   Dylan publishes his autobiographical prose work, *Chronicles: Volume One*.

2005   The four-hour Martin Scorsese documentary *No Direction Home* is shown on television to a wide US audience, released to DVD, and accompanied by new bootlegs from the early 1960s. Records "Tell Ol' Bill" for the film *North Country*.

2006   Records and releases *Modern Times*. The album marks his first number 1 album in thirty years. At 65, Bob Dylan becomes the oldest living artist to hit the top spot. He also begins eclectic weekly *Theme Time Radio Hour*.

2008   In September Dylan publishes two poems, "17" and "21," in the *New Yorker*, from a book titled *Hollywood Foto-Rhetoric: The Lost Manuscript* that does not appear. Bootleg Series *Vol. 8, Tell Tale Signs* – rare and unreleased recordings from 1989 to 2006 – is announced for October release by Columbia. On the night of

Barack Obama's election, Dylan tells a concert crowd that "it looks like things are going to change now."

2009   End of *Theme Time Radio Hour* series. Releases *Together Through Life* and co-writes the lyrics for all but one of the songs on the album with Robert Hunter of the Grateful Dead; it too reaches number 1 in the USA and UK. In October, releases *Christmas in the Heart*, a holiday album filled with covers of songs such as "Winter Wonderland"; the royalties are donated to charity.

2012   *Tempest* is released, an album of original songs filled with quotations and allusions to everything from classical poetry to mid-century folk songs and John Lennon. In May, Dylan receives the Presidential Medal of Freedom from President Barack Obama in a White House Ceremony.

2014   Release of *The Basement Tapes Complete* boxset, volume 11 in the Bootleg Series, which contains the most complete recordings of the fabled (and often bootlegged) tapes Dylan made with the Band in Woodstock in 1967.

2015   Dylan releases *Shadows in the Night*, the first of three albums filled almost entirely with covers of the Great American Songbook – a marked departure from his long affiliation with rock, blues, and folk.

2016   In March, the George Kaiser Family Foundation announces that it has purchased the Bob Dylan Archive and that the collection of over 100,000 objects (including manuscripts, film, tapes, and more) will permanently reside in Tulsa, Oklahoma. Two months later, Dylan releases the second album of American Songbook covers titled *Fallen Angels*. In October, the Nobel Prize committee announces that Dylan has won the literature award "for having created new poetic expressions within the great American song tradition." Dylan takes weeks to accept the award and does not appear at the ceremony. Instead, Patti Smith performs a moving version of "A Hard Rain's A-Gonna Fall."

2017   Releases *Triplicate* in March – a three-LP album and the third in the ongoing series of American Songbook covers. In June, Dylan submits a recording of his Nobel Lecture, which acknowledges influences ranging from Homer and Melville to Buddy Holly and Huddie Ledbetter. Volume 13 of the ongoing Bootleg Series appears, which contains eight discs of material from 1979 to 1981 along with *Trouble No More*, a film that combines documentary concert footage with evangelical sermons written by Luc Sante and performed by Michael Shannon.

2018   Collaborates on the creation of Heaven's Door Whiskeys that feature his elaborate iron sculptures on the label.

2019   Release to Netflix of *Rolling Thunder Revue: A Bob Dylan Story*, directed by Martin Scorsese. It mixes documentary footage from the 1975–1976 tour with fictional interviews. The first exhibition of material from the Bob Dylan Archive opens in Tulsa followed by a major exhibition of Dylan's artwork at the Modern Art Museum in Shanghai. Plans are announced for a Bob Dylan Center in Tulsa to open in 2021. Dylan continues to tour.

2020   The COVID-19 pandemic interrupts Dylan's tour schedule and leads to the cancellation of several dates. On March 27, he releases a new single titled "Murder Most Foul" about the Kennedy assassination – his first new song in eight years. "I Contain Multitudes" appears the following month followed by an album of entirely new material in June titled *Rough and Rowdy Ways*. The music receives broad critical acclaim and reaches number 2 on the US Billboard chart. In September, Dylan releases a new episode of *Theme Time Radio Hour* focused on whiskey.

CHAPTER 2

The Biographies

Andrew Muir

Biographies can be curiously unfulfilling publications. This is due partly to the ultimate unknowability of another person, and partly to the motivations and circumstances that bring these life-stories into being. The biographies of Bob Dylan are thus not only reflections of the artist's own life, self-promotion, and constant reinvention, but also interpretations that have been dictated by changing fashions in journalism, celebrity reportage, and the evolving nature of media and cultural studies in modern America and, by extension, the wider world.

This chapter will examine the major biographical studies of Dylan from 1972 to the present day, bookended by Dylan's own, verbal, filmic, and textual biographical constructs that eschew factual history in favor of what we might describe, biographer-like, as either poetic truth or self-serving mythologizing depending on our own biases and motivations. It will discuss what are considered the main biographies amidst a sea of partial ones of very varying value. For every labor of love, or side product from a serious biographer, looking at a particular period, are numerous editions with the sole intent of cashing in on Dylan's fame or a specific event or anniversary.

***

When Dylan arrived in New York's Greenwich Village, he continued his already established modus operandi of devising and disseminating various outlandish and impressive autobiographies. These ad hoc stories featured Dylan variously as being in a circus, part of a carnival, living on the road, playing with and for famous musicians, traveling on boxcars, and so forth. One common theme running through all these fanciful tales was that of Dylan running away from home. He immortalized this in a poem written for the program of his 1963 Town Hall concert: *Hibbing's a good ol' town /*

I ran away from it when I was 10, 12, 13, 15, 151/2, 17 an' 18 / I been caught an'
brought back all but once'.[1]

While none of this was true of Robert Allen Zimmerman, Dylan was
giving the back-story to an entirely different person(a). From Dylan's point
of view, then, Robert Allen Zimmerman's personal narrative was inappropriate and the tall tales he now spun were the 'true biography' of the
constructed character, Bob Dylan. He must have known that eventually
the truth would out, but he appeared never to consider this.

Dylan's real identity and family background remained hidden until
a mean-spirited exposé of his fabrications appeared in *Newsweek*, on the
relatively late date of November 4, 1963. The article included an outrageous
lie of its own in claiming Dylan had stolen the song "Blowin' in the Wind"
as well as being the first to uncover him as the son of respectable, middle-
class Jewish parents. After this, more of the truth about his background
began to appear in the fledgling music press. Then, just under a decade
later, the first biography appeared.

It is hard to imagine now, but back in the day, there were only two books
to which the Dylan fan could turn. Both were released in 1972. *Song and
Dance Man* by Michael Gray was the first study of Dylan's art, while
Anthony Scaduto, a long-time journalist from the *New York Post* who
specialized in crime reporting, wrote the first major biography of Dylan's
life.[2] In doing so, he also produced one of the first biographies of a popular
musician of the latter half of the twentieth century that treated its subject
seriously. Consequently, its effect was profound and not only amongst fans
but also amongst musicians.[3]

Scaduto's book stands up well even after all this time. What may now
strike us as, at times, a rather clichéd history of Dylan was then a revelation.
Indeed, that much of it has become commonplace stands as a testament to
the work Scaduto produced and the way his findings have been repeated ad
infinitum in the music press.

Even the tale of a celebrity who had grown up desperately wanting to be
famous and then hating fame, was less of a cliché back then. Moreover,
with the celebrity in question being as artistically talented as Dylan, and

---

[1] Bob Dylan, "My Life in a Stolen Moment" (1962), *Lyrics, 1962–1985* (New York: Alfred A. Knopf,
1985), p. 100.

[2] Michael Gray, *The Bob Dylan Encyclopedia* (London: Continuum, 2006); Anthony Scaduto, *Bob
Dylan* (London: Helter Skelter Publishing, 1996) (subsequently cited as *BD*).

[3] Bruce Springsteen excitedly recalled going to play for John Hammond Jr., the man who signed Dylan
for Columbia Records: "I'd just finished reading the Anthony Scaduto Dylan biography and I was
going to meet the man who made it happen!" *Born To Run* (New York: Simon & Schuster, 2016),
p. 170.

the important role fame has had on his life and career, the point was central to Scaduto's story. Dylan, as Scaduto succinctly put it, became "a personality before he could become a person" (*BD*, p. 179). Dylan, as we see in all these narratives, is forever a paradox. One reason for this is that his desire for fame was diametrically opposed to another core wish – that for total privacy. Scaduto quotes an early girlfriend, Echo Helstrom, on the innate nature of this: "He didn't want anyone to know anything about him – even before he was famous. He wanted everything to be kept secret" (*BD*, p. 5).

Scaduto produced a highly readable book that did not lack insight and, crucially, was underpinned and shaped by a succession of interviews he conducted with Dylan in 1971. These are, unsurprisingly, continually referred to in the text with frequent reminders to the reader that intimate discussions had taken place. How many were face to face and how many were phone calls is hard to tell. They would appear to have been surprisingly lengthy in total if a later project, mooted prior to Scaduto passing away, is correct in its claims. Provisionally called *The Dylan Tapes*, this promised amongst "hundreds of hours of tapes" some "Thirty-six hours of stories Dylan told Scaduto."[4]

The publication of this biography was also bolstered by positive Dylan quotes that were a goldmine for its publicity and dust jackets, including, "I read it. Some of it is pretty straight, some of it exactly the way it happened." Plus, with *Newsweek*, one feels, still hurting years later: "I used to pick up those magazines and see stories about me, and sometimes they used to hurt. Your book didn't cause me any pain at all, in fact I rather enjoyed it, because it's not that magazine bullshit" (*BD*, p. 1).

Scaduto made it abundantly clear that he was well aware that there was a price to pay for such co-operation and what were, effectively, endorsements: "there was an ulterior motive behind Dylan's friendliness . . . . That motive was manipulative self-protection, I felt . . . he would give me enough material to flesh out the portrait I had done of him in exchange for permitting him to edit material to which he objected" (*BD*, p. 294). Scaduto's work, then, existed within a delicate balance of Dylan's engagement and potential control.

Scaduto strikingly depicted the early 1960s Greenwich Village folk scene, and his interviews with key players around Dylan were revelatory

---

[4] The author was approached by a publisher's agent to comment on the viability of a publication under consideration. The undated flyer contains the following words, among others: "Anthony Scaduto is now working on a new exciting project, tentatively titled The Dylan Tapes, that will be able to expand and deepen the information given in Dylan's biography: a collection of the most interesting and never published before interviews that went into the making of Bob Dylan: An Intimate Biography. Thirty-six hours of stories Dylan told Scaduto; also stories from Suze Rotolo, Echo Helstrom, Joan Baez, Phil Ochs etc."

at the time. For example, you cannot find a clearer window into Joan Baez's conflicted feelings towards her lover, friend, and tormentor, outside of the, much later, song "Diamonds and Rust".

Another reason this take on Dylan still stands up so well is that so much of it uncannily prefigures what has since unfolded in the artist's life and career. Musically he begins the story playing piano on stage in Hibbing high school, and he now returns to that same instrument while on tour. The pull of the road struggles with the craving for a settled domestic life. The same fear of fans and mob mentality, which was to surface in Dylan's memoir *Chronicles*, is foreshadowed by Dave Van Ronk's: "his feeling, basically, was that the audience was a lynch mob" (*BD*, p. 149). Additionally, Dylan's move to explore Judaism is seen to be at least partly derailed by the actions of organized Jewish pressure groups just as the actions of those supporting Christian Evangelicals were to disillusion him later.

Scaduto also provides much sound lyrical analysis, probably steered by Dylan, something that has both positive and negative aspects to it. It would be reasonable to suggest that Scaduto labored to integrate these elements into his broader discussion. However, in that broader discussion he did add significantly to the store of crucial information on Dylan's work, such as the creation of the then recently released, controversial "George Jackson" single, a tribute to the Black Panther leader at a time when Dylan was being decried for his apparent disengagement with current concerns.

Scaduto remains to this day the biographer who concentrates solely on his subject and whose own personality is not allowed to intrude to detrimental effect. His solid effort stood alone for nearly fifteen years, after which three new biographies explored Dylan's life, but in strikingly divergent ways.

Robert Shelton was an important figure in the Greenwich Village scene who is credited with launching Dylan's career due to his well-written and laudatory review of Dylan supporting the Greenbriar Boys at Gerde's, on September 29, 1961.[5] Shelton, using his pen name, Stacey Williams, also wrote the sleeve notes to Dylan's first album. For the crucial first five years in Dylan's career, Shelton was his friend. This, however, turned out to be a major drawback when it came to writing the biography, despite bringing the obvious benefits. Shelton himself has said that a friend was not the best person to write such a book.[6] By protecting his friend from sometimes

---

[5] Robert Shelton, "'Bob Dylan: A Distinctive Folk Song Stylist: 20-Year-Old Singer is Bright New Face at Gerde's Club," *New York Times*, September 29, 1961.
[6] Robert Shelton, interviewed by John Bauldie in the Manchester-based Dylan fanzine, *The Telegraph*, 27 (Summer 1987).

uncomfortable historical incidents, Shelton raised crucial questions over what people want from a biography and contributed to the lengthy delay in it appearing in print by disagreeing with prospective publishers over this question.

Shelton's book provides a detailed account of Dylan up to 1966, but then staggers on to the end of the decade and jumps to 1978, when Shelton dined with Dylan in London. Finally, there is another jump to tack on a limp ending in a vain attempt to make it appear that the biography covers Dylan's life up to the time of its publication. Had the book come out in 1970, it would have been a revelation by being the first to cover Dylan's upbringing, adolescence, and the first decade of his career. That is what the vast bulk of the book is concerned with, but it was no longer new or timely. An edited edition, in 2011, sensibly decided to make 1978 the concluding point.

The main draw of the book is Shelton's interviews with Dylan. An hours-long recording of their discussion on a flight to Denver in March 1966 provides many quotes from Dylan that are sprinkled throughout the biography. The most sensational of those finds Dylan recounting his time as a prostitute, and serving customers of any gender and any demands. This unappealingly titled passage, "11pm Cowboy,"[7] smacks of Dylan playing Shelton.[8] Shelton intimates he may not himself believe the story, but so gently that only readers who are familiar with Dylan's propensity to mythologize his past are likely to pick up on it. There is also no indication of Dylan's mental state at the time of the interview. Recordings from the time portray a wildly fluctuating, chemically challenged Dylan, and as such his utterances ought to be portrayed in that light.

Shelton fails in his attempt to provide a critical biography. The 1961 review for which Shelton became famous was an outstanding piece of insight and observation. Here, contrastingly, Shelton seems to have a loss of nerve despite having Dylan himself as a potential guide for much of the time. So much so that, presumably in an attempt at being taken seriously, Shelton quotes from a variety of academic dissertations that seem ill-fitting and pretentious when taken out of their context and plunged into a book

---

[7] The allusion is to *Midnight Cowboy*, James Leo Herlihy's 1965 novel centering around a male prostitute. The novel, very topical at the time of Shelton's interview with Dylan, was adapted into a hit 1969 movie. As it happens, Dylan wrote a song for the soundtrack, "Lay Lady Lay," but it was delivered too late to be included.

[8] Shelton Robert, *No Direction Home* (New York: Beech Tree Books, 1986), p. 90 (subsequently *NDH*).

with an already too-wide array of registers. Additionally, for a book that took so long to emerge, it is curiously disjointed, with inexplicable jumps in Dylan's narrative, even in the more coherent 2011 edition.

Most crucially, Shelton's compromises designed to sustain Dylan's friendship – understandable and commendable as they were – restrict his book. For example, on the breakup of Dylan's first marriage (there is no hint here of any later ones), Shelton asks: "Must I record it here for posterity? Do you really want to know the personal details of an argument they had here or there, or of some hysterics on Sara's part, or who slapped whom?" (*NDH*, p. 474). Regrettable though it may be, this is exactly what the vast majority of readers want from a biography.

***

Bob Dylan, after talking to the first two biographers, has thus far, refrained from doing so again, while Sara Dylan has never spoken to any biographer.[9] Our next two biographers cite Dylan's non-involvement as a positive in that it kept them independent from Dylan's controlling influence. You could be forgiven for seeing this as making a virtue out of a necessity. Whichever, it creates a definite demarcation line between the first duo and those who came afterwards, as the biographers' own voices necessarily become more prominent. This is a tendency that Dylan has noted more generally: "Everything people say about you or me, they are saying about themselves."[10] Additionally, biographies usually tell us a significant amount about the publishers, consumers, and society involved in their production and reception.

Bob Spitz, in *Dylan: A Biography*, provided a vivid contrast with Shelton. Albert Goldman had recently caused a sensation with a highly successful hatchet job on Elvis Presley and was following that up with one on John Lennon.[11] Goldman described both these objects of widespread desire and devotion as pathetic men with appendages of clay. Spitz admitted, "Goldman helped enormously along the way." Conveniently, their "books were overlapping – he gave me a lot of stuff from Lennon, I gave him a lot of stuff from Dylan."[12] Consequently, we are presented with, as

---

[9] "Sara Dylan said something like 'Oh come on now' in a weary voice before plopping the phone down." "An Exclusive On the Tracks Interview: Howard Sounes, *On the Tracks*, 21 (Summer 2001), pp. 44–47.

[10] Mikal Gilmore, "Bob Dylan Unleashed," interview with Bob Dylan, *Rolling Stone*, September 27, 2012, www.rollingstone.com/music/music-news/bob-dylan-unleashed-189723/.

[11] Albert Goldman, *Elvis* (New York: Viking, 1981) and *The Lives of John Lennon* (New York: William Morrow and Co., 1988).

[12] John Bauldie, "A Conversation with Bob Spitz," *The Telegraph*, 31 (Winter 1988), p. 66. Spitz reveals this while simultaneously claiming not to be like Goldman at all.

Greil Marcus put it, "the horribly detailed night a lonely man supposedly spent with a woman in 1975," which Marcus describes as "a violation, an atrocity."[13]

That scene is one reason Marcus calls the book, "obnoxious" and Michael Gray terms it "malevolent."[14] Others include the relentlessly mean-spirited approach to people from all walks of life and descriptions peppered with disrespectful comments on racial, religious, and gender grounds. Women are demeaned and stereotyped throughout, including in descriptions such as "the object of Dylan's affections was as devoted to him as a cocker spaniel in heat" and "High, wide Finnish cheekbones, Siamese eyes, pale, chalky skin, and a full steamy mouth that hung limply and begged for masculine sustenance of any kind – Oh Lord, she was a hot little number!"[15]

Spitz's approach was built around the idea that sleaze sells and sleazy writing matches sleazy content. Nonetheless, his research included many, long interviews. The interviewees were very far from the pre-publicity promise of "inner entourage," but this meant much background detail was uncovered from lesser-known parts of the Dylan tale.

At first glance there does appear to be one major inner source, Dylan's mid-1960s near ever-present sidekick, Bobby Neuwirth. However, this is an illusion, as what we are being told is what someone else claims to remember Neuwirth telling them.[16] We do not know, therefore, in what tone Neuwirth claimed that he wrote some of Dylan's lines', including that most Dylanesque phrase: "When you're lost in the rain in Juarez and it's Easter-time, too." Perhaps he was just trying to impress someone.

This is not a book to approach if you are expecting artistic insight. We are told that "The influence of LSD is everywhere on *Bringing It All Back Home*" (*DaB*, p. 274). Apparently, this is shown in its very opening lines where, according to this biographer, "The guy was gonged out of his nut" (*DaB*, p. 274). Surely the writing of no other Nobel laureate can ever have been discussed in such a manner.

In this biography too, the story is focused firmly on the past. The final chapter takes us from the 1979 conversion to Christianity to 1986 in less than twenty pages. On page 542 you are in 1981, and by 546 you are at the

[13] Greil Marcus, "Bob Spitz, *Dylan: A Biography*," *Washington Post Book World*, January 8, 1989.
[14] Gray, *The Bob Dylan Encyclopedia*, p. 630.
[15] Bob Spitz, *Dylan: A Biography* (New York: McGraw-Hill, 1988), pp. 57–58 (subsequently *DaB*).
[16] "Bobby Neuwirth was another person I didn't talk to. . . . Yet people who Bobby confessed to almost as a therapist, revealed to me almost everything about those discussions, so I feel like I've gotten very close to Bobby Neuwirth." *The Telegraph*, 31 (Winter 1988).

1986 conclusion. Two years are skipped over without any indication that they even existed. Bewilderingly there is an epilogue set at one show in 1987 while significant events such as the 1986 Live Aid and Farm Aid are left unmentioned. Even by the end of the 1980s, the three major biographies remained focused on Dylan's early life and had almost nothing to say about the more recent decades. This situation was about to change, but the male-centric view of the biographers, to use a term so kind as to approach the euphemistic, has persisted even through the twenty-first century thus far.

***

John Hinchey celebrated the publication of the next biography with the words: "Clinton Heylin's *Dylan: Behind the Shades* is the fourth full-length biography of Bob Dylan, but it so far outclasses its predecessors that it may as well be the first."[17] Prime among Hinchey's reasons was that here, finally, was an account that came up to the current date. There were other virtues. Like Shelton before him, Heylin places Dylan in the top flight of artists from across the centuries. Unlike his predecessor, however, the sense of this comes across in his biography and its subsequent updates in 2001 and 2011.

Heylin's obsessive fan's knowledge of session and concert dates and their content proved, from the first, invaluable in correcting myths and long-held misconceptions. Thereafter, Heylin spent years criss-crossing the Atlantic from his UK base; tirelessly researching, listening, and uncovering alternate takes while also conducting an extraordinary number of inter-views. Consequently, there is a clear development through his editions. As one example, in the first edition, we are told that an authoritative source has reported that the song "You're Gonna Make Me Lonesome When You Go," hitherto always quoted as being addressed to Dylan's first wife, Sara, was instead for Ellen Bernstein. The 2001 edition reports this as a fact with Ashtabula, referenced in the song as her birthplace, as one of a "number of elements" personal to Ms. Bernstein. Then, in the 2011 take, Heylin provides a substantive quote from his lengthy interview with her that absolutely proves his case. Multiply this one example across the whole work, and you can visualize the overall progress.[18]

Over the three iterations, Heylin developed considerably as a writer. As his research became ever more formidable, the positives in his biographies

---

[17] John Hinchey, "Dylan's Shadow: A Review of Clinton Heylin's *Behind the Shades*," *The Telegraph*, 39 (Summer 1991), p. 82.

[18] The full interview was reproduced in *Judas!* 2 (2002), pp. 31–44, www.a-muir.co.uk/Dylan/Judas/J2 .pdf.

have increased as the negatives have diminished, excepting the misplaced and distracting attacks on others, especially other authors. Heylin's many books on Dylan, and a wide range of musical artists, many of whom have Dylan connections, including the history of Dylan's songs and recording sessions bolster these positives. These chronologies all fed into his later biographical volumes. This deepening and enriching, aligned to his depth of coverage and attention to detail, means, simply put, that the 2011 edition is currently the only biography to which to turn. As Richard Thomas wrote, it is Heylin "to whom scholars and fans of Dylan, myself not least, are most in debt."[19]

It would be safe to assume Heylin thought that was that as far as full biographies went. He has continued to write on Dylan, especially either for, or books coinciding with, the release of Dylan's long-running *Bootleg Series* collections. The establishment of the Bob Dylan Archive collections in Tulsa, however, will surely have overturned that assumption, but more of that later, after turning to alternative streams of biographical accounts of Dylan.

Back at the time of Dylan's 60th birthday, Howard Sounes's *Down the Highway: The Life of Bob Dylan* accompanied Heylin's *Take Two*. Adopting an odd familiarity with his subject by continually referring to its subject as "Bob," Sounes's take is bolstered by a heavy reliance on official documentation. His other research includes new interviews, or more extensive ones with previous interviewees, including Sally Grossman, wife of one-time manager Albert and long-time friend of Dylan's first wife, Sara.

What his publication will forever be remembered for was the uncovering of a hitherto secret wife and child. Dylan's most dedicated fans had long believed there were a number of these, with some even claiming to have photographs, but had kept such things to themselves. Sounes, in contrast, hit the front pages with his revelation that Dylan had been married to Carolyn Dennis, from 1986 to 1992, the couple having had a child together in January 1986. The spilling of this secret takes us back to the conundrum posed by Shelton regarding how far biographers have a right to invade privacy. Ted Perlman is quoted as saying that everyone who knew was "sworn to secrecy never to mention it."[20] Sounes not only goes on to trumpet it but also to print the address where Dennis and her previously shielded daughter were currently living. Dennis declared that Sounes's portrayal of their family relationship was "malicious and ridiculous,"[21] a charge which Sounes flatly denied.

[19] Richard Thomas, *Why Bob Dylan Matters* (New York: Dey Street Books, 2017), p. 320.
[20] Howard Sounes, *Down the Highway: The Life of Bob Dylan* (London: Doubleday, 2001), p. 372.
[21] Hugh Davies, "Bob's a Terrific Father, Says Dylan's Secret Wife," *The Telegraph*, April 13, 2001, www.telegraph.co.uk/news/worldnews/northamerica/usa/1316089/Bobs-a-terrific-father-says-Dylans-secret-wife.html.

This overview has not taken into account those many publications on Dylan's life that feature little or no original research. Chief amongst these is Ian Bell's two-volume *The Lives of Bob Dylan* published in 2012–2013.[22] Bell had the advantage of encompassing the 2012 *Tempest* album and is correct in making much of this, though also takes claims for its importance further than is credible.

There is a breezy, even cozy familiarity in the narrative that is very misleading. We are told, parenthetically, and as though intimately when referring to Sara that "Mr. Tambourine Man" was "always her favourite." Bell never spoke to Sara Dylan, nor, it appears, to anyone who would have at that time, so how he knows this is not explained. Whole scenes are similarly reported as though the author was privy to what had happened. There are plusses, such as a mordant wit that brightens the retold stories. Bell also succinctly raises again the question Shelton posed. Regarding the state of Dylan's marriage in the mid-1970s, Bell asks: "Who really knows or has the right to know?"[23]

Artistic judgments outside the critical orthodoxy are always welcome if justified. Such justification is often sadly lacking herein, not least in the risible claim that *Tempest*, fine achievement though it is, should be considered Dylan's best album since *Blonde on Blonde*. This contention becomes bizarre when Bell derides the last two tracks, which comprise over 21 minutes, and so constitute a hefty percentage of that album.

Bell's derision extends to fans of Dylan's live performances, especially those who have followed the tours since he reconceptualized his live work in 1988, and which constitute the most sustained creative output of Dylan's artistic life. In the second volume, we therefore have a biographer disdaining the majority of his subject's life work as well as the fans who source some of his information. Perhaps this should not come as a surprise, as Bell talks dismissively of Dylan's "biographical stalkers"[24] while writing a book out of said stalkers' research and interviews.

As a cursory glance at the biographers' differing takes on key events such as the Newport Festival in 1965 or Dylan's motorcycle accident in 1966 clearly demonstrates, grasping the Dylan story is difficult. Dylan is a shape-shifter *extraordinaire*, a generator of myths both directly and indirectly. Additionally, his films – *Eat the Document, Renaldo and Clara*, and *Masked*

---

[22] Ian Bell, *Time Out of Mind: The Lives of Bob Dylan* (Edinburgh: Mainstream, 2013); Ian Bell, *Once Upon a Time: The Lives of Bob Dylan* (Edinburgh: Mainstream, 2013).
[23] Bell, *Time Out of Mind*, p. 36.   [24] Bell, *Once Upon a Time*, p. 36.

and Anonymous – are extremely illuminating documents of artistic autobiography. Meanwhile, his teasingly subtitled "volume one" book of often-fictive memoirs, *Chronicles*, continued his tendency to produce self portraits that defy genre, chronology, and analysis. Wonderfully allusive, from time-saving historical and geographical lifts to full literary intertextuality, and all stages in between, the book is awash with guessing games and deliberately misleading almost-facts.[25] Dylan's *Bootleg Series* and especially the 2006 Scorsese directed documentary *No Direction Home* have afforded Dylan further steerage on the way his tale might be told in the future.

Until recently it had seemed inevitable that for a life-story of Dylan that also took us into the heart of the mystery of his artistic expression, we could only look to the future. The writer of such a book would have to be extraordinary skilled in interpreting a range of disciplines; a historian somehow able to see his own information-drenched time clearly; and a first-rate biographer able to sift the mountains of runes to grasp and explain our age and Dylan's place in it. You would have to assume that somebody that multi-talented would be a creative artist themselves rather than a mere chronicler. Consequently, Dylan's claim that: "I don't think I'm gonna be really understood until maybe 100 years from now"[26] seemed unchallengeable. Then came the game-changing announcement that the George Kaiser Family Foundation and the University of Tulsa had acquired the Bob Dylan Archives.

This precious store of material offers a unique insight into the man and, far more importantly, the artist, containing as it does an enormous quantity of writing drafts, recording tapes, and film of Dylan creating his legacy. Consequently, while this overview has been of pre-Tulsa narratives, the future of Dylan biographies is clearly going to be "post-Tulsa." Already Clinton Heylin is gearing up to rewrite Dylan's life-story in the light of this cornucopia of new material. *Rolling Stone*'s Douglas Brinkley will become the latest in the line of journalists turned Dylan biographers, and Dylan, himself, if he wants to keep his hand on the tiller of his life-story, as he did in the 2006 *No Direction Home* documentary, may well be tempted to be interviewed for such narratives once again, just as he was at the beginning of the first cycle of biographies.

---

[25] A similar approach was adopted by Martin Scorsese for his 2019 "mockumentary," *The Rolling Thunder Revue: A Bob Dylan Story*.

[26] Mick Brown, "Bob Dylan: The Way He Sang Made Everything Seem Like a Message," *The Telegraph*, May 1, 2011, www.telegraph.co.uk/culture/music/bob-dylan/8480252/Bob-Dylan-The-way-he-sang-made-everything-seem-like-a-message.html.

CHAPTER 3

Songwriting

Sean Latham

"Where do the words come from?" Bob Dylan has been asked some version of this question hundreds of times over the years by journalists, fans, and critics, all hoping to glimpse the origin of his seemingly boundless capacity for lyrical invention. When he first arrived on the New York folk music scene, Dylan typically responded by crafting an ever-more colorful history for himself and attributed some of his early tunes to a life lived on the road. He claimed, for example, to have studied at the feet of a nameless Chicago bluesman after running away from home and also suggested that he gathered material from his (entirely fictitious) years spent working in traveling circuses and carnivals.[1] In 1962, just after the release of his first album, he playfully fended off Cynthia Gooding's initial attempts to explore his creative process by complaining about the studio temperature when she asked how much of "Fixin' to Die" he had written. When she got him back on track and again pressed the question, Dylan unwound a tale about a woman working in a side show known as the "elephant lady" before explaining that he wrote a song about her called "Won't You Buy a Postcard" but somehow lost it. Two months later, he employed similar tactics with Pete Seeger when the leader of the folk movement asked about "some of the songs Bob Dylan has made up." The young man again squirmed a bit before claiming that "I write a lotta stuff. In fact, I wrote five songs last night, but I gave all the papers away ... someplace."[2]

As his fame blossomed, Dylan met these kinds of questions with ever-increasing irritation. At a 1965 press conference in Los Angeles, he vaguely put off a question about his technique by explaining, "I just sit down and the next thing I know, [a song] is there."[3] The reporters doggedly pressed ahead, asking him if there was a message in his music, if he was honest

---

[1] *Oscar Brand Show*, WNYC Radio, New York City, October 29, 1961.
[2] WBAI Radio, New York City, March 11, 1962.
[3] Bob Dylan, Los Angeles Press Conference, December 1965. YouTube video, www.youtube.com/watch?v=8qEXRYsEj5Y.

about his emotions, and even if he wrote just to get rich. Not surprisingly, Dylan became hostile, explaining that he's "just an entertainer" who doesn't "have to explain [his] feelings."[4] The press conference then devolved into the same kind of strangely aimless stories he used when Gooding tried to explore his process. He ended it by telling the crowd that he had not come to California to perform, but was instead "looking for some donkeys."[5]

On the few occasions Dylan has tried to answer such questions directly, he too seems mystified, which might help explain why he has been so evasive on this point for so long. "I don't know how I got to write those songs," he confessed to Ed Bradley in a 2004 television interview. "All those early songs were almost magically written," he says, before reeling off from memory some of the most haunting lines from "It's Alright Ma."[6] It almost sounds like he's invoking a spell as the words spill from him, and then he abruptly breaks it with a shrug. "Try to sit down and write something like that" he challenges Bradley, letting us catch just a glimpse of that infamous snarl, now shadowed by age and his own genuine sense of puzzlement about the "penetrating magic" his younger self had once conjured.[7]

In one of his most masterful tricks, Dylan has recently turned the question of creativity back on us – on the fans, scholars, and performers who have held out hope that there might be some kind of special formula for inventing the painterly world of "Tangled Up in Blue" or a semi-biblical parable like "All Along the Watchtower." Starting in 1991, he has steadily released what has now become fifteen volumes of "official bootleg" collections that include live concert performances, rehearsals, demos, and studio tapes. Taken together, they constitute a massive catalog of his sixty-year career that often allows us to see the songs in the process of creation. On *The Cutting Edge* (2015), for example, we can listen to the now iconic "Like a Rolling Stone" first struggle to life in a crowded New York studio as a mournful waltz, abruptly fall apart into confusion within a few takes, then flash again briefly at a faster tempo before settling finally into a slow, bluesy groove. Dylan and his patchwork band then suddenly set the song in its more familiar 4/4 signature, allowing the lyrics to wrap themselves around a distinctly rock sound. Then, in the seventh recorded take, that iconic snare shot crashes through the speakers, Al Kooper's organ moans

---

[4] Ibid.   [5] Ibid.
[6] *60 Minutes*, "Bob Dylan Gives Rare Interview," December 5, 2004, www.cbsnews.com/news/60-minutes-bob-dylan-rare-interview-2004/.
[7] Ibid.

just a bit behind the beat, and the song explodes in its essentially finished form.

Similar moments of invention flash throughout the Bootleg series. On *The Basement Tapes Complete* (2014), for example, "You Ain't Goin' Nowhere" locks immediately into its laconic groove, but with seemingly random verses about feeding the cat as Dylan clearly experiments with sound and meter. When the tape next starts, these dummy lyrics give way to the fully formed pastoral vision of a song that has now been covered by dozens of major artists. In this case, the chorus and music appear to develop alongside one another and Dylan then steps back to fill in the verses after he has a sense of the song's sound and rhythm. On *More Blood, More Tracks* (2018), we hear a different kind of creative process at work. Among Dylan's most famous bootlegs, these recordings include spare acoustic versions of "Tangled Up in Blue" and "Idiot Wind" that return to the songwriter's folk roots and to a mode of writing shorn of the star's anger and irony. Tantalizingly, this release also includes photographs of a red pocket note-book that contains three different versions of "Idiot Wind," allowing us to see how the lyrics first took shape then morphed on the page into the final, recorded version.

As if this long sonic dive into the artist's workshop wasn't enough, Dylan sold his extraordinary archive to the George Kaiser Family Foundation and the University of Tulsa in 2016. This collection (discussed at length in Chapter 27), contains some 100,000 items ranging from photographs and session tapes to correspondence, promotional material, and even the leather jacket Dylan wore on that muggy seaside night in 1965 when he plugged in his electric guitar at the Newport Folk Festival. At the heart of it all are stacks of notebooks like the one photographed for *More Blood, More Tracks* as well as page after page of manuscripts on which songs – both familiar and unreleased – take shape. Where do the words come from? What's the source of the magic? We might not yet be able to answer those questions, but this archive now allows us to at least trace the spell as it is cast, to see how clusters of ideas gel into songs, to understand how some concepts wither, and to explore the kinds of things Dylan himself was reading and thinking about as he wrote. Unlike the Bootleg tapes, this material reveals that much of Dylan's music does not emerge mystically in the studio, but is instead the result of arduous work, deep research, and careful craftsmanship.

The sheer size and depth of the Bob Dylan Archive® means that unraveling Dylan's writing processes will take decades of work. Even a brief survey of the materials, furthermore, makes it clear that there is no magic formula since the songwriter has plainly experimented with many different writing techniques over the years. As he told Bradley in that 2004 interview, he might no longer be able to summon the surreal lyrics of "It's Alright Ma," but "you can't do something forever . . . and I can do other things now."[8] As we will see, there is no single well from which the words emerge – no simple pattern of invention, composition, and revision. Indeed, one of Dylan's greatest strengths as a songwriter might be his studied resistance to habit and formula. He tries desperately not to repeat himself and thus appears to be regularly in search not just of new songs and sounds, but new techniques for distilling his imagination into music and performance.

Know My Song Well

On September 20, 1962, Dylan tried out a new song for a few friends – a test just ahead of his first major concert at Carnegie Hall, which took place just two days later. "A Hard Rain's A-Gonna Fall" is many things: a terrifying journey through a surreal landscape, a dense mass of wide-ranging allusions, a brutal coming-of-age narrative, and a savage indictment of a modern world filled with bloody confusion that both echoes and updates Allen Ginsberg's "Howl." Although written just before the Cuban Missile Crisis, it immediately resonated with a generation first learning to think about global destruction through nuclear war, climate change, and extinction. Fifty-four years after its premiere, Patti Smith stepped to the microphone at the Nobel Prize ceremony in Stockholm and performed it in place of the curiously absent Dylan (see Chapter 25). Despite initially stumbling over the lines, she revealed the strange and haunting power of a tune that seems just as urgent now as it did in 1962.

"A Hard Rain's A-Gonna Fall" is among Dylan's greatest creations because it is essentially a song about the process of creation itself – about the courage required to see, hear, and feel the world and then try to give honest voice to that experience. It takes shape, after all, around a young man – a "blue-eyed son" – who has ventured out and now returned, making it into a kind of epic poem, a modern retelling of Homer's *Odyssey* condensed into a bare 554 words. "Where have you been?" "What did you see?" "What did you hear?" "Who did you meet?" the bewildered mother asks. The singer steadily relates his experiences before being faced with a more challenging question: "What'll you do now, my darling young one?" He vows to go back into the world again, to bear

---

[8] Ibid.

witness one more time, "to tell it, and think it, and speak it, and breathe it." But he also promises to do more than simply describe what he sees. In the final line of the last verse he promises, "I'll know my song well before I start singin'."

Dylan was only twenty-one when he wrote those lines and yet he had already immersed himself in a deep, albeit uneven, education in American folk and popular music that encompassed country, pop, gospel, and the blues. Growing up in Hibbing, Minnesota, he spent his days listening to popular crooners like Frank Sinatra and Bing Crosby as well as the first wave of rock 'n' roll ushered in by Elvis. Thanks to a trick of the atmosphere, at night he could twist his radio dials carefully to capture the AM signals that bounced their way to him from Arkansas and Louisiana. They carried a different kind of sound defined by black voices from the American South, a wide collection of styles and sounds loosely called the blues made by performers with what sounded then like mythical names: John Lee Hooker, T-Bone Walker, Howlin' Wolf, and Muddy Waters. He took it all in and set himself the stern task of learning these many styles and sounds.

His friends and collaborators have long described Dylan's talents as a mimic and his unusual ability to perform a song after hearing it just once or twice. One of the oldest items in the Bob Dylan Archive, in fact, is a scratchy recording of the young man pounding out a cover of Little Richard in the high school auditorium, a performance so wild that the principal worried it would damage the piano. As he finished high school and left home, he abruptly shifted his focus to the growing folk music boom and sought its source material on any record he could find – the older and more obscure the better. He plundered record collections, dug deeply into the idiosyncratic *Anthology of American Folk Music* (1952) compiled by the avant-garde artist Harry Smith, and kept an ear out for anything new, obscure, or unexpected. During his brief stint as a college student in Minneapolis, a beatnik named David Whittaker handed him a copy of *Bound for Glory* (1943), Woody Guthrie's half-remembered and half-invented hobo's idyll. The young man who a few months earlier had styled himself after a queer black rock star as he pounded on the piano, now adopted what he hoped might pass for an Oklahoma drawl, dressed in ragged work clothes, and listened to every Guthrie song he could find.

Before he arrived in New York in January 1961, Dylan had spent only a few years studying the kind of folk songs that would first catapult him to fame, but his research had been broad and often meticulous. In the Greenwich Village coffee houses where he first performed, this education continued, as he gathered songs from other performers and from the dusty corners of Izzy Young's Folklore Center – a tiny storefront and informal archive that played a pivotal role in the 1960s Folk Revival (see Chapter 5). Dylan not only learned new sets of songs, but also came to understand the folk and blues tradition of floating lyrics, in which performers grab key words, riffs, and images and then remix them with others. Such songs are less fixed compositions than scaffolds on which new and familiar ideas can be arranged and Dylan experimented creatively with this system.

When he entered Columbia's famous New York studios to record his first album in 1962, he had indeed learned his songs well and he flaunts that education in the seventeen tracks he cut in a pair of three-hour sessions. All but two of these are covers of extraordinary works from the American folk and blues canon, the tracks often made remarkable by Dylan's uncanny mimicry. "See That My Grave Is Kept Clean" (first recorded by Blind Lemon Jefferson in 1927) and "In My Time of Dying" (first recorded by Blind Willie Johnson in 1927) both offer terrifying visions of a singer facing death, and perhaps even reporting back from the other side. In the original versions, the distinctive intonation of black blues singers invokes not just a spiritual reckoning, but also the terrors of the Jim Crow South and the haunted vision of lynched men shocked by the violence suddenly visited on them. Dylan's own performance pays homage to these early recordings through his mimicry, but he is also manipulating and perhaps even exploiting what Jennifer Lynn Stoever calls "the sonic color line" – a way of "racializing" sound that codes certain ways of listening and performing as black while effectively producing 'the inaudibility of whiteness.'[9] In mimicking both Guthrie and Jefferson on these early covers, we see a student still studying and still trying to come to grips with the vast gap between his experiences and those of a Dust Bowl hobo or a blues singer suffering the terrors of American racism.

The two original tracks on that same album, however, suggest that Dylan began to see a way past mere imitation and the moral hazards of borrowing another person's tragedy. Both are musical homages to Woody Guthrie and the first, "Talkin' New York," is built entirely from the older singer's toolbox complete with a talking-blues format, open guitar chords, and a feigned aw-shucks humor about big city life. It even has a few floating lyrics borrowed from Guthrie, including the title (from "Talkin' Dust Bowl Blues"), the line about getting ripped off by a fountain pen ("Pretty

---

[9] Jennifer Lynn Stoever, *The Sonic Color Line: Race and the Cultural Politics of Listening* (New York: NYU Press, 2016), pp. 7, 12.

Boy Floyd"), and the closing image of taking a train out of the city ("New York Town"). The song is clever, funny, and shows off Dylan's talents for improvisation while also acknowledging – as many of the songs on this first album do – his debts to the earlier performers.

The second original song on the album is also an homage to Guthrie, but is entirely different in tone and structure. It plainly marks the moment Dylan comes into his own as a songwriter, acknowledging that to know a song well means more than just mastering lyrics, melody, and intonation. "Song to Woody" takes its tune from the older performer's "1913 Massacre" (1941). As Daniel Wolff has demonstrated in *Grown-Up Anger*, this early Dylan original only grows richer with each hearing, as the young man unpacks his complex relationship to the folk movement, its 1930s labor politics, its unexpected intersections with the iron mining town he once called home, and his own dawning sense of outrage at the world's injustice.[10] Once again, he floats in lyrics from Guthrie's great ballads. In its powerful closing lines, however, it also marks Dylan's decision to be more than just a mimic, more than just a copy artist trying to warble like an Okie or sound the agonies of blackness. In a voice much closer to his own flat Minnesota accent, he admits that "the very last thing that I'd want to do, / Is to say that I'd hit some hard travelin' too." With this deft lyric, he honestly confesses that so far he has only imitated others and lacks the kind of experiences that hurt those before him into art. His studies had been deep, in effect, but they also revealed to him what he still lacked – a vision of the world that emerged from his own ideas and experiences.

That first album of covers was essentially a flop, and as its sales limped along, Dylan turned from studying music to inventing it, writing a collection of entirely new songs that would shortly launch him to fame. Building on what he now knew to reach for, a vision of his own, he crafted one of his first and most enduring masterpieces: "Blowin' in the Wind." A manuscript version of this song in its earliest form exists, but shows little evidence of revision or evolution.[11] Contemporary witnesses, furthermore, seem to confirm that it sprang from Dylan's mind almost fully formed. Gil Turner, a distinguished folk singer who also worked in Greenwich Village, reports that on April 16, 1963, Dylan brought him a copy of the song with only the first and last verses that he had just worked out in a back room. Turner was astonished by what he saw scrawled on the pages and agreed to

---

[10] Daniel Wolff, *Grown-Up Anger: The Connected Mysteries of Bob Dylan, Woody Guthrie, and the Calumet Massacre of 1913* (New York: Harper, 2017).

[11] Autograph manuscript of "Blowin' in the Wind," 1962, in *A Rock & Roll Anthology: From Folk to Fury*, Sotheby's, www.sothebys.com/en/auctions/ecatalogue/2016/rock-roll-n09587/lot.51.html.

test it out that evening for a crowd that shared his sense of wonder. Dylan soon added another verse and his manager, Albert Grossman, then offered it to his new folk super group, Peter, Paul and Mary. By the summer, it had become a Billboard number 1 hit and would become an anthem of the civil rights movement and part of the "brand" of the 1960s (see Chapter 20). It also helped create the mythos of Dylan as Romantic genius – not a hardworking craftsman or a student of the past, but a genius who could dash off an extraordinary work like this at a moment's notice.

As the image of the dedicated blue-eyed son in "Hard Rain" suggests, however, the truth is rather more complicated. We may not have a deep manuscript record for "Blowin'," but the song reflects careful study, a deep knowledge of the blues process, and a talent for bricolage that is ultimately more interesting than mere inspiration. As Pete Seeger and others soon realized, Dylan built the song around "No More Auction Block," a nineteenth-century marching tune likely created by black soldiers in the Civil War. That older song had been covered by performers like Paul Robeson and Odetta, whose deep and languorous intonation of its horrifying chorus about the "many thousands gone" powerfully mixed music, politics, protest, and resilience in the face of ongoing racial violence.

Here, Dylan once again borrows sounds and ideas from these predecessors, but crucially, he gives up on the idea of trying simply to imitate them. He does not sound the blackness of the original at all, in fact, but instead speeds up the tempo considerably to remove the mournfulness and fashions a new set of more ambiguous lyrics that replace the repeated verses of the original with a set of open-ended questions. The words themselves are biblical and their emphasis on doubt and uncertainty echo everywhere from Genesis and Exodus to the Psalms and even to Jesus crying out on the cross, "My God, my God, why have you foresaken me?"[12] As Michael Gray argues, they find a more specific origin in the book of Ezekiel, the record of a Hebrew prophet who foresaw the destruction of Jerusalem and its eventual return to glory. After proclaiming the city's end, he cries out that the people "have eyes but do not see and ears to hear but do not hear, for they are a rebellious people."[13] Dylan's three verses build around similar questions about a contemporary (if also timeless) America that cannot see or hear – and might already be in the kind of wandering exile that Ezekiel predicted for the Jewish people.

---

[12] Matt. 27:46 (NIV).
[13] Ezek. 12:1; Michael Gray, *Bob Dylan Encyclopedia* (New York: Continuum, 2006).

Although we cannot trace the evolution of these lyrics directly in the archival record, we can see just how essential Dylan's arduous studies have been to his songwriting. By blending a mournful black protest song with open-ended but biblically inflected lyrics, he creates what has now become an effectively timeless protest song.[14] And the borrowing doesn't stop with just this song. As we've already seen, Dylan returned to a similar set of questions when he composed "A Hard Rain," but in that slightly later song, they feel more desperate, more deeply rooted in the prophetic tradition, and more committed to using song in order to tell hard truths rather than simply wonder about the world's injustice.

This distinctive method of composition, which involves looking to the past as a source of innovation, is part of what makes Dylan's writing so distinctive. Unlike many of the other performers in the early Greenwich folk scene, he wanted to do more than faithfully imitate or preserve the past; instead, he sought to use it, just as Guthrie did, to make something new. This procedure has led some critics and reviewers to condemn him as a plagiarist (see Chapter 17). A particularly scandalous *Newsweek* article in 1963, in fact, wrongly claimed that he had stolen "Blowin' in the Wind" from a high school student in Boston.[15] These allegations wounded Dylan at the time, causing him to turn sometimes savagely on the press and the hurt is still evident decades later in a 2012 *Rolling Stone* interview when he recounts that original *Newsweek* allegation, and then tells Mikal Gilmore, "Fuck 'em. I'll see them all in their graves."[16]

My Prayer Book

Borrowing, repurposing, and reassembling the past is fundamental to Dylan's method and reflects his commitment to the kind of dedicated study he described in "Hard Rain." When he withdrew to Woodstock, NY in the late 1960s, he brought with him most of the touring group that weathered the tumultuous 1966 tour and that would later be known as the Band. Together, they created the now legendary *Basement Tapes* (captured in their entirety on Bootleg v. 11). These sessions are legendary for producing songs like "This Wheel's on Fire," but the bulk of the material is

---

[14] The song's open-ended nature means it can be used for nearly any cause demanding change. In 2017, for example, Regina Spektor performed it – with powerful accompaniment from the crowd – at the Women's March in Los Angeles.

[15] "I Am My Words," *Newsweek*, November 4, 1963, p. 95.

[16] "Bob Dylan Unleashed," *Rolling Stone*, September 27, 2012, www.rollingstone.com/music/music-news/bob-dylan-unleashed-189723/

actually a graduate seminar in American music in which Dylan takes his
fellow musicians through dozens of old songs, including prison tunes ("Po'
Lazarus" and "The Auld Triangle"), labor songs ("The Bells of Rhymney"),
sea shanties ("Ol' Roison the Beau"), and country-gospel numbers
("Belshazaar"). Others who have played with Dylan at various times have
described not only his seemingly encyclopedic knowledge of American folk
song, but also his interest in teaching potential bandmates old covers like
these that never made it onto a concert set list.

This kind of musical pedagogy not only belongs to bootlegs and
rehearsal rooms, however, but also constitutes an important strain of
Dylan's recorded output, stretching from that first self-titled album full
of covers to his more recent releases that draw almost exclusively from the
Great American Songbook (see Chapter 11). When it appears he might be
stuck in a rut or struggling for inspiration, in fact, Dylan often turns to his
past self, allowing us to hear him actually study his songs right in front of
us. In fact, what many critics have long called Dylan's endless process of
reinvention or transformation – from folk icon to rock star to country
singer to gospel performer to unlikely crooner – can also be seen as an
ongoing process of self investigation. As the hippies descended on
Woodstock in 1969, for example, Dylan took flight from the madness
and started making what might initially seem like fantastical lists of songs
for *Self Portrait*, a double album filled with covers that prompted a startled
Greil Marcus to ask in *Rolling Stone*, "What is this shit?"[17]

At the time, Dylan had been suffering from an apparent lack of inspiration and his notebooks from this period are filled with fragments of
abandoned songs, abstract doodles, and even complaints about how long
the days can be. In a 1978 interview, he described this as a period of
"amnesia" in which "it took [him] a long time to get to do consciously
what [he] used to be able to do unconsciously."[18] Even as he filled the
notebooks with lyrical experiments, he also began compiling playlists from
which he would eventually pull the tunes that appeared on *Self Portrait*. Its
appearance may have shocked listeners and critics like Marcus, but in
retrospect we can now see that Dylan used that final year in Woodstock
to once again start studying in order to prepare for something new. This
album, in fact, now stands as part of a string of releases that includes the
publication of his lyrics as *Writings and Drawings* (1973), the release of his
largely abandoned novel *Tarantula* (1971), and the *Greatest Hits Vol. II*

---

[17] Greil Marcus, "Self Portrait," *Rolling Stone*, June 8, 1970.
[18] Cited in Clinton Heylin, *Behind the Shades Revisited* (New York: Harper, 2001), 295.

album (1971) – all of which provided the artist with a sweeping retrospective of his first decade of work. In the wake of this plunge into his own archive, he returned to the studio in 1974 to record what would become *Blood on the Tracks* – one of the most widely admired albums of his career.

This process played itself out again in the early 1990s when the songwriter again seemed to lose his creative spark on albums like *Under the Red Sky* (1990), which inspired little interest. A year later, the first official Bootleg release appeared, which contained work ranging from an amateur tape made in 1961 to a remixed song from the most recent album. Dylan then set to work on two new albums that emerged from yet another plunge deep into musical history similar to the one he undertook before making *Self Portrait*. This time, he covered a wealth of traditional American folk songs on *Good as I Been to You* (1992) and *World Gone Wrong* (1993). These tunes are tragic, mournful, and filled with a kind of gnostic symbolism that he plainly hoped to tap into in an effort to restart his own writing. As Dylan told John Pareles for a *New York Times* interview in 1997, "Those old songs are my lexicon and my prayer book . . . . You can find all my philosophy in those old songs."[19]

Once again, Dylan's deep commitment to studying the past – to learning his song well before he starts singing – began to yield new and even transformative work, first in *Time Out of Mind* (1997) and then in the extraordinary *"Love and Theft"* (2001). The title of this album, eerily released on September 11, 2001, appears in quotes, acknowledging that it had been borrowed from a book of the same name by the historian Eric Lott about the origins of popular music in black performance and especially in the deep racism of blackface minstrelsy.[20] All of the dozen songs on this double album are steeped in historical and cultural references that reveal an extraordinary depth of learning. In some cases, these debts are made apparent, so that in a song like "High Water (For Charley Patton)," we can recognize the early black blues singer in the title. He famously coaxed an extraordinary range of sounds from his voice and guitar to describe the devastation of a 1927 flood on the Mississippi that killed hundreds and displaced hundreds of thousands of black families, thus helping to propel a new wave of the Great Migration. In Dylan's version of the song, the waters crash through the entire sweep of human history, from the biblical flood to the Civil War, the Jim Crow South, and even

---

[19] "A Wiser Voice Blowin' in the Wind," *New York Times*, September 28, 1997.
[20] Eric Lott, *Love and Theft: Blackface Minstrelsy and the American Working Class* (Oxford: Oxford University Press, 1993).

modern philosophy. Charley Patton thus jostles with Charles Darwin, Big Joe Turner (the blues shouter who sang "Shake, Rattle, & Roll"), and the English materialist philosopher George Lewes.

This same density of sonic, lyrical, cultural, and historical allusion appears everywhere on the album, making each song not only an act of love and theft, but also a history lesson carefully designed to resist the idea that Dylan – or any other artist – simply invents songs out of his head or can operate independently from the entwined traditions of the blues, folk, gospel, and country that weave together to create American popular music. Over the next decade, in fact, Dylan's writing process led him ever deeper into this entangled history and, as David Yaffe writes, "sometimes it is fascinating just to hear him work the archives."[21] As was the case at the start of his career, allegations of plagiarism again emerged. Two lines from an otherwise obscure book about Japanese organized crime, for example, were discovered in "Floater." But this accusation ignores the fact that Dylan used a whole jumble of cultural references as floating blues lyrics to construct the album. These include, the story of Tweedle Dee and Tweedle Dum in the opening track; the rockabilly riff that drives the nostalgic lament of "Summertime"; and the classic floating blues line "dust my broom" that drifts into "High Water." Dylan is schooling himself and us in these songs – a process that accelerated on the next two albums and took extraordinary shape in *Theme Time Radio Hour*. This latter series of 100 shows produced for XM radio from 2006 to 2009 took the form of an old-time radio show with Dylan himself serving as a wry DJ reading (mostly fake) fan mail, delivering corny one-liners, and offering a deep lesson in the history of American popular music. He had once insisted at the start of his career that a singer or writer must know a song well before singing, and here he insists that his listeners too should be part of this same process so that they can understand the density and deep learning of his work.

Still Studying

Even as he led his fans down these wandering musical pathways into the source of his own creative energy, he also turned that analytical process on himself and his own history. By the 1990s, Dylan had become an integral part of American music – the towering influence of "Blowin' in the Wind" and *Highway 61 Revisited* still helping define the boundaries of rock as a now mature genre. Faced with the looming presence of his own persona,

---

[21] David Yaffe, *Bob Dylan: Like a Complete Unknown* (New Haven: Yale University Press, 2001), p. 113.

Dylan again set out to study the tradition – this time the tradition he himself had helped create. We see this process most powerfully at work in the so-called Never Ending Tour, a term that loosely encompasses the steady set of touring performances that still take him around the world each year, through venues both large and intimate. (In yet another return to his roots, his 2019 tour included a series of twenty-eight college venues.) Ever fearful of becoming a mere parody of himself – a kind of Vegas act who pumps out his old standards night after night – Dylan has used these tours to reinvent his own music in what has become a now annual ritual. One of the great pleasures of attending a Dylan concert, in fact, is trying to guess the song: to suddenly realize that a surf-rock sound has now been wrapped strangely around his foundational gospel song, "Gotta Serve Somebody," or that the slow tune with the bowed bass reeking of a dusky nightclub is actually "Like a Rolling Stone."

This always surprising, and sometimes unsettling, tendency to rearrange or even partially rewrite songs has long been a part of Dylan's practice, going back at least to the 1975–1976 Rolling Thunder Revue tour. Michael Denning, in fact, argues that "Dylan's fundamental long form, the frame for his songs, is not the album, but the concert and the concert tour."[22] This extraordinary show followed the release of *Blood on the Tracks* and took shape as a traveling circus that mixed headliners (including Roger McGuinn and Joan Baez) with startling new talents like the violinist Scarlett Rivera and guitarist T Bone Burnett. Tapes from various stops on the tour have been collected in a 2019 box set and it is the subject of an extraordinary film directed by Martin Scorsese that mixes riveting live concert footage with all kinds of patently false interviews and stories about what actually happened. Dylan designed the original tour with director Jacques Levy, brought along the playwright Sam Shepard and even performed first in a plastic mask and then in bright white grease paint – all of which lent a sense of improvisation, spectacle, and performativity. After Rolling Thunder, his performances only became more theatrical as he rearranged the sound, lyrics, tempo, and mood of even his greatest works.

In the last several years, as Richard Thomas has argued, his concerts have once again started to feel like carefully choreographed dramatic productions.[23] The improvised *commedia dell'arte* feel of the 1970s, however, has given way to

[22] Michael Denning, "Bob Dylan and Rolling Thunder," in *The Cambridge Companion to Bob Dylan*, ed. Kevin J.H. Dettmar (Cambridge: Cambridge University Press, 2009), p. 31.
[23] Richard Thomas, *Why Bob Dylan Matters* (New York: Harper Collins, 2017), p. 274.

something more spare and more formal. The stage is typically dressed entirely in black; there are no introductions, opening acts, or attempts to prime the crowd. Dylan and his band simply walk onto the stage in darkness, the lights come up, and they play a fixed list of songs that rotates by season but rarely changes between performances. He never says a word to the audience and simply leaves after the encore – usually to roaring applause. Like all great actors, he refuses to break character and instead pours his energy into creating "Bob Dylan" in front of us, so that his songwriting, as Anthony Decurtis suggests, becomes "something that he enacts as much on stage as in the studio."[24] This is nothing like the image of the Romantic genius rattling off song after song on his typewriter. Instead, we see Dylan still studying his song, pursuing an increasingly recursive journey through the sounds and traditions of American popular music that now include his own works – not as museum pieces to be preserved, but as source material for a new cycle of writing and revision.

In 2018, a forty-seven-year-old song unexpectedly returned to Dylan's concert set lists and has remained there ever since. He first wrote "When I Paint My Masterpiece" in 1971 and gave it to the Band for their album *Cahoots*, then, perhaps ironically, added his own version (backed by Leon Russell) on *Bob Dylan Greatest Hits Volume II*. The lyrics describe a trip to Rome in which the past collapses into the present as the singer wanders the alleyways of both the ancient city and his own lively imagination. Struggling for inspiration among the ruins, he sings that "Someday, everything is gonna be different / When I paint my masterpiece." In performances separated by nearly five decades, we can hear Dylan still struggling with the creative process, still attempting to sing his song well, still trying to describe the world around him, still seeking to craft his masterpiece and have done. The towering rock star of 1971 who first sang these lyrics sounded confident in his performance, convinced that his long pursuit and careful study would yield something. The cracked yet glorious ruin of Dylan's voice in 2018, however, sounds far more uncertain.

He confesses as much in his Nobel Lecture, itself a wandering meditation recorded over a free-form piano that makes it feel like we might be listening to an old, rambling man in a smoky jazz bar. At the very end, he seems to conclude that his quest for that masterpiece will fail, in part because songs are not paintings or ancient Roman buildings that take permanent form. "Our songs are alive in the land of the living," he says.

---

[24] Anthony Decurtis, "Bob Dylan as Songwriter," *Cambridge Companion to Bob Dylan*, ed. Dettmar, p. 54.

"They're meant to be sung, not read." He then turns to Homer and quotes the first line of the *Odyssey* – itself a song that had been chanted for generations before the ancient Greek poet set it down in script: "Sing in me, O Muse, and through me tell the story."[25] Dylan, it seems, can never quite paint his masterpiece, never study his song enough, in part because performance itself is part of the creation. Like the young man from Minnesota who gathered up old songs and rewove them for decades into something new, he invites us at the end of this speech to listen to the music – and in listening, hear something new. Here then, is his best answer to the question, "Where do the words come from?" They come from a tradition that can be endlessly pillaged, rearranged, and renewed – a tradition that now includes Dylan himself.

[25] Bob Dylan, *The Nobel Lecture* (New York: Simon & Schuster, 2017), p. 23.

CHAPTER 4

The Singles: A Playlist for Framing Dylan's Recording Art

Keith Negus

Bob Dylan began his career as a performing musician during a period when the vinyl LP was being adopted as a medium for creating an atmosphere and ambience. Frank Sinatra's themed albums that evoked specific moods began appearing as 78 rpm disc collections from 1946.[1] The more robust 12-inch, 33⅓ record was introduced by Columbia Records in June 1948, and allowed Sinatra to introduce albums on one long player (LP) with a series of acclaimed collections during the 1950s. Dylan has acknowledged Sinatra's work throughout his career, even paying homage by performing "Restless Farewell" at the older performer's 80th birthday celebrations in 1995, and releasing *Shadows in the Night* in 2015. The album featured renditions of songs popularized and defined by the interpretations of Sinatra and his imaginative arrangers and it was followed by *Fallen Angels* (2016) and *Triplicate* (2017) with further selections from the Great American Songbook (see Chapter 11).

Like Sinatra's collections, Dylan's individual albums are characterized by an overall feel and ambience rather than a concept or a narrative. This is partly why he has omitted the recordings of critically acclaimed songs from albums – tracks that have appeared on later official bootlegs. For example, the austere piano and acoustic guitar version of "Blind Willie McTell" would have been incongruous on *Infidels* if placed amongst the bland lite reggae and soft rock textures of the album, regardless of its quality as a song. A Dylan album typically takes shape not around a unity of narrative, but a sound world and ambience: whether the casual vocals, loose acoustic guitar strumming, and irregular pulses throughout *Another Side of Bob Dylan* (1964) or the claustro-phobic and murky amalgam of saxophone, trumpet, keyboards, percussion, electric and acoustic guitar, mandolin, and gospel vocals pervading *Street Legal* (1978). Dylan's approach was unlike those rock musicians who adapted the

---

[1] Charles Granata, *Sessions with Sinatra: Frank Sinatra and the Art of Recording* (Chicago: Chicago Review Press, 2004).

album as a frame for conceptual ideas and narrative suites of songs, such as The Who's "rock opera" *Tommy* (1969) and Genesis's *The Lamb Lies Down on Broadway* (1974) – the latter indebted to Leonard Bernstein's and Stephen Sondheim's *West Side Story*. The Beatles' *Sgt. Pepper's Lonely Hearts Club Band* (1967) has sometimes been presented as a concept album. Yet, the fictional Edwardian brass band was merely a mask to distance the group from their Beatles personas. It was not so much a concept as "a convenient way of packaging twelve randomly collected tracks."[2]

Dylan neither had the repertoire of a variety entertainer nor the inclinations of a conceptual rock musician. His well-known response to *Sgt. Pepper* was to accentuate his place in an "old weird America"[3] of country, blues, and folk with a series of plainly recorded and unadorned songs, populated by mysterious or marginal characters in Southern gothic settings on the album *John Wesley Harding* (1967), followed by reveries of domestic contentment and rural tranquility on *Nashville Skyline* (1969), *New Morning* (1970), and *Self Portrait* (1970). This was a rejection of the album as concept, the trend toward rock as art, and the use of the studio for baroque ornamentation and sonic effects. Dylan has never sought to be an innovator of studio recording techniques, release formats, or cultural trends. He has either followed the prevailing technologies and ethos of recording at the time, or simply ignored them. Yet, his late 1960s recordings introduced a casual and convivial recording aesthetic that has influenced generations of folk-rock, lo-fi, and Americana musicians.

When recording songs, Dylan has sought to capture a tone and a groove, rather than to trouble with the technicalities of precise arrangements, to separate instruments in a mix, or to find the flawless definitive version. When recordings have circulated of Dylan performing or rehearsing songs – whether through official releases or bootlegs – it is clear that the aim is to create an atmosphere and a sound world. He has spoken of this often in interviews over a period of years, from his desire to create a "thin, wild mercury sound" that is "metallic and bright gold"[4] – a sound that characterized few actual recordings; and his belief that "the old Chess records, the Sun records. I think that's my favorite sound for a record ... I like the mood of those records – the intensity. The sound is uncluttered. There's power and suspense. The whole vibration feels like it's coming from inside your mind."[5]

[2] Charlie Gillett, *The Sound of the City* (London: Souvenir Press, 1983), p. 267.
[3] Greil Marcus, *Invisible Republic, Bob Dylan's Basement Tapes* (New York: Henry Holt, 1997).
[4] Robert Shelton, *No Direction Home: The Life and Music of Bob Dylan* (New York: Da Capo, 1986).
[5] Bill Flanagan, "Bob Dylan Talks About Together Through Life with Bill Flanagan," www.bobdylan.com.

This search for a favored sound guided his approach and direction to band members and engineers under the pseudonym of producer Jack Frost on "*Love and Theft*" (2001) and *Modern Times* (2006). Dylan has clearly attempted to evoke contrasting moods, from the slickly recorded *Slow Train Coming* (1979) with its funk gospel organ and brass textures (produced by Jerry Wexler and Barry Beckett), to the reverb heavy, multi-layered and "swampy" (Dylan's term) murk of guitars and keyboards on *Time Out of Mind* (produced by Daniel Lanois). His most consistent sound has been a blend of the smoother metallic bright timbres of country, the directness and irregularities of folk, and the abrasive blues sonorities of electric guitar and harmonica.[6] Sound, tone, and feel are more important than variety or concept. Dylan has never been an album artist in the same way as some of his contemporaries, such as the Beach Boys or Marvin Gaye who aspired to make coherent thematic musical statements, or in the way in which the album as idea was developed by artists such as Prince or Rubén Blades, Kate Bush or Kendrick Lamar or Björk. Even Dylan's most critically acclaimed albums – *Highway 61 Revisited* (1965), *Blood on the Tracks* (1974), *Oh Mercy* (1989), or *Time Out of Mind* (1997) – are collections of songs with an overall ambience rather than thematic or conceptual links connecting tracks.

And, there are alternatives to the album as a way of framing Dylan's songs and recordings. Paul Williams argued that Dylan should be appreciated as foremost a performer rather than a recording artist, constructing his argument through set lists, live shows, and analysis of different renditions of the same song. Dylan's songs can also be framed as poetry, in book collections of lyrics arranged as printed verse on a page or subject to analysis by scholars of poetry.[7] In 2018, his songs appeared as an exhibition of framed handwritten lyrics with graphite illustrations on the walls of the upmarket Halcyon Gallery in London's Mayfair (a suitably elitist cultural space for a winner of the Nobel Prize in Literature). All of these frames influence how Dylan is understood as an artist and perceived by listeners, readers and viewers, and guide the way his life and work are interpreted. In this chapter, I take a different approach by framing his songs with an argument that the recorded single (now accessed as a track) can afford a distinctive cluster of insights into Dylan's creative life.

---

[6] For a more detailed discussion of Dylan's production in the studio, see Keith Negus, *Bob Dylan* (London: Equinox, 2008) and Negus, "Bob Dylan's Phonographic Imagination," *Popular Music*, 29 (2010), pp. 213–228.

[7] Christopher Ricks, *Dylan's Visions of Sin* (London: Viking, 2003).

Singles have been important to Dylan since he grew up listening to radio in the late 1940s and 1950s. He remembered this experience when presenting *Theme Time Radio Hour*, broadcast from 2006 to 2008 and comprising themed programs featuring recordings of songs about different subjects, including weather, drinking, mothers, cars, radio, moon, and hair. These programs illustrate Dave Marsh's point that "Singles are the essence of rock 'n' roll. They occupy the center of all the pop music that came after it. They're the stuff of our everyday conversations and debates about music, the totems that trigger our memories."[8] The first 7-inch, 45 rpm single was released by RCA in March 1949, and although a key to understanding so much popular music, it has generally been neglected by critics and academics. The single reached listeners who only liked one or two songs and who were not devoted fans of any artist. Many people's single collections were as eclectic as the charts in the 1960s, 1970s, and 1980s. Marsh's comment about albums is entirely applicable to Dylan's discography: "most albums (including many of the most successful and creative in history) remain singles separated by varying amounts of filler, though nobody likes to admit it."[9] Singles can be arranged into playlists, a way of organizing music that forms a continuous thread linking pre-rock 'n' roll radio programming to streaming platforms. Dylan's career has traversed the epoch from broadcast radio list to the digitally streamed list. His recorded songs now appear on playlists set up by curators, corporate bots, and consumers according to their own preference for mood and activity – 1970s Road Trip, Love Songs, Rock 'n' Roll All Night, Coffee Morning Vibes, and Chillout were all found within minutes of a quick spin through one streaming platform. Such lists are a useful way of succinctly and pragmatically conveying aspects of a fifty-year plus career as a recording artist. Here, then, is my Dylan playlist: ten singles that give an insight into his recording art.

"Mixed Up Confusion"(1962)

"Mixed Up Confusion" was the first single released by Dylan in December 1962, and was produced by John Hammond. It is evident that he, his management, and his record label, Columbia, had no clear idea that he was to be a "folk" singer or even a "protest" singer. In some

---

[8] Dave Marsh, *The Heart of Rock and Soul: The 1001 Greatest Singles Ever Made* (London: Penguin, 1989), p. ix
[9] Ibid.

ways it is a deceptively throwaway track. Yet, Dylan and the band of two guitars, bass, drums, and piano managed to create a harmonica-driven amalgam of rockabilly, country boogie, blues holler, and bar-room jazz piano that suits the shout and fall vocal delivery of a minimalist list of clichés (taken in turn from other songs) about people being too hard to please, looking for a woman, and feeling like a stranger. It would take Dylan a little longer to grasp how to resuscitate such lyrical clichés (which he would use again). Although it would be two and a half years before he faced condemnation for "going electric" at the Newport Folk Festival, he was electric on his first single. In fact, he was electric since his performances with rock 'n' roll bands at school. The electric performance of R&B and that blurry mixture of country and blues became a continual thread running throughout his recording life.

"Blowin' in the Wind" (1963)

"Blowin' in the Wind" has defined Dylan for many people, thanks initially to a cover by Peter, Paul and Mary who had a chart hit with it in 1963. Dylan's own recording is intimate, with casually played acous-tic guitar and harmonica, and the conversational tone reinforced by the repeated "yes, and ... " in the delivery of the lyrics. It has been sung solemnly by choirs in Christian cathedrals, bellowed at school assem-blies, and endlessly adapted to comment upon and satirize politicians. Lyrically it conveys stoic acceptance of the impossibility of changing a world of war and conflict, whilst offering vague hope that an "answer" is out there somewhere – blowin' in the wind. Like many of Dylan's creations, it is based on an existing song, the tune of "No More Auction Block" from the spiritual or slave songs tradition. Dylan was impressed by Odetta's recording of the song, and inspired more generally by the way she fused folk, blues, and gospel into her power-fully strummed guitar style. Sung by freed slaves in Canada after the abolition of slavery in 1833, to a melody traceable to the Ashanti tribe of West Africa, the lyrics were printed in the *Atlantic Monthly* in 1867 after the USA completely abolished slavery in 1865.[10] It is just one enduring testament to the profound influence of slavery on US culture and popular music more generally.

---

[10] Oliver Trager, *Keys to the Rain: The Definitive Bob Dylan Encyclopedia* (New York: Billboard Books, 2004).

"Subterranean Homesick Blues" (1965)

"Subterranean Homesick Blues" combines two of the most common melodic vocal patterns of blues-inspired, rhythmically driven lyrics – the chant on one pitch, with occasional drops down to a minor third below. Dylan has often mentioned the inspiration for this song: "It's from Chuck Berry ... A bit of 'Too Much Monkey Business' and some of the scat singers of the '40s."[11] Dylan tried an acoustic guitar version and then recorded it with a band of guitars, bass, drums, and electric piano. He took Berry's country R&B arrangement and reworked complaints about mundane jobs, obligations to conform, and debt into a paranoid, absurdist rant inspired by Beat poetry. Distrustful and vaguely defiant of authority – whether institutional, counter-cultural, or street wisdom – the moral is "don't follow leaders." This structured rhyming architecture has endured in Elvis Costello's "Pump It Up" and REM's "End of the World As We Know It." The single is also notable for the way it was integrated into the opening scene of the film *Dont Look Back* (1967), featuring Dylan in an alleyway holding up cards containing words from the song. This short clip was used to promote the song and has inspired many homages and parodies in music video and advertising.

"Like a Rolling Stone" (1965)

"Like a Rolling Stone" was based on a rage-driven poem Dylan had edited down, experimenting with a 6/8 piano-based ballad version in D♭ before recording it as a snare drum-backed 4/4 rock song in C. It builds on an oceanic blend of metallic electric guitar, hesitant swirling organ, insistent harmonica, and barroom bluesy piano indebted to Phil Spector's "wall of sound" technique. The song contains a character type that features in quite a few Dylan songs: the person (by implication, a woman) that has done him wrong, betrayed him, misunderstood him, wanted too much from him – another walking dead cliché constantly reworked in blues and rock music – sardonically addressed as "doll," "Miss Lonely," and "babe." The recording is nearly six and a quarter minutes long and was released to radio split over two sides of a 7-inch single, but available publicly as unedited on the A side. Once it started appearing in concert (it's his second most performed song), "Like a Rolling Stone" became less a howl of bile directed at someone unable to deal with their own decline, than a redemptive

---

11 Robert Hilburn, "When I Paint My Masterpiece," *Mojo*, September 2005, pp. 72–74.

anthem of belonging. During Dylan's 1974 tour, Betsy Bowden heard the audience singing along with "how does it feel?" as "reinforcing the feeling that each listener is not alone but rather part of a community all of whom know how it feels."[12] Of the stately large band performance recorded in Tokyo for *Live at Budokan*, Wilfrid Mellers observed that the song "transformed from a gleeful song of rejection into a powerful, almost hymnic paean which has only a vicarious connection with the words."[13] "Like a Rolling Stone," more than any other Dylan composition, demonstrates the way in which a musician tangibly and audibly connects with an audience in the here and now of the concert.

"All Along the Watchtower" (1968)

"All Along the Watchtower" is based on a familiar repeated loop of three chords (C#m, B, A) and circular verses that Dylan called a "cycle of events." It allows us to hear two important characteristics of Dylan's recorded songs and provides the only significant example of another musician profoundly changing the way Dylan performed his own songs. First, is the influence of the Christian Bible on his lyrics. Dylan has used phrases from the Bible to evoke the way narrators and characters seek redemption in their unfilled quest for salvation.[14] "All Along the Watchtower" draws its verses from Isaiah 21 and the Book of Revelation. The second characteristic illustrates Dylan's skill at using the harmonica as a mournful comment on the bleak landscapes conveyed by the minimal lyrics, and to subtly echo the "wind began to howl" with the sonic stylization of howling wind on the harmonica. The original released recording was musically sparse (featuring acoustic guitar, bass, and drums) with a conversational, understated vocal. Jimi Hendrix put out a recording of the song a month or so after Dylan's and removed the frailties, ambiguities, and ominous mood, thereby turning it into an assertive and defiantly declamatory rock anthem.[15] The subtleties and nuances of the original disappeared in concert as Dylan follows Hendrix by playing it as bombastic stomp of crowd-pleasing mainstream rock. It has

---

[12] Betsy Bowden, *Performed Literature, Words and Music by Bob Dylan* (Lanham, MD: University Press of America, 2001).

[13] Wilfrid Mellers, *A Darker Shade of Pale: A Backdrop to Bob Dylan* (Oxford: Oxford University Press, 1984), p. 219.

[14] Michael Gray, *Song and Dance Man III: The Art of Bob Dylan* (London: Continuum, 2000).

[15] Clinton Heylin, *Revolution in the Air: The Songs of Bob Dylan, 1957–1973* (Chicago: Chicago Review Press, 2009).

become Dylan's most performed song, with 2,268 performances by February 2020.

"If Not for You" (1970)

"If Not for You" is one of Dylan most relaxed and celebratory love songs, aptly described by Clinton Heylin as a serenade to his then wife Sara. The recording provides glimpses of another narrative about the singer's important connections with the Beatles, and especially George Harrison. The Beatles and Dylan had influenced each other, and musically commented on each other's work throughout the 1960s. Dylan and Harrison were spending considerable time together during the period when this song was being composed and the two musicians recorded a version together (unreleased at the time), before Dylan included the laidback, downhome bluesy country shuffle that appears on *New Morning*. That same year (1970), Harrison put out a slower rendition, with the blissful quality of contented love expressed through his characteristically melodic slide guitar. When Harrison died in 2001, Dylan began including a moving performance of "Something" in his live shows. Like so many of his songs, "If Not for You" was performed by many other artists and illustrates his ability to take everyday phrases and remove them from the mundane when expressing ordinary human sentiments, as well as his grasp of the value of singable melodies in popular song.[16] "If Not for You" was released as a single by Olivia Newton John the following year, with a recording that drew from both Dylan's and Harrison's versions. It was an important hit for Newton John who was named Country Music Association vocalist of the year in 1974 and had a big influence on the style of the country pop mainstream during this period. This sometimes overlooked single is part of yet another story about the importance of country music in Dylan's artistic life.

"Tangled Up in Blue" (1974)

"Tangled Up in Blue" is also musically grounded in country, folk, and blues, and Dylan recorded it using an open tuned guitar played higher up the neck to create a shimmering, bright and ringing sonority. He initially set the song in E at a series of New York sessions that were characterized by a melancholic and restrained ambience. The released version was recorded later in Minneapolis with different musicians and raised to the key of A, the

---

[16] See Gino Stefani, "Melody: A Popular Perspective," *Popular Music*, 6 (1987), pp. 21–35.

higher pitch allowing Dylan's voice to reach upwards and outwards, addressing an epic tale to an audience rather confiding in a more confessional manner. The relaxed urgency of the recording, propelled by the constantly returning suspended fourth chord motif, allowed Dylan to adopt a more upbeat storyteller's voice to deliver what is widely acclaimed as his most accomplished narrative lyric. The song draws from old ballads, with its familiar opening line of "early one morning" and in the technique of shifting perspectives with verses that can tell a story by being delivered in different sequences. Yet Dylan had also been reflecting on perspective in painting following art lessons with Norman Raeben and this inspired him to write lyrics in a way that allowed for the viewpoints of multiple protagonists and for constant shifting between present and past. The released single is narrated in the first person singular and plural (I, us/ we). In later live performances, however, Dylan would stretch the song in different directions, changing the scenes and settings while narrating it in first and third person, as if he – the Bob Dylan persona – is both telling the tale and observing himself from outside. In "Tangled Up in Blue" past events are not simply memories evoked through sentiment or nostalgia, but experiences profoundly present in the here and now.

"Gotta Serve Somebody" (1979)

"Gotta Serve Somebody" caused controversy and seemed to challenge many of the principles that people assumed Dylan held. It was a pivotal song during a period of about two years (1979–1980) when the songwriter became committed to an evangelical strand of Christianity. Dylan was brought up in a Jewish household and had his bar mitzvah at 13. Ever since his earliest songs, he had drawn on biblical imagery to evoke moods, emotional landscapes, and paint characters. After a course of Christian study, he now used and embraced the Bible in his songs in a much more literal way. The lyrics dispensed with wordplay, subtleties, absurd or grotesque juxtapositions, evocations of the inner self, and the clever use of ambiguity. "Gotta Serve Somebody" was a message to his listener, addressed in the second person "you." It doesn't matter who you are – ambassador, gambler, champion boxer, rock star poseur, or thief – you are going to have to "serve somebody." That "somebody" is not open to debate, it's either the "devil" or "the lord": good or evil. Yet, the stark lyrical choice is undercut by uplifting funk rhythms, bright horns, warm devotional organ motifs, slick bluesy guitar, and a crisp production that allows specific instruments to shine as they move in and out of the mix.

Dylan had asked Jerry Wexler to produce his recordings during this period due to the sound he had created with Aretha Franklin and Wilson Picket at Atlantic Records, and Wexler (with co-producer Barry Beckett) brought in the Muscle Shoals Horns, acclaimed for their brass playing on numerous rock, pop, and soul recordings. The unease in the lyrics about human corruption, futility and sin is alleviated and almost redeemed with a soulful, danceable groove set in a joyful gospel arrangement. Dylan himself used the song as a vehicle for some passionate performances and a statement of belief as the opening number in concert, and it again inspired outstanding covers, as can be heard on recordings by Etta James and Mavis Staples. This single illustrates the importance of the sonorities of gospel as yet another musical thread in Dylan's career as a recording artist (see Chapter 7).

"Make You Feel My Love" (1997)

"Make You Feel My Love" draws its lyrical and musical inspiration from the Tin Pan Alley ballad, the Great American Songbook, and nineteenth-century protestant hymns (the three are all musically related). It is a song of devotional love in which the protagonist lists the sacrifices offered for their feelings to be sensed and accepted. It has a prominent, yet slightly under-stated, descending chromatic pattern characteristic of laments and songs of unrequited love (and also found in "Simple Twist of Fate"), falling in semitones from the note Db to F throughout each verse. The chords also waver between their major and minor form in keeping with the singer's uncertainty about their love being felt (itself an old songwriting trick). The song is in Db/C♯, consistent with Dylan's preference for the black notes when composing on the piano, and the production is informed by Sun and Chess recordings.[17] Produced in collaboration with Daniel Lanois, the vocals have a sixteenth note delay with delicate reverb applied to accentuate the singer's lone voice calling out across empty space (and perhaps the resonance of an old church). The song was dismissed by rock critics, mainly (but not only) for its words, with variants of the phrase "greeting card lyrics" that originated in a review by Greg Kot in *Rolling Stone*. But this is not a greeting card. Even if, ironically, the words have become incorporated into romantic valentine presents and wedding gifts, these offerings of sacrificial love only exist because it is heard as sung words. It is another illustration of how, despite the world's poetry, most of the time we

---

[17] See Negus, *Bob Dylan*.

use ordinary language to express our most profound feelings, emotions, and desires. Regardless of the critics, acclaimed popular songwriters recognized its value and released their own versions – notably Billy Joel, Garth Brooks, and Adele. As Johnny Borgan has written, "Make You Feel My Love" was pivotal in Dylan's re-exploration of the "pre rock 'n' roll American song tradition," a thread that Borgan traces back to his appreciation of Willie Nelson's 1978 album *Stardust* and to a song Dylan recorded in the late 1960s.[18] "Make You Feel My Love" is central to Dylan's re-engagement with the Great American songbook, and links back to the earlier Sinatra influence and forward to *Shadows in the Night* (2015).

"Things Have Changed" (2000)

"Things Have Changed" was written as a commission – and won an Oscar – for the film *Wonder Boys* featuring Michael Douglas as the lead character Grady Tripp, a professor with anxieties about writing a new novel, messy intimate relationships, and a liking for marijuana. Director Curtis Hanson approached Dylan as an admirer of his work and, according to various accounts, believed the songwriter would be able to empathize with the lead character. Having viewed rough cuts of the movie, Dylan did indeed become "a worried man with a worried mind," narrating the song from the first person and demonstrating once more his ability to breathe new life into well-worn musical patterns and lyrical clichés ("Worried Man Blues" being one of various references to older songs) and use them to inhabit characters. The lyrics to the song, and the accompanying promotional video, cleverly fuse and play with aspects of both Dylan's persona and Grady Tripp's onscreen identity. The video shifts from Dylan to Douglas, merging Tripp with Dylan's voice and guitar playing. Too often these subtle nuances were lost when critics predictably assumed that the song's sentiment "I used to care but things have changed" is being voiced by the "I" of Bob Dylan and not a character inhabited by the persona of Dylan in a song. The song was produced quickly by Dylan as Jack Frost during a day off with his touring band. The production and performance contribute to the characterization and narrative of the film. The vocals give the impression of the singer addressing himself (and whoever will listen) from within a murky and uncertain physical and existential place. Engineer Chris Shaw recalled that Dylan did not like an

---

[18] Johnny Borgan, "Bob Dylan + The Great American Songbook = True!" *JohnnyBorganBlog*, July 21, 2017, https://johnnyborgan.blog/2017/07/21/bob-dylan-the-great-american-songbook-true.

initial mix of the song and instructed the engineer that "everything was too clear" and to "mush it up."[19] At Dylan's request the vocal was run through a guitar amplifier and Shaw routed the signal via a fuzz box, mixing this into the vocal track to heighten the vaguely distant, murky vocal mood. The "mushed up" ambience was further crafted by allowing leakage of drums into the vocal microphone and by raising the percussive guitar and mandolin to levels unusually and unnaturally loud in relation to the drums and bass. The deceptively quirky production of a lilting, minor key, country blues shuffle enhances the way Dylan delivers the lyrics in keeping with the character's world-weariness and increasingly stoned and cynical outlook. As the song progresses it's as if the narrator is becoming too tired to finish a phrase, leaving a pregnant pause before dropping the final words – but, then again, Dylan may also be adopting a trick perfected by Sinatra when stretching lines and hesitating before singing the final word or phrase.

***

This list of ten singles offers a way of thinking about the range, qualities, and depth of Dylan's recordings. They allow us to hear the *stories in songs* – the tales told by narrators, the scenes, the action, the drama, the emotions. They allow us to hear the *stories about songs* – the influences on Dylan, the deliberate way in which he constructed and recorded the tracks. And, they allow us to hear the *songs in stories* – the way Dylan's recorded songs embed themselves in our lives, histories, memories, and futures, becoming part of a narrative about who "we" are, where we came from, and what we might become.

---

[19] Dan Daley, "Recording Bob Dylan," *Electronic Musician*, December 31, 2008, www.emusician.com /gear/recording-bob-dylan.

PART II

Musical Contexts

CHAPTER 5

Folk Music

Ronald D. Cohen

> Folk songs played in my head, they always did. Folk songs were the underground story.[1]

Bob Dylan grew up in Hibbing, Minnesota, during the 1950s, where the opportunity to hear folk music was something of a rarity. Indeed, the young Robert Zimmerman was hooked on R&B (black) and rock 'n' roll (white). This was the soundtrack for teens at that time, and he even played the piano, as well as the acoustic and electric guitar, in local bands. It was not until Dylan moved to Minneapolis in 1959, he long contended, that he discovered folk music, particularly its early roots in recorded blues and country music, and especially Woody Guthrie, who would become his role model. In his 2017 Nobel Lecture, however, Dylan explained that he first heard a Lead Belly Folkways record while still in Hibbing:

> And that record changed my life right then and there. Transported me into a world I'd never known. It was like an explosion went off. . . . I must have played that record a hundred times. It was on a label I had never heard of with a booklet inside with advertisements for other artists on the label: Sonny Terry and Brownie McGhee, the New Lost City Ramblers, Jean Ritchie, string bands. . . . I still had a feeling for the music I'd grown up with, but for right now I forgot about it. For the time being it was long gone.[2]

Dylan's growing attraction to folk music can be understood through defining its musical style. Most simply, folk songs and ballads have always dealt with real-world actions and feelings, in contrast to the "moon, spoon, June" romantic lyrics of the plethora of commercially published songs, including R&B and rock 'n' roll. Folk music includes old songs with no

I would like to thank Bob Riesman, Kate Blalack, Nancy Cohen, Will Kaufman, Melinda Russell, Barry Ollman, and Jim Lane, for their expert editorial advice.
[1] Bob Dylan, *Chronicles, Volume One* (New York: Simon & Schuster, 2004), p. 103.
[2] Bob Dylan, *The Nobel Lecture* (New York: Simon & Schuster, 2017), pp. 2–3.

known composers, but also labor songs of the nineteenth and twentieth centuries, blues, gospel, cowboy, and hillbilly songs, as well as singer-songwriters (such as Woody Guthrie), songs from foreign countries, and so much more. Acoustic instruments, such as the guitar, banjo, harmonica, and mountain dulcimer, were important folk music components. Electric guitars, drum sets, and the piano were highly unusual (until the 1960s). Folk music attracted an increasing number of college students by the late 1950s, with its real-world attributes. Moreover, it was notably not dance music, which teens had long preferred, but would be listened to or even individually played on folk instruments. Descriptive words, usually stories, not rhythms, were its essence. The accelerating volume of record albums, folk music magazines, live performances, and radio programs made the music readily available.[3]

In 1950, Gene Bluestein moved to Minneapolis and entered the graduate program of English and American Studies at the University of Minnesota. Influenced by leftwing politics and folk music in New York, he brought to the Twin Cities a talent for banjo playing, quite rare at the time, and a knack for teaching folk music to children as well as to adults. The university had a few faculty members who studied folk music, but Bluestein was the first to connect with a broad population through his local radio and TV shows in 1958 and 1959. As a folklorist, he made field recordings of traditional performers in the South as well as in Minnesota. In 1958 he released the Folkways album *Songs of the North Star State*, performing all of the tracks in various languages, including Ojibwe, French, and Swedish. After obtaining his PhD in 1959, Bluestein moved to Michigan and then California, leaving behind a vibrant folk music legacy for Dylan.[4]

"Now at last I was in Minneapolis where I felt liberated and gone, never meaning to go back," Dylan writes in *Chronicles*, his stylish memoir. "First thing I did was go trade in my electric guitar, which would have been useless to me, for a double-O Martin acoustic." While not previously aware of the community's burgeoning folk music scene, he quickly discovered a welcoming home. "I found the local record store in the heart of Dinkytown," the student neighborhood adjoining the university campus. "What I was looking for were folk music records and the first one I saw was Odetta on the Tradition label. . . . I had never heard of her until then." He was hooked.[5]

[3] Ronald D. Cohen, *Folk Music: The Basics* (New York: Routledge, 2006).
[4] Melinda Russell, "Dinkytown Before Dylan: Gene Bluestein and the Minneapolis Folk Music Revival of the 1950s," *Minnesota History* (Winter 2017–2018), pp. 289–301.
[5] Dylan, *Chronicles*, p. 238.

A group of young scholars and musicians, mostly attracted to traditional blues and country music, was forming in Dinkytown, some performing at a local venue called the Ten O'Clock Scholar. Dylan, a quick study, soon began playing songs he had picked up from Odetta's records. He met "Spider" John Koerner, an urban bluesman a few years older (who would later join Dave "Snaker" Ray and Tony "Little Sun" Glover in a popular blues revival trio, Koerner, Ray, and Glover). "I learned a lot of songs off Koerner," Dylan recalled, "by singing harmony with him and he had folk records of performers I'd never heard at his apartment. I listened to them a lot, especially to The New Lost City Ramblers," a hugely influential string band composed of Mike Seeger, John Cohen, and Tom Paley. "At the time, I didn't know that they were replicating everything they did off of old 78 records, but what would it have mattered anyway?"[6]

Barry Hansen (who later became the radio personality "Doctor Demento") was a devotee of Chicago urban blues, who left Minneapolis to attend Reed College in Oregon in 1959, then returned for the winter holidays. He had received a letter from his friend Glover: "Barry, you gotta go to the Ten O'Clock Scholar. . . . You gotta go and hear Dylan." So he did. "I certainly remember his style as being very different from anything else I'd ever heard on records or live. Not totally traditional, but definitely nothing like the commercial folk singers who had recorded at that time." Hansen refers here to the Kingston Trio, which beginning in 1958 had kickstarted the popular folk music revival, but for traditionalists such as Hansen and his friends, including Dylan, they were musically unacceptable. He preferred Folkways Records, including *Foc'sle Songs and Sea Shanties*, which included his future friend Dave Van Ronk. "The record knocked me out," Dylan recalled.[7]

As Dylan became immersed in traditional songs and performers, the Twin Cities folk scene continued expanding, and grew to include his new friends Jon Pankake and Paul Nelson. In 1960, these two undergraduates at the university with a penchant for roots music launched their tiny fanzine *The Little Sandy Review*. They specialized in record reviewing, often with a critical slant. They had introduced Dylan to Harry Smith's *Anthology of American Folk Music*, a six record set released by Folkways Records in 1952. The album included eighty-four hillbilly, blues, gospel, and Cajun songs commercially recorded in the later 1920s and early 1930s.

In March 1960, Pankake "went to New York to personally deliver the first shipment" to Izzy Young's Folklore Center. "As Young said," Pankake continued, "we were even geographically isolated, out there in flyover

---

[6] Ibid.   [7] Ibid., p. 239.

land – geographically remote from places like the Ash Grove [in Los Angeles] and the [Greenwich] Village. . . . We liked the distance from the center that gave us the freedom inherent in the fanzine medium to say anything we wanted." Hansen was soon reviewing blues albums for his friends. Pankake preferred the friendly, and somewhat remote, confines of the Twin Cities, while Dylan, who was quenching his musical thirst from his friends' record collections, began thinking about becoming immersed in a wider musical world.[8]

Dylan now discovered Woody Guthrie's songs, including "This Land Is Your Land" and "Pastures of Plenty." As Dylan put it, "All these songs together, one after another, made my head spin. It made me want to gasp." Reading Woody's semi-fictional autobiography, *Bound for Glory*, was the final element in completing Dylan's new folk persona: "I went through it from cover to cover like a hurricane, totally focused on every word, and the book sang out to me like the radio." Dylan also discovered the records of Guthrie's friend Jack Elliott, who became Dylan's performing model.[9]

During the summer of 1960 Dylan traveled to Denver, where he met the black folksinger Walt Conley, who taught him some Pete Seeger songs, and he opened for the Smothers Brothers, a popular folk/comedy duo. *The Little Sandy Review* published an issue featuring Guthrie, including some of his letters from the New Jersey hospital where, because of the debilitating effects of Huntington's disease, he was confined. That was all that Dylan needed: "it was time for me to get out of Minneapolis."[10] While heading east he made a crucial stop in Madison, Wisconsin, a folk music and activist center, the home of the University of Wisconsin. He first met the leftwing student Ron Radosh, who had taken banjo lessons from Pete Seeger. "[H]e sounded and played like Woody, and wore a workingman's cap that he had copied from one Guthrie wore in a famous picture," Radosh recalled.[11] Dylan met a talented group of folk musicians, including the blues guitarist Danny Kalb, Marshall Brickman, and the banjo wizard Eric Weissberg. After ten days he moved on to New York, arriving on January 24, 1961.[12]

---

[8] Ronald D. Cohen, ed., "Jon Pankake," in *"Wasn't That a Time!" Firsthand Accounts of the Folk Music Revival* (Metuchen, NJ: Scarecrow Press, 1995), p. 109.

[9] Dylan, *Chronicles*, pp. 244–245. For the set lists from some of Dylan's performances in Minneapolis, see Todd Harvey, *The Formative Dylan: Transmission and Stylistic Influences, 1961–1963* (Lanham, MD: Scarecrow Press, 2001), pp. 131–132.

[10] Dylan, *Chronicles*, p. 257.

[11] Ronald Radosh, *Commies: A Journey Through the Old Left, the New Left and the Leftover Left* (San Francisco: Encounter Books, 2001), pp. 76–77.

[12] Stuart D. Levitan, *Madison in the Sixties* (Madison: Wisconsin Historical Society Press, 2018), pp. 53–54.

"Greenwich Village was full of folk clubs, bars, coffeehouses, and those of us who played them all played the old-timey folk songs, rural blues and dance tunes," Dylan affirmed. "There were a few who wrote their own songs."[13] While New York City more broadly was the country's folk music hub, the Village was its heartbeat, having long attracted musicians from around the country performing a variety of styles as the national folk revival began to pick up steam. Topical songs, many connected to the emerging civil rights and anti-war movements, were just becoming popular. As soon as Dylan arrived he began performing in the local basket houses, where the patrons contributed money if they liked the music, beginning at the Cafe Wha?, where he did Guthrie imitations. He was soon jumping from the Commons, to the Gaslight, the Lion's Head, Mills Tavern, and even the cramped back room of Izzy Young's Folklore Center. When first arriving in the city he had stopped by the Folklore Center, a folk music crossroads where Dylan was welcomed, and then quickly visited Woody Guthrie's hospital bedside. His educational influences had come from scores of recordings as well as an increasing number of musical friends. Dave Van Ronk, an established Village musician, guitar teacher, and local character, with maverick politics but rather traditional musical preferences, heard that Dylan was playing harmonica behind Fred Neil, at the Gaslight, so he hurried over. "I made my first acquaintance with his famous dead-fish handshake, and we all trooped back to the Kettle [of Fish] for a drink," Van Ronk remembered. "The Coffeehouse Mafia had a new recruit."[14]

Van Ronk was quick to spot Dylan's musical promise, but a bit wary of his performing talents: "Looking back, what a lot of people don't understand is that it was tough for Bobby at first. He was a new kid in town and he had an especially abrasive voice, and no one had any way of knowing that he would eventually become BOB DYLAN – he was just a kid with an abrasive voice." As Van Rank put it, things soon calmed down and "within a short time after hitting the city, Bobby became a regular part of the gang. And the more I heard him perform, the more I was impressed with what he was doing."[15]

Dylan soon discovered Gerde's Folk City, the Village's premier folk establishment. On April 10, 1961, he joined Joan Baez, already an

---

[13] Dylan, *Chronicles*, p. 81

[14] Cohen, ed., "John Cohen II," in *"Wasn't That A Time!"* pp. 177–185; Dave Van Ronk and Elijah Wald, *The Mayor of MacDougal Street: A Memoir* (Cambridge, MA: DaCapo Press, 2005); Stephen Petrus and Ronald D. Cohen, *Folk City: New York and the American Folk Music Revival* (New York: Oxford University Press, 2015); Elijah Wald, *Dylan Goes Electric: Newport, Seeger, Dylan, and the Night That Split the Sixties* (New York: Dey St., 2015).

[15] Van Ronk and Wald, *The Mayor of MacDougal Street*, pp. 159, 161.

established star, along with Van Ronk and Doc Watson as part of the Monday night "hoot." He next opened for the bluesman John Lee Hooker. A few months later, on September 26, he began a two-week engagement opening for the Greenbriar Boys. *New York Times* critic Robert Shelton wrote a glowing review of Dylan, thereby launching his career. He still performed mostly older songs, such as "900 Miles," "Sally Gal," "House of the Risin' Sun," and "Dink's Song," but he did sneak in a few of his new talking-blues compositions: "Talkin' Bear Mountain Picnic Massacre Blues" and "Talkin' Hava Negeilah Blues."

There was nothing new about topical songs, even those with political connections, and they had formed a regular part of the repertoire for Guthrie, the Almanac Singers, and Huddie "Lead Belly" Ledbetter. In the early 1960s, however, they took on a new relevance because of the emerging civil rights and anti-war movements. Agnes "Sis" Cunningham, who had performed with the Almanac Singers in the early 1940s, and her husband Gordon Friesen, a blacklisted writer, with encouragement from Pete Seeger and Malvina Reynolds, launched *Broadside* magazine in February 1962. Cunningham and Friesen, poverty stricken, lived in public housing on the Upper West Side, and the performers would visit the apartment and record their new songs. With the subtitle "A handful of songs about our times," *Broadside* became the main source of topical songs. "The very first thin issue contained six songs, words and music, one had been written by Malvina Reynolds and one by Bob Dylan ['Talking John Birch']," Sis and Gordon recalled. "There was a Reynolds and a Dylan in nearly all of those early issues. ... Bob Dylan came to these monthly meetings for well over a year. Gil Turner, emcee at Gerde's Folk City, brought him to the first one."[16]

Another important influence on Dylan was Rev. Gary Davis, a blind gospel and blues singer, and guitar wizard, who had arrived in New York from North Carolina in 1944. In early May 1961 Dylan met Davis at the exclusive Indian Neck Folk Festival in Connecticut, sponsored by students

---

[16] Agnes "Sis" Cunningham and Gordon Friesen, *Red Dust and Broadsides: A Joint Autobiography* (Amherst: University of Massachusetts Press, 1999), p. 276; Jeff Place and Ronald D. Cohen, *The Best of Broadside, 1962–1988: Anthems of the American Underground from the Pages of Broadside Magazine* (Smithsonian Folkways Recordings, SFW CD40130, 2000). See also James Sullivan, *Which Side Are You On?: 20th Century American History in 100 Protest Songs* (New York: Oxford University Press, 2019); Richard A. Reuss and Joanne C. Reuss, *American Folk Music and Left-Wing Politics, 1927–1957* (Lanham, MD: Scarecrow Press, 2000); Ronald D. Cohen, *Work and Sing: A History of Occupational and Labor Union Songs in the United States* (Crockett, CA: Carquinez Press, 2010); Ronald D. Cohen and Will Kaufman, *Singing for Peace: Antiwar Songs in American History* (Boulder, CO: Paradigm, 2015).

at Yale University. He picked up numerous songs from Davis, including "Death Don't Have No Mercy," "It's Hard to Be Blind," and "Baby, Let Me Follow You Down." In the fall, Dylan would open for a Davis concert at Bennington College in Vermont. Also that fall Dylan occasionally backed the bluesman Big Joe Williams at Gerde's Folk City. This relationship led Dylan to lend his vocals and harmonica for a blues recording session with Williams and Victoria Spivey, the classic blues singer who had recently come out of retirement, in March 1962 for Spivey Records.[17]

Dylan's first official concert, as distinct from the clubs and coffee houses, came on November 4, 1961, when Izzy Young organized an appearance at the Carnegie Chapter Hall, a small theatre that was part of the prestigious Carnegie Hall. His rather ragged performance, included a lineup of older songs such as "Pretty Peggy-O" and "Gospel Plow." His professional life then began to accelerate quickly as his clever topical songs started dominating his repertoire. While Dylan began crafting new verses, he often linked them with older, familiar tunes.

In the summer of 1961 Dylan began dating Suze Rotolo, who had first heard him at Folk City, where he was performing with Mark Spoelstra. "Their repertoire consisted of traditional folk songs and the songs of Woody Guthrie," she recounted in her autobiography. "They weren't half bad. Bob was developing his image into his own version of a rambling troubadour, in the Guthrie mode."[18] They actually met following a folk concert at the Riverside Church in late July, which also included Van Ronk, Tom Paxton, and Ramblin' Jack Elliott. Through Rotolo's sister, Dylan soon became acquainted with Alan Lomax, the legendary folklorist who had been collecting traditional rural music since the 1930s and was now hosting twice-monthly parties. Even as the older musicians, some of whom had been included on the Harry Smith *Anthology*, were being rediscovered, Dylan now had the opportunity to hear them in person. He had amazingly found himself not only in the midst of the upcoming topical songwriters, but also among the older blues and hillbilly singers whose concerts were locally sponsored by the Friends of Old Time Music. Moreover, Rotolo's work for CORE, the civil rights organization, brought Dylan directly into activist politics.[19]

Despite Dylan's new-found political awareness and engagement with the rising popularity of topical songwriting, he still continued his interest

[17] Ian Zack, *Say No to the Devil: The Life and Musical Genius of Rev. Gary Davis* (Chicago: University of Chicago Press, 2015), pp. 138–140.
[18] Suze Rotolo, *A Freewheelin' Time: A Memoir of Greenwich Village in the Sixties* (New York: Broadway Books, 2008), p. 13.
[19] John Szwed, *Alan Lomax: The Man Who Recorded the World* (New York: Viking, 2010), p. 338.

in more traditional tunes, particularly through his friendship with Paul Clayton. Born in New Bedford, Massachusetts, in 1931, early on he became familiar with whaling songs, then Southern songs when he became a student at the University of Virginia. By the mid-1950s he combined his interests in a prolific series of folk albums, such as *Whaling Songs and Ballads*, *Cumberland Mountain Folksongs*, and *American Folk Tales and Songs*. "There can have been few singers as unlike one another as Paul and myself," according to Van Ronk, who had met Clayton soon after his arrival in the Village in the late 1950s, "yet he had a considerable influence on me, as he had some years later on Bob Dylan."[20] In September 1961, Dylan and Clayton appeared together at a club in Washington, DC, and soon after performed with Mike Seeger, a member of the influential revival string band the New Lost City Ramblers, and the bluegrass musician Bill Clifton, in Charlottesville, Virginia.[21]

The first notice of Dylan in Izzy Young's influential column in the magazine *Sing Out!* appeared in the December–January 1961–1962 issue: "Carolyn Hester has signed with Columbia Records. She will be accompanied on her newest LP by Bob Dylan on the Harmonica."[22] This session came a day after the publication of Shelton's rave review of Dylan's opening performance for the Greenbriar Boys at Gerde's Folk City, which led to his meeting Columbia's famed producer John Hammond, who quickly signed Bob to a contract. His first Columbia recording sessions began in late November, but Young didn't get around to a full recognition of Dylan's promise until the next issue of *Sing Out!* in early 1962: "Bob Dylan blew into New York just a year ago. . . . Bob is another example of how complete commitment to folk music as a way of life can be recognizedly commercial forces long before the 'folk' forces." Young was not yet aware that Dylan had made up much of his history (see Chapter 2), but realized that a non-traditional performer could yet be accepted as a folk singer. For some, however, the two were mutually exclusive.[23]

In 1962 folk music was picking up commercial steam, due largely to the rising civil rights movement, which Dylan and *Broadside* magazine were quick to promote. This was a transition period for Dylan, since he continued to select from his older folk repertoire while expanding his

---

[20] Van Ronk and Wald, *The Mayor of MacDougal Street*, p. 84.
[21] Bob Coleman, *Paul Clayton and the Folksong Revival* (Lanham, MD: Scarecrow Press, 2008).
[22] Scott Barretta, ed., *The Conscience of the Folk Revival: The Writings of Israel "Izzy" Young* (Lanham, MD: Scarecrow Press, 2013), p. 65.
[23] Ibid, p. 67.

growing collection of original compositions. He now rarely appeared in folk clubs, except for Folk City and the Gaslight, where he was recorded probably in late 1962.[24] Then he mixed together his newly written "A Hard Rain's A-Gonna Fall" and "Don't Think Twice It's All Right" with the older "The Cuckoo" and "Barbara Allen." Earlier in the year, however, he began recording a series of sessions for his second Columbia album, *The Freewheelin' Bob Dylan*, including "Rambling, Gambling Willie," based on the Irish ballad "Brennan on the Moor." Although it did not appear on the album, for Izzy Young, the song "is as good as any bad-man ballad I can think of. He [Dylan] has a true poetic touch that smacks of the best folk traditions in many of his songs. He has also recently written on 'Emmett Till' and the 'John Birch Society.'" Young plainly relished Bob's creative reworking of older ballads as well as his timely topical songs.[25]

Throughout 1962, Dylan juggled performing topical songs along with the older songs in his repertoire. As he would later state: "By listening to the early folk artists and singing the songs yourself, you pick up the vernacular. You internalize it. You sing it in the ragtime blues, work songs, Georgia sea shanties, Appalachian ballads, and cowboy songs."[26] For example, in a March audition for the Ed Sullivan television show, he included the early twentieth-century Southern ballad "Man of Constant Sorrow" along with "Song to Woody." He also performed such old chestnuts as "No More Auction Block" and "House Carpenter." In April at Folk City he included the traditional "Corrina, Corrina" alongside his own new composition, "Blowin' in the Wind." He also recorded Robert Johnson's "Milkcow's Calf Blues," but *The Freewheelin' Bob Dylan* when it appeared contained only original compositions as well as his rendition of "Corrina, Corrina." "Of all the precipitously emergent singers of folk songs in the continuing renascence of that self-assertive tradition, none has equalled Bob Dylan in singularity of impact," Nat Hentoff wrote in the album's liner notes. "The irrepressible reality of Bob Dylan is a compound of spontaneity, candor, slicing wit and an uncommonly perceptive eye and ear for the way many of us constrict our capacity for living while a few of us don't." "Blowin' in the Wind," the opening song, set the stage for a truly remarkable album. As Hentoff concluded: "It is this continuing explosion of a total individual, a young man growing free rather than absurd, that makes Bob Dylan so powerful and so personal and so important a singer."[27]

---

[24] *Bob Dylan: Live at the Gaslight 1962*, Columbia Legacy A96016, 2005.
[25] Barretta, ed., *The Conscience of the Folk Revival*, p. 70. [26] Dylan, *The Nobel Lecture*, p. 4.
[27] Nat Hentoff liner notes, *The Freewheelin' Bob Dylan*, Columbia CL1986, 1963. For a partial list of Dylan's recorded concerts, see Harvey, *The Formative Dylan*, pp. 137–144.

Dylan plunged into 1963 bristling with new songs and creative energies. His topical work quickly gained popularity, particularly after the release of the new album. The civil rights and peace activist Howard Zinn noted in his diary that he had attended a concert by Joan Baez in Atlanta. She sang "a new song written by Bob Dylan, powerful, bitter about the wars our country has fought, always with God on our Side, and Germans, now our friends, killed 6 million Jews, but God is on their side now, Wow."[28] Dylan also became more deeply involved with the civil rights movement, traveling to Mississippi where he performed "Only a Pawn in Their Game" in July. Pete Seeger had now become an eager fan. At year's end, in the midst of a world-wide family trip, Seeger wrote to Dylan: "When I sang 'Hard Rain' for 3,000 folks in a public park here [in India] yesterday, it got an ovation – far more than any other song I sang. . . . I have sung the song everywhere on this trip [Australia, Japan] but here it hit home the most."[29]

Dylan's already hectic schedule accelerated through the year. He did some performing in Chicago, appearing on Studs Terkel's WFMT radio show, then in mid-May he ventured for the first time to the West Coast. At the Monterey Folk Festival he joined the Weavers and the New Lost City Ramblers on stage, performing "A Hard Rain's A-Gonna Fall" and "Masters of War," then "With God on Our Side" joined by Baez. Thus began their intense relationship. In late July, he appeared at the Newport Folk Festival, the first since 1960, along with Baez, Joan Collins, Pete Seeger, Jack Elliott, and Mississippi John Hurt. "Bob was the new, fast-rising star and after his performance at the festival it was clear that the folk world was his oyster," Rotolo explains. "Bob's songs were in the folk idiom yet they were definitely and undeniably written in the present."[30] Dylan appeared in an evening performance with Peter, Paul and Mary, Seeger, and others, as well as the ballad and topical songs workshops. He now only performed his own songs, although, following in Woody Guthrie's footsteps, many derived from older melodies. For example, "A Hard Rain's A-Gonna Fall" was based on the seventeenth-century ballad "Lord Randall," while "Ballad of Hollis Brown" was related to "Pretty Polly." For Rotolo, and many others, "Folk music had won the day, moving out to unite discontented kids everywhere who were waiting for a ticket to ride."[31]

[28] Robert Cohen, *Howard Zinn's Southern Diary* (Athens: University of Georgia Press, 2018), p. 163.
[29] Rob Rosenthal and Sam Rosenthal, eds., *Pete Seeger: In His Own Words* (Boulder, CO: Paradigm, 2012), pp. 316–317. It should be noted that Zinn was a veteran of the Army Air Corps during the Second World War, having flown many missions over Germany and Eastern Europe as a bombardier.
[30] Rotolo, *A Freewheelin' Time*, p. 231.
[31] Ibid., p. 232. See also Barney Hoskyns, *Small Town Talk* (Philadelphia: DaCapo Press, 2016), pp. 41–50.

After Newport Dylan's career continued to escalate. "Joan Baez and Bob Dylan are doing a lot of playing together recently," Izzy Young wrote following Newport. "Bob's singing becomes less strident and Joan's singing becomes more forceful so that when you hear them singing it is hard to identify their voices and the result is quite happy for the listener."[32] In early July, he began the first of his recording sessions for *The Times They Are A-Changin'*, to be released in early 1964. Dylan was now appearing in large auditoriums and at civil rights events including the landmark 1963 March on Washington. He continued to turn out topical songs through 1964, along with a growing list of increasingly personal songs that would mark his turn to folk-rock the following year. His appearance at Newport in 1965 with an electric guitar is considered a musical landmark, as well as controversial event. For Ed Sanders, a poet and member of the band The Fugs: "Maybe it was too quick a transition from Woody to Fender [guitar] for the fans of folk clinging to the image of artisans in cabins building banjos out of turtle shells. I could never figure out what the booing was about."[33]

Folk music had taken many twists and turns during the early 1960s, characterized by Dylan's explosive, highly creative career. The music's style and substance would pave the way toward Dylan's subsequent Nobel award. Still, he always remained indebted to his immersion in the historic development of folk music in the British Isles and the United States. Folk songs, old and new, have remained popular throughout Dylan's long career, and something he never abandoned. The recorded historical selections for his *Theme Time Radio Hour* (2006–2009) were a strong indication of his fascinating, eclectic musical tastes. While folk music, broadly defined, reached its peak of popularity by the mid-1960s, it continued to resonate into the twenty-first century, along with Dylan's career.

---

[32] Barretta, ed. *The Conscience of the Folk Revival*, p. 86.
[33] Ed Sanders, *Fug You* (Philadelphia: Da Capo Press, 2011), p. 154; Wald, *Dylan Goes Electric*.

CHAPTER 6

The Blues: "Kill Everybody Ever Done Me Wrong"

Greil Marcus

I'm going to be playing some songs tonight, but I'm not going to play excerpts or snippets, because when I play a song I'm playing it not as a way of illustrating a point, but as a fact: as a document of an event that took place at a certain time and place, involving certain people.[1]

But to start, I want to play – I need to play – a video of a song by a string band called 3 Penny Acre – they named themselves after the price of the Louisiana Purchase. The song is "Tulsa 1921," about the white pogrom that destroyed the black community in Tulsa ninety-eight years ago this weekend – ninety-eight years ago, June 1, the day after tomorrow.

3 Penny Acre's "Tulsa 1921" Plays

It's 2011. They seem to be in a radio station. They're guitarist and song-writer Bryan Hembree, originally from Tulsa, now Austin, who introduces the song as part of a play; bass fiddle player Berenice Hembree; and mandolin player Bauyard Blaine. The music comes out as living history, with no sense of words jammed into a line to convey information, to get the facts lined up: as you listen, the event takes place. Bryan Hembree sings earnestly, with anger inside his mournful tone, as he tells the whole story. The spurious newspaper item about a black worker supposedly accosting a white female elevator operator – which could have meant he spoke to her, but which was translated into an attack, or rape. The man's arrest. The lynch mob immediately forming, and then, blocked by the sheriff, turning on Greenwood, north Tulsa, literally the other side of the tracks, the flats, famous as Black Wall Street, the most prosperous black community in the nation and bane of white Tulsa, which over two days burned black Tulsa to

This chapter is the text of a keynote lecture delivered on May 30, 2019 at the University of Tulsa's World of Bob Dylan conference.
[1] All of the performances played as part of this talk can be found on YouTube.

the ground. Thirty-five blocks of businesses and well-kept homes left as ash. The newspapers reporting a death toll under forty, and, after Tulsa was cleansed, with men, women, children, and former slaves scattered to other parts of Oklahoma or having left the state altogether, three hundred never accounted for – buried in mass graves, so today, when you stroll the Arts District in north Tulsa, passing the restaurants, the bars, the vinyl record shop, the Woody Guthrie Center, you are walking on death. The worst single racial crime in the United States after slavery, and buried in white memory, not taught in Tulsa schools, not marked, a collective silence that did not begin to break until the murderers' generation was gone.

Bryan Hembree lets his words out as if the story is merely using him to pass itself on, making his craft invisible. "They were shooting left and they were shooting right," he sings, reversing the normal speech where right comes before left – he needs it for a rhyme, but it throws you off, takes you right out of the drama, putting you on the street as it melts. Berenice Hembree leans in on the last lines of the verses, adding an empathy, adding gravity. There's no tone that can hit you in the gut, as a kind of physical recognition of truth, a tone that makes you flinch with pleasure, like that of the mandolin when a player knows what the instrument is for; Bauyard Blaine begins the music on that plane and never drops. Speaking of five-string open G tuning on electric guitar, Keith Richards explains how the whole song feels as Blaine shapes it: "If you're working with the right chord, you can hear this other chord going on behind it, which actually you're not playing. It's there. It defies logic. And it's just lying there saying, 'Fuck me.'"[2]

What was done in Tulsa in 1921 went into every blues made or recorded in the years that followed. There wasn't a black man or woman in America who didn't know what happened here. The *Chicago Defender* and every other black newspaper in the country printed what the white papers didn't. What was a one-day story in the white papers was a year-long story or more in the black papers – and so there wasn't an American citizen whose ancestors were slaves, let alone those who had been slaves themselves, who didn't take the message of the Tulsa massacre to heart. It was an event that was part of the decades of twentieth-century lynching and mass murder of black people throughout the country – as in Okemah, Oklahoma, Woody Guthrie's hometown, in 1911, of a thirty-five-year-old woman and her fourteen-year-old son; as in 1920 in Duluth, Minnesota, when three black circus workers were hung in front of hundreds of

---

[2] Keith Richards, *Life* (London: Weidenfeld & Nicolson, 2010), p. 243.

townspeople, who might have included Bob Dylan's grandfather, and his father – especially throughout the 1920s, when the Ku Klux Klan took over the governments of towns and states from Indiana to Colorado, Georgia to South Carolina. Lynchings were civic events, and if you didn't show up people were going to ask why. My own grandparents were in the crowd for the lynching in San Jose in 1933; they figured their business might suffer if they weren't.

But Tulsa sent the loudest message: anything you have, anything you are, can be taken away at any time. Life is contingency and doubt. That was the world of black Americans, but it was also the modern world – in a century defined by world wars, genocide, and the threat of nuclear war. It was an African American sensibility that became an African American art form that after not that long a time could speak for anyone.

I want to start with something John Lennon said in 1970, in an interview in *Rolling Stone* with Jann Wenner. The blues, he said, is "not a concept. It is a chair, not a design for a chair or a better chair or a bigger chair or a chair with leather or with design," he said. "It is the first chair, it's chairs for sitting on, not chairs for looking at or being appreciated. You *sit* on that music." He went on: "We didn't sound like everybody else, that's all. I mean we didn't sound like the black musicians because we weren't black and because we were brought up on a different kind of music and atmosphere. And so 'Please Please Me' and 'From Me to You' and all those were our version of the chair. We were building our own chairs."[3]

What is Bob Dylan's version of the chair?

To me it's "I Am a Lonesome Hobo" on the 1967 *John Wesley Harding* – which begins in "Poor Boy, Long Way from Home" and a hundred other blues and folk songs, and anyone could name three dozen other performances that would be just as valid. But most of all it's *Time Out of Mind*, released thirty years later. That is Bob Dylan's great blues album – where, as John Lennon says, whoever you are, black or white, English or American, Jamaican or Nigerian, you have to draw from your own atmosphere, and add it to the form.

The blues is a chair. You sit on it. The blues is also a well, a bottomless pit of invention, disguise, impersonation, play, japery, dead-pan, as serious as death, as fast as death when it's in a hurry, slowed to a crawl because it can't be rushed, because the story is too good to let it end. The blues is a well, and you swim in it.

---

[3] Jann S. Wenner, *Lennon Remembers* (London: Verso, 2000), pp. 78–79.

It's all in the beat, the way a song rolls over itself. There is no end to the rabbits the blues can pull out of its hat, that the blues can put there for others to find.

Fly by night, here and gone, lucky to catch their name – a lot of the people who made blues records in the 1920s and 1930s recorded once, and were never heard from again. Colson Whitehead captures it perfectly in his novel *John Henry Days*, where some time in the early 1930s a Deep South blues singer who's been playing joints in Chicago finds himself the next day in an upstairs room of a blues record store run by a young white man who has a tape recorder. They walked in, they walked out, they got their twenty dollars, names written down, almost always, not necessarily heard or spelled right, addresses, maybe, maybe not – as with Will Bennett.

He recorded once, on August 28, 1929, at weekend sessions the Brunswick label set up in the St. James Hotel in Knoxville, Tennessee – obviously the same St. James Hotel that shows up in the last verse of Bob Dylan's "Blind Willie McTell," unless that was one of a hundred other St. James hotels scattered around the country, half of them seemingly in Jim Thompson novels set in Oklahoma.

Will Bennett left behind one 78 rpm disc, "Railroad Bill" backed with "Real Estate Blues," issued on the Vocalion label. His life was just as singular. He was a farmer from the next county over from Knoxville. He was over fifty: he was born in 1878 in Georgia. He died in 1955. For a long time, nothing was known about him, outside of a tiny item in the *Knoxville Journal* as one of several local musicians ("Will Bennett, negro, of Loudon") set to record. When blues researchers finally reached the right place, they found people who remembered Bennett as a trick guitar player: like Charley Patton or Jimi Hendrix he could play it behind his back or between his legs. People said what they always say about great guitar players: "He could make it talk." He loved ballads – "John Henry," "Casey Jones," who he could have read about in the newspapers. He sang early blues, like "Poor Boy, Long Way from Home." He sang "Mississippi Heavy Water Blues," about the 1927 Mississippi flood.

The sessions at the St. James Hotel included white string bands – the Smoky Mountain Ramblers – and the black ragtime combo the Tennessee Chocolate Drops. There was the blues singer Leona Manning, a play about the Hatfield-McCoy feud, and a spoken word record by Col. J.G. Stretchi, who owned the recording studio. In this company, Will Bennett was no professional.

In 1895 a turpentine worker and circus roustabout who went by the name of Morris Slater was thrown off a moving train in Alabama. He pulled a pistol and fired at the guard. He began a vendetta against the Louisville and Nashville Railroad. They called him Railroad Bill. He became a gunfighter to put Billy the Kid in the shade. Again and again throughout Alabama he stood down police and escaped, twice with a dead sheriff behind him. As an African American folk hero, he was the hoodoo trickster who can change shape, turn himself invisible, some people can see him and some people can't. In 1896, when the bounty on his head went so high that Pinkertons and amateurs came from half the country to kill him, he was set up and ambushed inside a grocery store – while carrying two loaded pistols and a Winchester rifle. His body was put on a cart and trucked around from county to county. You could see it for a quarter.

As a folk hero he became a folk song: "Railroad Bill, Railroad Bill / He never worked and he never will." It emerged while he was still alive; if he'd stopped in a levee camp after one of his escapes from a county posse, he could have heard the workers singing about him. He could have sung along.

Over the years, the tune took on a pretty melody, picked out mournfully by the Virginia banjo player Hobart Smith in 1942, or by Bob Dylan in Minneapolis in 1961, with both Smith and Dylan letting pieces of Charlie Poole's 1927 "If I Lose, I Don't Care" float through it: "If you lose your money," they sing, "learn to lose."[4]

But nobody ever sang "Railroad Bill" with the glee of Will Bennett, who Hobart Smith might have heard; when I asked if Bob Dylan had heard Bennett, he said no. What went into Bennett's record? "Railroad Bill" was already a country market standard by 1929 – Riley Puckett and Gid Tanner put it out first, in 1924 ("He shot the light out of the poor brakeman's hand"), and the great West Virginia guitarist Frank Hutchison cut his version just weeks before Bennett made his. As far as anyone knows, Will Bennett was the first African American to record it – you might say to take it back.

He was, after all, old enough to have followed the story as it happened. And there were elements of the tall tale and the black outlaw in his own life. In Tennessee, people in Gordon County liked to say he could "drive a nail into a board with his fist, then pull it out with his teeth." When he was about twelve, in about 1890, in Alabama, five years before Railroad Bill began shooting up the state, he accidentally shot a white friend – they were

---

[4] Even that note, along with the charm of the melody, was gone when in 1970, with Al Kooper and David Bromberg in the room, Dylan took up the song again, in a take left off his "I just threw everything I could think of at the wall" *Self Portrait* – as colorless a performance as one will ever hear, with a vocal lacking even the will, or the alcohol, of a karaoke singer where it's mixed in with "Feelings" and "You Can Call Me Al."

playing cowboys and Indians, and every family had a gun on the kitchen table. His mother tried to get him out of Alabama, but a white gang caught him. They cut his throat and left him for someone else to bury. He was saved by a woman who brought him back to health; she hid him on her farm, gave him a job, and eventually gave him a guitar. When Railroad Bill appeared, Will Bennett wasn't merely old enough to follow the story as it happened, he had already lived part of it out.[5]

Will Bennett's "Railroad Bill" is more like the numbers "Pretty Peggy-O" or "Freight Train Blues" as Bob Dylan sings them on his first album, recorded in late 1961, than Dylan's own reflective "Railroad Bill" from just a few months before, Dylan singing, as the homemade tape was first described, in a Minneapolis hotel room, when everybody in the Dinkytown folk music milieu knew the song "St. James Infirmary," when everybody would have loved it if they'd been in a St. James Hotel, but they were about fifty miles short – there was a St. James Hotel in Redwing, Minnesota, and there still is, but not in Minneapolis.

In his high, worried-man voice, the character Will Bennett is acting out is so charged by the story he's telling you can't tell him from the character. The man singing envies Railroad Bill – "Railroad Bill, took my wife / Threatened on me that he would take my life," he sings, as Bob Dylan would sing "Railroad Bill took my wife / If I said a word he'd take my life." But Will Bennett seems to think it'd be worth it, that it'd be a badge of honor, a story he could dine out on for eternity: you can see him up in heaven, down in hell, people asking, "So, how'd you get here?" and him answering, "*RAILROAD BILL killed me! Top that!*"

He envies Railroad Bill, he admires him, and within three verses he's crossed over and he is Railroad Bill, just like Ronnie Van Zant turning into the junkie in Lynyrd Syknyrd's "That Smell." There it's shocking, with the accusatory voice – *you, you, you* – suddenly shifting into the first person: "One more blow for my nose." But as Will Bennett makes the change you're watching a Western. It's a thrill to see the poor victim turn into the Sundance Kid.

> Buy me a gun
> Just as long as my arm
> Kill everybody ever done me wrong
> Gonna ride, my Railroad Bill

[5] Information on Will Bennett from Tony Russell, "Will Bennett," in Ted Olson and Tony Russell, *The Knoxville Sessions 1929–1930*, included with the box set *The Knoxville Sessions 1929–1930 – Knox County Stomp* (Bear Family, 2016), pp. 43–45.

Railroad Bill has become the singer's animating spirit. Railroad Bill is the train that's going to take the singer away from whoever's chasing him. Railroad Bill is the ghost of the dead man whose back the singer is riding, who as the singer clatters his suites of commonplace verses about guns (five), alcohol (three), and women (four) gives him the power to get away with anything he can think of.

I found this song on a little collection the Catfish label put together in 2000 called *The Early Blues Roots of Bob Dylan.* There were Bukka White's "Fixin' to Die," Blind Lemon Jefferson's "See That My Grave Is Kept Clean," songs Dylan recorded for his first album, and Sleepy John Estes's "Broken Hearted, Ragged and Dirty Too," Blind Willie McTell's "Broke Down Engine," and Blind Boy Fuller's "Step It Up and Go," all of which Dylan recast for *Good as I Been to You* (1992) and *World Gone Wrong* (1993) more than thirty years later.

***

Will Bennett's "Railroad Bill" is one of those rabbits in the blues hat – one that jumps out and runs away. You can't catch it. Bob Dylan didn't have to hear this particular record to hear in countless other blues records the swirl of possibilities it speaks for, that it embodies – the way it says, *This is blues, say your piece, get in and get out.* Blow into town at one end of main street and blow out at the other, always leave them wondering, "Who was that masked man?" So I don't hear Will Bennett's "Railroad Bill" in Bob Dylan's "Railroad Bill." I hear it in "Bob Dylan's 115th Dream," in "Subterranean Homesick Blues," in "Tombstone Blues," that fabulous momentum, the ten-car crash of verses building on each other, that rush to an ending, the desperado as a desperate man, laughing at himself. Think of how funny "Memphis Blues Again" is, and how even if in Will Bennett's "Railroad Blues" you can feel that the singer is going to be shot to death at the end, in the verse just after the record is over that the singer left out, shot down by the people chasing him, for the money and to uphold the honor of the community, or by himself, to show them that he can get the last word first – for all of that, Will Bennett's smile never breaks.

Will Bennett's "Railroad Blues" Plays

But any account of Bob Dylan and the blues, even if it points toward *Time Out of Mind,* starts with that first album, in 1962 – with a 20-year-old claiming he can somehow get away with singing "See That My Grave Is Kept Clean" and "Fixin' to Die," not to mention Emry Arthur's "Man of Constant Sorrow," which ends with the singer singing from his grave. Or "In My Time of Dying," which is Blind Willie Johnson's "Jesus Make Up My

Dying Bed." Or Memphis Slim's "Highway 51," which is where the singer asks to be buried. Or "House of the Risin' Sun," which, Tony Glover said, Dylan likely learned from John Koerner or Dave Ray in Minneapolis in 1959 or 1960, and then learned again, in New York in 1961, from an arrangement by Dave Van Ronk. "It was common currency back then," Tony said – Tony "Little Sun" Glover, who died yesterday in St. Paul at seventy-nine.

In the blues, words first came from a common store of phrases, couplets, curses, blessings, jokes, greetings, and goodbyes that passed anonymously between blacks and whites after the Civil War. From that, the blues said, you craft a story, a philosophy lesson, that you present as your own: *This happened to me. This is what I did. This is how it felt.*

You make it up. The blues mandate that you present a story on the premise that it happened to you, so it has to be written not autobiography but fiction. The structure mandates a simple format into which absolutely anything can fit. Anything can be said – and with a range of feeling that is up to the performer, to the degree of his or her imagination and facility.

This is John Simon, the producer of the Band's first two albums, of Big Brother and the Holding Company's *Cheap Thrills*, and countless signal albums after that, in his *Truth, Lies & Hearsay: A Memoir of a Musical Life in and out of Rock and Roll*, published in 2018:

> A little math. The Blues is a unique song form. It's 12 bars long. It's made up of three sentences, *but the first two sentences are exactly the same.* Like:
>
>> *Oh, Baby, what you do to me*
>> *Oh, Baby, what you do to me*
>
> So, since the words are the same, what makes those first 2 sentences different?
>> Well, the difference is a musical one: *the chord underneath each of those sentences is different.*
>> When the chord under the second sentence changes, it changes *one single note* in the melody – and that tiny change expresses all the pain, possibility, poignance that you now can hear in every Blues cover band in the world.
>> The first time [the sentence is sung it] doesn't give the listener much information about what the singer feels. BUT, when the chord changes for that second sentence, and *one* note in the melody changes, it gives the lyric a minor-key, sadder cast, and all of a sudden the same sentence, "*Oh, Baby, what you do to* me," becomes ironic, sadder.
>> The Blues song form has now become a vehicle to express the Blues sadness.[6]

---

[6] John Simon, *Truth, Lies & Hearsay* (Self-published, 2018), pp. 215–216. The quotation is compressed from a longer discussion about the blues with Taj Mahal.

I might say it's more modern than that – that change allows the singer, the guitar player, the piano player, to express the human condition as it revealed itself in the revolutions of the eighteenth century that put all order in doubt, to express alienation, to express a fundamental and inexplicable estrangement from his or her familiar, inherited world. With a glaring blues light over your head and blues cops staring you in the face, that change allows you to question, to interrogate your estrangement from your own self – for which, as Stanley Booth described the blues sensibility, you "are only partly responsible." That change all but demands that you confront the paradox of being born with free will into an unfree world.[7]

As a modernist art, the blues is kin to Cubism, Dada, *Finnegans Wake* (1939), or Louise Brooks in *Pandora's Box* (1929). L.V. Thomas was a Houston blues singer who was born in 1891; she began playing blues guitar when she was eleven, in about 1902. "There were blues even then," she told the Houston blues researcher Mack McCormick in 1961, when, having heard one of the records she and the guitarist Geeshie Wiley made in 1930, and guessed her accent might be Houston, he found her in the telephone book. "There were blues even then" – which meant she remembered when there weren't.

With the template John Simon describes – with that foundation, that blues Constitution, subject to amendments and interpretations, precedents and reversals – the form could alter, shift, push its boundaries, because that foundation stone, a place to touch, was always there. The form was not made more complex, only, as with Robert Johnson, deeper – with greater technique, a technique that had its sources in a greater imagination, because thoughts that had never been expressed demanded a technique to say what had never been said before. Here is the British musicologist Wilfred Mellers on Johnson's 1937 "Hellhound on My Trail":

> We have reached the ultimate, and scarifying, disintegration of the country blues . . . voice and instrument no longer comfort one another in dialogue, but stimulate one another to further frenzy. On the words "gotta keep moving" the blues-form is literally disrupted, the harmony displaced, the modulations weirdly awry . . . The expression of loneliness – the singer speaking with and through his guitar – could be carried no further.[8]

---

[7] Stanley Booth, "Even the Birds Were Blue," *Rolling Stone*, April 16, 1970. Collected as "The 1969 Memphis Blues Show: Even the Birds Were Blue," in Booth, *Red Hot and Blue: Fifty Years of Writing About Music, Memphis, and Motherf**kers* (Chicago: Chicago Review Press, 2019), p. 106.

[8] Wilfred Mellers, *Music in a New Found Land: Themes and Developments in the History of American Music* (New York: Oxford University Press, 1964, 1987), p. 272.

The form has been pushed too far, Mellers is saying, as if the form can't contain the volcanic emotion that has been poured into it. But it is still the blues.

Line by line, note by note, a language has been constructed. Luc Sante argues that the blues did not emerge, they did not evolve, they did not appear spontaneously because of the humming motor of culture after the Civil War as an inevitable sociological development, but that as with, in the same decade, the 1890s, "the x-ray or the zipper," the blues were invented, in a single time and place, by a single person, or maybe two – one person and another backing him or her up. The form was so expressive it hit like a blast of light, and so portable in its form that it traveled instantly – so that, to paraphrase Sante, from the first blues song on Monday there were ten by Tuesday and a hundred by Sunday, when people leaving church were already saying it sounded like the Devil's music.[9]

Maybe, maybe not. But by a certain point in the 1890s, possibly in Mississippi, probably in Texas, the language was becoming public, accessible to anyone. Anyone could speak it.

The question Bob Dylan's first album raises is – Ok, anyone can speak it. But does just anyone have the right?

***

"He cut through that scene like a scythe," the late folk singer Sandy Darlington once said of the arrival of a 19-year-old Bob Dylan in Greenwich Village in early 1961. You can hear that arrival, that wind at the singer's back, on that first album – in its audacity, its flair, its refusal to countenance the slightest modesty in the face of songs *he* should have had no right to sing, let alone live up to. What could the kind of person David Hajdu called "a Jewish kid from the suburbs" – one of the stupidest things anyone has ever said about Bob Dylan, given that Hibbing, Minnesota, is not a suburb of anything, but maybe not that far from what a lot of people in Greenwich Village were saying about this person who called himself Bob Dylan in 1962 – know about death?[10] What could a callow know-it-all really know about the death that is feared, chased, refused, and embraced in the original recordings of "Fixin' to Die," "Man of Constant Sorrow," "In My Time of Dying," "See That My Grave Is Kept Clean," and the rest, most of them put down well before he was born?

[9] Luc Sante, "The Invention of the Blues," in *Kill All Your Darlings, Pieces 1990–2005* (Portland, OR: Verse Chorus Press, 2007).

[10] David Hajdu, *Positively Fourth Street: The Life and Times of Joan Baez, Bob Dylan, Mimi Fariña, and Richard Fariña* (New York: Picador, 2011), p. 193.

What the songs taught him, maybe – something they had somehow failed to teach any of the scores of other people who were singing them in the same clubs Bob Dylan was singing them in. "In that music is the only true, valid death you can feel today off a record player," Dylan said in his famous *Playboy* interview with Nat Hentoff in 1966, speaking of what he called traditional music, though he could as well have been speaking of the blues – and prompting more than one person then to respond, as Rafael Alvarez did in the *Baltimore Sun* when he came across the statement more than thirty years later, "A record player!"[11] You take what you can find.

In a time when folk music was a commercial force – in a year when Joan Baez's second album reached number 13 on the pop charts and stayed on the charts for 125 weeks; when Peter Paul and Mary's first album reached number 1 and charted for more than three years; when the Kingston Trio, the Bay Area guitars-and-banjo combo that had taken the traditional North Carolina murder ballad "Tom Dooley" to every town in the USA four years before, had three albums in the top ten – in that time, *Bob Dylan*, with the distribution and marketing clout of the biggest and most prestigious label in the country, with the name John Hammond on the back as producer, the man who had worked with Billie Holiday, Count Basie, Charlie Christian and Big Joe Turner, Benny Goodman and Lionel Hampton, initially sold about five thousand copies.

But as a commercial failure it was also a rumor, and its commercial obscurity gave the rumor its force. Everybody knew Joan Baez and the Kingston Trio – in 1962 she was on the cover of *Time*, in 1959 they'd been on the cover of *Life* – but if you knew the Bob Dylan album you knew something other people didn't, something that soon enough everybody had to know. Within a year, an album title could put an adjective in front of the singer's name as if *it* were already common currency.

You can hear why all of this happened as, on *Bob Dylan*, everything, from "Pretty Peggy-O" to "Talkin' New York" to "Freight Train Blues" to "Fixin' to Die" falls into "See That My Grave Is Kept Clean," the last song.

As Blind Lemon Jefferson recorded it in 1928, he started off with a few jaunty picked notes that sound like a fanfare from an old-timey string band. Then a faraway, moaning voice takes over – a voice that seems to be addressing itself to no audience, that seems to be singing to itself. It's the sound of someone thinking more than performing.

[11] Nat Hentoff, "Bob Dylan: The Playboy Interview," *Playboy*, March 1966. Collected in *Bob Dylan: The Essential Interviews*, ed. Jonathan Cott (New York: Wenner Books, 2007), p. 98. Rafael Alvarez, "Invisible Republic: Nobody Understands Dylan," *Baltimore Sun*, May 11, 1997.

He keeps up a quick, cantering pace throughout, the simple but irreducibly definite strum telling you that everything in the song is inevitable. That this is a story that was told before you were here to hear it. That to more than barely form a word – and you hear how the words barely escape Jefferson's mouth – would be to betray the song.

It would be to pretend that any meaning could ever be clear, when what the singer is saying is that that is a lie. In some way, Jefferson's timing says, this is a story that is older than humanity itself – or that if the first people ever to hear the story were still here to tell us about it, they wouldn't be able to remember who they heard it from.

> Have you ever / heard a coffin sound
> Have you ever / heard a coffin sound
> Have you ever / heard a coffin sound

There's just a slight pause between "ever" and "heard," stronger the second time. As John Simon says, the slightest musical change under the repeated line gives it a new weight, a new gravity, but as Jefferson seemingly helplessly draws out the words in the line – "*everrrrrr*," "*hearrrrrred*" – that new chord, that one-note shift, also adds a feeling of suspense, and this is what Jefferson is playing with. It pays off two verses later, when the slight indication of uncertainty turns into pure melodrama –

> Have you ever heard the church bell toll
> Have you ever heard the church bell toll
> Have you ever heard the church bell toll

– and after the last word of each line, after each toll, he strikes two reverberating notes – *drummm, drummm* – the precise touch Robbie Robertson will hit just after Bob Dylan sings "Where the cape of the stage once had flowed" in "Visions of Johanna" on *Blonde on Blonde* almost forty years later.

Blind Lemon Jefferson's "See That My Grave Is Kept Clean" Plays

Inside the quickened pace of the song there is something slow and burdened – a three-minute funeral march – and that is how young singers in Minneapolis, Cambridge, Berkeley, Austin, Philadelphia, Chicago, and New York were singing the song in the early 1960s. If they had the nerve, maybe they'd even go for that church-bell note – but usually they didn't, because it would sound fake, like a cheap effect, blowing up a point you already got, as it almost does when Blind Lemon Jefferson does it.

As Dylan begins the song, he places that bet and clears the table with the unexpected, dramatic, scary dip of a bass note – which turns into a swoop, then a rumble. It barely repeats a moment later, then invades the music three times more, and every time the music hasn't prepared for it, hasn't dropped a cue, and it throws you off. The tiny riff communicates a harsh and bitter fatalism, but it disappears each time almost before you can register it, leaving behind that feeling of suspense – in this case, the feeling that the song is breathing down your neck.

As Dylan sings, his voice is scraped and braying: frantic, enraged, immediate, *noisy*. Despite the formally measured pace everything feels rushed. He drops all of Jefferson's most colorful verses – there are no coffins, no church bells. *I don't need that*, the song says now. *You don't need that*. It's almost as if the singer is saying that now, in 1962, with the specter of annihilation hanging over his audience and him, he and his audience know more about death than Blind Lemon Jefferson did, and maybe they did: forty-one years later, in 2003, in Erroll Morris's film *The Fog of War*, Robert MacNamara, President Kennedy's Secretary of Defense, speaking of the Cuban Missile Crisis, held up his hand and bent his thumb to his forefinger, until they almost touched, to show how close the specter had come to turning into fact.

Within the strictures of what folk music was supposed to be, of what it was it was supposed to mean, what Bob Dylan did to this hallowed song – the Cambridge singer Geoff Muldaur wasn't just going to sing it, he said, someday he was going to go to Texas and find Blind Lemon Jefferson's grave and sweep it off, and eventually he did – was vulgar, disrespectful, ignorant, conceited – that 1960s word – and vain. But outside of those strictures, in the bigger world where Bob Dylan would soon enough be heard, it was daring, frightening, and exciting, and its defiance of the rules of its time and place was as much an engine of its performance as its defiance of death – and thirty-five years later, in 1997, when Bob Dylan releases *Time Out of Mind*, and the first song comes on, "See That My Grave Is Kept Clean" will be inside of it. Like a ghost, at first – and then like a body.

Today, after its 1998 Grammy for album of the year, after it has become, to some degree, familiar, after people who make lists have fit it nicely into the inevitable progression of Bob Dylan's career, it's necessary to go back to 1997 and re-experience, or imagine, just how damned *Time Out of Mind* sounded and felt. I can't recall a major artist – someone with something to lose – offering people anything as bleak, as barren, as hopeless as this record. Jerry Lewis may have made *The Day the Clown Cried*, his movie about a clown entertaining Jewish children in Auschwitz on their way to the gas chambers, but he never released it. Faulkner published *The Sound and the Fury* – but before, really, anyone cared, or knew who he was.

As the characters in the songs moved across the landscape Dylan had laid out for them, it was hard to believe they could say what they had to say and go on living. That blues imperative that you take phrases from a vast tradition, shuffle them, and then make a story that you present as your own holds here. There's a displacing familiarity, but a familiarity with deadly limits – with everything you hear, it's as if you've heard it before, but not like this. "Highlands," the sixteen-and-a-half minute shaggy dog story that ends *Time Out of Mind* might be a comedy, but it's the story of a man walking streets that are just as dead as the streets in the first line of the first song on *Time Out of Mind*, and the man who's talking to you in "Highlands," who like Blind Lemon Jefferson seems to be talking to himself, sounds like someone who hasn't been out of his SRO hotel in weeks.

I first heard the album in the spring of 1997, five or six months before it was released. I was told it might not be released at all – Bob Dylan hadn't decided. After I listened to it twice, alone in a room in an office building, I could believe it – and I couldn't believe an album with producer's credit to the so-proper Daniel Lanois was going to come out, that year or ever, sounding like this sounded: with fraying notes, broken tones, as if wherever they recorded it there was dirt on the floor and flies on the window panes. It was hilarious, and kind of disgusting, to read Lanois's memoir years later and find out how much better *Time Out of Mind* would have been if Dylan had simply done what Lanois told him to do, instead of running off and doing something else.

When *Time Out of Mind* did appear, the kind of people who reduce all art to biography – because, as John Irving once put it, talking about people who thought everything that happened to his character T.S. Garp, short of being shot to death, happened to him, people without an imagination can't imagine anyone else could have one – knew exactly what it was. It was a breakup album – and the only real question was to find out who Bob Dylan had broken up with.

It's stunning what people will do to protect themselves from art, from music, from a song. In 2000 I taught a class at Berkeley called "Prophecy and the American Voice" – not prophecy as in predicting the future, but prophecy as in the Old Testament, Isaiah and Amos, promising the people of Israel ruin for their sins – and *Time Out of Mind* was one of the texts, along with speeches by John Winthrop and Lincoln and Martin Luther King, three versions of *Invasion of the Body Snatchers*, and *Saved!* a collection of Bob Dylan's onstage gospel sermons from 1979 and 1980, when he was performing as a born-again Christian. The students were destroyed by *Time Out of Mind*. They heard the void it was affirming in an instant, and no matter how long they listened, the burden it insisted on – as always in the blues tradition, some private tragedy working as a metaphor for a tragedy that has everyone in its grip – never lifted. But somebody did say, *Well, it's a breakup album,* and another student, Amy Vecchione, slammed her hand on the table. "Sure, it's a break-up album," she said. "But it's not about breaking up with a woman. It's about breaking up with God." Song by song, it went that far; it was that hard.

As soon as Dylan began performing the songs, especially in 1997 and over the next few years, they expanded. They claimed more territory. They became more of what they wanted to be; they told the person who wrote them how to play them. There's a performance of "Cold Irons Bound" from the Bonnaroo Festival in Manchester, Tennessee, in 2004, that's so much a Sam Peckinpah Western, so much the final shootout in *The Wild Bunch*, that you can't tell if the cold irons bound phrase Dylan keeps roping a steer with means he's bound in irons or if it means he's bound for a cold iron bed, which in blues phrasing means a death bed. Whatever it is, he's going to get there fast. "With a certain kind of blues music," he once said, "you can sit down and play it … you may have to lean forward a little." In this performance he's halfway off the earth.

But "Lovesick," the first song on *Time Out of Mind*, is his own chair, his own version of the blues. The cadence is hobbled, as if to move a single foot forward involves the resolution of a moral dilemma: framing it, finding the real question, trying to determine the answers, and then realizing you don't care. Though the song isn't based on the blues structure of a repeated first line – not "I'm walking, through streets that are dead / I'm walking, through streets that are dead" but "I'm walking, through streets that are dead / Walking, with you in my head" – the first line is so much stronger than the second you feel it in its place anyway. The image of dead streets floods your mind in an instant, and you see them, you're on them. That "you" he says is in his head isn't in yours – with dead streets already there there's no room for it.

In *Masked and Anonymous* (2003), which Dylan, using the name Sergei Petrov, wrote with Larry Charles, the director, Owen Wilson's Bobby Cupid gives Bob Dylan's Jack Fate what he claims is Blind Lemon

Jefferson's guitar. As "Lovesick" grows, grows as it opens up and spreads out as the song plays on *Time Out of Mind*, but far more so as the song was acted out onstage, you can hear the rhythms of "See That My Grave Is Kept Clean" inside of it – underpinning the song, like a ship moving through it. Other songs appear and disappear, like faces in the portholes of the ship of the hidden song. "Sometimes I want to take to the road and plunder," says the singer, with "Kill everybody ever done me wrong" under his breath.

You can ask the same question Bob Dylan's first album challenged you to ask: what does "Lovesick," what does all of *Time Out of Mind*, know about death? What the songs taught it – the old songs, recorded well before the singer was born, the same songs. Songs that told him he had to build his own chair, and how.

This is "Lovesick," as Bob Dylan performed it in Bournemouth, in the UK on October 1, 1997, the day after *Time Out of Mind* was officially released. You can hear the song come into its own body: the voice searching its way through the sound the song has called up from the band, the words like weights the singer has been forced to bear, the guitarist's notes fracturing as they twist into the air, the pieces trying to find their way back to the chord they came from, and never quite making it, speaking that language of suspense.

Bob Dylan's "Lovesick," Bournemouth, October 1, 1997, Plays

I have other songs I'd love to play for you, but that's all I have to say.

CHAPTER 7

Gospel Music

Gayle Wald

Of all of the musical genres with which Bob Dylan has engaged in his long career, gospel is the least examined and, in many ways, the most poorly understood. To say that anything in the meticulously combed-over Dylan oeuvre has resisted interpretation may seem foolhardy. A lineage of distinguished scholars and dedicated fans has scrutinized Dylan's musical archive, detailing his source material as well as his literary uses of the Bible and other sacred texts. Others have explored his complex engagements with Christianity, ever mindful of Dylan's resistance to attempts to impose labels such as "born again" on his practice or theology. In general, however, discussions of Dylan and gospel tend to home in on his musical production of the late 1970s and early 1980s, during the brief but important era when he limited himself, both in the recording studio and in live shows, to songs of Christian witness. Observers of Dylan's career tend to call the three albums he released in quick succession during this period – *Slow Train Coming* (1979), *Saved* (1980), and *Shot of Love* (1981) – his "gospel" or "Christian" LPs, positing them as a musically and thematically distinct body of work. Many have regarded these albums as belonging to a creatively fallow decade (roughly 1978 to 1988) of Dylan's career, a period bookended on one side by the albums *Blood on the Tracks* and *Desire* and on the other side by *Oh Mercy* (1989).

Yet in much of this work, *gospel* functions primarily as a shorthand for the "Christian" Dylan without contributing to a discussion of the music. Likewise, while a focus on Dylan's lyrics and repertoire can shed light on the Nobel Prize winner's songwriting technique and influences, approaches that focus on the written text overlook the performativity of gospel, in which a song's meaning is inseparable from singers' delivery of the lyrics and their ability to ignite the spirit in listeners. And for all of the insights it can yield, the practice of mining Dylan's enormous oeuvre – which includes live

Thank you to Lauren Onkey, Scott M. Marshall, and Kathryn Lofton.

performances, archived ephemera, and online fan documentation of set lists – can cause us to lose sight of the bigger picture, which is Dylan's rich and complex relation to gospel as an African American musical practice. It also hinders us from attending to the centrality of black women as creative agents who facilitate Dylan's engagements with gospel. For although male vocal harmony groups and male soloists are important to the story of Dylan and gospel, the protagonists of this story are women – more specifically, gospel chanteuses.

Like rock 'n' roll, gospel originates as a hybrid, the musical offspring of blues and spirituals. Emerging in the late nineteenth and early twentieth centuries, in the context of Protestant Christian renewal movements, migration, and urbanization, it expressed new varieties of black Christian experience and subjectivity. Musically speaking, gospel has roots in the oral tradition of slave spirituals and in African American appropriations of English hymns, but is distinct from these, in part because its form and content reflect the influence of secular sounds and traditions. The biography of the music is crystalized in the story of Thomas A. Dorsey, an acknowledged "father" of the genre. The Georgia-born son of a minister and a piano teacher, Dorsey was a trained musician who began his music career as a Paramount Records agent and sideman for blues queen Ma Rainey, touring with her Wild Cats Jazz Band under the stage moniker Georgia Tom. In collaboration with the Chicago-based bluesman and slide guitar player Tampa Red, he produced dozens of the bawdy blues numbers known as "hokum," including a 1928 million-seller called "It's Tight Like That."[1]

Dorsey also contributed his talents to church music, performing at a 1930 National Baptist Convention; but his association with gospel springs from his penning of a single song, "Take My Hand, Precious Lord," at a moment of profound personal grief, when he lost his wife as she was giving birth to their son. Based on a melody attributed to the white American composer and Oberlin College professor George N. Allen, "Precious Lord" (as it is known) is a slow moan of a song, indebted to blues and yet, in its commitment to an image of a compassionate God who will alleviate human suffering, less earth-bound than blues songs bemoaning the various troubles of the world. As Dorsey's fame as a composer of spiritual songs grew, he directed his energies to music publishing and to the direction of gospel choirs and choruses, endeavors that would solidify

---

[1] Michael W. Harris, *The Rise of Gospel Blues: The Music of Thomas Andrew Dorsey in the Urban Church* (New York: Oxford University Press, 1994).

gospel as a new *genre* with its own rules, institutions, and traditions. Yet while Dorsey, who understood the inspiration behind "Precious Lord" as God-given, never returned to the freewheeling, secular world of the traveling tent shows, he did not renounce secular *sounds*. "No, no, I'm not ashamed of my blues," he once said. "It's all the same talent, a beat is a beat whatever it is."[2]

Even if he did not know about Dorsey, Dylan would have come to understand some of these complexities of gospel from his own musical experiences. The young man portrayed in *Chronicles, Volume One*, experiences music with an acute, even supernatural, receptivity. Bobby Zimmerman does not just hear music, he is metaphysically *struck* by it, in ways that are memorable half a century later. Johnny Cash's "I Walk the Line" called out to the Hibbing, Minnesota teenager, asking "What are you doing there, boy?" Woody Guthrie's voice "was like a stiletto," making a sound that "would come like a punch . . . it was an epiphany, like some heavy anchor had just plunged into the waters of the harbor." "The stabbing sounds" from Robert Johnson's guitar "could almost break a window."[3] This youthful Dylan, voraciously curious about African American music, tuned in to late-night gospel radio shows from distant cities, where deejays spun disks by the Famous Ward Singers, the Caravans, the Swan Silvertones, and Mahalia Jackson. He would have encountered popular records by the likes of the Highway QCs, the jubilee quartet that launched a young Sam Cooke's career, and Sister Rosetta Tharpe, an early crossover artist who drew secular audiences with her "swinging" spirituals and dexterous guitar picking. (John Hammond, the impresario who brought Tharpe to wide popular attention by featuring her in his landmark 1938 Carnegie Hall concert "From Spirituals to Swing," would in 1961 sign an untested Bob Dylan to Columbia Records, over the objections of label executives who dubbed the scruffy folk singer "Hammond's folly.") The indissolubility of secular and sacred black music would have been further exemplified for a young Dylan in the music of Tharpe acolyte Little Richard, who spurred some of the teenager's earliest forays into musical performance and inspired a now-famous dedication ("to join – 'Little Richard'") in his Hibbing High School yearbook. Like Tharpe, Richard Penniman was a product of black Pentecostal

---

[2] Anthony Heilbut, *The Gospel Sound: Good News and Bad Times* (New York: Simon & Schuster, 1971), p. 34.

[3] Bob Dylan, *Chronicles, Volume One* (New York: Simon & Schuster, 2004), pp. 217, 244, 282. It is notable that in *Chronicles, Volume One*, Dylan omits mention of his investments in Christianity and skips over the "Christian" period.

religion, which endorsed syncopated music and the vivacious dancing that indicated Holy Spirit possession. His famous trick of playing the piano standing up, his right leg thrust over the lid, translated the physical manifestations of spirit-filled Pentecostal worship for youthful rock-and-roll fans like Dylan, who reportedly flustered his earliest bandmates by doing his best imitations not only of Richard's singing but of his visually arresting stage antics.

Yet while Little Richard provided one important blueprint for Dylan's musical trajectory, even anticipating the mature Dylan's turn to Christianity and renunciation of secular music, Dylan drew a different and no less important sort of inspiration from two women. The first was Odetta, the operatically trained singer whom Dylan first encountered in a listening booth in a Minneapolis record store in 1958. *Odetta Sings Ballads and Blues* (1957) made such an impact on the young musician that, as he later told a journalist, "Right then and there, I went out and traded my electric guitar and amplifier for an acoustical guitar, a flat-top Gibson."[4] Her expansive repertoire included African American spirituals and traditional Christian hymns, and for Dylan she exemplified important connections between folk music and civil rights that would later become more central to his popular persona. His admiration for her singing and guitar-playing found expression in his inclusion of the song "Gospel Plow" on *Bob Dylan* (1961), his eponymous Columbia Records debut LP; a year earlier, she had released it as "Hold On" on the live album *Odetta at Carnegie Hall*. Dylan also channeled Odetta's dramatic approach to African American folk material, exemplified by her famous version of the convict song "Waterboy," with its articulate yelps and hammering guitar. She returned the compliment by being the first major artist to release an album of Dylan songs, *Odetta Sings Dylan*, in 1965.

The second woman who figures centrally in Dylan's gospel formation was a startlingly precocious contralto only two years his senior. As Dylan once described it, hearing "Uncloudy Day," the 1956 Staple Singers hit featuring a young Mavis Staples, was akin to a religious experience. It was "the most mysterious thing I'd ever heard," he once told an interviewer. "It was like the fog rolling in. What was that? How do you make that? It just went through me like my body was invisible."[5] Dylan first met Staples backstage at the taping of a 1963 television special, when he was being

---

[4] Roy Rosenbaum, "Bob Dylan: The Playboy Interview," *Playboy*, November 1978.

[5] Robert Love, "Bob Dylan: The Complete AARP Interview," *AARP*, February 2, 2015, www.aarp.org /entertainment/celebrities/info-2015/bob-dylan-magazine-interview.html.

lauded as the prophet of the Folk Revival and she was the standout soloist in the hippest and most politically plugged-in gospel group in the nation, a family outfit led by her father, the formidable Roebuck "Pops" Staples. By both of their accounts, Dylan found Staples's presence as electrifying as her voice, and the two began a several-year-long "court-ship," although Dylan was then in a relationship with Suze Rotolo, the young artist who facilitated his knowledge of politics and radical theatre, and would soon be linked romantically to Joan Baez.[6] Indeed, at the same 1963 Newport Folk Festival where Baez performed two duets with Dylan, using her sterling reputation to give a significant boost to his burgeoning career, Dylan spontaneously proposed marriage to Mavis Staples at a backstage lunch buffet.[7] Although she rebuffed the proposal, worrying about how her marriage to a white man would be received at the height of the civil rights movement, the two became lifelong friends and musical collaborators.

Dylan's sexual attraction to Staples is not incidental in this context. For while his relationship to male gospel performers – from Hank Williams, Johnny Cash, and Elvis Presley to Little Richard and Cooke – has been characterized in terms of respectful admiration and earnest imitation, Dylan's relationship to female gospel artists as backup singers has been defined by romantic as well as creative attachment. In many instances, these two varieties of attachment are inseparable, making it impossible to separate Dylan the "man" from Dylan the "musician." For example, during the 1978 *Street Legal* tour, around the time Dylan experienced Christian Revelation, he would periodically introduce his backing vocal-ists, a group that variously included Hilda Harris, Albertine Robinson, Maretha Stewart, Jo Ann Harris, and Carolyn (aka Carol) Dennis – all black women – as "my ex-wife, my next wife, my girlfriend, and my fiancée."[8] His acknowledged love affairs with Staples and Dennis, as well as his less public (rumored or "known") romantic relationships with Regina McCrary, Helena Springs, Clydie King, and Mary Alice Artes,

---

[6] Greg Kot, *I'll Take You There: Mavis Staples, the Staple Singers, and the Music that Shaped the Civil Rights Era* (New York: Simon & Schuster, 2014).

[7] Greg Kot, "I Got a Lot More to Give," *Chicago Tribune*, August 1, 2004; Peter Sagal, "Not My Job: Mavis Staples Gets Quizzed on Office Supplies," *Wait Wait . . . Don't Tell Me!*, August 16, 2014, www .npr.org/2014/08/16/340647455/not-my-job-mavis-staples-gets-quizzed-on-office-supples.

[8] David Yaffe, "Tangled Up in Keys: Why Does Bob Dylan Namecheck Alicia Keys in His New Song?" Slate.com August 11, 2006. Michael Gray has a slightly different version, in which Dylan is more playful and more flirtatious with Dennis, identifying her during concerts as "my current girlfriend," "my ex-girlfriend," "my fiancée – wishful thinking!" and "the true love of my life, my fiancée." See Michael Gray, *The Bob Dylan Encyclopedia* (New York: Continuum, 2006), p. 174.

suggest that gospel music provides a useful starting point for a different story of "love and theft" than the male homosocial one that usually features in discussions of Dylan's cultural practice. Howard Sounes quotes the musician Maria Muldaur speculating that Dylan pursued intimacy with black female gospel singers because, as women with limited interest in "white" folk and rock music, they were not invested in his star persona. "I think he dated some of these black girls because they didn't idolize him . . . . They were real down to earth, and they didn't worship him. They are strong women who would just say, cut your bullshit."[9] Dennis and McCrary would lend credence to Muldaur's conjecture, separately reporting that when they auditioned to be Dylan's backup singers, neither cared enough about the artist to be in thrall to his mystique.

While such speculation is consistent with what we know as Dylan's lifelong aversion to celebrity, it does not allow for the more interesting possibility that Dylan was attracted to the *creative authority* of the gospel chanteuse. The scholar and gospel performer Horace Clarence Boyer has characterized gospel vocalizing as "energetic, florid, and 'spirit-induced,'" in the sense that "the spirit dictate[s] the amount of embellishment, volume, and improvisation that [is] applied" to a given performance.[10] Gospel singing, that is to say, demands performers who imbue the inert musical text with a creative energy and intelligence derived from personal faith. Listeners who have not grown up with gospel music often imagine that gospel singers are at their best when they "let it all hang out." But in fact, as Boyer and the gospel scholar and producer Anthony Heilbut remind us through their careful attention to the signature techniques of such gospel luminaries as Clara Ward, Dorothy Norwood, Mahalia Jackson, and Marion Williams, spirit-induced singing is a matter of profound artistic discipline and personalized creativity.[11] Just as important, black women historically have found ways to seize upon gospel's elevation of the *singing voice* to carve out prominent roles for themselves. Particularly in denominations that forbid women from pastoral roles, these singers wield their power as performers to amplify, echo, or even muffle the pronouncements of male ministers with their inspired performances. This sonic authority of black women in church is linked to the public prominence of female gospel soloists in the music's mid-twentieth-century Golden Age.

---

[9] Howard Sounes, *Down the Highway: The Life of Bob Dylan* (New York: Grove Press, 2001), p. 371.
[10] Horace Clarence Boyer, *The Golden Age of Gospel* (Champaign, IL: University of Illinois Press, 2000), pp. 40, 43.
[11] Ibid., 50; Heilbut, *The Gospel Sound*.

It stands to reason, then, that in his collaborations with gospel vocalists, which came into full flowering in 1978–1979, when he began to compose, record, and then perform the material from *Slow Train Coming*, Dylan was both seeking out a certain sound quality associated with gospel and looking to harness the energy and magnetism of these singers for his own musical ends. Indeed, notwithstanding fans' deep resistance to Dylan's fire-and-brimstone persona of the Christian era, Dylan's gospel catalog contains a host of notable recordings, from "Precious Angel" (from *Slow Train Coming*) to "Solid Rock" (a highlight of *Saved*) to "Every Grain of Sand" (a ballad from *Shot of Love*). *Slow Train Coming* was a commercial success despite some critical pushback, eventually being certified platinum in the USA. Even those who turned up their noses at his pugnacious proselytizing found Dylan to have been in particularly fine voice in his early 1980s concerts.

The most famous work from the period is "Gotta Serve Somebody," from *Slow Train Coming*. A call-and-response between Dylan and his backup singers, who affirm his lyric's critique of false idols, the song was derided by the likes of John Lennon, who composed an acerbic answer song, "Serve Yourself." But "Gotta Serve Somebody" earned Dylan considerable popular acclaim, peaking at number 24 on the Billboard Hot 100 chart (a particularly good showing for an artist who did not reliably break into the Top 40) as well as a 1979 Grammy Award, ironically in this context for Best *Rock* Vocal Performance by a Male. (Apparently the National Academy of Recording Arts and Sciences, the group overseeing the Grammys, could not imagine "Gotta Serve Somebody" as a gospel song.) Later that same year, backed up by Terry Young, Helena Springs, Monalisa Young, and Regina McCrary (then Havis), Dylan sang "Gotta Serve Somebody" on *Saturday Night Live*, following it with a moving performance of "I Believe in You" and "When You Gonna Wake Up." The album even earned Dylan a following among white fundamentalist Christians, who read about Dylan's "born-again" experience in religious publications.

The recent release of *The Bootleg Series, Vol. 13: Trouble No More*, a box that documents Dylan's Christian period, lends credence to the notion that Dylan's backup singers not only supported him sonically in this era through their arresting vocal arrangements and skillful percussive accompaniment, but also pushed him to be a better – that is, more spirit-infused – singer. This is evident in the set's featured live recordings (from 1979 to 1981) of "Solid Rock," a spirit-filled romp with irresistible vocal and guitar hooks, as well as from a rehearsal outtake of Dylan and Clydie King performing an affecting duet of "Abraham, Martin and John."[12] Part of *Trouble No More: A Musical Film*, a documentary included in the box set, the song and video warrant special attention, first because the song, as a 1968 Dion composition written in remembrance of Abraham Lincoln, Martin Luther King, Jr., and John and Robert Kennedy, is not usually considered to be gospel. More important, the performance footage reveals the palpable intimacy of the two musicians, who convey an aura of eroticized spiritual communion that is simultaneously carnal and transcendent of mundane romantic attraction. "She was my ultimate singing partner," Dylan told *Rolling Stone* in the magazine's obituary of King, who died in January 2019. "No one ever came close. We were two soulmates."[13]

Dylan's respectful remembrance of King, offered at a time when he was in the process of establishing a Bob Dylan Archive in Tulsa, Oklahoma (and thus conceivably taking stock of earlier eras in his career) contrasts with the representation, in some writing about Dylan, of his black female gospel singers as a variety of eye candy, or as interchangeable "girl singers" defined by race and gender.[14] Yet in addition to sounding a sour note of misogyny, such commentary flies in the face of these singers' impressive musical achievements, both with and without Dylan. King, a one-time backing singer for Ray Charles, had a solo LP to her name before she began collaborating with Dylan, and both she and Springs, who wrote more songs with Dylan than anyone else in his career, recorded duets with him.[15] McCrary, daughter of an original member of the Fairfield Four gospel group, sang and co-wrote with Dylan and, at his request, routinely performed a spoken homily (based on a story of her father's) as an opener to Dylan's live shows. With Dennis and Monalisa Young, all of these singers would at some point contribute to the mini gospel-concerts, usually consisting of five songs with Terry Young's piano accompaniment, that followed McCrary's homily. The "backgrounding" of Dylan's backup singers in some Dylan scholarship, whether through a minimization of their talents or misrecognition of their roles, thus belies their musical agency as co-creators of Dylan's music, before, during, and after his Christian period.

[12] Jennifer LeBeau, dir. *Trouble No More: A Musical Film*, 2017.
[13] David Browne, "Clydie King, Unsung Backup Singer for Ray Charles and Bob Dylan, Dead at 75," *Rolling Stone*, January 10, 2019, www.rollingstone.com/music/music-news/clydie-king-ray-charles-bob-dylan-singer-dead-777417.
[14] Clinton Heylin, *Trouble in Mind: Bob Dylan's Gospel Years: What Really Happened* (New York: Lesser Gods, 2017).
[15] Gray, *Bob Dylan Encyclopedia*, pp. 380, 632.

This is not to suggest that Dylan's investment in his female collaborators has been innocent of the plunderous desire that characterizes the "theft" side of the love-and-theft dialectic. If we have learned anything from Eric Lott's seminal study of blackface minstrelsy, the source of the title phrase of Dylan's 2001 *"Love and Theft"* album, it is that white attraction to "blackness" is inseparable from a certain white quest for ownership of and power over those who would seem to possess it. David Yaffe, one of the few to write about Dylan and black women, has characterized his relationship with his backup singers in transactional terms. "When Dylan found his inner soul sister, the Queens of Rhythm lost a gig," he writes, using the moniker Dylan used for the backing vocalists (some combination of Queen Esther Marrow, Louise Bethune, his new wife Carolyn Dennis, and Dennis's mother Madelyn Quebec) who sang on his 1986 and 1987 tours with Tom Petty and the Heartbreakers.[16] By late 1987, Dylan had bottomed out creatively. "My own songs had become strangers to me," he recalls in *Chronicles*, "I didn't have the skill to touch their raw nerves."[17] But as he confessed to David Gates in an interview for *Newsweek*, a creative epiphany occurred during an October show in Locarno, Switzerland:

> It's almost like I heard it as a voice. It wasn't like it was even me thinking it. I'm determined to stand, whether God will deliver me or not. And all of a sudden everything just exploded. It exploded every which way. And I noticed that all the people out there – I was used to them looking at the girl singers, they were good-looking girls, you know? And like I say, I had them up there so I wouldn't feel so bad. But when that happened, nobody was looking at the girls anymore. They were looking at the main mike. After that is when I sort of knew: I've got to go out and play these songs. That's just what I must do.[18]

Leaving aside for a moment Dylan's image of "girl singers" (a group that included his wife and mother-in-law) and the complicated ways that attraction and objectification dovetail in this story, his description of the function of his backing vocalists – "I had them up there so I wouldn't feel so bad" – is still striking. What does it mean that Dylan no longer needed "the girls" for the artistic or psychological cover they provided? And what are we to make of Dylan's narration of this moment as one of quasi-religious revelation, as an "explosion" of consciousness over which Dylan had no control? Is Dylan as an artist being expelled from the Garden or, in

---

[16] Yaffe, "Tangled Up in Keys."   [17] Dylan, *Chronicles*, p. 148.

[18] David Gates, "Dylan Revisited," *Newsweek*, October 5, 1997, www.newsweek.com/dylan-revisited -174056.

expelling his backup singers, is he recreating himself as Adam? Whatever the answers to these questions, by the time he initiated his Never Ending Tour in June 1988, Dylan was no longer featuring the central sonic sources of his gospel sound.

Dylan's recollections of the late 1980s position his black female collaborators as artistic proxies: women who alternately lifted him up, covered him, or spoke on his behalf. There is evidence that audiences during the Christian period also indulged such projections, heckling the women during their opening gospel sets. Ostensibly this reflected fans' hostility toward the man who had once snarled "I ain't gonna work on Maggie's farm no more," but who was now snarling at audience members who did not share his faith in the End Times. The musician Nick Cave memorably called *Slow Train Coming* "a great record, full of mean-spirited spirituality … a genuinely nasty record, certainly the nastiest 'Christian' album I've ever come across," and fan accounts of Dylan's gospel-era rants from the stage suggest that the musician gave as well as he got.[19] Yet even if Dylan's apocalyptic preaching between songs alienated fans who felt the voice of the counterculture had finally capitulated to Authority, the anger directed at his female singers suggests fans were also expressing antipathy toward gospel music.

Certainly, those who screamed at Dylan and his backing vocalists to "play rock music" were unaware of both the profound irony of this demand (in terms of rock's history) and the fact that most African Americans who grew up in the church would not necessarily have understood Dylan's music, despite its Christian lyrics, as gospel. Indeed, Pops Staples was more than a little impressed by Dylan's sensitive lyrics in "Blowin' in the Wind," especially the line about one day being called "a man." Arguably, for Pops and other black listeners, *this* was Dylan's real gospel song, one no less anthemic than "This Little Light of Mine." Moreover, by the time Dylan ventured into his gospel period, the music and its market had changed. The phenomenal success of "Oh Happy Day" by the Edwin Hawkins Singers in 1969 meant that gospel had entered a new phase of commercial popularity in the Age of Aquarius. The deaths of Ward, Jackson, and Tharpe within a few years in the early 1970s signified the end of the era of the Golden Age gospel diva. By the mid-1980s, the gospel hymns of the Freedom Singers (with whom Dylan had performed "Blowin' in the Wind" at Newport)

---

[19] The quote attributed to Cave is from *Mojo*, January 1997, according to the user "Callahan" on ExpectingRain.com. See "Street Legal is Nick Cave's Favorite Dylan Album" thread, www.expectingrain.com/discussions/viewtopic.php?f=6&t=35812.

were about to give way to the stylings of Whitney Houston, daughter of the gospel singer Emily "Cissy" Houston.

In 2003, *Gotta Serve Somebody: The Gospel Songs of Bob Dylan*, a collection produced by Jeffrey Gaskill, convened prominent African American gospel musicians to breathe new life into Dylan's by-then old gospel songs. Featuring dazzling interpretations of the late 1970s and early 1980s material by stalwarts like Shirley Caesar and the Fairfield Four, the album was less a tribute to Dylan than an argument for the songs themselves. It is thus fitting that among the album's many powerful tracks, the standout is "Gonna Change My Way of Thinking," a hard-driving, funky duet that reunites Dylan and his idol and one-time sweetheart Staples. The performance is built around a skit whose premise is that Staples had wandered into Dylan's Malibu home, interrupting a recording session that is already in progress. Her arrival sets off an extended dialogue, in which he welcomes Staples to his beachfront manse ("You can sit on this porch and look right straight into Hawai'i," he quips), offers to slaughter and "fry up" some chickens to satisfy her hunger, and confides that he is battling a case of the blues by staying up nights and reading *Snoozeweek*. On cue Staples responds: "That ain't gonna get rid of no blues. Let's do some singing!" Following her exhortation, the two continue where Dylan had left off, their time-honed, jagged voices conveying both world-weariness and a determination.

The skit that ushers Staples into this performance with Dylan is a winking reprisal of a 1931 recording that begins with a similarly staged impromptu duet between country-gospel singer Jimmie Rodgers and the Carter Family, and it is both supremely silly and unabashedly nostalgic. We hear band members cracking up in the background as Dylan and Staples deliver their lines with hammy relish, enjoying the cornball quality of their banter. But while it is a comic trifle, the skit is also richly instructive, revealing gospel music as a vital touchstone and a shared musical language in the careers of *both* performers. In representing Staples as a visitor who knows what to do to ease Dylan's blues, the skit betokens their intimacy, a familiarity born of a long and occasionally difficult history. It also hints at Dylan's collaborations with gospel chanteuses as a balm for his own emotional and creative vulnerability; after all, it is Staples who suggests the curative value of singing together. In their lovely version of a song about the necessity of self-renewal, neither voice is "backgrounded." Nor is there a sense of Dylan as leader and Staples as follower; the magic emerges from the music they make together. "Here's the thing with me and the religious thing," Dylan told *Newsweek* (not *Snoozeweek*). "This is the flat-out truth: I find the religiosity and philosophy in the music. I don't find it anywhere else. . . . I don't adhere to rabbis, preachers, evangelists, all of that. I've learned more from the songs than I've learned from any of this kind of entity. The songs are my lexicon. I believe the songs."[20] In this moment, Staples would seem to believe the songs, too.

[20] Gates, "Dylan Revisited."

CHAPTER 8

Country Music: Dylan, Cash, and the Projection of Authenticity

Leigh H. Edwards

Dylan's explicit foray into country music in his recordings in the late 1960s evolved out of his earlier interest in the genre, which he grew up listening to in childhood. He has described country artists such as Hank Williams and Johnny Cash as childhood heroes; cited the Carter Family as an early influence; and recorded three albums in Nashville – *Blonde on Blonde* (1966), *John Wesley Harding* (1967), and *Nashville Skyline* (1969) – using some of the city's famed session musicians.[1] Of those albums, two are most relevant to Dylan's interest in country as a genre: *John Wesley Harding* was Dylan's more pared down genre mix of folk and rock inflected by country that drew on American roots music and shared similarities with Cash's signature sound with the Tennessee Three, while *Nashville Skyline* was an explicitly mainstream country album. The latter especially is often cited as a pioneering work in country-rock that influenced other musicians and sparked a boom in that hybrid genre. Dylan has continued to incorporate country into his oeuvre over his career, in some of his own country-inflected compositions and, notably, in tribute songs for Williams, Cash, the Stanley Brothers, and Jimmie Rodgers. In his live performances, he has included country instrumentation on his tour since the late 1990s, including banjo, fiddle, mandolin, and pedal steel guitar, and he has also toured with Willie Nelson (2004).

His work on *Nashville Skyline* is important for his collaboration with Cash since the men did two joint recording sessions. Their duet of Dylan's "Girl from the North Country" is the only one that ended up on this album, although there had been talk of doing a full album of their duets, a project that was later abandoned. Some of their recordings from those

---

[1] Jay Orr, ed., *Dylan, Cash, and the Nashville Cats: A New Music City* (Nashville: Country Music Foundation Press, 2015), p. 14.

joint sessions are now available as part of the new Bob Dylan Bootleg Series, on *Travelin' Thru, 1967–1969: The Bootleg Series Vol. 15* (2019). From the February 17, 1969 Dylan–Cash session, the bootleg release includes the vital recording they made of Dylan's 1962 song "Don't Think Twice, It's All Right" with Cash's 1964 song inspired by it, "Understand Your Man." Cash used some of the melody from Dylan's earlier song in his later tribute composition, as this unique joint performance of these two songs show- cases. The bootleg release from that session also includes their duets of Cash's "I Still Miss Someone," "Big River," "I Walk the Line," and his hit "Ring of Fire" (penned by June Carter Cash and Merle Kilgore). Likewise, it contains Dylan's "One Too Many Mornings," their take on Carl Perkins's "Matchbox" (with Perkins there playing guitar), and their arrangement of "Mystery Train" (written by Junior Parker) and Woody Guthrie's "This Train is Bound for Glory." Most crucially, from the February 18, 1969 session, the Bootleg Series features the first known recording of the song Dylan wrote for Cash, "Wanted Man," with Perkins on guitar. Also included are their renditions of key influences for both, such as two Jimmie Rodgers medleys, including "Blue Yodel No. 1."

Their important collaboration grew out of the mutual respect they had built over the years. Cash admired *The Freewheelin' Bob Dylan* (1963), and wrote the younger performer a letter to praise him as "the best country singer I've heard in years,"[2] noting the common folk culture roots of country and Dylan's own early-1960s folk music. Building on their corres- pondence, Cash gave Dylan his guitar, a traditional country artist's sign of respect, when they saw each other at the Newport Folk Festival in 1964 and came to his defense amid the controversy around his electric performance a year later. In response to outraged fans who felt Dylan was betraying acoustic instrumentation and folk modes of address as well as the folk revival, Cash's reply in *Broadside* magazine was: "Shut up and let him sing!"[3] Dylan paid homage to Cash on his *Nashville Skyline* album, and Cash wrote its Grammy-winning liner notes. On June 8, 1969, Dylan appeared on the first episode of *The Johnny Cash Show* (1969–1971) and their duet of "Girl from the North Country" was memorable and influen- tial. Rosanne Cash later recalled as a teen watching her father and Dylan sing together on television, saying that duet "seared itself into the minds of

---

[2] C. Eric Banister, *Johnny Cash FAQ: All That's Left to Know about the Man in Black* (Milwaukee: Backbeat Books, 2014), p. 85.

[3] Quoted in Peter Lewry, *A Johnny Cash Chronicle: I've Been Everywhere* (London: Helter Skelter, 2001), p. 49.

[her] generation" and was like a "nuclear reaction had occurred in the musical foundations and entrenched loyalties of the entire country."[4]

The Dylan–Cash duet shocked some audiences at the time because it yoked icons of rock and country together, bridging two musical cultures that were stereotypically seen as disparate, melding the folk-rock counterculture's revolutionary, avant-garde critiques with the supposedly conservative, nostalgic, establishment values of the country genre. This high profile collaboration, however, quickly inspired more artists to record vibrant work with Nashville session players, including Neil Young, Simon & Garfunkel, Linda Ronstadt, George Harrison, Leon Russell, Paul McCartney, and the Nitty Gritty Dirt Band.

When Dylan did his country album, some fans saw it as a simplistic embrace of a stereotypically conservative genre, but recent academic studies have found a complex range of political affiliations across the history of the genre, including progressive content. Scholars such as Nadine Hubbs, for example, have identified progressive alliances involving working-class advocacy, LGBTQ+ rights, and cross-racial class alliances. Citing examples like Cash's prison reform and Native American land rights advocacy, Hubbs finds a long progressive history in the genre that questions a stereotype of bigotry imposed by middle-class narratives.[5] Cash himself often held conflicting political positions, with some audiences hoping Cash could be a Woody Guthrie-style organic intellectual, or organizer for his class. Others, however, were disillusioned by his seemingly vocal support for Nixon and his ties to big business, although he also supported Vietnam protestors. Cash's political affiliations, in other words, were more complex than a conservative stereotype would allow and he used contradiction to critique stereotypes of Southern white working-class masculinity and to complicate country music's narratives of authenticity.[6] Dylan exploits similar kinds of contradiction, often using them to question the very idea of authenticity as he plays a trickster figure with constantly changing personae. Barry Shank has argued convincingly that Dylan in the 1960s embodies the

[4] Orr, *Nashville*, p. 9.
[5] Nadine Hubbs, *Rednecks, Queers, and Country Music* (Berkeley: University of California Press, 2014). Mark Allan Jackson, ed., *The Honky Tonk on the Left: Progressive Thought in Country Music* (Amherst: University of Massachusetts Press, 2018).
[6] Leigh H. Edwards, *Johnny Cash and the Paradox of American Identity* (Bloomington: Indiana University Press, 2009).

contradiction of a countervailing search for both autonomy and authenticity in American culture.[7]

In the reception of *Nashville Skyline*, Dylan faced another common stereotype about country music: that the lyrics are simplistic or transparent.[8] Dylan, however, talked about using more direct language in a creative way to achieve the storytelling effect he sought, as recounted by Allen Ginsberg.[9] More generally, scholars have argued that critics must address country music's complexity and use of figurative language rather than relegating it to overly simplistic transparency or literal realism.[10]

Dylan's late 1960s foray into country music thus exemplifies how the country genre was one of the wellsprings of a more broadly conceived folk tradition. It also illuminates how he toys with different projections of authenticity in his stage persona and media image, and how he critiques those poses to undermine the very idea of authenticity. He found the search for authenticity and purity in the folk revival constricting and looked with suspicion at the movement's nostalgic quest for roots that were never actually pure. In country music, Dylan found a different take on authenticity and the tension between folk culture and mass culture, tensions that he had more freedom to navigate as an outsider. Dylan himself framed his country album as part of his well-documented efforts to disrupt his own media image and undermine any one clear persona, as well as to derail the hagiography of him as a folk prophet. In *Chronicles*, he argues that he did *Nashville Skyline* to throw off fans, saying he wished to dispel unwanted narratives about him as the voice of his generation.[11] Country music's mode of address involves what Jimmie N. Rogers terms the genre's "sincerity contract," entailing the idea of staying true to one's roots and not selling out, which signals loyalty to an audience imagined to be working class.[12] Dylan tried on country music's sincerity as one of his many performance masks, one that is particularly well-suited to his long critique of authenticity, where he implies that it can only ever be faked or at

[7] Barry Shank, "'That Wild Mercury Sound': Bob Dylan and the Illusion of American Culture," *boundary 2* 29, no. 1 (2002), pp. 97–123.

[8] Sean Wilentz, *Bob Dylan in America* (New York: Doubleday, 2010). Christopher Ricks, *Dylan's Visions of Sin* (London: Penguin, 2003).

[9] Barry Miles, *Ginsberg: A Biography* (London: Viking, 1990), p. 392.

[10] Barbara Ching, *Wrong's What I Do Best: Hard Country Music and Contemporary Culture* (New York: Oxford University Press, 2001).

[11] Bob Dylan, *Chronicles: Volume One* (New York: Simon & Schuster, 2004). David Gates, "The Book of Bob," *Newsweek*, October 4, 2004, p. 56.

[12] Jimmie N. Rogers, *The Country Music Message: Revisited* (Fayetteville: University of Arkansas Press, 1989), pp. 17–18.

least multiple and changing. I will return to the challenges and contradictions of country music's quest for authenticity in a moment, but first we need to look more carefully at the biographical and cultural contexts for Dylan's Nashville albums.

Biographical and Cultural Contexts

Dylan's first experience working with a Nashville session musician was with Charlie McCoy on *Highway 61 Revisited* (1965). Dylan used mostly New York musicians on that album, but Columbia producer Bob Johnston invited his friend McCoy to a recording session, perhaps as a way to lure Dylan to record at Columbia's Nashville studios.[13] McCoy described the improvised acoustic guitar performance he contributed to "Desolation Row" as an imitation of Grady Martin's famous sound on Marty Robbins's hit song "El Paso" (1959). When Dylan wanted to record *Blonde on Blonde* and was not getting the sound he wanted with his touring band, the Hawks, in New York, Johnston urged him to record in Columbia's Nashville studio with some of its legendary session musicians. In February 1966, Dylan went to Nashville, bringing musicians Robbie Robertson and Al Kooper. He recorded with McCoy and his band, the Escorts. Dylan infamously described that album as "the closest I ever got to the sound I hear in my mind," as the "thin . . . wild mercury sound" and "metallic and bright gold, with whatever that conjures up."[14] McCoy and his band had a requisite stylistic range not only in country music but also for Dylan's own synthesized take on rock, R&B, blues, and folk.

The fact that Dylan used Nashville session musicians for these albums is important, because they were often creating arrangements on the spot while also using their facility with different musical styles to help achieve the sound that musicians sought. As Travis Stimeling has argued of Nashville session musicians more generally, they could be seen as collaborators with artists.[15] Dylan used musicians informally referred to as the Nashville Cats, which included McCoy, Charlie Daniels, and Kenny Buttrey. He used McCoy, Buttrey, and Pete Drake on *John Wesley Harding*. On *Nashville Skyline* he was backed by McCoy, Buttrey,

[13] Charlie McCoy with Travis Stimeling, *Fifty Cents and a Box Top: The Creative Life of Nashville Session Musician Charlie McCoy* (Morgantown: West Virginia University Press, 2017), pp. 80–81.
[14] Orr, *Nashville*, p. 23.
[15] Travis Stimeling, *Nashville Cats: Record Production in Music City, 1945–1975* (New York: Oxford University Press, 2020).

Drake, Norman Blake, Daniels, and Bob Wilson, with Cash listed as "guest artist."

While the established Nashville session protocols generated quick, highly efficient recordings, the musicians described the Dylan sessions as much more laid back, with room for creative exploration, although Dylan liked to work with little discussion.[16] For *Nashville Skyline*, Daniels said Dylan arrived with only four songs and had quickly to write new material and then give it to the session musicians to create an arrangement: "Bob would come in with songs. We'd sit and listen to what he had, and throw together an arrangement, almost immediately."[17] Stimeling notes that for *Blonde on Blonde*, Dylan did more than a dozen takes on some songs, which suggests that he was still looking for his sound.[18] Guitarist Wayne Moss remarked, "We used to think of Nashville sessions as being relaxed, but Dylan changed our whole approach. He was so relaxed and laidback that your creative juices took on an entirely different aspect . . . . Anything we wanted to try, have at it."[19] Significantly, Dylan listed all session musicians by name on the album, one of the first artists to do so.[20]

Recorded at Columbia's Nashville studios in three sessions, *John Wesley Harding* offered a sparser, more straightforward approach to rock influenced by folk, country, and Dylan's long interest in the ballad form. The spare instrumentation included Dylan on acoustic guitar, harmonica, and piano, accompanied by Charlie McCoy on bass and Kenny Buttrey on drums. Pete Drake played pedal steel guitar for two songs, "Down Along the Cove" and "I'll Be Your Baby Tonight," both of which foreshadow the mainstream country of *Nashville Skyline*. Dylan purposefully used more direct lyrics, with more concise imagery. His smoother vocals prefigured the surprising tenor he used for *Nashville Skyline*, where he departed from his instantly recognizable nasal twang rooted in his early homage to Woody Guthrie. *John Wesley Harding* appeared in stark contrast to the elaborate psychedelic rock albums of that moment, such as the Beatles' *Sgt. Pepper's Lonely Hearts Club Band* (1967). It prompted other rock musicians to seek out the folk sources of blues and country and helped spark the flowering of alternative country and Americana roots music in the 1990s (see Chapter 10).

[16] Orr, *Nashville*, p. 21.
[17] Peter Doggett, *Are You Ready for the Country: Elvis, Dylan, Parsons and the Roots of Country Rock* (New York: Penguin, 2000), p. 10.
[18] Stimeling, *Nashville Cats*, p. 245; from his notes on session recordings for *Blonde on Blonde*, Bob Dylan Archives, New York, NY, May 24, 2016.
[19] Orr, *Nashville*, p. 23.   [20] Ibid.

Received as a country-rock hybrid and one of his most political albums, *John Wesley Harding* shares some thematic affinities with Cash's proletarian concept album, *Blood, Sweat and Tears* (1963), with similar social advocacy, working-class themes, and folk roots. Dylan's social protest is evident in "I Am a Lonesome Hobo" and "I Pity the Poor Immigrant," as well as the highly influential "All Along the Watchtower." Dylan's ballads on the album also draw inspiration from Williams and Cash.

While that album reflects Cash's influence more implicitly, in themes and form, Cash's influence on *Nashville Skyline* is explicitly front and center, since Dylan used his Cash duet and Cash's liner notes as his entrée to country music. Dylan included songs that sound like mainstream country, such as the instrumental "Nashville Skyline Rag"; "Lay, Lady, Lay," originally written for the *Midnight Cowboy* (1969) soundtrack but completed too late to be included; "I Threw It All Away," his lyrical nod toward shedding his folk hero image; and "Country Pie," whose lyrics jokingly list different pies, which seemed particularly to vex critics looking for his previous poetic complexity. While some were disappointed by lyrics focused more on domestic bliss than social justice, the album was a commercial success, reaching number 3 on the *Billboard* top 200 albums chart. Cash's liner notes vouch for Dylan's sincerity and country chops, describing him as "a hell of a poet," vast, like Whitmanian "leaves of grass," and someone who is both "alike" "yet unalike," seemingly a reference to Dylan's practice of taking source material and reworking it to generate his own synthesis. Again, Cash had earlier undertaken that process himself, shaping Dylan's "Don't Think Twice, It's All Right" (1962) into "Understand Your Man" (1964). Dylan's song itself drew on earlier ones, including Paul Clayton's "Who's Goin' to Buy You Ribbons When I'm Gone?" that itself built on "Who's Gonna Buy Your Chickens [Flowers] When I'm Gone?" Trying to shield Dylan from potential criticism, Cash writes in the liner notes that Dylan is not imitating but rather emulating,

> At times, to expand further the light
> Of an original glow.
> Knowing that to imitate the living
> Is mockery
> and to imitate the dead
> is robbery.

He then invokes those beings who are "complete unto themselves" to categorize Dylan. Moments from the Cash and Dylan recording sessions are captured on film in the documentary *Johnny Cash: The Man, His World, His Music* (1969), and their easy rapport is evident as they ramble through a duet version of Dylan's "One Too Many Mornings," laughing and joking with each other. There, Dylan is clearly trying to be respectful and Cash looks admiring at Dylan. That mutual respect extends from their personal relationship to their investments in bringing the country and rock genres together, and this historic moment of collaboration has itself become part of an authenticity story for country-rock, that "nuclear reaction" moment Rosanne Cash describes.

Authenticity

To draw out this story of authenticity, it will be helpful to turn to a case study of Dylan's titular song from *John Wesley Harding*, because that song thematizes authenticity and exemplifies points of comparison and contrast with Cash, who had earlier done his own Hardin song. Thus, the song's cultural context warrants further explication. Dylan famously changed the story, and the spelling of Hardin's name, in a way that brought in mythologies and pondered how Wild West stories were made and circulated. Cash's song about Hardin was for his Western concept album, *Johnny Cash Sings the Ballads of the True West* (1965). That album, one of his four concept albums from the 1960s that traced his views on US history, celebrated the cowboy.[21] However, it followed on the heels of his album *Bitter Tears: Ballads of the American Indian* (1964) that decried the dispossession of American Indian land and culture. Thus Cash forwards a view of the frontier that both lauds and critiques aspects of it. In this song, he focuses on frontier masculinity, frontier justice, and violence; his Hardin draws a gun to get back money he had lost shooting dice, is arrested for it the next day, but keeps the money. Both artists explore ideas of storytelling in ballad form, thinking through versions of American history.

Dylan's song strangely reflects on how he himself toys with authenticity, because it mimics his own tendency to create embellished personae throughout his career. Authenticity is the keyword here because that idea is central to country music, while it is a recurring complex problem for Dylan. Dylan recounts his composition process for this song: "I was gonna write a ballad . . . like maybe one of those old cowboy . . . you know, a real

---

[21] *Ride This Train* (1960) thematizes Western expansion and railroad culture; *Blood, Sweat and Tears* (1963) highlights working-class folk songs and labor; *Bitter Tears: Ballads of the American Indian* (1964) advocates for American Indian land rights and culture; and *Johnny Cash Sings the Ballads of the True West* (1965) searches for cowboy experiences behind the mythology.

long ballad. But in the middle of the second verse, I got tired. I had a tune, and I didn't want to waste the tune, it was a nice little melody, so I just wrote a quick third verse, and I recorded that."[22] The historical John Wesley Hardin was a Texas outlaw sent to prison in 1877 for murder; he wrote an autobiography embellishing his life story, thereby turning himself into a mythological outlaw. He was eventually pardoned and practiced law before being shot dead in an El Paso saloon after he pistol-whipped a lawman who had accused his prostitute friend of brandishing a gun in public.

Dylan follows Hardin's lead by making up stories to embroider his mythological status. He does more, however, than turn the outlaw into a recognizable trope, since he creates a new character that provides a metacommentary on Hardin's own self-fashioning. The song describes the outlaw as a noble character, "a friend to the poor," almost a Robin Hood type. Dylan's second verse can perhaps function as a light reference to the dispute involving Hardin's female friend: "With his lady by his side / He took a stand." The song's third verse quickly resolves the ballad by saying they could not prove a charge against him and that his exploits garnered him fame through the media: "All across the telegraph / His name it did resound." Dylan focuses on storytelling through mass media communication, here the telegraph, to reflect how Wild West mythology was created and circulated. He went on to compose more songs in this vein and he later played a movie cowboy in Sam Peckinpah's film, *Pat Garrett & Billy the Kid* (1973), composing the Grammy-nominated country-rock and folk-rock soundtrack album that featured "Knock' on Heaven's Door." In the film, Dylan portrays a character called Alias, who refuses to give his name and instead plays with notions of identity.

This work in both film and music reveals how country music has evolved into an intricate mixture of folk and mass culture. The iconic Western cowboy became popular, in part, through 1930s Hollywood films, with singing cowboys like Roy Rogers and Gene Autry, and the musical influences came from a combination of earlier nineteenth-century folk cultures. In his liner notes to *Johnny Cash Sings the Ballads of the True West*, which was received as part of the folk revival movement, the now iconic "Man in Black" describes trying to return to original folk sources rather than simply using the mass-marketed Hollywood film fantasies about the American West. Yet when he looks for "pure" folk sources, he can only find sources that reflect this mixture of folk culture and mass culture. He read folk

---

[22] Jann Wenner, "Interview with Jann S. Wenner," *Rolling Stone*, November 29, 1969.

culture sources in John Lomax, Carl Sandburg, and every issue of *True West* magazine, but he also consulted Tex Ritter, who was famous as a Hollywood singing cowboy in films, although he was also a folk music preservationist and stylist. Cash argues that if modern audiences listen to his updated versions of Old West ballads on their modern radios, they will still hear the "true west" coming through that mass media communication and that the songs were "meant to be heard" via sound recordings.[23] His description of using modern mass media to deliver what he felt was a "pure" structure of feeling of the "Old West" speaks to a central contradiction in country music. Despite its investment in rural origins and the idea of a "pure" folk culture, country music originated in the 1920s thanks to the decidedly urban, mass culture forces of recording technology and radio.[24]

Country music's ongoing debates about authenticity in folk culture and mass culture have long been fixated on what counts as genuine country music versus what is a manufactured fake or sellout. Drawing on the rhetoric of a pure, untainted country music, the genre's origin stories keep insisting on a rural, folk culture basis for the music as opposed to a commercialized, tainted, fallen mass culture.[25] That tension manifests itself in lyrics that express nostalgia for a supposedly simpler time and an earlier, often agricultural way of life set in opposition to a contaminating modernity rooted in industrialization and capitalism. Ironically, country songs are mass commodities, yet the lyrics are often about the wistful nostalgia for some non-commercial, simpler life on the farm. That contradictory dynamic, in which modern mass culture expresses nostalgia for previous folk culture that it has commodified or marginalized, is part of a larger trend evident in mass culture more generally.[26] Country music stages that nostalgic fantasy via mass media, the very form that helps

---

[23] Johnny Cash, "Reflections," *Johnny Cash Sings the Ballads of the True West*, Columbia/Sony Legacy ([1965] 2002).

[24] Bill C. Malone, *Singing Cowboys and Musical Mountaineers: Southern Culture and the Roots of Country Music*, 2nd edn (Athens: University of Georgia Press, 2003), p. 7.

[25] Ching, *Wrong's*. Richard Peterson, *Creating Country Music: Fabricating Authenticity* (Chicago: University of Chicago Press, 1997). Joli Jensen, *The Nashville Sound: Authenticity, Commercialization, and Country Music* (Nashville: Country Music Foundation/Vanderbilt University Press, 1998). Aaron Fox, *Real Country: Music and Language in Working-Class Culture* (Durham: Duke University Press, 2004). Diane Pecknold, *The Selling Sound: The Rise of the Country Music Industry* (Durham: Duke University Press, 2007). Kristine M. McCusker and Diane Pecknold, eds., *A Boy Named Sue: Gender and Country Music* (Jackson: University Press of Mississippi, 2004).

[26] George Lipsitz, *Time Passages: Collective Memory and American Popular Culture* (Minneapolis: University of Minnesota Press, 1990), pp. 3, 22.

perpetuate the conditions of modernity that the country genre expresses alienation from in its search for the folk and the pure. Of course, country music never had "pure" folk origins, because it has always had commercial elements, and the idea of a distinction between folk music and mass culture was itself an arbitrary one imposed by early twentieth-century academics and "folk" song collectors.[27]

When Dylan reimagines and further fictionalizes the story of a cowboy outlaw, one whose tale is transmitted through mass media – the telegraph in the past and Dylan's mass-marketed song recording in the present – he is engaging with this contradictory mix of folk and mass cultures. He also comments on and enacts the creation of authenticity myths. Just as the larger cultural history of country music affects Dylan's country output and its reception, Dylan's intervention reinforces the problems always lurking just behind country's rhetoric of authenticity.

Legacies

Dylan's engagement with country adds layers to his oeuvre while illuminating the genre's complex dynamics. His Nashville albums, furthermore, inspired other important work in country, folk, and rock. Ramblin' Jack Elliott and Pete Seeger came to record in Nashville, for example, and Dylan's influence is evident in Buffy Sainte-Marie's *I'm Gonna Be a Country Girl Again* (1968). Notably, Joan Baez's double album of Dylan songs, *Any Day Now* (1968), includes four songs from *John Wesley Harding* and features distinctly country sounds thanks to the steel guitar, fiddle, and dobro, all directed by session leader Grady Martin. The Byrds, who had covered Dylan's songs in earlier pioneering folk-rock recordings of "Mr. Tambourine Man" and "All I Really Want to Do," explored country-rock in *Sweetheart of the Rodeo* (1968), including Dylan covers like "You Ain't Goin' Nowhere."

One final example can help illustrate the way in which the Dylan–Cash collaborations activated new creative potential in the sound and rhetoric of country music. The documentary footage from the *Nashville Skyline* record-ing sessions in 1969 is in stark contrast to film footage from the D.A. Pennebaker documentary *Eat the Document*, which covers Dylan's 1966 UK tour. The film captures Cash visiting Dylan backstage; the visibly gaunt and, at that time, amphetamine-addled Cash sings his "I Still Miss Someone" with Dylan but labors to get through it, with Dylan playing

[27] Malone, *Singing*. Benjamin Filene, *Romancing the Folk: Public Memory & American Roots Music* (Chapel Hill: University of North Carolina Press, 2000).

piano. In bonus footage included at the film's end, Dylan rides in the car with John Lennon and brags about having Cash in his film. In this sequence, Dylan seems to be struggling to flip between two very different kinds of authenticity, from a pose of ironic jaded rocker, trying to impress Lennon, to a sincere collaborator when thinking of Cash and his far more sincere mode of performance and address. In the sequence, as Dylan brags to Lennon about having Cash in his film, as if holding Cash up as a symbol of roots authenticity, he and Lennon are both excited about Dylan having seen Cash. Then, he makes a joke and mimics Cash's abrupt, jerky movements caused by his drug-addicted state. Dylan then quickly reverses himself and tells Pennebaker to cut that moment from the film, because "I like him" and, implicitly, he doesn't want to be seen as making fun of a man he plainly admires. He then turns his comment about Cash's movement into an awkward remark about "all good people" moving that way. His remarks about liking Cash, which implies his obvious concern that Cash know he respects him, are the most sincere comments Dylan makes during that sequence; he had been joking around, performing the role of ironic hipster satirizing fame, the press, and the rock star trappings. The fact that he chose to leave the sequence in the footage after his editing of the film is also telling. The interlude actually humanizes Cash: rather than being a symbol, he is someone facing human challenges. Likewise, it humanizes Dylan, who is trying on different modes of address and is unsure of them as he shifts from the ironic to sincere. The awkward segment encapsulates the idea that as Dylan slides between different performances and modes of address, he questions the authenticity of them all. His encounters with Cash, like his encounters with country music, thus bring even more complexities to his work. He has also used his engagement with country music in his other work, from storytelling techniques to the musical influences and cultural history he references. Likewise, Dylan's work in country has influenced other artists, as when Dylan sparked more country-rock hybrids with his Cash collaborations, and his metacommentary on country authenticity questions any easy embrace of authenticity in the genre.

CHAPTER 9

Rock Music

Ira Wells

Bob Dylan's relationship to rock 'n' roll was once the most hotly disputed subject in twentieth-century popular music. By January 20, 1988, however, those disputes must have seemed like a distant memory to the celebrities jamming on the stage of New York's Waldorf-Astoria hotel. It was the third annual induction ceremony of the Rock & Roll Hall of Fame, and Bob Dylan had just taken his place in the pantheon. "Bob freed your mind the way Elvis freed your body," Bruce Springsteen declared in a speech that framed Dylan as a musical trailblazer: "He invented a new way a pop singer could sound, broke through the limitations of what a recording artist could achieve."[1] In his own speech, Dylan thanked both the ethnomusicologist Alan Lomax *and* Little Richard: folk and rock 'n' roll were once conceived as mortal enemies, but things had changed. Despite the blandly celebratory mood, few could deny that this was, paradoxically enough, a low point in Dylan's career. As Springsteen implied – "If there was a young guy out there writing 'Sweetheart Like You,' writing 'Every Grain of Sand,' they'd be calling him the next Bob Dylan" – the assembled rock royalty were not there to celebrate *this* Bob Dylan, the Dylan of *Infidels* and *Empire Burlesque.*[2] This Dylan – the 46-year-old man in the long black coat – was almost incidental to the proceedings. As Mick Jagger, George Harrison, Neil Young, Jeff Beck, Tina Turner, Elton John, and others belted out a billowy "Like a Rolling Stone," the event could not help but recall that earlier, more contentious era, when Dylan's first forays into rock had been greeted (by some) as a form of apostasy.[3]

The story of Dylan "plugging in" at the 1965 Newport Folk Festival has seared its way into the American cultural imagination: it's the Bob Dylan

---

[1] Bruce Springsteen, "The Rock and Roll Hall of Fame Speech," in *Studio A: The Bob Dylan Reader,* ed. Benjamin Hedin (New York: W.W. Norton, 2004), p. 203.

[2] Ibid, p. 203.

[3] "Bob Dylan – Rock 'N' Roll Hall of Fame 1988 (Speech + HQ Performance)," YouTube video, 16:38, November 2, 2018, www.youtube.com/watch?v=LGProNXknsk.

story known by those who don't know anything about Bob Dylan. Clinton Heylin describes it as "the most written about performance in the history of rock."[4] Elijah Wald argues that the performance "split" the 1960s, while Mike Marqusee calls it the "fulcrum" of the decade, when "the early unity and idealism of the civil rights movement gave way to division and pessimism" and "the media was discovering that rebellion could sell."[5] While fans and critics still debate the meaning of Newport, most agree on the basic facts: Dylan appeared on the Sunday evening stage at about 9:15 pm with a Fender Stratocaster electric guitar. He had cast off what Dave Van Ronk called his "romantic hobo" look, wearing a black leather jacket and motorcycle boots.[6] He was joined by Al Kooper, Barry Goldberg, and members of the Paul Butterfield Blues Band. They played three songs: "Maggie's Farm," "Like a Rolling Stone," and an early version of "It Takes a Lot to Laugh, It Takes a Train to Cry." Peter Yarrow beckoned Dylan back on stage, and he played two more numbers using an acoustic guitar borrowed from Johnny Cash: "It's All Over Now, Baby Blue" and "Mr. Tambourine Man."

What remains the subject of debate is the extent to which Dylan's electric numbers offended, horrified, or satisfied the audience. According to the story handed down from the folk establishment, Dylan's electric performance was nothing less than an act of aesthetic vandalism. In *The Mansion on the Hill*, Fred Goodman describes the audience as being "struck dumb" and "pummeled" by the opening chords of "Maggie's Farm." "People were just horrified," according to Peter Yarrow. "It was as if it was a capitulation to the enemy – as if all of a sudden you saw Martin Luther King Jr. doing a cigarette ad."[7] "I ran to hide my eyes and ears," Pete Seeger wrote days after the performance, "because I could not bear either the screaming of the crowd or some of the most destructive music this side of Hell."[8] Decades later, Seeger remembered telling people backstage that he would have cut the cables if he'd had an axe; in some more fanciful memories, an axe-wielding Peter Seeger was literally trying to hack the cables.[9] Some people remember that Dylan was "booed off the stage" – at times, Dylan himself even seems to remember it that

---

[4] Clinton Heylin, *Bob Dylan: Behind the Shades: The Biography – Take Two* (New York: Viking, 2000), p. 206.
[5] Mike Marqusee, *Chimes of Freedom: The Politics of Bob Dylan's Art* (New York: New Press, 2003), p. 141.
[6] Dave Van Ronk and Elijah Wald, *The Mayor of MacDougal Street* (New York: Da Capo Press, 2005), p. 162.
[7] Fred Goodman, "Excerpt from *The Mansion on the Hill*," in *Studio A*, ed. Hedin, p. 43.
[8] Seeger quoted in Elijah Wald, *Dylan Goes Electric* (New York: Dey St., 2015), p. 282.
[9] Ibid, p. 281.

way.[10] According to Paul Nelson's famous review in *Sing Out!*, the folk publication, that evening's performance "split apart forever the two biggest names in folk," and forced the audience to choose between Seeger's sugary middlebrow Norman Rockwell vision of America and the more avant-garde, Beat-inspired vision offered by Dylan. The folk audience had to choose, Nelson argued – and it chose Seeger. But if Dylan's folk audience rejected what Nelson called a "difficult stab of art," they did so partly because they suspected that commerce, rather than art, motivated the thrust.[11]

The folk establishment's allergic reaction to this new incarnation of Dylan had less to do with the electrified music than a sense that the movement itself was at stake. From the beginning, the folk revival ethos, with its roots in the Popular Front left, was animated by a powerful vision of equality and fraternity: as Goodman records, every performer at the festival "played for scale: fifty dollars a day. Bob Dylan did it for the same money as prisoners from a Texas chain gang."[12] Far from the utopian, folk-sanctioned vision of communal fraternity, Dylan's new rock songs proclaimed a radical sense of individualism, alienation, and withdrawal – a literal and metaphorical rejection of the symbolic pieties of an earlier time: "your diamond ring, you'd better pawn it babe." Worse, from the perspective of folk's old guard, was that the heretical message appeared to be blatantly commercial: going electric was an aesthetic decision that allowed Dylan to plug into a larger audience.[13]

The familiar story of Dylan's treasonous performance at Newport, shimmering with allegorical richness, has long struck critics as incredulous. As David Hajdu and others have observed, *Bringing It All Back Home*, Dylan's first (partial) foray into rock, had been out since March, while "Like a Rolling Stone" was on heavy radio rotation and would hit number 2 on the *Billboard* charts within weeks.[14] Dylan was not the only, or even the first, electric act to play at Newport that weekend – Lightnin' Hopkins, the Chambers Brothers, and the Paul Butterfield Blues Band (two of whom stuck around to back Dylan) had already played well-received electric sets.[15] Even the most obvious questions – such as whether Dylan was

---

[10] Both Seeger and Dylan reflect on the episode in *No Direction Home*, dir. Martin Scorsese (Paramount Pictures, 2005).

[11] Paul Nelson's "Newport Folk Festival, 1965," originally in *Sing Out!*, reproduced in *The Pop, Rock, and Soul Reader: Histories and Debates*, 3rd edn, ed. David Brackett (New York: Oxford University Press, 2014), p. 158.

[12] Goodman, "Excerpt," p. 41.

[13] On the commercialization of rock, see, for instance, Marqusee, *Chimes of Freedom*, p. 146.

[14] David Hajdu, *Positively 4th Street* (New York: Farrar, Straus and Giroux, 2001), p. 259.

[15] Wald, *Dylan Goes Electric*, p. 6.

booed off the stage – are difficult to answer with certainty. Some suggest that people were booing because of poor sound quality, or because Dylan wasn't proficient at the electric guitar.[16] "Documentary" evidence is of limited use in setting the record straight: as Elijah Wald points out in *Dylan Goes Electric*, most film clips of the performance splice "the anguished shouts after Dylan left the stage into other parts of the performance to create the illusion that the mythic confrontation was captured on tape."[17] Regardless of the extent or reason for the booing, the suggestion that these songs would have incited such spontaneous public outrage seems far-fetched. "My own view, and I was sitting there," says John Cooke, "was that most people in the audience had heard 'Like a Rolling Stone,' and they probably bought tickets purposely to see Bob Dylan and hear it, not in some weird hope that Dylan would go back in time to do the stuff he hadn't done on his last two albums."[18]

If the broad contours of the Dylan "sellout at Newport" myth were defined by the folk establishment, revisionist accounts have emphasized the naivety required to presume that Dylan had ever been an authentic folkie. In *The Mayor of MacDougal Street*, Dave Van Ronk describes how the adoption and adaptation of personas was de rigueur in a 1960s Greenwich Village folk scene in which "personal reinvention was the order of the day."[19] Dylan's carefully cultivated Dust Bowl ragamuffin image – and the Chaplinesque stage humor that frequently attended it – were crucial to his early act, but impediments to the more expansive, sophisticated version of himself he was developing. "Myself, I thought that going electric was a logical direction for Bobby to take," Van Ronk recalls. "I did not care for all of his new stuff, by any means, but some of it was excellent, and it was a reasonable extension of what he had done up to that point. And I knew perfectly well that none of us was a true 'folk' artist."[20] While some fans are still eager to conserve Dylan as the paragon of folk, first-hand accounts of his time in the Village highlight his contingent, even opportunistic, relationship with the movement. In high school, as his biographers reveal, Dylan was a Little Richard and Chuck Berry-inspired rocker who performed "Rock and Roll is Here to Stay" in the school gym; the performance was supposedly so loud that the principal cut the PA system.[21]

---

[16] Hajdu, *Positively 4th Street*, p. 260.   [17] Wald, *Dylan Goes Electric*, p. 2.
[18] Hajdu, *Positively 4th Street*, pp. 259–260.
[19] Van Ronk and Wald, *The Mayor of MacDougal Street*, p. 163.
[20] Ibid, p. 215. Also quoted by Louis Menand in "Bob on Bob," *New Yorker*, August 28, 2006, www .newyorker.com/magazine/2006/09/04/bob-on-bob.
[21] Dennis McDougal, *Bob Dylan: The Biography* (New York: Wiley, 2014), p. 20.

"When you hear a good rhythm and blues song," Dylan says in a 1958 taped conversation, "chills go up your spine ... you want to *cry* when you hear some of those songs."[22] Given his early musical touchstones (Jimmy Reed and Clyde McPhatter among them) and his later career arc, Dylan's brief dalliance with folk has struck some critics as a mere accident of history. Benjamin Hedin speculates that had Dylan arrived in New York a few years later, during the British invasion, he would have skipped his "folkie debut" and plugged in from the start.[23]

Dylan's embrace of folk songs may have been tactical, temporary, and careerist, and he would of course famously disavow any assertation that he was the "voice of a generation," but the music itself was received by many in a spirit approaching total sincerity and earnestness. It may be true, as Van Ronk suggests, that Dylan never thought of himself as a true folk artist, but the anti-racist and anti-war sentiments behind "The Lonesome Death of Hattie Carrol" and "Masters of War" rang true with his audience, and it's hard to imagine why anyone listening to Dylan in 1964 would have heard these songs as anything other than sincere expressions of social consciousness. Was "Blowin' in the Wind" just a formal exercise in songcraft? Was Dylan's performance of "When the Ship Comes In" in front of 200,000 people at the March on Washington in 1963 simply a good PR move – a way to build his profile until something better came along? Festival organizers at Newport, some of whom had been persecuted under McCarthyism, certainly didn't think so – nor did they conceive of folk listeners as a market subject to manipulation. They understood their audience "not merely as an aggregate of consumers, but as a participatory community," Marqusee writes, and "they believed, not without reason, that this was a community whose bonds – based on shared values – would dissolve if it was invaded by market forces."[24] Dylan's participation in this community cannot be dismissed as merely incidental, a historical accident that he might have "skipped" on his journey to rock, because it is precisely the rejection (some saw it as betrayal) of this community and its ideals that provided his form of rock with its anarchic edge. The sense of reckless abandon coursing through these frayed, chaotic performances was made credible by the fact that Dylan really was abandoning something. Whether he was crying when he returned for his acoustic encore is yet another subject of

---

[22] Wald, *Dylan Goes Electric*, p. 38.
[23] Benjamin Hedin, "Introduction," in *Studio A*, ed. Hedin, p. xii.
[24] Marqusee, *Chimes of Freedom*, p. 145.

debate, but the songs must have felt, to some, like a goodbye kiss: "Strike another match, go start anew / And it's all over now, baby blue."

"I'm Not Part of No Movement"

In grappling with Dylan's impact on the rock genre, critics often begin with the words, and for good reason. *Billboard* magazine's top single of 1965 – the year in which "Like a Rolling Stone" peaked at number 2 on the charts – was Sam the Sham and the Pharoahs' "Wooly Bully" – a song that makes a fetish of lyrical juvenescence.[25] "Matty told Hatty about a thing she saw / had two big horns and a wooly jaw. Wooly bully, wooly bully / Wooly bully, wooly bully, wooly bully," and so on. There is of course a vast aesthetic gulf separating the rhyming couplets and nonsense lyrics of "Wooly Bully" from the "skippin' reels of rhyme" that lead us down the "ancient empty streets too dead for dreaming" in "Mr. Tambourine Man." Whether the lyrics of "Gates of Eden" are more "poetic" than those of "Blowin' in the Wind" depends, of course, upon the critical priorities of the listener. But starting in the mid-1960s, artists, fans, and critics tended to agree that the often surreal, allusive, dense, phantasmagoric turn in Dylan's song writing – a lyrical experimentation that coincided with his embrace of electric instruments – represented a more "poetic" form of writing.[26] For some critics, the *sine qua non* of Dylan's contribution to rock resides in his lyrical innovation; indeed, in 2016, when the Swedish Academy awarded Dylan the Nobel Prize in literature, it was precisely "for having created new poetic expressions within the great American song tradition."[27] Of course, Dylan's poetic expressions did not just exist "within" the American song tradition: they also changed that tradition, helping to inaugurate an artistically credible "rock" music as distinct from "rock 'n' roll."

The lyrical innovations of Dylan's early rock period are clearly prodigious. In the hands of a critic trained in methods of close reading and steeped in the poetic tradition, Dylan's fever-dream lyrics can be made to bear an almost infinite variety of interpretive fruit. Take a relatively straightforward line

---

[25] "Top Singles," *Billboard 1966 International Record & Talent Showcase*, p. 22, www.americanradiohistory.com/Archive-Billboard/60s/1965/Billboard-1965-International-Record-&-Talent.pdf.

[26] For a contemporary articulation of this argument, see Mikal Gilmore's assertion: "What set Bob Dylan apart from everybody was something more outlandish: It was how he wielded language." "Why Bob Dylan is a Literary Genius," *Rolling Stone*, December 9, 2016, www.rollingstone.com/music/music-features/why-bob-dylan-is-a-literary-genius-105108/.

[27] "The Nobel Prize in Literature 2016," Nobel Prize, www.nobelprize.org/prizes/literature/2016/summary/.

from "It's All Over Now, Baby Blue": "The highway is for gamblers, better use your sense / Take what you have gathered from coincidence." Christopher Ricks uses the juxtaposition between "gambler" and "better" ("a gambler *is* a better") to make the point that every rhyme is a kind of bet, and whether you hear the "cents" in Dylan's "sense" or see the "coin" in "coincidence," Ricks believes that Dylan's rhyme highlights something essential about the nature of rhyme itself, which converts linguistic coincidence into a new sense.[28] Some critics contend, not without reason, that Dylan's lyrics shouldn't be considered in isolation from his music. But the formal approach exemplified by Ricks (and whatever its limitations, it is infinitely preferable to the longstanding impulse in Dylan fandom to attempt to pinpoint the "real" subjects of these songs or what various arcane images are supposed to represent – just *who was* the one-eyed midget shouting the word "now"?), the turn toward a more Romantic, Beat-inspired mode of lyrical composition enabled a generation of critics who would create a shared understanding of Dylan as rock's "poet laureate."

Dylan's lyrical metamorphosis in his first great trilogy of albums (*Bringing It All Back Home, Highway 61 Revisited*, and *Blonde on Blonde*) performed other kinds of valuable work for the emergent rock culture – one of which was to import high cultural touchstones into the popular lyric. While song writers associated with Tin Pan Alley had long incorporated promiscuous cultural references into their songs (Cole Porter, after all, rhymed "symphony by Strauss" with "Mickey Mouse" and "Mahatma Gandi" with "Napoleon brandy" in "You're the Top"), Dylan's invocation of T.S. Eliot, William Blake, Bertolt Brecht, and Jack Kerouac provided the blossoming genre of the "rock lyric" with a new intellectual credibility. These trappings of cultural distinction were especially useful in the mid-1960s, when "rock 'n' roll" was still strongly associated with the twisting, shimmying, locomoting teenybopper bands who dominated the charts. Yet perhaps the most culturally significant feature of Dylan's lyrical development in these years isn't the sophistication of the lyrics – critics often point out that even Dylan's best compositions contain filler lines[29] – but the way in which the lyrics gesture toward a Romantic ideal of the individual self as the authentic wellspring of creativity.

Dylan had been on record repudiating the "finger-pointing songs" since October 1964, when Nat Hentoff reported on the recording of *Another Side of*

---

[28] Christopher Ricks, *Dylan's Vision of Sin* (New York: Ecco Press, 2005), pp. 34–35.
[29] Alex Ross, for instance, contends that "Dylan's strongest verbal images occur toward the beginning of a song, and it falls to his musical sense to make something of the rest." "The Wanderer," *The New Yorker*, May 10, 1999.

Bob Dylan in Columbia's Studio A for the *New Yorker*. "Me, I don't want to write *for* people anymore. You know – be a spokesman," Dylan said. "From now on, I want to write from inside me," he continued, to write "the way I walk or talk … I'm not part of no Movement."[30] It would take Dylan another six months to develop his own rock sound, but he had already discovered an essential part of the ethos. Looking back, we can recognize how Dylan's "finger-pointing" songs allowed him to pivot from a preservationist idea of folk to an activist topical song movement that was, in turn, more aligned with rock. But the notion that rock is incompatible with organized structures and movements, that it emerges organically from a radical, unfettered individualism, would become an important strand of the genre's DNA over the next decade. It wasn't that the lyrics of "Queen Jane Approximately" or "Ballad of a Thin Man" were "about" Dylan in any literal sense, but that their very artifice and intertextuality could illuminate something about the soul of the artist. Later critics (Stephen Scobie and Lee Marshall among them) would apply some discerning critical pressure to the assumption that Dylan's "poetic" lyrics of 1965–1966 were more "authentic" than those of previous albums. Rather, proceeding from the influence of the Beats (and more distant influences that ran back through Whitman and Emerson in America and the English Romantics), Dylan's rock lyrics privileged personal and interior conceptions of authenticity over the social and communal understanding of authenticity that had united the folk singers. Of course, many of Dylan's early R&B influences, including Chuck Berry, had been singer-songwriters; moreover, as critic Carl Wilson points out, Dylan had probably learned from The Beatles "how commercially and reputationally advantageous it was to be viewed and paid as writers as well as performers."[31] But Dylan's public persona (developed in his playful confrontations with journalists and in his evolving personal style) gave the public an icon of the individual poet-genius, while his lyrics provided rock critics and their readers with an occasion to hone their own cultural distinction, cementing the notion that rock lyrics could be a vehicle for the sophisticated, radical, and highly personal exploration of the individual self within a mass cultural form.

In the American cultural imagination, Dylan is often conscripted to play a symbolic role within the accepted teleology of rock. In its mythic renderings, "rock" is the soundtrack of the counterculture, anathema to the stifling conformity of the buttoned-up 1950s, reflexively opposed to political corruption at home and warmongering abroad, devoted to the

[30] Nat Hentoff, "The Crackin', Shakin', Breakin' Sounds," in *Studio A*, ed. Hedin, p. 37.
[31] Carl Wilson, author interview, May 9, 2019.

romantic exploration of psychic recesses of the individual mind. But as Keir Keightley argues in "Reconsidering Rock," "What is truly at stake in rock culture is the differentiation of taste, not an affiliation with forms of cultural action."[32] Rock allowed listeners to oppose mass culture from within a mainstream form that manifested primarily as a pattern of consumption: what rock (as opposed to rock 'n' roll) resisted, in the end, was music that wasn't rock. "Once rock broke the symbolic link between mass culture and mindless conformity," Keightley writes, "it became possible to build new distinctions within and upon the terrain of the popular, to express oppositional sensibilities via commercial, mass mediated culture."[33] Dylan's rock became the primary criterion that would ground every subsequent cultural distinction within the field. As the "uber rock-star," in Lee Marshall's words, Dylan

> unites the contradictory elements of self, community, and commerce: an individual who rejects politics in favor of inner-consciousness yet still manages to be political; an artist who follows his own unique vision regardless of the consequences yet found new audiences and commercial success; a self-conscious artist speaking for no one except for his own self yet upheld as the leader of a youth movement.[34]

With the passage of years and albums, Dylan seemed increasingly central to rock culture even as rock music grew increasingly peripheral to Dylan. His initial rock phase – consisting of that first trilogy – was over only fourteen months after it had begun. His most exhilarating rock performances took place in a 1966 world tour that re-staged the drama of "plugging in" each night: after serenading audiences with a poignant acoustic set (including "She Belongs to Me" and "Visions of Johanna"), Dylan returned with the Band to excoriate them with "I Don't Believe You (She Acts Like We Never Have Met)" and "Like a Rolling Stone." It was the loudest, most confrontational phase of Dylan's career – and then it was over. After a period of bucolic self-recreation, he returned with the countrified sounds of *John Wesley Harding* (1967) and *Nashville Skyline* (1969), sang melodic duets with Johnny Cash, and explored a universe of American musical influence with the Band in what would become the Basement Tapes.[35] In the mid-1970s, after eight years away from live

[32] Keir Keightley, "Reconsidering Rock," in *The Cambridge Companion to Pop and Rock,* ed. Simon Frith, Will Straw, and John Street (Cambridge: Cambridge University Press, 2001), p. 129.
[33] Ibid, p. 141.
[34] Lee Marshall, *Bob Dylan: The Never Ending Star* (Cambridge: Polity, 2007), p. 114.
[35] See Greil Marcus, *Invisible Republic: Bob Dylan's Basement Tapes* (New York: Henry Holt, 1997).

performance, Dylan would introduce rock renditions of songs like "Tonight I'll Be Staying Here With You" in shows designed for stadiums and arenas. The 1970s albums that followed might all be considered rock in some loose sense – *Blood on the Tracks* routinely appears on lists of the best rock albums of the decade – but the "rock" elements on Dylan's 1970s albums feel increasingly marginal to their success as albums.

If Dylan's strung-out performances in 1966 had a serrated edge, his early 1980s rock sounded like something that had been manufactured and bubble-wrapped. Listeners often associate the period with the soulful gospel captured in *Trouble No More – The Bootleg Series Vol. 13*. But Dylan's studio work of the era – the chunky guitar riffs and cowbell on "Gonna Change My Way of Thinking," the bluesy chord progressions on "Shot of Love," the solid rock of "Solid Rock" – included the most conventional rock of Dylan's career. The Christian content of these songs may have been another radical swerve against audience expectation, but the glossy production on these records stands out in Dylan's *oeuvre* for the degree to which it conforms to the musical aesthetic of the moment. In *Chronicles: Volume One*, his memoir, Dylan writes frankly about the sense of artistic ennui he experienced while playing packed stadiums with Tom Petty in 1986. "My own songs had become strangers to me," he writes, "I didn't have the skill to touch their raw nerves, penetrate their surfaces."[36] Perhaps unexpectedly, it would take the producer Daniel Lanois, most famous at the time for his work with Irish rockers U2, to break Dylan's rock habit and send him off in new musical directions in *Oh Mercy* and *Time Out of Mind*.

Dylan's fans will have their personal favorite rock performances of recent decades: his punk-like execution of "Jokerman" with The Plugz on Letterman in 1984; an MTV "unplugged" session in 1995; a gritty rendition of "Love Sick" at the 1998 Grammys (interrupted by an interpretive dancer with "soy bomb" written on his chest, who Dylan may have hired). For decades, Dylan's music has been given the hard rock treatment – most famously by Jimi Hendrix's canonical interpretation of "All Along the Watchtower," but also by the Ramones ("My Back Pages"), Rage Against the Machine ("Maggie's Farm"), and the White Stripes ("One More Cup of Coffee"). Yet the general musical tendency in Dylan's music since his late 1990s "comeback" has been toward diversity, tradition, and eclecticism. In the 1960s, Dylan famously ridiculed the idea of generic fidelity: "[W]hat does it mean, rock 'n' roll? Does it mean

---

[36] Bob Dylan, *Chronicles: Volume One* (New York: Simon & Schuster, 2004), p. 148.

Beatles, does it mean John Lee Hooker, Bobby Vinton, Jerry Lewis's kid?" Dylan asked in a 1966 *Playboy* interview.[37] "What about Lawrence Welk? He must play a few rock 'n' roll songs."[38] Despite his mockery of the generic terms themselves ("folk music is a bunch of fat people," he said in the same interview), Dylan's artistic decisions in 1965–1966 told the opposite tale: plugging in was a symbolic act of material consequence. Over the past twenty-five years, as Dylan's music has forked into the blues, Irish outlaw ballads, Tejano music, country and western, and pop standards, his sound achieved the generic promiscuity he hinted at in 1966: a "traditional music" that "comes about from legends, Bibles, plagues, and revolves around vegetables and death."[39] If there is an advantage to using *rock* as a generic label for Dylan, it is that rock itself is now capacious and "generic" enough to allow us to forget about such labels.

In his 1988 Rock & Roll Hall of Fame induction speech, Bruce Springsteen had defended Dylan as a pioneer. "Without Bob," he said, "the Beatles wouldn't have done *Sgt. Pepper*, the Beach Boys wouldn't have made *Pet Sounds*, the Sex Pistols wouldn't have made 'God Save the Queen,' U2 wouldn't have done 'Pride in the Name of Love,' Marvin Gaye wouldn't have done 'What's Going On?'" – and Springsteen goes on.[40] In explaining Dylan's importance to rock history, critics frequently employ a similar formula: without Dylan, famous band *x* would never have made classic album *y*. The problem with such pronouncements is not only their counterfactual logic – we'll never know the world in which Bob Dylan did not exist, and presumably the cultural influences operating on him were also operating on everyone else – but also that they locate the essence of his achievements outside of his own songs. While reinforcing the "I'm not there" reading of Dylan's artistic identity, such an approach risks missing what *is* there. Critics sometimes reflect on that iconic 1965 performance at Newport and bemoan that our own musical culture, while fleetingly captivated by the latest PR-driven feuds and outrages, is incapable of caring about anything as deeply as one community of listeners once cared about Dylan plugging in. But what we have lost in intensity is perhaps made up for in perspicacity, in our ability to hear in Dylan's live performances the interpenetration of style and influence and genre that now exists, thrillingly, in the moment of our own musical present.

[37] Bob Dylan, "*Playboy* Interview with Bob Dylan," interview by Nat Hentoff, *Playboy*, www .interferenza.net/bcs/interw/66-jan.htm.
[38] Ibid.   [39] Ibid.   [40] Bruce Springsteen, "The Rock and Roll Hall of Fame Speech," p. 203.

CHAPTER 10

Roots Music: Born in a Basement

Kim Ruehl

In 1975, piggybacking on the game-changing sound of Bob Dylan's four-teenth studio album, *Blood on the Tracks*, Columbia Records released a collection of his home recordings. Though the songs had already been circulating for the better part of a decade as bootlegs, the release splashed deep enough in the waters of mainstream music to continue rippling to this day.

Recorded in 1967, in the basement of a pink house in upstate New York, *The Basement Tapes* captured a creative meeting of minds between Dylan and a group of players who were, at that point, just his touring band. Dylan had some sense before these sessions that the group, which called itself Levon and the Hawks after parting ways with original frontman Ronnie Hawkins, had something more to give. Yet, he hadn't encountered the amalgam of the players' talents until the lot of them congregated in the basement of Big Pink.

But first, they started rehearsals in a red room in Dylan's Woodstock home. Though their movement from red room to pink house is notable mostly just in its symbolism, the progression from something basic and bold to something new, beautiful, and intrinsically collaborative should not be glossed over. As it would turn out, the style of music that emerged from those sessions – now called roots or Americana music – would become celebrated for the way it brings so many different pieces of American music together, the extent to which it often feels undefinable.

In his introduction to *The Old, Weird America*, his ethnographic study on *The Basement Tapes*, Greil Marcus explains, "The music was funny and comforting; at the same time, it was strange, and somehow incomplete. Out of some odd displacement of art and time, the music seemed both transparent and inexplicable."[1]

---

[1] Greil Marcus, *The Old, Weird America* (New York: Picador, 2011), p. xxi.

Indeed, the sessions were not intended to be released commercially but were rather meant to be demos of new songs that Dylan's publisher might be able to sell to other artists. Through them, however, we can hear Dylan's delight in discovering the velvet-smoothness of Richard Manuel's vocals, the shape-shifting qualities of Robbie Robertson's guitar, and the deep pocket of Rick Danko's bass and Levon Helm's drumkit. We hear the way these musicians awakened something in each other which had been stirring for years. We hear the glee of a group of people creating a vortex of styles that would prove to be a pivotal moment in the history of American music. "Bob Dylan," Marcus observes, "seemed less to occupy a turning point in cultural space and time than to be that turning point."[2]

At the point in Dylan's career when he entered that basement, he had only been recording professionally for five years. Though he had produced an impressive amount of material in that time – seven albums – and amassed the kind of celebrity that affected his personal life, he was growing frustrated with an evolving recording process. His studio experiences were becoming more complicated, more divorced from his artistic personality. The heads of studios were moving away from the one-take standard that existed when he made his first couple of albums, toward a more layered, sophisticated, and technological approach. Fed up with the folk establishment, such as it was, and not feeling exactly at home in what was happening with rock 'n' roll either, Dylan had taken to recording in Nashville to get a more homey atmosphere in the studio while still working with some of the finest players he could find.

Among them Mike Bloomfield, whose roaring electric guitar helped Dylan inadvertently alienate fans at the 1965 Newport Folk Festival. He had Al Kooper on Hammond organ, Charlie McCoy on harmonica, and an assortment of country session players. As a result, with this blending of styles, *Blonde on Blonde* became widely touted as the album that changed Nashville. It provided an opening there for some of the outlaw players who were rolling into town around that time and didn't fit neatly into the Nudie suits of country establishment: Kris Kristofferson, Willie Nelson, Jessi Colter, and others who would come to blur the line between country, folk, and rock – human ripples behind Dylan's creative wave.

Dylan's own musical roots were grounded in these elements – folk, rock, and the blues – and he explored them anew over the course of the albums he recorded in Nashville: *Blonde on Blonde*, *John Wesley Harding*, and *Nashville Skyline*. Each was full of acoustic guitars, slide guitars, pedal

² Ibid, p. xvi.

steels, that driving 4/4 snare-and-hi-hat rhythm punctuated infrequently by tom and cymbals. This handful of albums recorded before, during, and after the basement demos introduced and endeared him to the country music process and granted him the opportunity to toy with his vocals, explore their more languid reaches, channel his inner Roy Orbison.

Still, he was searching for a sound, trying to make his music better approximate what he heard in his head. When he released *Blonde on Blonde* in 1966, he seemed pleased with what he referred to as "that thin, wild mercury sound." But there was something unfinished about its artistic statement that he went on looking for, enlisting the help of Robertson and Helm, and eventually the rest of their band.

When Dylan capped their tumultuous tour with a traumatic motorcycle accident around a month after *Blonde on Blonde* was released, he understandably shifted his focus inward and started looking for more satisfying ways to be an artist while he recovered. The Hawks had meanwhile moved near Dylan's home in Woodstock and had set up a makeshift studio in the basement of the house where many of them lived.

"The goal," Robertson wrote in his 2016 memoir, *Testimony*, "was to use whatever gear we could from our live show to create a setup that would let us discover our own musical path. . . . When I asked a recording engineer to take a look at the basement, he said the concrete walls, glass basement windows, and big metal furnace could make for the worst sound anybody ever used for recording music. To me, that was good news. This was all about breaking the rules, and the more unacceptable the setting, the more it felt right."[3]

Thus, while the sessions were meant to produce demos, it was clear to all those involved that they were hoping to land on a new kind of songwriting that would defy the trends of the day. They succeeded, as Dylan-penned originals like "I Shall Be Released," "Quinn the Eskimo," "You Ain't Goin' Nowhere," "This Wheel's on Fire" (co-written with Danko), and "Tears of Rage" (co-written with Manuel) were picked up by other artists and became some of the most formative songs in the advent of popular roots music. But it was those songs' proximity to tunes by traditionalists (Johnny Cash, Hank Williams, and others) on the tapes that made clear these musicians knew well the roots from which they were growing. Still, Robertson recalled, "This wasn't the folk traditionalist Dylan; this was the emergence of a new species."[4]

[3] Robbie Robertson, *Testimony* (New York: Three Rivers, 2017), p. 268.
[4] Ibid, p. 165. Though Robertson was referring here to the day Dylan first hired him, he frames the encounter as a bit of foreshadowing as to what the Band would wind up doing with Dylan in the years to come.

Screaming at the Sky

It's easy to pinpoint *The Basement Tapes* as the advent of roots music in the mainstream because it brought an American artist with an allegiance to the deep roots of his nation's folk music together with a mostly Canadian band that had cut its teeth on rockabilly and the blues. The particular brand of music they cobbled together, with its balance of darkness, narration, emotion, and humor, had never been heard before that point, not in that way. It was certainly miles away from the psychedelia that was dominating mainstream rock 'n' roll, and lightyears from the disco that was on the horizon by the time it was released.

In the basement was where Levon and the Hawks became the Band. It would be on the heels of those sessions that the group would finally record its first album, *Music from Big Pink*, cementing classics like "The Weight" in the American roots canon. It provided the Band a springboard toward a sound they, too, had been chasing ever since they parted ways with Ronnie Hawkins.

In his memoir, Robertson writes about his final days playing behind Hawkins: "I was trying to do something with my playing that was like screaming at the sky. Levon understood on a deep level what I was going for, and in those moments when I doubted my progress, he showed the generosity and willingness to hold up a mirror and wink approvingly."[5] Meanwhile, if anyone was truly screaming at the sky in the mid-to-late-1960s, it was Bob Dylan – his collaboration with the Hawks was bound to result in something notable taking flight.

And this all came roaring forth in the basement of Big Pink in a way that was missing from many of Dylan's previous studio albums. As the lyrics of 1965's "It's All Over Now, Baby Blue" suggest, Dylan had never been the straight folksinger that the folkies thought they saw. They were drunk on the second coming of Woody Guthrie, but Dylan wasn't the man they sought; he was a student extolling the virtues of his teacher before he struck out on his own, found his own way. And his way led to the creation and full realization of what would come to be known as American roots music.

But, for prophetic hints about the coming of this sound, one need to look no further than Dylan's 1962 self-titled debut, wherein he recorded songs by Blind Lemon Jefferson, traditionals he'd heard from Dave Van Ronk and Eric Von Schmidt, and his own originals, including "Talkin' New York." The album was like a deconstructed take on roots music: all the ingredients laid out on the counter.

---

[5] Robertson, *Testimony*, pp. 75–76.

It was "Talkin' New York" which especially hinted at the artist Dylan would become – the writer who could start with tradition and haul it forward, kicking and screaming, into the future. That very motion would become the cornerstone of modern roots music, the vortex of tradition and progress, the place where folk music ducked into a phone booth and came out wearing the clothes of commercial viability. The folkies of the day fixated on "Song to Woody" because it sung of an unsung hero. But if there had been any such thing as "rootsies," they would have seized upon "Talkin' New York," and championed it for its forward motion using backward-reaching themes.

Laying a Foundation

Across the next several years, Dylan's work awakened other artists to the possibilities inherent in mixing musicological styles, so that when Dylan nailed the sound and aesthetic, they were ready to take up guitars and follow him down that dusty road. Indeed, the sprouts of roots music that showed up in his early 1960s albums helped to create context for the sharp departure he would soon enough take from the prevailing folk boom. Between 1965 and 1967, Dylan released four albums that became the foundation for what would swell soon enough as the emergence of roots music: *Bringing It All Back Home, Highway 61 Revisited, Blonde on Blonde*, and *John Wesley Harding*. Though he wouldn't begin to cement all these styles into a logical, persistent genre for another decade, these four albums are routinely cited among roots musicians as the foundation of their craft.

Another Side of Bob Dylan (1964) ends with "It Ain't Me Babe," a kind of Dear John letter to the image the folk crowd and mainstream media had attached to Dylan ("I'm not the one you want babe / I'll only let you down"). It's a clear poetic apology, issued before he walked away, his rhythm guitar creaking the hinges as a proverbial door closed behind him. "Subterranean Homesick Blues," which opens *Bringing It All Back Home* (March 1965), enters with a couple of strums from Dylan's acoustic before an electric guitar asserts itself and the drums come in. Dylan's vocals have a more insinuated melody, more emphasis on rhythm, though there's plenty to dissect from the lyrics. But it was the third track, "Maggie's Farm," that Dylan chose to open his set at Newport Folk Festival that year. It's a rock song in a blues format, with lyrics that decry power differentials, driven by a narrative context that depicts a rural setting using urban electrification – all recognizable now as the kinds of roots music juxtapositions we routinely hear from artists like Lucinda Williams and Steve Earle.

There are so many layers of artistry in "Maggie's Farm," but the important point is the way Dylan and his band string together various musicological elements to create a new sound and make a statement – something rock 'n' roll was not supposed to do. One stinging line in particular condemns the whistle-while-you-work mentality of tradition-only folk music: "They say sing while you slave and I just get bored / I ain't gonna work on Maggie's Farm no more." With history's hindsight, it's difficult to definitively call *Bringing It All Back Home* a rock 'n' roll album. It has its moments, and at the time it was decried as rock or pop or – worse – mainstream. Dylan's subcultural folk music fans hated it for its departure, but we can hear in it the seeds of Tom Petty, Bruce Springsteen, and even more niche Americana artists like Buddy Miller or the Drive-By Truckers. This influence is particularly underscored by "Outlaw Blues," with its mesh of distorted backup sounds, where the melody feels buried under layers of stone and steel.

Ultimately, though, *Bringing It All Back Home* is an inspired but directionless collection of songs. It's a stab in the dark, a fumbling for the light, for the sound for which Dylan was searching. He culminated the recording with a pair of songs that would have made just as much sense on any of his previous albums – "It's Alright Ma (I'm Only Bleeding)" and "It's All Over Now Baby Blue." It's hard to tell if he included these songs because he ran out of steam with the new sound, or whether he just had so many songs and went with the best selections, regardless of any pursuit of a comprehensive artistic statement.

Thematically, there's a connection between the close of *Bringing It All Back Home* and the opening of *Highway 61 Revisited*, which was released just five months later, in 1965. The actual Highway 61 ran from Dylan's home state of Minnesota down toward New Orleans -- a convenient thematic and stylistic handoff from the previous album, where he took it "back home." *And now, before you get too comfortable, I'll up and leave again*, he seemed to be saying. The next musical statement many listeners received was "Like a Rolling Stone," which opens *Highway 61*. It provides the full band sound that was introduced on "Maggie's Farm," but with more organization. Al Kooper's organ is the oar in the water with its long, languid strokes as the singer blows about in the wide-open sky overhead, distant and untamable.

In 2012, Tom Petty, who grew up to become a friend and frequent collaborator of Dylan's, told *American Songwriter* magazine

> We hadn't heard Dylan [growing up in Florida] until "Like A Rolling Stone" came out as a single. And we loved that right away. We learned

that, did it in the show. We learned all his singles. . . . I had heard *Highway 61 Revisited*. A friend of mine had that. I actually bought *Blonde on Blonde*. That's where I really got into Bob. And I started to really dig his thing. He influenced my songwriting, of course. He influenced everybody's songwriting. There's no way around it. No one had ever really left the love song before, lyrically. So in that respect, I think he influenced everybody, because you suddenly realized you could write about other things.[6]

Petty wasn't the only one. It was in a New York recording studio that Robbie Robertson first encountered Dylan, on a day when he was listening back to early mixes of "Like a Rolling Stone." "I'd never heard anything like this before," Robertson wrote. "The studio lit up with the sound of toughness, humor, and originality. It was hard to take it all in on one listen."[7] Granted, it would be another couple of years before he would join forces with Dylan, but the sound he had heard that day was certainly at the front of his mind when he tried to convince his bandmates, who were sick and tired of being someone else's backup band, to step in behind Dylan for a tour.

Indeed, when Dylan hit the road later in 1965, touring the UK with the Hawks, he began with one solo acoustic set and followed it with a full-band electric set of this new sound he was chasing. The crowd loved the former and booed their way through the latter except for "Like a Rolling Stone," which they cheered their way through – the song was at the top of the charts at the time – before resorting to booing for all the rest of the songs.

As jarring as that moment must have been for fans who were watching from the beginning, the effect of listening back to that era of Dylan albums, knowing the wealth of American roots music that unfolded in the wake of *The Basement Tapes'* official release, we can hear how each of these entries offers the listener two steps forward and one step back. Indeed, for the folkies, each includes a few deep cut gems toward the end of the disc. These acoustic tracks show how Dylan's roots music sound was coming together in his mind, though the brisk pace at which these albums were released clearly gave a portion of his audience whiplash.

Then again, the development of roots music wasn't exactly news to Dylan. He had spent his entire career – and has since – playing with sounds and traditions, occasionally one at a time, sometimes layering them over one another to see how they'd play. When he delved into Dylan's universe as it became organized around *The Basement Tapes*, Greil Marcus explored

---

[6] "Tom Petty on the Enigma Called Bob Dylan," *American Songwriter*, February, 2011, https://americansongwriter.com/tom-petty-on-the-enigma-called-bob-dylan/paul-zollo/.
[7] Robertson, *Testimony*, p. 160.

the influence of Doc Boggs, Clarence Ashley, the Carter Family and others, all of whom can be found among those Dylan himself regularly mentioned in interviews. Dylan added Charley Pride, Jelly Roll Morton, Ian and Sylvia. With Robertson, Helm, and company in the room came the additional influence of Buddy Holly, Bo Diddley, Buddy Guy, and various other big-time bluesmen. We hear all these influences in Garth Hudson's organ and Richard Manuel's vocals, against the meandering beat poetry of Dylan's devil-may-care lyricism.

But all of this was always there, lurking below the surface, slowly coming up for air across the handful of albums that led Dylan through the mid-1960s. Jumping from the last track of each to the following release's opening tune feels so jarring as to be shocking. But if we leapfrog from ending tracks to ending tracks, the progress toward roots music is more incremental and provides more links in a chain: "It's Alright Ma (I'm Only Bleeding)" and "It's All Over Now Baby Blue" (*Bringing It All Back Home*), to "Queen Jane Approximately" and "Desolation Row" (*Highway 61 Revisited*), to "Just Like a Woman" and "Sad Eyed Lady of the Lowlands" (*Blonde on Blonde*), to "Down Along the Cove" and "I'll Be Your Baby Tonight" (*John Wesley Harding*). The same holds for the next handful of albums, all the way to 1970s *New Morning*, which sounds like it could just as well be a Wilco project.

Following these links through the cyclical nature of Dylan's songwriting, we can see how artists may have pieced together all of his sounds well before the official Columbia Records release of *The Basement Tapes* nearly a full decade after Dylan laid down his tracks in Big Pink. Following this chain, we can see how Dylan landed on the perfect formula for roots music in real time, as he was tinkering in the basement with the Hawks. It was as though Dylan's artistic vision was a wind-up toy, and he had been cranking its gear for so long, there was no remaining option but to set it down in that basement and let it go where it might.

Of course, as with everything Dylan has ever done, other people came to take it far more seriously than he did. If we consider the context of the basement, we must remember that Dylan was recovering from a neck fracture and getting back in the swing of singing and playing. His songwriting chops were loosened up from time off the road, his retreat from the city, and what Robertson reported was a large amount of marijuana. Dylan has always been best when given room to stretch outside of expectations – his audience's expectation as well as his own.

The Basement Tapes, he told Kurt Loder for *Rolling Stone* in 1984, "were just songs we had done for the publishing company, as I remember. They were used only for other artists to record those songs. I wouldn't have put 'em out. But, you know, Columbia wanted to put 'em out, so what can you do? . . . People have told me they think it's very Americana and all that. I don't know what they're talking about."[8] The Americana Music Association defines Americana music as "contemporary music that incorporates elements of various American roots music styles, including country, roots-rock, folk, bluegrass, R&B and blues, resulting in a distinctive roots-oriented sound that lives in a world apart from the pure forms of the genres upon which it may draw. While acoustic instruments are often present and vital, Americana also often uses a full electric band."[9] And though this definition seems to be all over the place and include everything, it is personified and made more aurally specific by the music Dylan and the Band set in motion in that basement, however unintentionally, whether Dylan knows what they're talking about or not.

That the ingredients for roots music came together in that basement was indeed kismet, but it was something artists who were listening closely, alive to Dylan's determination to forge his own way rather than stick to the template provided by folk or rock tradition, were already tracking. There was a sense that he was onto something, though it wasn't clear yet exactly what. The musical movement that has long since become roots music would have occurred without *The Basement Tapes* because Dylan was moving so strongly in that direction anyway, and artists who were open to his influence had already noticed. Among them was Gram Parsons, who is often credited with being one of the chief forefathers of Americana and roots music. His band, The Byrds, released their breakthrough roots music album, *Sweetheart of the Rodeo*, a year after the basement sessions were recorded but seven years before they were released, and opened it with Dylan's "You Ain't Goin' Nowhere." Though some of the tracks dripped out in 1969 on the *Great White Wonder* bootleg, the official release of *The Basement Tapes*, coming as it did on the heels of *Blood on the Tracks*, offered a missing puzzle piece and granted other artists the opportunity to not waste time trying to connect those dots; Dylan and the Band did it for them.

Something Brand New

Dylan's use of rock 'n' roll to deliver philosophical, self-deprecating lyricism, to raise questions about the world instead of questions about puppy love, was

---

[8] Kurt Loder and Bob Dylan, "Bob Dylan, Recovering Christian," in *Dylan: The Essential Interviews*, ed. Jonathan Cott (New York: Simon & Schuster, 2007), p. 299.
[9] Americana Music Association, https://americanamusic.org/what-americana-music.

raising eyebrows. But his musical influence in this period went beyond what any artist had the language to discuss. There was something deliciously musicological, creatively seismic. When talking to Blair Jackson and David Gans, co-authors of *This Is All a Dream We Dreamed: An Oral History of the Grateful Dead*, in 1981, Jerry Garcia noted the "melodic renaissance" Dylan underwent during the making of *Blonde on Blonde*.[10] Garcia credited it, at least in part, to Dylan's collaboration with Robbie Robertson, but also recognized that Dylan was experimenting with something that had never been done before – an approach to performance that has long since become anything but unusual among singer-songwriters.

As Garcia asks:

> You know the *Planet Waves* album [1974]. The two versions of "Forever Young": the country-and-western version is Dylan's version, and the slow version is Robbie Robertson's version. So you can get some idea there of Robertson's contribution to the songs on *Blonde on Blonde*. All those passing chords ... the relative minor substitutions that sort of characterize those songs, the moving second lines that happen in them. All those things are signatures of that era of Dylan's writing – the kind of melody which you hear but he doesn't sing. There's a melody to all those songs, like "Stuck Inside of Mobile with the Memphis Blues Again" – those songs all have this melody which you will hear in your head, but he doesn't really sing. He really more speaks them, but the music so well frames them that there's this melody that you imagine they have.

As the 1970s unfolded, artists like Bruce Springsteen, who borrowed this way of singing, began to make their way up the pop charts. Petty would perfect it a decade later, when he leaned away from the melody in select moments of songs like "I Won't Back Down." And as Dylan collaborated more and more with Petty, Orbison, George Harrison, and Jeff Lynne as the Traveling Wilburys, we would see each of those men – who together characterized the heart of contemporary roots music – taking this vocal technique even further.

On "At the End of the Line," the Wilburys' biggest radio hit, the person taking the lead vocal would sing-speak the lead line at one tone while the rest of the singers would repeat "at the end of the line" in a lower, near-spoken register. It gave the impression of melody without any of them actually singing, as all their interwoven guitars held down a languid under-pinning like a river that flows underground. The sound they created was decidedly more accessible than 1980s rock 'n' roll, more hip than

---

[10] Cloud Surfing Blog, "Jerry Garcia on Bob Dylan 1981," http://cloudsurfing.gdhour.com/archives/4339

traditional folk. And it became a roadmap for singer-songwriters who wanted to stay true to their musical influences even as they sought to create new material. As the media has erred on the side of calling any artist with an acoustic guitar a folksinger, there have been real musicological implications to separating "folk" from "roots" music. The former sticks to its origins while the latter gives artists more room to move – a stylistic overture that was fought for and won, once upon a time, in an upstate New York basement.

In 2015, the organizers at the Newport Folk Festival filmed a session with singer-songwriter Jason Isbell, a defining force in American roots music for his generation – a role that may not have existed if not for Bob Dylan. He talked about the influence Bob Dylan's music has had on his own, ruminating on the gulf between rock and folk and the way roots music exists so that artists don't have to fit in neatly delineated boxes. Dylan, Isbell said, is

> a mysterious character. When he shifted his focus to rock 'n' roll music, if it happened now it wouldn't scare anybody. . . . If that hadn't happened there would be [a] very obvious division between people who made electric music and people who made acoustic music. Probably still to this day. So it gives me an opportunity to sing my sad, narrative, folk-driven songs and still play rock and roll guitar solos, which is kind of my favorite thing in the world.[11]

Toward the middle of the session, the interviewers handed him the Fender electric guitar that Dylan played at the 1965 festival. "Holy geez," Isbell exclaimed, turning the "time capsule" over in his hands, recognizing the way many complex layers of music history, many intersections of styles, and many moments which changed music forever, can be contained in the well-polished curves of a single instrument. The guitar's previous owner understood all these things intimately, as though he were a roots music oracle who poured them out through those same six strings.

---

[11] Jason Isbell, "Behind the Walls, Newport Folk 2015," www.youtube.com/watch?v=Hy5h_2YUE84.

CHAPTER 11

The Great American Songbook

Larry Starr

Better Duck Down the [Tin Pan] Alley Way, Lookin' for a New Friend.[1]

Should we have been surprised? Bob Dylan himself says no, in his exceptionally useful "Uncut Interview."[2] Indeed, by the time of the release in 2015 of *Shadows in the Night*, the first in what has become a series of Great American Songbook albums by Dylan, we should have been well past the point of surprise at anything this amazing musical and stylistic chameleon chooses to do.[3] (I am not holding my breath for an album of Dylan opera excerpts, but I know better than to make any predictions at this point!)

Hindsight inevitably is 20/20, but it is legitimate to look for the signposts along the trajectory of Dylan's recorded career that might now be regarded as harbingers of his interest in this traditional repertoire. It turns out that there are many such signposts, if we widen our purview to include considerations of singing style and song form.[4] To begin, it is useful listening with fresh ears to what has long been regarded as an

---

[1] Bob Dylan, "Subterranean Homesick Blues" (1965). At the time of this writing, Bob Dylan has released three albums of Great American Songbook repertoire (one of which is a three-disc set, *Triplicate*), presenting his interpretations of fifty-two songs. If an attempt were initiated to discuss these recordings thoroughly in the dual contexts of Dylan's overall output of recordings, and of the recorded history of the Great American Songbook, potential material for several books becomes readily apparent. What follows here should be regarded simply as my own initial probing into an area of riches, offered as a modest guide to further investigation, for myself and for interested readers.

[2] Jeff Burger, ed., "Bob Dylan: The Uncut Interview" (with Robert Love), in *Dylan on Dylan: Interviews and Encounters* (Chicago: Chicago Review Press, 2018).

[3] "Great American Songbook" is a term employed for a significant body of American popular songs, created mainly during the decades spanning the 1920s to the 1950s, that has continued to be frequently performed and recorded to the present day. The songs were published as sheet music, making it readily available to multiple interpreters.

[4] For the purposes of this article, I am not including Dylan's *Christmas in the Heart* (2009) album. Although there are surely intersections between Christmas repertoire and the Great American Songbook (such as "White Christmas" and "The Christmas Song," the latter included on the Dylan album), *Christmas in the Heart* seems essentially a one-off project in Dylan's catalog.

anomalous selection from Dylan's anomalous, notoriously ill-received 1970 album *Self Portrait*.

Bob Dylan Croons Rodgers and Hart's "Blue Moon"? Really?

For the young folk and rock music fans of the 1960s, who constituted Bob Dylan's initial core audience, the music of Tin Pan Alley supposedly was their parents' music: stylistically old-fashioned, sentimental, utterly unconcerned with pressing matters of either the present or the past.[5] But it's important to realize that the advent of rock 'n' roll in the mid-1950s and the popularization of urban folk music in the 1960s never totally eclipsed the Tin Pan Alley repertoire, even in music specifically marketed to youth. Elvis Presley himself recorded the Rodgers and Hart classic "Blue Moon" during his early sessions at Sun Records in 1954, and this version was released both as a single and on an album by RCA Victor in 1956. It seems certain that the teenage Dylan – who was, along with millions of others, an enthusiastic Presley fan – knew of this recording. (And Presley's own early idol was crooner Dean Martin!) In addition, "Blue Moon" was one of dozens of Tin Pan Alley standards revived in doo-wop or up-tempo rock 'n' roll arrangements during the late 1950s and 1960s. The Marcels' recording of this song was one of the most successful examples of this, a massive hit that was virtually inescapable on radio during the spring of 1961. In this sense, "Blue Moon," along with other analogous examples (Fats Domino's "My Blue Heaven"; "Twilight Time" and "Smoke Gets in Your Eyes" by the Platters; as late as 1967, the Happenings' "I Got Rhythm"), demonstrates that this repertoire remained "contemporary" pop music throughout the period of Dylan's ascendancy.

Nevertheless, Dylan in the 1960s was seen, rightly or wrongly, as the anti-establishment, tradition-shattering anti-hero of the youth-oriented counterculture. His metamorphosis into the country crooner of *Nashville Skyline* in 1969 came as shock enough, but *Self Portrait*, an album dominated by folk and country music cover versions sung in a crooning style, seemed designed to rub salt in the wound (and perhaps it was). As the sole Tin Pan Alley-vintage song released on *Self Portrait*, Dylan's "Blue Moon" attracted little notice at the time. Indeed, it was the only Great American Songbook selection to appear on any officially released Dylan album prior

---

[5] "Tin Pan Alley" was the catch-term for a street of music publishing houses in New York City, where the sheet music for popular songs was mass produced during the era of the Great American Songbook. "Tin Pan Alley music" is frequently employed as a virtual synonym for the Great American Songbook, or for songs evocative of that style and era in popular music.

to 2015's *Shadows in the Night*. Precisely for that reason, however, it merits attention here, and it also rewards that attention.

"Blue Moon" stands as a fine example of typical Tin Pan Alley song form. The refrain, which is the only part of the song usually performed, consists of four sections that may be represented as A–A–B–A: three identical, or very similar, musical stanzas, the second and third of which are separated by a contrasting "bridge" section. Dylan's recording respects the totality of Rodgers and Hart's original composition, which might seem a trivial observation were it not for the fact that both Presley's and the Marcels' versions – the ones most likely to be familiar to Dylan and members of his 1970 audience – do not. Presley omits the bridge section entirely, performing only the first half of the refrain. The Marcels do sing the bridge section, but inaccurately, simplifying (I am tempted to say "dumbing down") its melodic and harmonic structure. Arguably the most affecting passage in the entire song as originally written comes with the striking, unexpected melodic turn and chord change in the bridge, on the lyrics "please adore me." Dylan is unfazed by this; he handles the passage appropriately and with obvious ease, an indication both of his musicianship and of his regard for the song as a composition, characteristics abundantly evident in his much later Songbook albums.

Throughout his performance of "Blue Moon," Dylan's vocal evokes the relaxed phrasing of a jazz singer, playing conversationally against the steady background beat and even improvising subtly around the basic melodic structure. His smooth crooning tone conjures to some extent the Sun-era Presley's recording of the song. The formal arrangement is also worthy of attention, since it obviously reflects some thought on Dylan's part. It would have been typical to position any instrumental break in a recording of "Blue Moon" after the entire refrain has been sung through once. Instead, in Dylan's version, a striking fiddle solo takes place immediately following the bridge, separating the "B" section from the singing of the final "A." This may be heard as illuminating musically what the lyrics have just told us: that the blue moon has "turned to gold." The solo also highlights, via a delaying tactic, another essential transformation conveyed in the concluding lyrics: that the singer at last is "no longer alone." After the last "A" section is sung, an additional, final fiddle solo is heard, providing in effect an instrumental frame around the crucial change in the singer's fortunes.

Crooning, Song Forms, and Dylan's *Nashville Skyline*

Crooning is not the only vocal style associated with the Tin Pan Alley repertoire; Al Jolson, the extravagant belter who introduced many now-classic American songs during the 1910s and 1920s, was anything but a crooner. The later ascendancy of singers like Bing Crosby and Frank Sinatra helped assure, however, that crooning became the standard interpretive approach to Tin Pan Alley songs. This was especially true for the interpretation of love ballads, naturally enough, and such ballads in turn came to constitute the vast majority of songs that endured to establish themselves as the Great American Songbook. Crooning also entered the stylistic vocabulary of some very prominent country singers, such as Gene Autry and Eddy Arnold, whose employment of it helped them attain crossover success into the mainstream pop music market.

The cross-fertilization between country and pop was not limited to vocal style. Country songs of sentiment and heartbreak frequently employed a lyric vocabulary largely indistinguishable from that of Tin Pan Alley-style songs. When A–A–B–A song forms also began to be employed by country songwriters, the distinctions between country and traditional pop songs came more and more to hinge upon the diction of the singers and the instrumental arrangements, not upon the words and music of the songs themselves. A helpful instance here is Patsy Cline's first crossover hit (which was a big one), "Walkin' after Midnight" (1957). Arguably, only the twang in Cline's voice and in her accompaniment marked this record specifically as a country song. And by the early 1960s, Cline herself was recording Tin Pan Alley classics like "Heartaches," Irving Berlin's "Always," and "You Made Me Love You (I Didn't Want to Do It)" – the last introduced originally by Al Jolson, as early as 1913! Conversely, singers with a Tin Pan Alley orientation discovered that they could achieve pop success with country material; young crooner Tony Bennett had a huge early hit with "Cold, Cold Heart" (1951), a song written and originally recorded by as solid a country musician as ever was, Hank Williams. Eventually, country "outlaw" Willie Nelson released a complete album of American Songbook standards, *Stardust*, in 1978. Should we have been surprised?

All this helps explain why Dylan's country album *Nashville Skyline* may be seen as one significant step toward his later full-hearted embrace of Tin Pan Alley repertoire. Throughout the album, Dylan showcases an expert, even refined, croon in performing eight of his own new songs, and in his duet with Johnny Cash on the much older "Girl from the North Country." (Listen, for example, to his assured, unexpected leap into his upper register during the concluding stanza of "One More Night," which expressively portrays the wind blowing "high above the tree.") Noteworthy also is the fact that all eight of the new songs, and even the new instrumental "Nashville Skyline Rag," are in A–A–B–A form, a formal arrangement that had appeared only sporadically in Dylan's earlier songs; previously, he tended to utilize the simple, repetitive strophic forms commonly found in folk music. In effect, the Bob Dylan of *Nashville Skyline* is a singer and songwriter who, in embracing contemporary country aesthetics, has also moved suddenly much closer to long-established Tin Pan Alley conventions. This is readily evident as well in the album's conventionally themed lyrics, and in its broadened harmonic vocabulary (especially prominent in "Lay, Lady, Lay" and in the bridge section of "Tonight I'll Be Staying Here with You").

With *Nashville Skyline*, Dylan, who had established himself by the mid-1960s as an artist pushing all the established boundaries of songwriting, daringly set himself the challenge of working within a tradition-based genre of popular music. From a certain standpoint, he embraced an analogous kind of challenge when he undertook, much later, the extensive recording of Great American Songbook standards. In any case, the push-back from his fans that Dylan encountered upon releasing *Nashville Skyline* was predictable. Nobody seems to have considered what might have been the reaction had this album been the work of a previously unknown country artist. I venture to suggest that, if such had been the case, *Nashville Skyline* – while it may not be a "great" album, whatever that is – would have been heralded as the debut of a major new talent who was producing very fresh work within the genre. (Apart from the fine singing, the expert instrumental playing, and the harmonic surprises, there is the humorous wordplay in "Peggy Day.") But of course, this album had to bear the burden of being a *Bob Dylan* album, and its reception was inseparable from that hard truth. In evaluating the Songbook albums of decades later, their status as Bob Dylan albums is similarly inescapable and that much heavier. It would seem problematic to evaluate them in any other light, if such an attempt could even be made.

These issues might have presented themselves much earlier, had Dylan made a Songbook album in the late 1970s, as he apparently wanted to do. After seriously considering *Nashville Skyline*, I don't think we should be surprised to learn that Dylan was sufficiently impressed by Willie Nelson's *Stardust* to want to follow Nelson's example and record his own album of standards.[6] But Columbia Records would have none of it at that time, and soon Bob Dylan was off creating his own gospel music instead. The Songbook would have to wait. When he eventually returned to the long-postponed project, he went for it in spades! And he presented his own

[6] Burger, "The Uncut Interview," p. 489.

version of "Stardust" on the third record of his *Triplicate* set.[7] Prior to considering Dylan as a Songbook interpreter, however, we should look briefly at Dylan's own neo-Tin Pan Alley creation, "Beyond the Horizon," from the album *Modern Times* (2006).

Remodeling a Tin Pan Alley Standard

After *Nashville Skyline*, Dylan occasionally wrote songs that combined Tin Pan Alley-like lyric sentiments with the standard A–A–B–A song form, such as "If Not for You" (*New Morning*, 1970) and "Hazel," a tribute to a woman with "stardust" in her eye (*Planet Waves*, 1974). Surely the most striking example of this is the much later "Beyond the Horizon," because it is modeled so closely on "Red Sails in the Sunset," an evergreen song with a long history of successful recordings. Beginning with hit versions by Bing Crosby and Guy Lombardo, both in 1935, it was revived by Nat "King" Cole in the early 1950s and by both the Platters and Fats Domino in the early 1960s. Using a pre-existing song as the melodic basis for a new one was a familiar practice for Dylan, dating back to his folksinger days (and he was just one among many to employ it). But his remodeling of "Red Sails in the Sunset" is particularly intriguing, since it encompasses not simply the melodic line, but also the lyric subject matter, and even the relationship between the music and the verbal imagery.

Like its source, "Beyond the Horizon" presents the scenario of a singer staring out to sea, seeking something in the distance that is emblematic of love and its return. In "Red Sails in the Sunset," the details are very specific: the longed-for sight is that of the sailboat carrying the loved one back to shore for a wedding. With "Beyond the Horizon," the longing is for something broader and more elusive: the singer looks "behind the sun, at the end of the rainbow" and "o'er the treacherous sea," "through countries and kingdoms," for a place where "love waits forever for one and for all." There, at last, "the sky is so blue," and there's "more than a lifetime to live lovin' you." "Beyond the Horizon" also borrows the A–A–B–A form of the source, and Dylan sings through this music a total of four times, with new words for each iteration, thus marrying Tin Pan Alley song form with his own long-favored strophic form. Dylan employs the melody of "Red Sails" quite literally; the ascending lines of the "A" sections, which evoke very

---

[7] Following the release of Dylan's Songbook albums, Willie Nelson himself released an album of standards, *My Way* (2018), which included both "Blue Moon" and "Young at Heart." Dylan had recorded the latter song on his *Fallen Angels* (2016). Was Nelson, in effect, returning Dylan's long-delayed compliment to Nelson's own *Stardust*?

effectively the sense of looking up and out into the distance, serve the purposes of both songs equally well. Throughout, Dylan croons the old melody and his fresh lyrics very tenderly.[8] In terms of both composition and performance, "Beyond the Horizon" is a deeply touching song.

For the listener, "Beyond the Horizon" has an affect very different from that of "Red Sails in the Sunset," despite all the similarities. Dylan adopts a faster tempo than would be typical for "Red Sails," and the performance has a gentle swing that is much more appropriate for his song of active seeking than it would be for portraying the rather static situation of one planted on the shore, awaiting the return of a specific boat. The winding, chromatic little instrumental hook that starts off "Beyond the Horizon," and recurs regularly, also contributes its touch of restlessness. But perhaps Dylan's most sophisticated alterations involve his re-conceiving of the phrasing in his source. The ascending vocal phrases in "Red Sails" follow strong downbeats, as if metrically representing the singer firmly placed on shore, gazing out from a fixed location toward a fixed point. The analogous phrases in Dylan's song *anticipate* the strong downbeats, starting from a metrically weak position, and represent rhythmically the much less definite setting of his song and its push toward onward movement. These may seem technical details, but their musical impact is obvious and visceral.

The Album as Remodel: Dylan's *Shadows in the Night*

If Woody Guthrie served as Dylan's acknowledged lodestar for his earliest albums, Frank Sinatra occupies a parallel position in relation to the Songbook albums.[9] Working with arranger/conductors Billy May, Nelson Riddle, and Gordon Jenkins, Sinatra in the 1950s helped pioneer the "concept album," a long-playing record with songs chosen to sustain a particular mood, or theme: *Songs for Swingin' Lovers!*, *Frank Sinatra Sings for Only the Lonely*, and many others. The first of Dylan's Songbook albums, *Shadows in the Night*, is a kind of meta-concept album designed as a tribute to Frank Sinatra's concept albums. The ten songs on *Shadows* are all associated with Sinatra – some more closely than others, but he recorded them all. And to be sure, Dylan's album has an unbroken ambience: the ten slow ballads are crooned with the consistent, sensitive

---

[8] A delicious moment in the lyrics comes with Dylan's reference to "the theme of a melody from many moons ago"! And in his first strophe, Dylan mentions the "stardust above."

[9] Burger, "The Uncut Interview," pp. 492–494.

accompaniment of a five-piece band, evoking an intimate, late night cabaret atmosphere. Soft horns added to three selections enhance this sonic environment, without disrupting it.

Dylan offers a veiled clue to his source of inspiration with the album title itself, which recalls Sinatra's surprise later-career megahit "Strangers in the Night," a song that is *not* present on the album (and a song with a purely optimistic resolution that would have mixed uncomfortably with the melancholy and equivocal moods of the songs that are present). *Shadows in the Night* is a good name for this darkly tinged album. Dylan's recording has the closest kinship with Sinatra's 1957 LP *Where Are You?* with which it shares four songs: "I'm a Fool to Want You," "The Night We Called It a Day," "Autumn Leaves," and "Where Are You?"[10] Sinatra's album has a tighter unity of theme than Dylan's, insofar as all of its twelve songs take loneliness, and specifically the absence of love, as their subject. *Shadows* spreads a wider net, including two songs with significant spiritual content, "Stay with Me" and "That Lucky Old Sun" – not at all surprising for Dylan. A brief discussion of one song the albums share in common, "Autumn Leaves," will illuminate how closely Dylan may adhere to Sinatra's model, while "That Lucky Old Sun" demonstrates how Dylan can also create an interpretation that is very personal and distinctive.

Dylan's "Autumn Leaves" is a virtual re-creation of Sinatra's version, down to the details of the instrumental arrangement: the extended, mournful introduction; the little chromatic swirls that evoke falling leaves, following each sung line in the first stanza; the absence of a marked pulse in every stanza but the second; and the four-note tag at the very end. Dylan's vocal, as well, takes nearly all of its cues from Sinatra. Each of Dylan's four opening vocal phrases starts softly, and then drifts off. Both Dylan and Sinatra lean expressively on the word "winter" in stanza three, and both slow down markedly toward the song's conclusion, as if reluctant to leave the cherished memory of the loved one behind. Who could fault Dylan for paying obvious homage to Sinatra's subtle, yet devastating, interpretation of a remarkable song (and to Gordon Jenkins's equally remarkable arrangement of it)? Dylan upends criticism along these lines with his own words: "Comparing me with Frank Sinatra? You must be

---

[10] There is arguably a fifth common element, insofar as both Sinatra's and Dylan's albums include one song based on a melody from the same classical composition! *Shadows* offers "Full Moon and Empty Arms," derived from the lyrical second theme in movement III of Rachmaninoff's Second Piano Concerto, while *Where Are You?* has "I Think of You," adapted from the second theme of the first movement in that concerto. Coincidence? Very probably, but in the case of Bob Dylan, who would dare say for certain?

joking. To be mentioned in the same breath as him must be some sort of high compliment. As far as touching him goes, nobody touches him. Not me or anyone else."[11]

Nevertheless, it would be a mistake to claim that Dylan offers nothing to "Autumn Leaves" other than a pale reflection of Sinatra's version. He sings so quietly in the second and third stanzas (avoiding Sinatra's slight swells) that it seems as if he can hardly bear to articulate the words in his anguish. His voice quivers on the last word of the first stanza ("gold") and on the final word of the song ("fall"), and Dylan allows it to crack on the lines "I miss you most of all, my darling." In effect, while Sinatra, then in his early forties, articulated a song of mid-life regret, Dylan in 2015 (more than three decades older than the Sinatra of *Where Are You?*) sang the song of an old man facing the winter of his life, a man who has lost all hope.

It might be argued that Dylan has simply exposed his inevitable, age-related vocal limitations in "Autumn Leaves," but I would suggest instead that he manages to turn these limitations into virtues. Sinatra, throughout his own late career, provided a model of how this could be done, most spectacularly in his famous interpretation of "Theme from *New York, New York*" (recorded in 1979, when the singer was in his mid-sixties). Here, Sinatra takes what was originally the song of a young person setting out for the first time to make it in the big city, and turns it into the song of an older entertainer who refuses to become a has-been. Starting out in a lower register that deliberately emphasizes the rough edges in his voice, Sinatra becomes audibly more energized and "younger" as the song progresses, arriving finally at a blazing, triumphant high note, which he hits not once, but twice!

Dylan achieves something analogous performing "That Lucky Old Sun" on *Shadows*. His version is modeled closely on Sinatra's 1949 recording, and Sinatra did his best there to portray the resigned, world-weary toiler who longs to "roll around heaven all day." But Sinatra, try as he might, could not disguise that he was a full-throated singer in his early prime when he interpreted the song. Dylan, in contrast, does not have to adjust his voice to sound as if he is "wrinkled and gray," and he allows all the coarseness and crackle to emerge, in perfect service to the song. The obvious strain when he reaches for the high note on "lift me to *paradise*" is heartbreaking. But (unlike Sinatra) Dylan smooths out his voice, relishing and prolonging all the long, open vowels every time he sings "roll around heaven all day," as if he is transfigured by the vision. It is a striking

---

[11] Burger, "The Uncut Interview," p. 494.

performance, and a wonderful conclusion for an album that is characterized throughout by great tenderness and by a deep respect for the chosen repertoire.[12]

The Dylan albums that followed *Shadows in the Night* retained Frank Sinatra as a dominating background presence, if not as the omnipresence he seems in the first Songbook album. *Triplicate*, for example, shares four songs with Sinatra's 1965 album *September of My Years*, three of them on the first *Triplicate* disc (titled "'Til the Sun Goes Down"). There are surprising appearances of up-tempo songs on the later albums, such as "Polka Dots and Moonbeams" (modeled on Sinatra's 1940 recording) and "That Old Black Magic" (this one modeled on the 1958 hit by Louis Prima and Keely Smith) from *Fallen Angels*. The preceding discussion of *Shadows* suggests some starting points for approaching the many riches of the succeeding Songbook albums.

Questions, Not Conclusions

What additional insights into Dylan's earlier career might be gleaned from his Songbook albums? And how much does Dylan add to the interpretive history of this repertoire? These and many other questions present themselves to animate the meaningful investigations that Bob Dylan's Great American Songbook albums demand, and that this chapter has been able only tentatively to suggest. Perhaps the chief significance of these recordings may lie simply in the fact that Dylan is helping to keep this repertoire alive, especially given the likelihood that many listeners may receive their introduction (or their reintroduction) to the Songbook through them. Arguably, that would be achievement enough for one who (surprisingly?) now appears to be a "grand old man" of American popular song.

---

[12] Dylan also employs his aging vocal instrument to advantage on the *Shadows* track "Some Enchanted Evening." Obviously lacking the operatic voice for which the song was originally written, Dylan interprets the song as tenderly given wisdom, such as a respected elder might offer to a young man first seeking love.

PART III

Cultural Contexts

CHAPTER 12

American Literature

Florence Dore

When Bob Dylan won the Nobel Prize in Literature in 2016, the rehearsal of familiar axioms about the relationship between so-called "high literature" and popular song followed. As the *Nation* writer David Hajdu put it just after the world's most prestigious literary prize was handed to a rock icon, "the old categories of high and low art, they've been collapsing for a long time, but this is it being made official."[1] If the 2016 Nobel established that Dylan's songs qualify as "high" art, what is their status as American literature in particular? In his Nobel Lecture in 2017, Dylan points to *Moby Dick* as an influence. Are Dylan's songs therefore to be admitted to the canon of American authors that includes the likes of Herman Melville? In the same speech, he also acknowledges that he has drawn on sources that fall outside the bounds of American literature – including the poetry of John Donne, Homer's *The Odyssey*, and Erich Maria Remarque's *All Quiet on the Western Front*.[2] So what should we make of Dylan's mention of Melville's tome? If Dylan's songs are a species of "literature," how, given his myriad literary influences, can they be understood as American literature? What he admires about Melville, he explains, is the author's ability to create an aesthetic with "everything thrown in," so it hardly makes sense to put too fine a point on Dylan's relation to any single author. Given his kitchen-sink approach to literary influence, why should we consider Bob Dylan's work in relation to American literature at all?

Some of the material in this chapter is adapted from *Novel Sounds: Southern Fiction in the Age of Rock and Roll*, by Florence Dore. Copyright © 2018 Columbia University Press. Reprinted with permission of Columbia University Press.

[1] Ben Sisario, Alexandra Alter, and Sewell Chan, "Bob Dylan Wins Nobel Prize, Redefining Boundaries of Literature," *New York Times*, October 13, 2016, www.nytimes.com/2016/10/14/arts/music/bob-dylan-nobel-prize-literature.html.

[2] Bob Dylan, "The Nobel Prize in Literature 2016," www.nobelprize.org/prizes/literature/2016/dylan/lecture/.

Perhaps we should turn the question around and ask instead how Dylan has influenced lauded contributors to the American canon. The flow from Dylan's oeuvre to contemporary American authors has not been nearly as opaque, after all, as the reverse trajectory. In his 1973 novel, *Great Jones Street*, Don DeLillo fictionalizes the theft of Dylan's *The Basement Tapes* in a plot involving the thinly veiled Dylan-protagonist Bucky Wunderlick and his "Mountain Tapes." Dana Spiotta lifted the title for her 2006 novel *Eat the Document* directly, naming it after Dylan's elusive 1966 documentary for ABC. Jonathan Lethem names the protagonist of his 2003 rock novel *The Fortress of Solitude* "Dylan," explicitly after Bob, planting the lyrics to "Chimes of Freedom" in his character's fictional unconscious.[3] In Michael Chabon's Blashfield address at the American Academy of Arts and Letters, later published as "Let it Rock" in the *New York Review of Books*, this acclaimed contemporary American author announced that Dylan's lyrics "have influenced my own writing as much as if not more than the work of any poet apart from O'Hara and maybe Edgar Allan Poe." Chabon goes on to expand outward from Dylan to suggest that rock 'n' roll matters more to his work than other novels: "In fact, song lyrics in general have arguably mattered to and shaped me more, as a writer, than novels or short stories written by any but the most crucial of my literary heroes."[4] So is the matter settled? Once we track Bob Dylan's influence on American novels, has the relation between Bob and American literature been fully plumbed?

Come gather round people, wherever you roam, for there is a longer story to tell. Although Dylan cites Melville in his Nobel Lecture, the real clue he offers about his relationship to American literature is his mention of Huddie Ledbetter, the African American musician otherwise known as Lead Belly. In analyses of a midcentury literary movement called the New Criticism, the literary scholar John Guillory makes it clear that ideas of the "high literary" were created in American English departments – that the conception of the "high literary" arose in those institutional spaces between the 1930s and the 1950s to reinforce economic divisions that seemed to be evaporating during the era.[5] How shall we read the recent incursions of popular music into the Ivory Tower? What are the Bob Dylan Archive and

---

[3] Don DeLillo, *Great Jones Street* (Boston: Houghton Mifflin, 1973); Dana Spiotta, *Eat the Document: A Novel* (New York: Scribner, 2006); Jonathan Lethem, *The Fortress of Solitude: A Novel*, 1st edn (New York: Doubleday, 2003).

[4] Michael Chabon, "Let It Rock," *New York Review of Books*, July 11, 2013, www.nybooks.com/articles/2013/07/11/let-it-rock/.

[5] John Guillory, *Cultural Capital: The Problem of Literary Canon Formation* (Chicago: University of Chicago Press, 1993).

the TU Institute for Bob Dylan Studies doing inside university walls? It is to this genealogy, which traces the surprising importance of vernacular and popular forms to institutional definitions of the high literary, that I will now turn, for only here can the Bard of Rock's role in American literature clearly be captured. More than a question of influence, Dylan and American literature share the same cultural lineage – and it all starts with Lead Belly.

Dylan notes his place in this history in his Nobel Lecture, but not when he cites *Moby Dick*. Rather, we learn how his songs should be considered American literature when he narrates the alchemical mixture of Buddy Holly and Lead Belly that he says took place in his person just after Buddy Holly died. Dylan explains that he went to see Buddy Holly the day before his plane crashed, when "out of the blue, the most uncanny thing happened":

> He looked me right straight dead in the eye, and he transmitted something. Something I didn't know what. And it gave me the chills.
>
> I think it was a day or two after that that his plane went down. And somebody – somebody I'd never seen before – handed me a Leadbelly record with the song "Cottonfields" on it. And that record changed my life right then and there. Transported me into a world I'd never known.[6]

As an answer to the stated goal in this speech, which is to "reflect on" how his songs "related to literature," and "see where the connection was," Dylan could not have been more precise. For in 1934, right around the time he recorded "Cottonfields," Lead Belly also performed for a group of white academics, on a panel called "Popular Literature," at the meetings for the Modern Language Association.

We will return to Lead Belly as Exhibit A at the 1934 Modern Language Association conference (MLA). For now, I will note that just before this appearance, the ethnomusicologist John Lomax discovered Lead Belly serving time for murder in the Louisiana State Penitentiary known as "Angola."[7] Lead Belly has of course been "transporting" white American musicians ever since. Nirvana's memorable 1993 performance of Lead Belly's 1933 "Where Did You Sleep Last Night" for *MTV Unplugged* begins with Kurt Cobain putting out his cigarette, saying, first, "Fuck you all," and then explaining that he had once asked the record mogul David Geffen to help him buy a guitar formerly owned by Lead Belly, his "favorite performer of all." When Nirvana turned the world's attention back to

---

[6] Bob Dylan, *The Nobel Lecture* (New York: Simon & Schuster, 2017), p. 2.
[7] Charles Wolfe and Kip Lornell, *The Life and Legend of Leadbelly*, new edn (New York: Da Capo Press, 1999).

this 1933 song, rock listeners had already become well accustomed to hearing the music of Lead Belly in recordings by white artists. Moving backward from Nirvana's celebrated homage, we find, for example, Robert Plant screaming his way through "Gallows Pole," Led Zeppelin's 1970 version of Lead Belly's 1939 "The Gallis Pole," and Elvis Presley's 1966 recording of Lead Belly's 1934 "Frankie and Johnny," from his Hollywood movie based on the song's plot. On a live recording made at Threadgill's Bar and Grill in Austin, Texas, in 1962, Janis Joplin can be heard belting out "CC Rider" and "Careless Lover," both apparently learned from versions by Lead Belly.[8] Lead Belly's influence has run right through the history of rock 'n' roll, at least since 1962 when Dylan penned the line "Here's to Cisco an' Sonny and Lead Belly too" in "Song to Woody," for one of the first songs he ever wrote.

Given Lead Belly's stature in rock, how can his oeuvre be important to American literature? Allegiance to Robert Plant, Janis Joplin, and for that matter to Dylan, has been understood as a badge of anti-institutional authenticity for white purveyors of rock music – a sign of renegade cultural identity apparently exonerating white scholars from Ivory Tower privilege and its overt participation in racial segregation. That Lead Belly has made his mark in American rock music is already well established. What has been more difficult to discern, in part because of this bad-faith understanding of the relation between rock and the institution, is Lead Belly's place in the definition of American literature. It is by examining Lead Belly's presence in the high literary, overlooked in accounts both of rock 'n' roll and America's literary institutions, that we can actually glimpse Dylan's place in this history. To literary critics and rock writers alike, Dylan winning the Nobel has seemed surprising and sometimes wrong. But tracing the story of American literature backward to the 1930s, we find an institutional conception of the literary even then as rooted in vernacular song, an idea that persisted even as electric microphones were replacing acoustic horns in musical recording – and as pioneers in the American music industry were dividing vernacular music along racial lines into "hillbilly" markets and "race records."[9] It was these early conceptions about vernacular music, generated by the very scholars who would later establish the New

---

[8] Holly George-Warren, *Janis: Her Life and Music* (New York: Simon & Schuster, 2019), pp. 34–35.

[9] See "The History of 78 RPM Recordings," Yale Library, www.library.yale.edu/cataloging/music/hist oryof78rpms.htm, for a timeline showing the introduction of electric microphones. On the marketing of race records and hillbilly music along racially divided lines, see Karl Hagstrom Miller, *Segregating Sound: Inventing Folk and Pop Music in the Age of Jim Crow* (Durham, NC: Duke University Press, 2010), pp. 206–214.

Criticism, that paved the way for Lead Belly's astonishing appearance at the 1934 MLA. On December 28, attendees were invited to a Friday night "smoker," a social gathering listed in the MLA program as featuring "Negro Folksongs and Ballads, presented by John and Alan Lomax, with the assistance of a Negro minstrel from Louisiana." At a panel held the next day on popular literature, Lomax gave the talk "Comments on Negro Folk Songs (illustrated with voice and guitar by Negro convict Leadbelly [*sic*] of Louisiana)."[10] In addition to making records with Lomax, it seems, during the 1930s the African American folksinger and twice-convicted murderer Huddie Ledbetter also performed as the "Negro minstrel from Louisiana" at the largest gathering of literature scholars in the world. Lead Belly and John Lomax visited a number of American colleges and universities during the 1930s and 1940s, and the stop at the MLA meetings in Philadelphia was part of that tour.

What was an African American singer who dropped out of school at the age of fourteen to play guitar in Texas juke joints with Blind Lemon Jefferson doing in the whites-only spaces of academe, decades before the passage of the Civil Rights Act? The answer lies in Nashville, Tennessee. Dubbed "Country Music, USA" in 1950, midcentury Nashville was also home to Vanderbilt University, which by 1950 was the center of institutional definitions of American literature. The idea of literature being generated at Vanderbilt turns out to have emerged out of a historical interest in ballads there – an interest going back at least to 1930. During that year, a group of twelve Vanderbilt professors published *I'll Take My Stand*, a book of essays lamenting the waning influence of Southern values on American culture generally. *I'll Take My Stand* advanced the case for ballads – the literary scholar Andrew Nelson Lytle called them "ballets" in his essay for the volume – as a remedy for this decline. Lytle's admiration for the ballad form involved a worry about sound technology in particular: Southern farmers should "throw out the radio and take down the fiddle from the wall," declared Lytle.[11] For him the problem was radio; for his colleague Donald Davidson it was the manufacture and distribution of records that caused cultural erosion. Lamenting in particular the "shop-girl" who listens to "a jazz record while she rouges her lips," Davidson argued that the "magnificent possibilities for distributing art

---

[10] See "Proceedings of the Modern Language Association of America," *PMLA* 49 (1934), pp. 1324–1325. Lead Belly's trip to the MLA is also chronicled in Charles Wolfe and Kip Lornell, *The Life and Legend of Leadbelly*, new edn (New York: Da Capo, 1999), 130–136.

[11] *I'll Take My Stand: The South and the Agrarian Tradition* (New York: Harper and Row, 1962), pp. 229, 224.

became appalling opportunities for distributing bad art." The US South is a model for changing what the distribution of jazz records has destroyed, said Davidson, because the region "has been rich in folk-arts, and is still rich in them – in ballads, country songs and dances, in hymns and spirituals." The "shop-girl" should throw away race records and radio, should cease listening to jazz and return to her own white ballads, ballads preserved in the geographical enclaves Davidson describes as "mountain fastness and remote rural localities."[12] Agrarians imagined that a return to ballads from the British Isles, those that had been preserved in mountain fastness, would allow Southern values to be restored to national prominence.

Lytle embellished this *volkish* call to "throw out the radio," moreover, with a racial epithet about a hidden African American in "the woodpile," clarifying that the call for pre-technological music is inextricable from a commitment to racial segregation.[13] Amid its messages about "ballets," *I'll Take My Stand* included complaints about the end of slavery, including Robert Penn Warren's declaration, "Let the negro sit beneath his own vine and fig tree."[14] Davidson's worry about record distribution and the spread of jazz carries with it a similar anxiety about the spread of black cultural forms into white spaces, a segregationist view that he expresses in his writings about ballad collecting as well. In 1934, Davidson wrote of his trek with Vanderbilt colleague Georgie Pullen Jackson into rural Georgia to find Sacred Harp songs, described by Jackson as "white spirituals":

> As for Dr. Jackson's argument that the Negro spirituals derive ultimately from the white spirituals, I thought as I listened that no one acquainted with the controversy between those who argue for a white origin and those who hold out for an exclusively Negro origin could remain unconvinced in the light of Sacred Harp performance. ... Doubtless the Negro had adapted them in his peculiar way, but he had first of all taken his songs from the source where he had got his Bible, his plow, his language.[15]

During the 1930s, the author and ethnographer Zora Neale Hurston made forays into rural locations to collect African American folk ballads, and Hurston's recordings clearly formed part of what Daphne Brooks describes

---

[12] Ibid, pp. 35–36, 55.   [13] Ibid, p. 205.   [14] Ibid, p. 264.
[15] Donald Davidson, "The Sacred Harp in the Land of Eden," *Virginia Quarterly Review* 10, no. 2 (April 1, 1934), p. 215. See also Samuel P. Bayard, "George Pullen Jackson," *Journal of the International Folk Music Council* 6 (January 1, 1954), pp. 62–63; Alton C. Morris, "George Pullen Jackson (1874–1953)," *Journal of American Folklore* 66, no. 262 (October 1, 1953); George Jackson, *White Spirituals in the Southern Uplands: The Story of the Fasola Folk, Their Songs, Singings, and "Buckwheat Notes"* (New York: Dover, 1965).

as an effort to "put black voices on the [scholarly] record."[16] But Davidson's "mountain fastness" indicates rather a different impulse, the desire to designate a natural refuge away from the reach of black sounds. The affirmation of "ballets" in *I'll Take My Stand* emerges as inextricable from this segregationist message, and Davidson associates ballads with national purity as well when he later writes that Sacred Harp spirituals are examples of "native American culture" originating in the British Isles. For Davidson, ballads found in mountain fastness confirmed links between white Southerners and their ancestors from England and Scotland.[17] His rejection of music with an "exclusively Negro origin" in 1934 clarifies that his goal was in part to establish racial essence through the ballad form and to make a claim for white superiority in rejecting the phonograph. Lead Belly's presence at the MLA registers this segregationist valorization of the oral.[18]

We find a link between these racialized ideas about ballads and later institutional claims about the "high literary." Eight years after declaring that "the negro" should "sit beneath his own vine and fig tree," Warren collaborated with Cleanth Brooks to edit the foundational New Critical tome *Understanding Poetry*. Along with poems by John Donne, William Shakespeare, T.S. Eliot, and John Keats, Warren and Brooks include a sampling of ballads in this text, most of them ancient Scottish and English instances of the form. But among these, remarkably, is one that Lomax recorded Lead Belly singing at Angola before traveling with him to the MLA: "Frankie and Johnny." Warren and Brooks do not credit any source for this ballad. No matter how they learned of it, however, whether from Lomax's recording or somewhere else, it is striking that the same ballad captured the notice of Lomax and these guardians of the high literary. For reasons that Guillory has explained, the New Critics attributed

---

[16] Daphne A. Brooks, "'Sister, Can You Line It Out?': Zora Neale Hurston and the Sound of Angular Black Womanhood," *Amerikastudien/American Studies* 55, no. 4 (2010), p. 623.

[17] Donald Davidson, "The White Spirituals and Their Historian," *Sewanee Review* 51, no. 4 (December 1943), p. 589.

[18] Paige A. McGinley analyzes Lomax's exercise of white privilege with Lead Belly. Paige A. McGinley, "'The Magic of Song!': John Lomax, Huddie Ledbetter, and the Staging of Circulation," *Performance in the Borderlands*, ed. Ramon H. Rivera-Servera and Harvey Young (Basingstoke and New York: Palgrave Macmillan, 2011), pp. 128–146; Paige McGinley, *Staging the Blues: From Tent Shows to Tourism* (Durham: Duke University Press, 2014). Lead Belly eventually sued John Lomax for unfairly withholding portions of his pay. For a comprehensive account of these legal dealings, see Wolfe and Lornell, *The Life and Legend*, pp. 178–185. Jennifer Lynn Stoever and Erich Nunn have offered readings of Lomax's exploitation of Lead Belly in terms of the violence against African American persons in the post-Reconstruction USA. Jennifer Lynn Stoever, *The Sonic Color Line: Race and the Cultural Politics of Listening*, reprint edn (New York: New York University Press, 2016); Erich Nunn, *Sounding the Color Line: Music and Race in the Southern Imagination* (Athens: University of Georgia Press, 2015).

to literature the power to unify secular culture, and they traced this power back through Eliot's modernist verse to Donne's metaphysical poetry. This New Critical program of poetic repair, as articulated in another of the important New Critical works, Brooks's influential 1947 *The Well Wrought Urn*, involved showing students how to appreciate the "miracle of which the poet speaks" by learning to make "the closest possible examination of what the poem says as a poem."[19] Donne's "The Canonization" is a good place to start, as Brooks's title, taken from the poem, suggests. Alongside "The Canonization," this manual of high literary practice contains a Lead Belly tune. Like Brooks and Warren, Bob Dylan brings both Lead Belly and John Donne into discussions about what counts as literary. Citing lines from one of Donne's Elegies, Dylan makes these remarks in his Nobel Speech in 2017: "I don't know what it means, either. But it sounds good. And you want your songs to sound good." For Dylan as well as for the New Critics, both Lead Belly and John Donne count as good literature. But taken together, the combination also produces an imprimatur, one that legitimates cultural production as "literary" both inside and outside the Ivory Tower.[20]

But Dylan's approach to Lead Belly's ballads obviously differs from that of Brooks and Warren. How do we account for this difference? Without treading again on the well-worn path traveled by Eric Lott, with his famed *"Love and Theft"* and the Dylan album that followed, I will briefly note that Donald Davidson wrote a novel in 1954, *Big Ballad Jamboree*, and based it on the ballad, "The House Carpenter," which Dylan recorded in 1961.[21] Davidson was an avowed segregationist to the end of his life. Whereas he reached for "The House Carpenter" for the same reasons that motivated him to collect ballads in the 1930s, Dylan's interest in ballads more closely resembled Hurston's. For Davidson, English and Scottish ballads preserved in the hills are the musical indication of an essential Southern whiteness; Bob Dylan's interest in the same repertoire took him toward racial integration. It was just a few years after Davidson wrote *The Big Ballad Jamboree* that Dylan began learning ancient Scottish and English ballads like "The House Carpenter," and he was at the same time

---

[19] Cleanth Brooks, *The Well Wrought Urn: Studies in the Structure of Poetry* (San Diego: Harcourt Brace, 1956), p. xi.

[20] Guillory describes Eliot's desire for a literature that was "unconsciously Christian." Guillory, *Cultural Capital*, p. 152.

[21] Eric Lott, *Love and Theft: Blackface Minstrelsy and the American Working Class* (New York: Oxford University Press, 1993); Donald Davidson, *The Big Ballad Jamboree: A Novel* (Jackson: University Press of Mississippi, 1996).

matriculating in the school of Lead Belly, admiring his songs well enough to pen the line, "Here's to Cisco an' Sonny and Lead Belly too," just one year after he recorded "The House Carpenter." Davidson's segregationist novel, one of whose characters is a sympathetic member of the Ku Klux Klan, presents an obvious contrast to Dylan's intentional melding of black and white ballads, for example on his 1962 debut album *Bob Dylan*, which includes songs by early African American blues artists like Blind Lemon Jefferson (Lead Belly's mentor) and pianist Curtis Jones alongside his arrangements of the traditional Scottish "Pretty Peggy-O" and "Man of Constant Sorrow." Dylan's second album, *The Freewheelin' Bob Dylan* (1963), follows suit in bringing ballads forward into rock's interracial present, this time with original compositions mixing black and white ballad traditions. "Masters of War," for example, was based on the ancient English tune "Nottamun Town," and Dylan acknowledged that "Blowin' in the Wind," also on this album, reworks a slave spiritual: "I took it off a song called 'No More Auction Block'," he said in a 1991 interview.[22]

Tracing the threads back from Elvis Presley and Chuck Berry to the musical origins of rock in a racially segregated past, Dylan delivered ballads into a present whose racial lines rock had already breached, explicitly flouting the ballad's earlier racial categories even as he delved into the songs that earlier confirmed them. While Davidson sought and failed to move the needle back to a more racially divided musical moment, Dylan embraced the mixture, building upon rock's practices to create songs of racial protest: "Oxford Town," on the 1963 *Freewheelin'*, for example, which narrates the University of Mississippi's integration; "The Death of Emmet Till," about a 14-year-old African American boy murdered for speaking to a white woman, recorded for *Freewheelin'* but released on volume 6 of Folkways' 1972 *Broadside Ballads*; and "Only a Pawn in Their Game," Dylan's lament about the death of Medgar Evers, on the 1964 *The Times They Are A-Changin'*. These early 1960s recordings show Dylan's interest in tracing ballads across the color line developing into full-blown political protest songs, a practice that culminated in Dylan's performance of "Only a Pawn in Their Game" as an opener for Martin Luther King Jr.'s "I Had a Dream" speech at the 1963 March on Washington. The very same ballad was thus employed by Davidson, on the one hand, in his effort to draw Southern literature in the rock era back toward white dominance; and by Dylan, on the other, *en route* to the

---

[22] Todd Harvey, *The Formative Dylan: Transmission and Stylistic Influences, 1961–1963* (Lanham, MD: Scarecrow Press, 2001), p. 15.

March on Washington. While for Davidson "The House Carpenter" was meant to return him to a moment when Southerners could imagine "throw[ing] out the radio," Dylan's version of the tune was recorded on his path toward the embrace of a Fender Stratocaster at the 1965 Newport Folk Festival.[23]

Far from breaking down the institutional divisions literary scholars are accustomed to rehearsing between the high literary and mass culture, then, Bob Dylan's win of the Nobel Prize in Literature confirms the deep overlap between American literature and rock 'n' roll. His Nobel does not rescue popular music from its status as low; nor does it constitute a scandalous breach of the boundary between rock 'n' roll and the high literary. Instead, Dylan's Nobel gives the lie to the familiar notion that a focus on high-cultural literary works misses rock's low truths, clarifying instead the genealogical overlap between American literature and rock – that nexus in the vernacular from which both Dylan and American literature emerged as apparently opposing modes of expression with irreconcilable histories. In the late 1980s, the literary scholar Andreas Huyssen charged that modernist "aesthetic practice" exhibits an "inherent hostility between high and low," asserting that modernism and the avant-garde "defined themselves in relation to two cultural phenomena: traditional bourgeois high culture ... but also vernacular and popular as it was increasingly transformed into modern commercial mass culture."[24] Acknowledging Lead Belly's role in American literature alongside rock unsettles the common assumptions that lead to this sort of mistake, indicating that on the contrary, vernacular forms of expression were never sequestered from institutional designations of the high literary. From the 1920s to the birth of rock, keepers of "bourgeois high culture" in the USA unfailingly traced literature to vernacular music. It is this practice that explains Bob Dylan's win and that clarifies how a rock 'n' roller could prevail in a contest of who makes the best literature. Without acknowledging Lead Belly's place in this history, as Dylan asks us to do in his 2017 Nobel Lecture, the claim that we are engaged in scandal when we discover rock 'n' roll in high-cultural domains can only repeat endlessly, caught like a needle on

[23] Greil Marcus, *The Old, Weird America: The World of Bob Dylan's Basement Tapes* (New York: Picador, 2011); Elijah Wald, *Dylan Goes Electric!: Newport, Seeger, Dylan, and the Night That Split the Sixties* (New York: Dey St., 2015); Charles McGovern, "The Music: The Electric Guitar in the American Century," in *The Electric Guitar: A History of an American Icon*, ed. Andre Millard (Baltimore: Johns Hopkins University Press, 2004).

[24] Andreas Huyssen, *After the Great Divide: Modernism, Mass Culture, Postmodernism* (Bloomington: Indiana University Press, 1986), pp. viii–ix.

scratched vinyl – playing back again and again the shock of the low, infinitely re-inscribing the divisions between "high" and "low" we pretend to overcome. The point here is not to declare, again, that we have finally closed the gap, but to attend to what governs the ascendance of rock into literature at any given moment, given popular music's constant presence within, or perhaps its repeated incursions into, literature's institutions. Does Bob Dylan's work count as American literature? The answer is blowin' in the wind.

CHAPTER 13

World Literature

Anne-Marie Mai

In Bob Dylan's *Tarantula* (1971), we read a message from the so-called Professor Herold to his students, one of the many strange and strangely amusing letters running through the Beat-inspired book. Herold writes:

> to my students:
> i take it for granted that youve all read
> & understand freud – dostoevsky – st.
> michael – confucius – coco joe – einstein –
> melville – porgy snaker – john zulu – kafka –
> sartre – smallfry– & tolstoy – all right then –
> what my work is – is merely picking up where
> they left off – nothing more – there you have
> it in a nutshell – now i'm giving you my
> book – i expect you all to jump right in –
> the exam will be in two weeks – everybody
> has to bring their own eraser
>
> your professor
herold the professor[1]

Wow! It's hard not to exclaim, that's some syllabus: European, Russian, and American classics mixed with some Christian legend material (St. Michael), Chinese philosophy (Confucius), perhaps an American musical (*Porgy and Bess*), art from Hawaii (Coco Joe), the religion of the Zulu people (John Zulu), and the basis of modern natural science (Einstein). In addition, there is Herold's own book, which is immodestly presented as a continuation of all the foregoing. And there are only two weeks to the exam! Professor Herold does not reappear in *Tarantula*, and we do not hear anything about how the students did at the exam.

Herold's syllabus looks like both a countermove to and a parody of a college syllabus. The objective is clear: to read, understand and be able to

---

[1] Bob Dylan, *Tarantula* (London: MacGibbon & Kee, 1971), p. 126.

write about the offered material, and yes indeed, there will be plenty of use for an eraser when all of this is to be put to paper and organized for the exam. Dylan can't resist making fun of the self-important teacher, whose book naturally continues where all the wisdom of the world has left off, and it's likely that the students will do better by repeating the professor's own words of wisdom rather than those of Freud, Confucius, and Tolstoy. But there is a built-in criticism in Herold's syllabus: it is not some Harold Bloomian *The Western Canon*. It is a collection of texts from various parts of the globe and several continents and perhaps also an outline of the broad orientation in all kinds of writing and thought that Dylan's own opus displays. He does not keep within a narrow canon, but instead makes liberal use of texts and sources from widely differing cultures and traditions. *Tarantula* indeed shows the complexity of the textural and cultural world through which Dylan effortlessly moves. Professor Herold's exhortation can perhaps also be the author's hip advice to his readers to pull their socks up and reach the same level as the books they are in the process of reading. And that makes considerable demands, for it is not only Herold's canon that files past. The Danish philosopher Søren Kierkegaard, the British crime writer Arthur Conan Doyle, the American Beat generation, and the master himself, William Shakespeare, along with itinerant Indian poets and impenetrable pseudonyms are all on the reading list in *Tarantula*. Everything is the further spiced up with popular culture, advertising language, fairy tales, jokes, and the mention of known and unknown musicians to constitute a whole panoramic landscape of art and language.

It feels as if all the literatures in the world are in *Tarantula* – and in Dylan's work more generally. The feeling for literary classics is particularly in evidence in the period after his breakaway from the folk music environment in 1965 and it leaves many subsequent traces. In Dylan's songs there are references to Eliot and Ezra Pound, seen in fights in "Desolation Row" (1965), to F. Scott Fitzgerald, whose books have been trawled through by Mr. Jones in "Ballad of a Thin Man" (1965), to Shakespeare, who appears dressed in pointed shoes in "Stuck inside of Mobile with the Memphis Blues Again" (1966), to the old Italian maestro Dante, whose poems are handed over to the singer by his beloved in "Tangled Up in Blue" (1975), to the French poets Rimbaud and Verlaine, who the singer compares his lovelife to in "You're Gonna Make Me Lonesome When You Go" (1975), and to Erica Jong, who the singer is asked about in "Highlands" (1997) – to name just a few of the best-known and direct references. In addition, there are a lot of indirect references and allusions that Dylan has embedded everywhere in his considerable opus.

Recent studies have shown Dylan's use of the writings from the classical world, and his references to Ovid, Homer, and Virgil have been mapped.[2] "Working Man's Blues #2" (2006) is a thought-provoking example of how lines from a new translation of Virgil become transformed and embedded into Dylan's blues about the American proletariat. The Roman poet's plaintive verse is simply included in Dylan's late lyrics as images that are attached to the depiction of desolation in the songs.[3] Furthermore, the Bible is an inexhaustible source for Dylan, and references to it become a linguistic structure and sounding board that reaches across his career.

Dylan himself credits the reading of his school years for his wide literary horizon. In the speech he gave in 2017 in connection with receiving the Nobel Prize, he said the following about himself as a young artist:

> I had principles and sensibilities and an informed view of the world. And I had had that for a while. Learned it all in grammar school. *Don Quixote*, *Ivanhoe*, *Robinson Crusoe*, *Gulliver's Travels*, *Tale of Two Cities*, all the rest – typical grammar school reading that gave you a way of looking at life, an understanding of human nature, and a standard to measure things by. I took all that with me when I started composing lyrics.[4]

The syllabus that Dylan lists in his speech appears comparable with that of Professor Herold, and we might imagine that Dylan as a schoolboy was exposed to excerpts from many classic works or eagerly devoured them in his spare time. But the story says nothing more about this. It has, however, been pointed out that Dylan, when working on his Nobel Lecture had made use of SparkNotes, a popular aid for students who want a quick overview of the characters, plot, and main themes in the works.[5] The story of Dylan's use of SparkNotes became an amusing detail of the events surrounding his reception of the Nobel Prize, a detail that took the edge off the self-importance of the institution and the situation by showing that even a Nobel Prize winner can need pedagogical assistance.

So, Dylan's literary horizon includes a whole series of classics with which he is extremely familiar, but he is also a reader of contemporary literature who uses it as a source of inspiration. The Japanese writer Junichi Saga, for example, discovered that Dylan had borrowed lines from his novel

[2] Richard Thomas, *Why Bob Dylan Matters* (New York: Harper Collins, 2017), pp. 227–267.

[3] H. Detering, "Stemmerne fra Limbo: Bob Dylans sene Song Poetry," in *Hvor Dejlige Havfruer Synger*, ed. A.M. Mai (Odense: University Press of Southern Denmark, 2013), pp. 75–99.

[4] Bob Dylan, *The Nobel Lecture* (New York: Simon & Schuster, 2017), pp. 5–6.

[5] Andrea Pitzer, "The Freewheelin' Bob Dylan. Did the singer-songwriter take portions of his Nobel lecture from SparkNotes?," *Slate*, June 13, 2017, https://slate.com/culture/2017/06/did-bob-dylan-take-from-sparknotes-for-his-nobel-lecture.html.

Confessions of a Yakuza (1991, translations by John Bester). The Japanese author felt honored rather than offended. Lines from Saga's novel occur on the album *"Love and Theft"*, the title of which has been placed in inverted commas because it is also a loan, from the historian Eric Lott's *Love & Theft: Blackface Minstrelsy and the American Working Class* (1993). Dylan's *"Love and Theft"* album is first and foremost a so-called "root rock" release that works with the roots of American music, particularly the musical and cultural tradition of the Southern states, but it also engages with various sources and the world-literary feeling that characterizes Dylan's universe.

So, there are various things to take into consideration when one wishes to describe Dylan's relation to world literature and his own position in a world-literary context, but in order to illustrate them, it is first necessary to take a closer look at the actual concept of world literature.

What is World Literature?

As early as the 1820s, the German writer Goethe had the idea that a modern world literature would replace the boundaries between national literatures, creating a new intellectual and cultural exchange between nations. The epoch of world literature is at hand, and everybody must strive to hasten its approach, Goethe declared.[6] Karl Marx and Friedrich Engels discussed the concept of world literature, which they saw as a result of a new capitalist order. While Goethe stressed the intellectual possibilities inherent in greater international exchange, Marx and Engels were more interested in the development of the business aspects of a world market.[7] At the end of the nineteenth century, the Danish literary figure Georg Brandes was concerned with the quality of the works that would be able to make an impact on an international literary market, since the authors who write in the languages that many people understand will have a better chance than other writers to gain worldwide recognition.[8] To Brandes's way of thinking, the concept of world literature has a fourfold significance: first, it can refer to the truly important works from various national literatures; second, to an increasing exchange between writers across nations and languages; third, to the emergence of authors that spring from many different cultural environments and do not have a national anchorage; and fourth, the

---

[6] J.W. Goethe, "Conversations with Eckermann on Weltliteratur," in *World Literature in Theory*, ed. David Damrosch (1827; London: Wiley Blackwell, 2014), pp. 15–22.

[7] Mads Thomsen, *Mapping World Literature. International Canonization and Transnational Literatures* (New York: Continuum, 2008), p. 13.

[8] George Brandes, "Verdenslitteratur," in *Samlede Værker* (København, 1902), pp. 23–28.

concept can also refer to the literature that can be distributed and sold worldwide with financial gain for the publishing and media companies.

The American literary scholar David Damrosch regards world literature as "literary works that circulate beyond their culture of origin, either in translation or in their original language."[9] He emphasizes that world literature also means that the work has readers and thereby an effective life for a global audience. In this view, world literature can be seen in three ways: an established body of classics, an evolving canon of masterpieces, or multiple windows on the world. The French literary scholar Pascale Casanova points more specifically to the Nobel Prize as an example of an institution that expresses and mediates world literature. The Nobel institution reaches out to a post-national present where literary innovation is often linked to politically and economically less noticed corners of the world, such as the Ireland of Samuel Beckett or Henrik Ibsen's Norway.[10] Casanova puts her trust in the Nobel Prize system as an indicator for a world literary space, but one can also claim that the institution has displayed a certain inertia when it comes to perceiving and rewarding new departures and changes among the world's authors, especially the extensive upheavals and changes of the writing of the 1950s and 1960s, of which Bob Dylan is a part. Neither Allen Ginsberg nor John Ashbery, for example, received the prize.

Signals of a recognition of a new change and openness in the institution with regard to literary genres was the awarding of the Nobel Prize to the Italian actor, producer, performer, and writer Dario Fo in 1997, and to the Russian documentarist Svetlana Alexievich, who received the prize in 2015 for works that blend journalism and literature in portrayals of people in the fallen Soviet Union – and finally to Bob Dylan in 2016. The Nobel Committee had at long last started to recognize art that moves across the well-known genre borders and, for example, unites musical expression, performance, documentary, and word-painting.

With folk music and ballads as his springboard, Dylan continues and develops an old tradition that cuts across national borders and cultures. Since the Middle Ages, ballads have circulated among bearers of tradition who traveled from country to country in Europe, although some of the motifs also have Indian and Buddhist sources.[11] Dylan made use of the Scottish ballad tradition in, for example, one of his best-known songs,

[9] David Damrosch, *What is World Literature?* (Princeton: Princeton University Press, 2003), p. 4.
[10] Pascale Casanova, "Literature of a World," *New Left Review* 31 (2005), pp. 71–90.
[11] Sigurd Kværndrup, *Den østnordiske ballade – oral teori og tekstanalyse* (Copenhagen: Museum Tusculanum, 2006), p. 363.

"Hard Rain's A-Gonna Fall," which is a variation on the ballad "Lord Randall." This tradition has been passed on to a number of other countries in Europe and later to the USA, and it is part of a ramified network of popular writing.[12] Dylan is thus a bearer of tradition in the popular verse and folk music sense, where the singer varies or improvises on the handed-down material. Dylan, however, is especially important, because he unites experimental romantic and modernistic traditions with the European ballad and American folk music.

Horace Engdahl, a member of the Swedish Academy, emphasized that it is precisely such a combination that produces the major turns in the world of literature:

> What brings about the great shifts in the world of literature? Often it is when someone seizes upon a simple, overlooked form, discounted as art in the higher sense, and makes it mutate.[13]

Dylan's opus is thus world literature in Damrosch's sense and a window on the world in Georg Brandes's sense since it derives from various cultural environments and does not have a single national anchorage. In Engdahl's sense, it changes prevailing ideas about literature.

Dylan's opus can of course also be seen as a contribution to the Nobel Prize's treasure trove of significant works from many countries and to the worldwide book-selling industry, the present dimensions of which neither Marx nor Engels could have imagined. Dylan's *Lyrics 1962–2012* is a global bestseller, as is his *Chronicles Volume One* (2004), and everywhere Dylan's books and lyrics are translated into national languages. The songs have, for example, appeared in a Norwegian version and even been adapted to include local references by Jan Erik Vold. "Maggie's Farm" from Dylan's album *Bringing It All Back Home* (1965), for example, becomes a hotel named after the old national naval hero Peter Tordenskjold![14]

Most significantly, Dylan's work can now be regarded as part of world literature because it contributes to the creation of an ongoing remapping of the world through literature and writing. As Pheng Cheah emphasizes, such work is sensitive to the fact that globalization can mean that people have their own world of political and economic leaders taken away from them.[15]

---

[12] F.G. Andersen, "Boots of Spanish Leather," in *Hvor Dejlige Havfruer Synger*, ed. Mai, pp. 33–59.

[13] Horace Engdahl, Banquet Speech (2016), www.nobelprize.org/prizes/literature/2016/ceremony-speech/.

[14] Jan Erik Vold, *Damer i Regn* (Oslo: Cappelen Damm, 2014), p. 45.

[15] Pheng Cheah, "World against Globe: Toward a Normative Conception of World Literature," *New Literary History*, 45 (2014), p. 326.

This brings us to one of the key themes of Dylan's songs, most recently expressed in "Early Roman Kings" from *Tempest* (2012), which portrays powerful criminals from various ages and cultures. The title expression refers to the Roman kings, predecessors of the Roman Republic and the Roman Empire, to a gang of criminals in New York in the 1970s, to the Sicilian mafia, to the colonial powers of the nineteenth century, and to cynical businessmen who wheel and deal with human lives in the present. Yet at the same time, another voice exists in the lyrics that directly contradicts the Roman kings and global criminals of all ages, the voice of the music itself. The song contains references to Homer's *Odyssey*, to folk music, to biblical expressions, everyday expressions, and erotic slang. It is Odysseus, Christ, the folk musician, and the poet, in other words, who contradict the global rulers – both now and across a vast temporal and global span.

Dylan's Mapping of World Literature

Dylan's narrative in *Chronicles* moves back and forth between various times and places – from the New York of the early 1960s back into the Duluth and Hibbing of the 1940s and 1950s, to life on tour in Europe, family life around the USA, a recording venue in New Orleans and back to New York. The book is not simply a texture of times and places, but also a texture of artists, musicians, and writers who are important to Dylan. At the end of the book, he lists his heroes from the North Country and they contain a motley company of the writers Scott Fitzgerald and Sinclair Lewis, the rock musician Eddie Cochran, the baseball star Roger Maris, and the man who flew the Atlantic, Charles Lindbergh. Back home, he did not hear all that much about these celebrities, but he did get to hear about them, and he concludes his book by stating that he shares their fidelity to their visions. He feels that he is one of them and all of them at one and the same time. He has an anchorage in a home area, the North Country, and its heroes, but his mental map is also full of lines that extend far beyond the North Country and the American continent. As an artist he is always on the road and interested in widely differing artists and forms of art. One can see this among other things in his accounts of how he gets immediately hooked by songs of Woody Guthrie and Bertolt Brecht, especially "Pirate Jenny's Song" from *The Threepenny Opera*. Here he speaks of an attunement to two works of art that become milestones for him. In both instances, his reaction is physical and dizzying.

He compares listening to Guthrie to experiencing an anchor plunged into the water, an experience reminiscent of his portrayal of the great ships in his childhood port of Duluth. Dylan feels dizzy and entranced and characterizes Guthrie as poetic, sharp, and rhythmic, with songs that have a sweep of humanity about them. As with Guthrie's songs, Dylan's reaction to Brecht's "Pirate Jenny's Song" is physical: he feels that the sentences are falling from a height of four meters, striking him on the chin. He sits there stunned and gasps for air. While Guthrie, according to Dylan, represents a humanistic popular tradition, Brecht stands for a modernistic, cabaret-inspired, jazzy way of singing that is stripped of all humanism. "Pirate Jenny's Song" is a wild, cruel song that deals with revenge, but Dylan feels at home with both songwriters.

The stories of his attunements bear witness to his open, receptive approach to literature from widely differing contexts. Dylan's narrative of his own history as an artist and of his work is full of a feeling for world literature and represents a mapping of the world through literature. This feeling is clearly based on his own curiosity and receptiveness, on the prior assets he gained from his school years, and on the opportunities to travel and tour at a global level that are part of his history.

Traveling the World

Dylan's Nobel Lecture is a well-considered testimony to his literary inspirations and fascinations, and, as is usual with Dylan, the listener is given a journey through time and space: from nineteenth-century American literature to modern Europe and the Greece of Antiquity. He begins by explaining that the awarding of the Nobel Prize caused him to ask himself how his songs link up with literature. But he does not begin his lecture in literature; instead, he starts in the song tradition of Buddy Holly, whom he listened to as a young man in Hibbing in 1959, shortly before he set out for New York, and shortly before Holly himself died in a plane crash. Something strange happens at the concert: Dylan gains eye contact with Holly and feels that something is being transmitted to him, and shortly afterwards he is handed a record of folk and blues musician Leadbelly's "Cottonfields." These two things change his world: he had been wandering around in the dark, but suddenly, almost explosively, a light has been lit. The two experiences have to do with inspiration, initiation, and illumination. There is an echo in the description, for example, of Percy Bysshe Shelley's characterization of poetry as "a sword of lightning."[16] Later, Dylan also mentions another Romantic metaphor for poetry – the wind,

---

[16] P.B. Shelley : "A Defence of Poetry," in *Selected Poetry and Prose Works of Shelley*, ed. B. Woodcock (London: Wordsworth Poetry Library, 2002), p. 645.

or the breath of the muse on the lyre. But at the beginning of the lecture he touches on the metaphors of light and fire.

Buddy Holly's particular quality as an artist is that he collects and uses a number of different genres: country and western, rock 'n' roll, and R&B merge, according to Dylan, into one mode of expression – one brand. Dylan starts by making it clear that it is precisely this musical poetics he himself later follows and develops. Subsequently, he declares that these are not his only sources of inspiration: there are also a whole series of literary works that he read at school, themes of which he has consciously or unconsciously incorporated into his songs.

The three literary works that Dylan examines differ from each other, but there are also aspects that unite them. *Moby Dick* is a novel about a whale-hunter in search of a great white whale in all the oceans of the world; *All Quiet on the Western Front* is a realistic description of life on the Front during the First World War; and Homer's *Odyssey* is the epic poem of Antiquity about the ten-year return journey of Odysseus from Troy to Ithaca after the Trojan War. The works all take place on a world stage. Melville's Captain Ahab, for example, criss-crosses the world's oceans, with a crew that comes from widely differing parts of the world and brings with them myths and adventures of their own. Remarque's novel has to do with the First World War and the young generation that lost all its illusions in the trenches. *The Odyssey* takes place in localities in and around the Mediterranean, which to the Greeks of Antiquity was the world sea. The main characters of the works all lose their direction toward home in the vast global arenas in which they find themselves.

Ahab is first and foremost intent on getting revenge on the white whale that devoured his leg; Remarque's young soldiers can go home on leave but are soon forced to return to the trenches and the no-man's-land between them; Odysseus' return journey is disturbed and delayed by the sea god Poseidon, and a number of gods and mythical figures get mixed up in his story. Dylan focuses on the travelers – both real and imagined – in all these adventures and each of them reveals an aspect of what literature is able to do: it can be adventurous and exciting, or it can be sensually realistic in an almost cruel way, as when Remarque gives the reader an experience of the universe of the trenches. Further, it can be narrative that moves between mythical and real localities, as in *The Odyssey*. Motifs of war and revenge are part of the works, giving the reader a feeling of the vastness, danger, and horror of the world. Dylan's preferred works, in other words, have been written by authors with a global awareness and they survey what is ugly and inhuman by looking it straight in the face.

With his preferred choice, Dylan stays within a Western canon, but he chooses books that look beyond an American and a Western culture and tradition. Melville's novel is the first modern American novel, but it is a global text, just as *The Odyssey* is the first European epic and a source of inspiration for all sorts of writers. Remarque deconstructs all heroizing of war – he was German, but he was also an international pacifist who gave all the soldiers of the First World War a voice. His novel was burnt by the Nazis, and he had to experience his sister being executed by them in 1943, after he himself had escaped to USA.

At the end of his Nobel Lecture, Dylan returns to the question of the relation between his songs and literature. He says that they are unlike literature because they are to be listened to, just as Shakespeare's plays are to be seen performed on stage. His argument is finely drawn. Is he suddenly trying to distance himself from literature? He is on the verge of doing so, but never quite makes the leap since he ends with Homer, " who says, 'Sing in me, oh Muse, and through me tell the story.'"[17] Songs naturally have to be sung, and Homer's work consists of songs, even though today his work is almost always only ever read. The concluding quotation from Homer, furthermore, refers back to Dylan's Romantic poetics. Shelley wrote about the lightning strike of poetry, but he also wrote under the inspiration of Homer's poetry as a breath of the spirit that plays on the writer as if on a lyre. Dylan's point is not a historical or theoretical one in terms of literature. First and foremost, he wishes to underscore the participation of art in a living world where songs and works both past and present are in use. The works that Dylan has chosen for the speech are, like his own writing, always "on the road" – they are read around the globe, have been translated into innumerable languages, and circulate around the world. They belong, as Dylan says, to "the land of the living" since they are discussed, interpreted, and performed and they also inspire other genres and art forms. Melville's, Remarque's, and Homer's works too have all given rise to films and plays and inspired the visual arts.

Bob Dylan belongs to a generation that grew up during and immediately after the Second World War. The world opened up for these young people and Dylan's own world trip started in 1959, when he left Minneapolis. Initially, he shrouded his journey in myths and adventures, becoming a latter-day Odysseus, but he later shared the harsh and realistic details of his personal history with his readers in *Chronicles*. In the Nobel Lecture,

---

[17] Dylan, *The Nobel Lecture*, p. 23.

Dylan mentions that he had a spiritual luggage of principles and sensibilities with him, and he gives literature the credit for it.

The Nobel Lecture is thus also a tribute to the formative task of education. The "Professor Herold" of reality has not lived in vain and has clearly been more inspiring than that of *Tarantula*. Many young middle-class people from the generation to which Dylan belongs gained completely new opportunities – both educationally and socially – compared with their parents and grandparents. World literature came within reach for a growing audience. Even now, Dylan helps to change the world literature in which he has learnt to move. His songs quickly become accessible to a worldwide audience that has both purchasing power and, especially by virtue of Dylan's songs, a completely new awareness of itself as a generation. What Goethe says about world literature – that it provides its age with an artistic expression, an artistic form – also applies to Dylan. Although the institutional and technological frameworks around art and literature have undergone enormous change in the last five decades, he helps restore the old, Orphic roots to popular music, while at the same time linking it to experimental literature. To understand the richness of this history and its promise, various Professor Herolds will continue to play their parts.

CHAPTER 14

The Beats

Steven Belletto

In 1983, pioneering scholar Ann Charters oversaw the publication of *The Beats: Literary Bohemians in Postwar America*, a two-volume collection of entries on more than sixty figures associated with the movement. Released roughly a quarter century after groundbreaking work like Allen Ginsberg's *Howl and Other Poems* (1956) and Jack Kerouac's *On the Road* (1957), this project staked a claim for the ongoing relevance of the Beats by presenting them not as a small clique of writer-friends, but as a more far-reaching literary movement and cultural phenomenon. In the spirit of such capaciousness, Charters brought Bob Dylan into the Beat fold, and contributing scholar Joseph Wenke argued that the songwriter merited inclusion because he shared Beat "attitudes toward social authority, politics, and drugs, emphasizing the primacy of the self and rejecting institutionally prescribed norms. . . . the style of Dylan's most characteristic lyrics unmistakably reveals that Beat poetry was a strong influence on him as he developed into the most provocative and imaginative lyricist of his generation."[1] This two-pronged notion, that Dylan shared both social "attitudes" with the Beats and that his work bears the marks of their formal techniques and thematic preoccupations, has been a starting point for those who have thought about him in a Beat context.[2]

Dylan's presence in *The Beats* represented a key critical recognition of his connection to the slightly older generation of literary iconoclasts, and Charters doubled down on this link again a decade later when she assembled

[1] Joseph Wenke, "Bob Dylan," in *The Beats: Literary Bohemians in Postwar America*, Vol 1., ed. Ann Charters (Detroit: Gale, 1983), p. 181.

[2] For useful discussions of Dylan's relationship with the Beats, see Sean Wilentz, *Bob Dylan in America* (New York: Anchor, 2011), particularly the chapter "Penetrating the Aether: The Beat Generation and Allen Ginsberg's America," pp. 47–86; Simon Warner, *Text and Drugs and Rock 'n' Roll: The Beats and Rock Culture* (New York: Bloomsbury, 2015), particularly "Chains of Flashing Memories: Bob Dylan and the Beats, 1959–1975," pp. 107–133; and Michael Goldberg, "Bob Dylan's Beat Visions (Sonic Poetry)," in *Kerouac on Record: A Literary Soundtrack*, ed. Simon Warner and Jim Sampas (New York: Bloomsbury, 2018), pp. 123–147.

The Portable Beat Reader (1992), a canon-making anthology showcasing what she took to be the movement's most significant texts and figures. She thought it essential to present Dylan among Beat "Fellow Travelers," a choice justified by the lyrics of "Blowin' in the Wind," "The Times They Are A-Changin'," "A Hard Rain's A-Gonna Fall," as well as brief excerpts from *Tarantula* (1971), Dylan's surreal, collage-like prose poem.

These selections might make intuitive sense to those familiar with Beat writing and Dylan's music, particularly his first seven albums, up through *Blonde on Blonde* (1966). Although Dylan is of course infamous for changing his styles and approaches, sometimes radically so, one through-line in the early to mid-1960s is an infusion and adaption of Beat themes, aesthetics, and techniques. Inasmuch as the Beat sensibility was always shifting and mutating, Dylan adapted the older writers' social postures and attitudes toward literary tradition to help him forge his own idiosyncratic vision. As Sean Wilentz has remarked, "Dylan's involvement with the writings of Kerouac, Ginsberg, Burroughs, and the rest of the Beat generation is nearly as essential to Dylan's biography as his immersion in rock and roll, rhythm and blues, and then Woody Guthrie."[3]

This involvement began as a teenager in Minnesota when Dylan read writers like Kerouac, Ginsberg, William S. Burroughs, and Gregory Corso, the four most well-known Beat figures. In *Chronicles*, Dylan credits his move to New York City as inspired at least in part by the Beats, noting that: "I suppose what I was looking for was what I read about in *On the Road* – looking for the great city, looking for the speed, the sound of it, looking for what Allen Ginsberg had called the 'hydrogen jukebox world.'"[4] The phrase "hydrogen jukebox" appears in Ginsberg's "Howl," but Dylan creatively misquotes it by appending "world," a move that suggests how the phrase, a kind of evocative encapsulation of the technologized doom underwritten by mainstream culture, opened new horizons for him as he embarked on his songwriting career.

These horizons stretched back to 1943 and 1944, when a small group of friends in and around Columbia University dubbed themselves the "libertine circle" and began exploring art and literature.[5] This circle included Columbia undergraduates Ginsberg and Lucien Carr, former Columbia student Kerouac, and the older Burroughs. Although they wrote piles of manuscripts and began publishing some work in the early 1950s, the Beats

---

[3] Wilentz, *Dylan in America*, p. 50.

[4] Bob Dylan, *Chronicles: Vol. 1* (New York: Simon & Schuster, 2004), p. 235.

[5] For a more detailed history of the Beat literary movement, see Steven Belletto, *The Beats: A Literary History* (New York: Cambridge University Press, 2020).

didn't break into national consciousness until 1957, after City Lights Books in San Francisco released Ginsberg's *Howl and Other Poems*. The book was subject to a well-publicized obscenity trial, which did what all such trials ironically do: direct far more attention to the book than it would have otherwise had, and the title poem came to be seen as a nightmare reflection of the experiences of a younger generation who did not view conformity or consensus as positive values. When *On the Road* was published in September 1957, it was seen as the testament of a "generation"; the *New York Times*, for instance, famously heralded the novel as "the most important utterance yet made by the generation Kerouac himself named years ago as 'beat,' and whose principal avatar he is."[6] In other words, Kerouac was deemed significant not merely for his novel as such, but because he was seen as the very embodiment of a more widespread social phenomenon, the rise of rebellious youth culture. The teenaged Dylan was thus hardly alone in considering *On the Road* "like a bible," as he put it – and yet in just five or six years, the American cultural landscape would be so altered that it was Dylan who would be seen as the voice of his generation, a correspondence that is an important way the Beats and Dylan are linked: they all had to negotiate tensions between what they wanted to produce artistically, and what the public or media thought they ought to be producing.[7] As Dylan wrote in *Chronicles*, "As far as I knew, I didn't belong to anybody then or now ... but the big bugs in the press kept promoting me as the mouthpiece, spokesman, or even conscience of a generation. . . . I had very little in common with and knew even less about a generation that I was supposed to be the voice of."[8]

When he arrived in Greenwich Village in 1961, Dylan encountered a physical and psychic space that had been the province of the Beats since the 1940s, the "underground" where they had incubated their literary revolution. Although Ginsberg, Kerouac, and Burroughs were not living in New York at the time, many other writers were, and the Village was still a hub of underground energy. Among its many clubs were old Beat haunts such as the Gaslight Café, where the likes of Ray Bremser and Diane di Prima had read their poetry before they were countercultural stars, and Café Bizarre, where tourists flocked to see beatniks in their supposedly natural habitat. I'm using the word "beatnik" purposively here and want to remind readers that it is distinct from "beat": the term was generally used derogatorily to mean something like a bongo-playing marijuana enthusiast

---

[6] Gilbert Millstein, "Books of the Times" (review of *On the Road*), *New York Times*, September 5, 1957.
[7] Dylan, *Chronicles*, p. 57.   [8] Ibid, p. 115.

who had dropped out of respectable society – not a Beat writer but a cultural caricature of one. But by the early 1960s, the word had become a catch-all, naming anyone with a whiff of non-conformity about him. This is why when Robert Shelton wrote his famous review of an early Dylan performance at Gerde's Folk City in 1961, he not only proclaimed Dylan a "distinctive folk-song stylist," but also noted that he looked like "a cross between a choir boy and a beatnik."[9]

Shelton had put his finger on an ethos Dylan shared with the Beats that went far beyond his perhaps too-shabby looks. The performer began his climb to fame in places notable for their association with the Beats, particularly the Gaslight Café, whose owner, John Mitchell, had capitalized on Beat mania in the late 1950s by self-publishing *Poetry of the Beat Generation: As Read in the Gaslight*, a volume featuring well-known hip writers like Ginsberg, Ted Joans, and Jack Micheline, as well as a host of local Village characters.[10] In 1959, newsman Charles Kuralt ventured into the Village for a story on coffeehouse culture and singled out the Gaslight as an epicenter of Beat poetry.[11] Thus if the young Dylan considered the Gaslight to have "more prestige than any place else" in the Village, it was a perception informed by the club's long association with the Beat underground.[12] His debut album, *Bob Dylan*, released in March 1962, included only two original compositions, "Talkin' New York" and "Song to Woody" – while the latter announced his debt to Woody Guthrie, the former writes him into the café culture that in the late 1950s had been most consistently linked to the Beats in popular imagination:

> I landed up on the downtown side
> Greenwich Village
> I walked down there and ended up
> In one of them coffee-houses on the block.

Over the next sixteen months, as he played venues like the Gaslight, Dylan worked on his second album, *The Freewheelin' Bob Dylan*, which featured two of the songs later collected in *The Portable Beat Reader*, lyrics that Charters perhaps included because they connect the social commentary of earlier Beat work such as "Howl" and the more explicitly political

---

[9] Robert Shelton, "Bob Dylan: A Distinctive Folk-Song Stylist," *New York Times*, September 29, 1961.

[10] See *Poetry of the Beat Generation: As Read in the Gaslight*, ed. John Mitchell (New York: John Mitchell, nd; probably 1958 or 1959).

[11] Charles Kuralt, "William Morris at the Gaslight Café," CBS News, June 9, 1959, http://gvh .aphdigital.org/items/show/227

[12] Dylan, *Chronicles*, p. 15.

and purposively topical folk-rock of the mid-1960s and later. "Blowin' in the Wind" is a plea for social equality and human recognition, and its series of questions without answers recalls Ginsberg's poem "America," which also features a series of (more specific) questions: "America when will you end the human war? . . . America when will you be angelic? . . . America when will you send your eggs to India?"[13] Dylan's questions ("how many deaths will it take till he knows / That too many people have died?") are similarly simple yet difficult to answer conclusively. Both sets of questions require imaginative engagement on the part of the reader/listener, and resonate with Kerouac's definition of "Beat" as "a state of beatitude . . . trying to love all life, trying to be utterly sincere with everyone, practicing endurance, kindness, cultivating joy of heart."[14] Although Dylan would quickly move beyond writing protest songs such as "Blowin' in the Wind," it is one of his early signature works and nothing if not an earnest exhortation to "love all life."

"Hard Rain" is generally interpreted as an imagistic response to the horrific possibility of nuclear war. In his discussion of the song, Shelton emphasizes its Beat connections, calling it both a "landmark in topical, folk-based songwriting" and "the promised fruit of the 1950s poetry-jazz fusion of Ginsberg, [Lawrence] Ferlinghetti, and [Kenneth] Rexroth."[15] Shelton is referring to these writers' earlier experiments reading poetry to jazz accompaniment (and sometimes writing poetry for this express purpose), but "Hard Rain" also has some formal affinities with other Beat work such as "Howl," which opens with the speaker asserting that "I saw the best minds of my generation destroyed by madness," and then pulls readers through an underground of dispossessed souls passed over by history and crushed by the weight of social and institutional regimentation.[16] Ginsberg places these "best minds" in specific locations, from the Village bar Fugazzi's to "Paradise Alley" (a shabby tenement on the Lower East Side) to the East River to the "horrors of Third Avenue."[17] The effect is that the figures in Ginsberg's catalogues seem at once mythic and particularized – that is, they both stand for wider generational trauma and seem inspired by real people in the poet's circle. In "Hard Rain,"

[13] Allen Ginsberg, *Howl and Other Poems* (San Francisco: City Lights Books, 1956), p. 39.
[14] Jack Kerouac, "Lamb, No Lion," in *The Portable Jack Kerouac*, ed. Ann Charters (New York: Viking, 1995), pp. 562–563.
[15] Robert Shelton, *No Direction Home: The Life and Music of Bob Dylan*, rev. edn, ed. Elizabeth Thomson and Patrick Humphries (Milwaukee: Backbeat Books, 2011), p. 117.
[16] Ginsberg, *Howl and Other Poems*, p. 9. [17] Ibid, pp. 10, 15.

Dylan adopts Ginsberg's position as witness, echoing the famous opening line of "Howl" when he repeats the phrase "I saw":

> I saw a newborn baby with wild wolves all around it
> I saw a highway of diamonds with nobody on it
> I saw a black branch with blood that kept drippin'
> I saw a room full of men with their hammers a-bleedin'.

But unlike "Howl," Dylan's nightmare world is depicted via surreal images unanchored from particularities of place, so that one doesn't have the sense of a subterranean community united in their abjection, but of a more universal vision of archetypes like babies and wolves, suggesting a distorted dreamscape in which no one, hipster or square, is safe. For Dylan, the existential threat of "hard rain" estranges individuals from one another, so while Ginsberg's "best minds" can include a "lost battalion of platonic conversationalists" who "talked continuously seventy hours from park to pad to bar to Bellevue to museum to Brooklyn Bridge," Dylan's characters have no such connections to others: "I saw ten thousand talkers whose tongues were all broken."[18] "Howl" offers a portrait of an underground "generation" defined in part by its opposition to and difference from dominant culture; "Hard Rain" offers a portrait of an entire world that has been devastated, portending a new epoch in which *everyone* is implicated in the potential destruction of civilization. In this way, Dylan took the Beat vision as articulated in "Howl" and transformed it into a more universal expression that would begin to reverberate more loudly through the anti-war counterculture of the latter 1960s. It may be thus fitting that Ginsberg should claim that when he first heard "Hard Rain," he wept because "it seemed that the torch had been passed to another generation. From earlier bohemian, or Beat illumination."[19]

Ginsberg always had a knack for promoting himself and others, and soon had a direct opportunity to cultivate the notion that Dylan's work represented a torch passing from the Beats to a new generation of socially conscious artists. In December 1963, Al Aronowitz, a journalist who had written a twelve-part feature on the Beats for the *New York Post* back in 1959, took an interest in Dylan and wanted to introduce him to Ginsberg. Aronowitz brought Dylan to a party at the apartment of Ted Wilentz, co-owner of the 8th Street Bookshop and brother of Elias Wilentz, who had edited the seminal anthology *The Beat Scene* (1960). During that meeting, the two discussed poetry and jelled enough that Dylan invited

---

[18] Ibid, p. 11.   [19] *No Direction Home*, dir. Martin Scorsese (Paramount Pictures, 2005).

Ginsberg to Chicago where his next concert was, but Ginsberg demurred, concerned, as he put it later, that he might become Dylan's "mascot."[20] But the two wound up becoming lifelong friends and sometime collaborators; Dylan would advertise their connection to emphasize his underground bona fides while Ginsberg would leverage that same connection to help him transform into an elder statesman of the 1960s counterculture.[21]

At the time of their first meeting in late 1963, Dylan was amidst an extraordinarily creative period: *The Times They Are A-Changin'* was released mere weeks later and he signaled that the album's sensibility is at least partly inherited from the Beats by including poems in lieu of traditional liner notes. One poem, "11 Outlined Epitaphs," namechecked, among other things, the "love songs of Allen Ginsberg / an' jail songs of Ray Bremser," and Dylan seems to take up their mantle by asserting a new social order in the album's title track, which of course has become an anthem and symbol of the momentous social and political upheavals of the 1960s. Like "Hard Rain," "The Times They Are A-Changin'" has a universal, prophetic quality to it, and it proclaims the ascendancy of a new consciousness. This announcement takes on a different tone in "With God on Our Side," an indictment of those who invoke God as a pretext for waging war. The *Times* album also has topical songs arguing for social justice such as "Only a Pawn in Their Game" and "The Lonesome Death of Hattie Carroll." Insofar as they promote ideals of racial equality, these songs are broadly comparable to the Beat social posture. More stylistically evocative are those songs like "Times" that aren't necessarily tied to specific current events, but in their very universality invite listeners to hear themselves in those sons and daughters who feel regimented and misunderstood by their old-fashioned, out of touch elders.

This is likewise the case in "Chimes of Freedom," an important song on *Another Side of Bob Dylan* that continues to explore differing facets of American society by focusing not on youth culture, but on marginal social figures such as the "outcast" and "underdog." The song's basic conceit is to figure thunder as "chimes of freedom" that toll for "the rebel ... the luckless ... the mistreated, mateless mother, the mistitled prostitute ... the misdemeanor outlaw." Dylan's list is a version of Ginsberg's "great minds," a beset underclass who don't seem to have a place in mainstream society, the sorts of figures who populate a wide swath of Beat literature. As

---

[20] Wilentz, *Dylan in America*, pp. 67–69.
[21] On this point, see Richard E. Hishmeh, "Marketing Genius: The Friendship of Allen Ginsberg and Bob Dylan," *Journal of American Culture* 29, no. 4 (December 2006), pp. 395–404.

Tuli Kupferberg put it in 1959: "Since the Beat is outside of society . . . he is sympathetic to, understanding with & seeks the friendship [of] . . . those others also on the outside [including] . . . anyone trapped or crushed by, or fighting the ballbreaking, spirit enervating forces of society."[22] "Chimes of Freedom" is Dylan's assertion of such sympathy: it takes seriously groups of people who tend to be reflexively dismissed or ignored altogether, suggesting that to truly understand freedom, "we" – and the song is narrated in the first person plural – must recognize "the countless confused, accused, misused, strung-out ones."

Bringing It All Back Home, released in March 1965, continued to advertise and remake Dylan's Beat sympathies, especially on the album's cover. On a fireplace mantel behind Dylan is a small volume with a distinctive, bright magenta cover that cognoscenti would have recognized as a little magazine called *GNAOUA*, published out of Morocco and showcasing such Beat luminaries as Burroughs, Ginsberg, Brion Gysin, Michael McClure, and Harold Norse. More obvious are the photographs on the back of the album, which feature, among others, Dylan wearing a top hat and another of Ginsberg wearing the same hat, thus sharing what Sean Wilentz has called "an odd 1960s bohemian crown."[23] Cementing the association, Dylan's poetic liner notes muse: "why allen ginsberg was not chosen t' read poetry at the inauguration boggles my mind."

Many songs on *Bringing It All Back Home* accordingly have a Beat cast, perhaps most palpably "Subterranean Homesick Blues," whose title loudly echoes that of Kerouac's *The Subterraneans*, a novel that recounts a conflicted interracial love affair against the backdrop of the "subterranean hip generation."[24] Both the novel and song share an interest in subterranean hipness, and like Kerouac's characters, Dylan's speaker exists on the social margins, "thinking about the government," and resigned that

> The phone's tapped anyway
> Maggie says that many say
> They must bust in early May
> Orders from the D.A.

As in "Chimes of Freedom," this song thematizes what Kupferberg called the "spirit enervating forces of society." Dylan also includes more direct references to the Beats: when the song advises "Don't wear sandals," it is a nod to the way the caricatured beatnik wore sandals, a notion perpetuated

---

[22] Tuli Kupferberg, *Beating* (New York: Birth Press, 1959), np.
[23] Wilentz, *Dylan in America*, p. 73.
[24] Jack Kerouac, *The Subterraneans* (New York: Grove, 1958), p. 23.

in countless places such as a notorious 1959 *Life* magazine article that characterizes a typical Beat as "a hot-eyed fellow in beard and sandals."[25]

Beyond the shared subject matter, there are also stylistic affinities between *The Subterraneans* and "Subterranean Homesick Blues" that have to do with the use of spontaneity to announce a repudiation of convention. *The Subterraneans* was written in just three days using what Kerouac called his "spontaneous method," a technique that, as he explained, should "Begin not from preconceived idea of what to say about image but from jewel center of interest in subject of image at *moment* of writing, and write outwards swimming in sea of language."[26] In *The Subterraneans*, Kerouac writes according to this principle, which allows him to follow chains of imagistic associations or to pursue the sounds of words without primary concern for their semantic meaning, hence lines like "let's go see friends, things, phones ring, people come and go, coats, hats, statements, bright reports."[27] The primary interest here is in rhythm, which certainly seems to prefigure the staccato punch of "Subterranean Homesick Blues" as it seesaws back and forth through the underground to echo the ways in which its characters are buffeted by institutions like the government or the DA's office. This approach to lyrical expression suggests that Dylan was announcing his own performative spontaneity – a later song on *Bringing*, "Bob Dylan's 115th Dream," even begins with a false start and laughter, with Dylan then restarting. That Dylan let the false start stand underscores the spontaneous, improvised feel of the album, an aesthetic inherited from Kerouac and the Beats. The visual imagery that was subsequently attached to "Subterranean Homesick Blues" again underscored the Beat–Dylan connection. D.A. Pennebaker's *Dont Look Back* (1967), a documentary about Dylan's 1965 tour of Britain, opens with a kind of proto-music video of "Subterranean Homesick Blues" that has Dylan standing in the foreground cycling through cue cards containing the song's lyrics while a heavily bearded Ginsberg chats in the background with Bob Neuwirth. The message is clear: Ginsberg and Dylan are of the same aesthetic circle, but it is now Dylan's moment in the spotlight.

Highway 61 Revisited, the other album Dylan released in 1965, continues the spirit of the great songs on the second half of *Bringing It All Back Home* – "Bob Dylan's 115th Dream," "Gates of Eden," and "It's Alright, Ma (I'm Only Bleeding)" – by, as Timothy Hampton puts it, undamming

---

[25] Paul O'Neil, "The Only Rebellion Around," *Life*, November 30, 1959, p. 116.
[26] Jack Kerouac, "Essentials of Spontaneous Prose," in *Portable Kerouac*, ed. Charters, p. 485.
[27] Ibid, p. 82.

a "flood of generalized vitriol aimed at everything that is 'square.'"[28] This begins with the lead track, "Like a Rolling Stone," which delights in Miss Lonely falling out of bourgeois society and having to contend with the sort of world populated by those "misused, strung-out ones" named in "Chimes of Freedom." Other songs such as "Tombstone Blues" strike at the heart of over-institutionalized and administered society, observing, for instance, that "the National Bank at a profit sells road maps for the soul / To the old folks' home and the college." "Ballad of a Thin Man" features Mr. Jones, Dylan's Everyman whose place in society is contingent on the approval of professors, lawyers, and the like, but who seems to be missing the real point of contemporary experience: "But something is happening and you don't know what it is / Do you, Mr. Jones?" Like the elders in "The Times They Are A-Changin'" who are warned not to level criticism because they "can't understand," Mr. Jones faces an existential crisis because he can never quite figure out what "something is happening." The song never reveals what this "something" is, but that's part of the point, because listeners are invited to fill in the blanks regarding the specifics of that something, thereby participating in an underground community if only in virtue of the fact that they are *not* Mr. Jones.

The album ends with "Desolation Row," a song Shelton argues "belongs beside Eliot's 'The Waste Land' and Ginsberg's 'Howl' as one of the strongest expressions of apocalypse."[29] Although the song does indeed share the epic quality of "Howl," it too borrows part of its title from a Kerouac novel, this time the just-released *Desolation Angels*, and attentive observers have noted the various ways Dylan borrows from that book. For example, Kerouac's description of David D'Angeli, a character modeled on Beat poet Philip Lamantia, includes the phrase "the perfect image of a priest," which is repurposed in "Desolation Row" as "The Phantom of the Opera in a perfect image of a priest."[30] *Desolation Angels* is about, in part, Kerouac's literary circle in 1956 and 1957, right before the "Beat Generation" was about to break into public consciousness; writing retrospectively, he laments that his original vision was already in the process of being diluted and bastardized by poseurs and hangers-on: "Nothing can be more dreary than 'coolness,'" he writes, "postured, actually secretly *rigid* coolness … this was about to sprout out all over America."[31] Dylan references *Desolation Angels* in "Desolation Row" to signal the passing

[28] Timothy Hampton, *Bob Dylan's Poetics: How the Songs Work* (New York: Zone Books, 2019), p. 106.
[29] Shelton, *No Direction Home*, p. 198.
[30] Jack Kerouac, *Desolation Angels* (1965; New York: Perigee Books, 1978), p. 187.   [31] Ibid, p. 321.

of the Beat era. Handsome D'Angeli (he has "perfect features") has been transformed into the deformed Phantom of the Opera – also known as the Angel of Music – who literally lives in subterranean passages and whose very being is defined by his social estrangement. In other words, "Desolation Row" imagines a world in which the promise represented by a character like D'Angeli – or the Beat phenomenon writ large – has remained unfilled, and in its stead linger tragic figures like the Phantom. We are left with a fractured, emotionally stunted dreamscape in which people cannot connect in meaningful ways: "the riot squad . . . [is] restless, they need somewhere to go" and "Everybody's shouting, 'Which side are you on?!'" The song thus does indeed seem to be Dylan's answer to "Howl" insofar as it presents a sweeping vision of social desolation; he even acknowledged this debt in 1969 when he said that Ginsberg had influenced his songwriting during "That period of . . . 'Desolation Row,' that kind of New York type period when all the songs were just 'city songs.'"[32]

Thinking about Dylan in a Beat context sheds a different kind of light on his multifarious, sometimes opaque work, and helps us see it as a part of a social attitude and literary intervention that stretched back to the 1940s. *Tarantula*, Dylan's strange foray into literary publishing, could certainly benefit from being read in the context of Beat aims and aesthetics. The general critical line on the work is that it is off-puttingly obscure, "an enigma wrapped in a question mark."[33] *Tarantula* is far from readily accessible, but its refusal to make sense is a Beat-like comment on the expectations that were being foisted on Dylan when he composed it (throughout 1965 and 1966), a time when he was being touted as the "conscience of a generation."[34] Rather than produce a prophetic generational manifesto, Dylan offered a surreal romp through language that repurposes fragments from his songs and that only seems to hang together in its refusal to hang together, an idea he signals in those moments when he addresses the (bewildered?) reader:

> how come youre
> so afraid of
> things that dont make any
> sense to you?[35]

[32] "Interview with Jann S. Wenner [*Rolling Stone*, November 20, 1969]," in *Bob Dylan: The Essential Interviews*, ed. Jonathan Cott (New York: Wenner Books, 2006), p. 148 [ellipsis in original].

[33] Shelton, *No Direction Home*, p. 166. [34] Dylan, *Chronicles*, p. 115.

[35] Bob Dylan, *Tarantula* (New York: St. Martin's, 1994), p. 39.

Tarantula is enigmatic and difficult to grasp, yes, but those readers "afraid" of its form are akin to the square Mr. Jones who knows "something is happening" but doesn't understand what, and so turns to familiar repositories of knowledge (professors, lawyers) who will never be able to help him. The same is just as true for those readers of *Tarantula* who approach it looking for answers – "unfortunately my friend," Dylan writes, "you shall not get / the information you seek out of me"[36] – as it was for those earlier readers who attempted to apply conventional, academic standards to their evaluations of Beat literature. Instead, Dylan asks us to fundamentally reconsider what we assume a literary work can mean or be, something that his best songs also ask with respect to popular music, a shift in consciousness and perspective that is part of his broad inheritance from the Beats.

[36] Ibid, p. 114.

CHAPTER 15

Theatre

Damian A. Carpenter

Dylan and the Off-Broadway Scene in the Early 1960s

As of 2020, Bob Dylan has performed 3,787 official shows since 1961, the year Robert Shelton hailed Dylan as "a bright new face in folk music" in a *New York Times* review of a show he performed at Gerdes Folk City. Shelton's landmark review gave Dylan a firm boost onto the public stage just eight months after he arrived in New York. Notably, his review describes Dylan's conscious dramatic style: "Mr. Dylan is both comedian and tragedian. Like a vaudeville actor on the rural circuit, he offers a variety of droll musical monologues." These deadpan comedic "monologues" spoken over guitar accompaniment were Dylan compositions in the talking-blues style he picked up from Woody Guthrie. Notably, the key to performances like these is not the singing but the "droll" delivery and timing. "In his serious vein," Shelton continues, "Mr. Dylan seems to be performing in a slow-motion film. Elasticized phrases are drawn out until you think they may snap. He rocks his head and body, closes his eyes in reverie and seems to be groping for a word or a mood, then resolves the tension benevolently by finding the word and the mood." Again, attention to performance style dominates Shelton's description, not just the singing, but also the physical dramatic delivery.[1]

It is instructive to consider the entire page of the *Times* on which the review, the only article present, appeared; occupying center stage in the upper third of the page, it is surrounded on the left, right, and bottom by numerous advertisements for, primarily, theatre shows. As Shelton's review reports, Dylan "has been sopping up influences like a sponge," most likely referring to musical influences.[2] However, the positioning of the article places him on a stage surrounded not just by "the theatre," but pointedly

---

[1] Robert Shelton, "Bob Dylan: A Distinctive Folk-Song Stylist," *New York Times*, September 29, 1961.
[2] Ibid.

significant theatrical influences that Dylan would "sop up," explicitly and implicitly manifesting in his body of work. Bertolt Brecht's *The Threepenny Opera*, in its seventh (and final) year at the Theatre de Lys, is advertised just below Dylan's picture, an auspicious placement considering the impact Brecht had on Dylan a year and a half later. Another Brecht play, *In the Jungle of the Cities*, is also advertised, appearing alongside a play Dylan would recall forty years later in *Chronicles Volume One* (2001), Jack Gelber's *The Connection* at the Living Theatre.

Dylan arrived in Greenwich Village when the Off-Broadway scene was dominated by dramatists who had been recently dubbed by Martin Esslin as practitioners of the "Theatre of the Absurd." Published in 1961, Esslin's book anatomizes the Theatre of Absurd at a watershed moment in which emerging playwrights in the 1960s Off-Broadway scene and their audience, including Dylan, are beginning to engage with its legacy.

By the end of the decade, poet, critic, and playwright Archibald MacLeish would ask Dylan to contribute songs for his play *Scratch* (1971). In *Chronicles*, Dylan comments that the prospect was not all that "far-fetched" for him: "I'd always liked the stage and even more so, the theatre. It seemed like the most supreme craft of all craft. ... the action always took place in the eternal 'now.'"[3] Dylan recalls his "first appearances in a public spectacle" on stage in his high school auditorium, filling extra roles like a Roman soldier in the *Black Hills Passion Play of South Dakota* when it came to town every Christmas.[4] His affinity for theatre did not mean that he would become an accomplished actor in the classic sense. For instance, in December 1962 he flew to England to play a role in a BBC teleplay called *Madhouse on Castle Street*, a foray that did not bode well for an acting career. Dylan "was uncomfortable with learning lines, saying he would rather express himself through song."[5] This resulted in the director hiring another actor to play Dylan's part, leaving the young singer to basically play himself and perform songs during the performance. Nor would he write significant plays, as abandoned play manuscripts circa 1964 seemed to foretell. His collaboration with MacLeish never came off either, although a few songs penned for the project did end up on *New Morning* (1970).

We can look to Dylan's budding relationship with Suze Rotolo, who he met two months before Shelton's review and later credited with inspiring

[3] Bob Dylan, *Chronicles Volume One* (New York: Simon & Schuster, 2004), p. 124.   [4] Ibid, p. 125.
[5] Howard Sounes, *Down the Highway: The Life of Bob Dylan* (New York: Grove Press, 2011), p. 132.

him to "broaden [his] horizons," for his important exposure to the theatre scene surrounding him on the *Times* page.[6] She spent some time working on the production side of Off-Broadway shows, and we know they attended several plays, including Genet's *The Balcony*, Gelber's *The Connection*, Brendan Behan's *The Hostage*, Bertolt Brecht's *Man Is Man* and *Brecht on Brecht* (George Tabori's compilation of Brecht works), Kenneth H. Brown's *The Brig*, Leroi Jones's (Amiri Baraka) *The Dutchman* and *The Baptism*, and Albee's *The American Dream*.

While helpful to have some idea of the theatre Dylan was exposed to during this time it leads us down mostly impressionistic paths to understanding how it contributed to his growth as an artist. For instance, what are we to make of Dylan ambling after Brendan Behan in Greenwich Village one night in early 1962, after Behan had disrupted a performance of his play *The Hostage*, with the hope of speaking to the playwright? Perhaps chasing this shadow leads us to recognizing the "jingle jangle" phrase in Dylan's "Mr. Tambourine Man" echoing Brendan Behan's song "The Auld Triangle" (included in his play *The Quare Fellow*), a song that Dylan would later cover in the 1967 Basement Tapes sessions. Or perhaps we can note the thematic similarities between Behan's *The Hostage* and Dylan's work that explores the absurd hypocrisies of political posturing.

Another instance: Rotolo specifically recalls that she and Dylan were "blown away by the force of" Living Theatre's production of *The Brig*. The play depicts a day in the life of a Marine Corps prison and its "ritual cruelty," as Rotolo describes it.[7] But it is not so much the subject matter that seems most relevant to Dylan's work. Rather, it is the effect of the production, which was central to Living Theatre's absurdist mission. In the spirit of Antonin Artaud's Theatre of Cruelty and Brecht's Epic Theatre, their productions sought to remove the boundary between actor and audience and, according to Living Theatre's co-founder Julien Beck (and Judith Malina), "to reach the audience, to awaken them from their passive slumber, to provoke them into attention, shock them if necessary."[8] According to Rotolo, "the unrelenting verbal assaults of the guards and the general din left the audiences with a feeling of exhaustion and defeat equal to that of the prisoners confined to the brig."[9] A similar "unrelenting verbal assault" affecting both actor and audience becomes a distinctive

---

[6] Dylan, *Chronicles*, p. 268.
[7] Suze Rotolo, *A Freewheelin' Time: A Memoir of Greenwich Village in the Sixties* (New York: Broadway, 2008), p. 206.
[8] Julian Beck, "Storming the Barricades," *The Brig* (New York: Hill and Wang, 1965), p. 21.
[9] Rotolo, *A Freewheelin'*, p. 21.

quality of songs Dylan wrote over the next few years, such as "It's Alright Ma" and "Like a Rolling Stone."

For his part, Dylan credits exposure to Brecht's work as a key factor in his development, commenting that "it might not have dawned on [him] to write" songs like "It's Alright Ma," "Mr. Tambourine Man," "Lonesome Death of Hattie Carroll," "Who Killed Davey Moore," "Only a Pawn in Their Game," and "A Hard Rain's A-Gonna Fall."[10] The last of these songs, included on his second album *The Freewheelin' Bob Dylan* (1963), was written the same month that Living Theatre's 1962 production of Brecht's *Man Is Man* premiered and bears the mark of Brechtian influence. When Widow Begbick, for example, sings "I spoke to many people and listened / Carefully and heard many opinions / And heard many say of many things," we can hear the reply (in spirit and rhythm) of Dylan's speaker in "Hard Rain" to his interlocutor's questions: "Who did you meet?" or "What did hear?"[11] Yet, it was not until the release of *The Times They Are A-Changin'* (1964) that the Brechtian influence became more pronounced, with at least half of the songs being traceable to the German playwright.

Brecht and Dylan's Theatre of the Absurd

On May 17, 1966 at the Manchester Free Trade Hall, Bob Dylan once again found himself on stage in a kind of passion play. Instead of playing a background Roman soldier, this time he was center stage, cast in the role of Judas. An audience member exclaimed, "Judas!" to which Dylan responded, "I don't believe you. You're a liar." He then instructed the band to "Play it fucking loud," and launched into a rousing performance of "Like a Rolling Stone."

By 1966 Dylan's work and performance style had taken a notable turn from the vaudevillian tragic-comic role Shelton highlighted to one that was, at times, confrontational. The performances were more in the spirit of Brecht's Epic Theatre and Artaud's Theatre of Cruelty, precursors, as Esslin argues, of the Theatre of the Absurd. Broadly, these theoretical approaches to drama broke down the barrier between performer and audience and ideally prompted critical (Brecht) and emotional (Artaud) introspection on the part of the audience. For instance, there is Dylan's vehement delivery of "Like a Rolling Stone" in the infamous Manchester

[10] Dylan, *Chronicles*, p. 287.
[11] Bertolt Brecht, *Collected Plays: Two* (London: Bloomsbury, 2015), p. 50.

performance and in a Newcastle performance four days later where he seems to assault both microphone and audience, cupping his hands around his mouth as if shouting into an abyss. Another example from tour footage that year captures the audience telling Dylan to go home before launching into "Ballad of a Thin Man," with the singer gesticulating like an orator after hammering a punishing chord on the piano. Clearly, some of this performance dynamic is a response to the audience, but it also mirrors the general direction his lyrics had taken since the end of 1962.

In an interview during the July 1963 Newport Folk Festival, Dylan commented on the theatrical shift in his craft: "Man, I don't write protest songs, I just react . . . I was influenced by Brecht. Used to be Woody, but not anymore."[12] Later, speaking with his first biographer, Dylan reiterated his early influences: "Brecht was important to me . . . But there were a lot of other things. Like, *The Hostage*. I don't know if it was the play itself, the action on stage, or what, but it really got me."[13] Dylan even began working on his own plays during this period.[14] In a January 1964 letter to *Broadside*, he praises its publication of Brecht lyrics in the previous issue and talks about his interest in theatre:

> I'm wrapped in playwriting
> for the minute, my songs tell only about me an how
> I feel but in the play all the characters tell how
> they feel. . . .
> I think at best you could
> say that the characters will tell in an hour
> what would take me, alone, two weeks t sing about.[15]

He would later note that in writing "Like a Rolling Stone" (sometime around May 1965) he no longer felt the need to work in other mediums, perhaps because he found a way to incorporate a troupe of characters in a song that is like a four-verse play.

Dylan's letter appeared two weeks after the release of *The Times They Are A-Changin'*. Not only does he mention Brecht (and Behan) in the album's sleeve notes, but the album's title song likely owes its name and some of its lines to Tabori's translation of Brecht's "The Song of Moldau": "times are

---

[12] Anthony Scaduto, *Bob Dylan: An Intimate Biography* (New York: Grosset and Dunlap, 1971), p. 149.

[13] Ibid, p. 150.

[14] One surviving fragment (included in James O'Brien's 2012 doctoral dissertation "Bob Dylan's Fugitive Writings: Selected Poetry, Prose, and Playscript 1963–64") echoes a number of the plays listed above, and it shares many similarities with the text of Leroi Jones's *The Dutchman*, which he saw in 1964.

[15] Bob Dylan, "A Letter from Bob Dylan," *Broadside* 38 (1964).

a-changing. The last shall be first. / The last shall be first."[16] Dylan was most likely introduced to this work during a performance of *Brecht on Brecht* about a month before he wrote the song and he comments in *Chronicles* that "my little shack in the universe was about to expand into some glorious cathedral, at least in songwriting terms."[17] Brecht's "Pirate Jenny," in particular, impressed him: "when the performance reached its climactic end the entire audience was stunned . . . I knew why it did, too. The audience was the 'gentlemen' in the song."[18] The song implicitly addresses the audience ("gentlemen") through the persona of Jenny who is disguised as a servant and suffering the abuse and sneers of the "gentlemen." All the while, a pirate ship is approaching the town, and when it arrives she will choose who dies.

Critics have generally concluded that Dylan's "When the Ship Comes In" was a direct result of the song's influence because of the ship imagery and revenge theme. Written about the same time as "The Times They Are A-Changin'," another song that has some of the same spirit of "come-uppance" to it, this seems a plausible connection. Dylan has also claimed that "The Lonesome Death of Hattie Carroll," his ballad (loosely based on facts) about the abuse and murder of a black maid by a Baltimore aristo-crat, was indebted to "Pirate Jenny": "The set pattern to the song I think is based on Brecht, 'The Ship, The Black Freighter.'"[19] Dylan, however, perhaps misremembers, since the likely source is "Concerning the Infanticide, Marie Farrar," another song included in *Brecht on Brecht*, with its refrain at the end of each verse: "And you, I beg you, check your wrath and scorn / For man needs help from every creature born."[20] Dylan's refrain at the end of each verse in "Hattie Carroll" clearly bears a resem-blance: "But you who philosophize disgrace and criticize all fears / Take the rag away from your face / Now ain't the time for your tears." But we should not be so quick to discount some presence of "Pirate Jenny" in the song, especially if we consider Rotolo's recollection of Dylan watching a rehearsal of the play. She singles out the unique impact of the song so memorably sung by Lotte Lenya in *The Threepenny Opera* (in the 1931 film and the Theatre de Lys revival), now being sung by Micki Grant, a black

---

[16] Bertolt Brecht, *Brecht on Brecht*, trans. George Tabori (New York: Samuel French, 1967), p. 95; also of note is that one of the Brecht lyrics *Broadside* published which prompted Dylan's letter comment, "To My Countrymen" (translated by Eric Bentley), contains some lines quite similar in sentiment as the fourth verse of "The Times": "You children that you may all stay alive / Your fathers and your mothers you must awaken."

[17] Dylan, *Chronicles,* p. 272.   [18] Ibid, p. 275.

[19] Bob Dylan, liner notes to *Biograph*, Columbia, 1985.   [20] Brecht, *Brecht on Brecht*, p. 34.

woman, which, Rotolo comments, resulted in the song taking "on another dimension."[21]

While Dylan's Brechtian works were publicly seen to be an extension of the protest songs he had been writing, they take on a new dimension when seen in a theatrical context. As Esther Harcourt argues, reckoning this Brechtian shift is pivotal to understanding how Dylan's work transformed to a more absurdist body of work starting in 1965 with *Bringing It All Back Home*, the cover of which symbolically makes this argument as Dylan stares into the camera and tucked away behind him just to his right is a Lotte Lenya album of Brecht songs.[22] With *Highway 61 Revisited* (1965) and its songs, like "Ballad of a Thin Man" and "Like a Rolling Stone," the symbolic journey from Brecht to the Theatre of the Absurd he was exposed to in the early 1960s theatre is complete. In fact, Esslin's description of Absurdist theatre could equally serve as a description of the album:

> the spectator is confronted with the madness of the human condition, is enabled to see his situation in all its grimness and despair. Stripped of illusions and vaguely felt fears and anxieties, he can face this situation consciously, rather than feeling it vaguely below the surface of euphemisms and optimistic illusions. By seeing his anxieties formulated he can liberate himself from them.[23]

Or, as Dylan sings in "Like a Rolling Stone" after Miss Lonely is stripped of all pretense and illusion: "When you got nothing, you got nothing to lose / You're invisible now, you got no secrets to conceal."

Dylan, Levy, and Shepard

A decade later, Dylan's symbolic dramatic concealment marked a new theatrical development in his craft. Take, for instance, his December 4, 1975 performance in Montreal. Dylan is on stage wearing a mask of white face paint singing "Isis," a narrative about both a marriage and a tomb robbery that had gone terribly awry. Surrounded by his band of gypsies, Dylan dramatically crosses himself at one point with stiff forearms like he is warding off a hex when he recounts burying his dead partner in the ancient tomb. The deed done, he resolves to return to his wife, riding a harmonica

---

[21] Rotolo, *A Freewheelin'*, p. 235.

[22] For an expansive consideration of the Brecht/Dylan relationship, see Esther Harcourt's "Bertolt Brecht and Bob Dylan: Influence and Identity," PhD diss. (Victoria University of Wellington, 2006).

[23] Martin Esslin, *The Theatre of the Absurd* (New York: Penguin, 1991), p. 414.

solo like a demon out of the tomb's darkness into the next verse. The crossed forearms now spread like looming wings of some amorous bird of prey, fingers fluttering as he makes his final approach to Isis waiting in a meadow.

Dylan's stage performance and persona on the 1975 Rolling Thunder Revue tour took on a dramatic dimension that resulted in his most theatrical shows to date. The bright new face in folk music of 1961 was now masked, punctuating his growing mysterious, mythic stature and adding a *commedia dell'arte* flair. Some of this new direction in dramatic style can be attributed to Dylan's fascination with Marcel Carné's film *Les Enfants du Paradis* (1945), set in the early nineteenth-century Parisian theatre scene and featuring a celebrated mime as a lead character. More immediately, however, this direction can be attributed to a collaboration with Jacques Levy. "Isis" was the first of their joint lyrical efforts. Dylan already had a draft of the song when he met with Levy, a Brechtian-styled theatre director, in July 1975, and they soon produced (by Levy's estimation) fourteen songs. Seven of these appeared on *Desire* (1976), making the album not only Dylan's most lyrically collaborative to date, but also, because of Levy's theatre background, one of his most dramatically minded.

Both men commented that their collaboration was so back and forth that it is difficult to say who is responsible for what elements of the songs. But Levy has suggested that one of his overall contributions was to impose a tighter dramatic structure.[24] For instance, Dylan wanted to write a song about the incarcerated boxer Rubin "Hurricane" Carter, but could not decide on the first step. Levy suggested that "a total storytelling mode" should first be established, and the result was that "the beginning of the song is like stage directions, like what you would read in a script: 'Pistol shots ring out in a bar-room night … Here comes the story of the Hurricane.' Boom! Titles."[25] These narratives were more cinematic in nature, lyrical scripts that would be difficult to reproduce on stage, but they could produce powerful theatrical results, as in the case of "Isis."

As Levy comments, "one of the things about [the co-written songs] that's so wonderful is that they give [Dylan] a chance to do some acting."[26]

---

[24] Dylan's previous album, *Blood on the Tracks* (1975), was already trending this way, especially in "Lily, Rosemary and the Jack of Hearts," one of the tightest dramatic narratives Dylan has ever written. Clinton Heylin notes that Levy's influence was retroactive as well, with Levy apparently inspiring Dylan to revise some of his older lyrics to tighten plot structure, as was the case when he revised "Simple Twist of Fate" soon after. Clinton Heylin, *Bob Dylan: Behind the Shades Revisited* (New York: HarperCollins, 2001), pp. 397–398.

[25] Heylin, *Bob Dylan*, p. 398.

[26] Larry Sloman, *On the Road with Bob Dylan* (New York: Three Rivers Press, 2002), p. 14.

And since Levy was the Rolling Thunder Revue stage director, he was in a position to add heightened drama to the cast's performance in general. One theatrical ploy Levy used during many of the shows was designed to play on audience nostalgia for the early 1960s, when Dylan and Joan Baez would sing duets in concert. After Dylan's first set, the circus-styled Rolling Thunder curtain would drop. Fifteen minutes later, Dylan and Baez begin their series of duets from behind the curtain, building an audience fervor to see them. Sam Shepard describes the dramatic unveiling and its effect: "The curtain slowly rises and there they are revealed. Baez and Dylan, like the right and left hand of an American epic. . . . The song they're singing can't even be heard through this thunder of emotion. The singers are doing a pantomime in front of an ocean of applause."[27]

Watching Dylan on stage during the 1975 tour, Shepard mused: "What is this strange, haunted environment he creates on stage, on record, on film, on everything he touches?"[28] A playwright who made his name in the Off-Off-Broadway scene (Levy had already directed two of his plays) around Greenwich Village after arriving in 1963, Shepard was hired to write dramatic scenes to be filmed during the tour. The end result was *Renaldo and Clara*, a four-hour fragmented musical/documentary/fictional narrative broadly revolving around the story of Renaldo (played by Dylan) and two love interests. As Shepard notes in the introduction of his impressionistic account of the tour, his role as scriptwriter "quickly dissolved into the background and was replaced by a much more valuable situation": a chance to observe and participate in the unique experience that was the Rolling Thunder Revue.[29] At the center of it all was the question of Dylan's mythic stage persona, with Shepard sounding like a philosophical detective: "Who is this character anyway?"[30]

In *Angel City* (1976), Shepard appears to be further contemplating the implications of this question and thinking of his tour experience. In the play, a writer named Rabbit, who avoids flying (like Shepard, who took a train to New York to join Dylan's tour) and is described as wearing a "tattered detective's type suit," is hired by Los Angeles filmmakers to fix their script by creating some mysterious element that "trancend[s] the very idea of 'character.'"[31] The play itself is concerned with the concept of character, as indicated by Shepard's note to the actors: "Instead of the idea of a 'whole character' with logical motives behind his behavior which

---

[27] Sam Shepard, *Rolling Thunder Logbook* (New York: Da Capo, 2004), p. 112.   [28] Ibid, p. 145.
[29] Ibid, p. 1.   [30] Ibid, p. 71.
[31] Sam Shepard, *Fool for Love and Other Plays* (New York: Dial Press, 1984), pp. 64, 67.

the actor submerges himself into, he should consider instead a fractured whole with bits and pieces of character flying off the central theme."[32] His further explanation of this concept echoes his observations of Dylan's mythic stage character: "he's mixing many different underlying elements and connecting them through his intuition and sense to make a kind of music or painting in a space without having to feel the need to completely answer intellectually for the character's behavior."[33] Shepard's description could very well serve as an explanation of Dylan's fragmented part in *Renaldo and Clara*, which the songwriter described as "a play-act based on reality. It hopes to transcend that reality and get something out of the ashes which . . . will be more true than reality."[34]

Speaking with Shepard in 1986, the question of character came up again as Dylan was preparing to play the role of an aging rock star past his prime in *Hearts of Fire*. He half-jokingly comments that playing his *Renaldo and Clara* character "really stretched [his] mental capabilities."[35] It also stretched the way the tour and movie audience received his performance, causing a Brechtian alienation effect in which the dramatic qualities of identity are brought to the forefront in an effort to make audiences critically analyze what they may have passively experienced previously. Dylan and Levy had played with this "Brechtian notion" in "Black Diamond Bay" (1976), as Levy comments, "Instead of being inside the story, as you think you are all along, all of a sudden you step out and look at it as an observer."[36]

In 1984, Dylan and Shepard likewise experimented with this effect when they co-wrote their epic ballad "Brownsville Girl" (1986). This song builds around three dramatic layers: 1) the present, which finds the speaker standing in line to see a Gregory Peck movie; 2) the past, as the narrator remembers his adventurous romance; and 3) a fictional story line that makes use of the conventions of the Peck Western, *The Gunfighter*. The story always returns to the speaker center stage, standing in line, while the other two layers of memory and fancy are like, to use Shepard's phrasing, "bits and pieces of character flying off the central theme."[37] Ultimately the narrative serves as a study of the private, public and mythic nexus of character and identity. The result, to echo Dylan, is a picture of the narrator's life that is "more true than reality" because it attends to the

[32] Ibid, pp. 61–62.   [33] Ibid.
[34] John Rockwell, "My Film Is Truer Than Reality," *New York Times*, January 8, 1978.
[35] Bob Dylan, interview with Sam Shepard, Texas State University, Wittliff Collection, 1987.
[36] Sounes, *Down the Highway*, pp. 289–290.   [37] Shepard, *Fool*, p. 62.

multiple identities of selfhood.[38] The narrator is able to step outside of himself and observe, as if part of the audience:

> Something about that movie though, well I just can't get it out of my head
> But I can't remember why I was in it or what part I was supposed to play
> All I remember about it was Gregory Peck and the way people moved
> And a lot of them seemed to be lookin' my way.

Thus, in this central moment (about halfway through the song), the lyrics increasingly include comments of self-evaluation as he critically contends with the many stages upon which his character played, beyond the passive experience of the physical moment.

"My True Home Is on the Stage"

During the 1986 Shepard/Dylan interview that Shepard would re-imagine as a one-act play titled *True Dylan* (aka *A Short Life of Trouble*, 1987), which also plays with the private/public/mythic identity nexus we see in "Brownsville Girl," Dylan says that "my true home is on the stage."[39] For Dylan, who has always respected the "eternal now" of the stage, there is a sense of freedom playing the role of performer. Decades later, he would comment, "The stage is the only place where I'm happy. It's the only place you can be what you want to be. When you're up there and you look at the audience and they look back then you have the feeling of being in a burlesque."[40] Not only is there a freedom to present whatever version of yourself you see fit, but this element of burlesque implies a critical observation of the role as well. And this dramatic boundary space between performer and audience, Shepard surmises during the Rolling Thunder Revue, is where the magic of Dylan's performance manifests:

> The only protected space is up on stage. Dylan says it's the only time he feels alone. When he's up there. When he's free to work his magic. No one can touch him. . . . You see [the audience] staring hard into his white mask, his gray-green eyes, trying to pick at the mystery. Who is he anyway? What's the source of his power? An apparition?[41]

Apparitions also manifest in Conor McPherson's play *Girl from the North Country* (2017), set in Depression-era Duluth and based on Dylan's catalogue of songs. As Ben Brantley observes in his *New York Times* review,

---

[38] Rockwell, "My Film."   [39] Dylan, interview with Sam Shepard.
[40] Bob Dylan, interview with Dave Fanning, *The Irish Times Magazine*, September 29, 2001.
[41] Shepard, *Rolling Thunder*, p. 79.

"What's created, through songs written by Mr. Dylan over half a century, is a climate of feeling, as pervasive and evasive as fog."[42] The characters are themselves ghosts and they step out of the fog, break out of the drama, to offer a commentary on the drama, like a Greek chorus. This kind of break characterizes the consistent way in which Dylan interacted with the theatre throughout his career, from his early attempt at acting in *Madhouse on Castle Street* to his affinity for Brecht, who also made use of songs as an alienating break from the drama, and his collaborations with Levy and Shepard. Far from merely an interesting side note to his growth as an artist, Dylan's interest in the theatre is, in the end, essential to understanding his work as songwriter and performer. After all, astute scholars and admirers of Dylan's craft ought to take heed of his description of theatre as "the most supreme craft of all craft."[43]

---

[42] Ben Brantley, "Fending Off Despair with a Choir," *New York Times*, October 1, 2018.
[43] Dylan, *Chronicles*, p. 124.

CHAPTER 16

Visual Arts: Goya's Kiss

Raphael Falco

In an envelope postmarked 5 Mar 2011, carrying a LOVE stamp, Tony Bennett sent Dylan a card with a note handwritten in brown ink:

> Hi "Bob",
> You are a wonderful painter. If Goya were alive he would kiss your hand. Always paint and thank you.
> "Tony"[1]

It is unclear which painting or exhibition Bennett is responding to in his note. Two exhibitions were open in 2011, although Bennett appears to refer to Dylan's painting in general and not to any current show. That year, *The Brazil Series* was shown at the Statens Museum for Kunst, Copenhagen, and the Gagosian Gallery, New York, exhibited Dylan's somewhat controversial paintings, *The Asia Series*. But there was a good deal more in the prior decade. After a forty-year gap following the publication of *Writings and Drawings*, during which he continued to paint, draw, and sculpt, Dylan's visual art was again publicly available.

Apart from four album covers – *Self Portrait*, *Music from Big Pink*, *Planet Waves*, and *Another Self Portrait* – Dylan didn't exhibit his work until 2007 when an exhibition called *The Drawn Blank Series* was held in Chemnitz, Germany. In 2008, the Halcyon Gallery in London, which currently represents Dylan, featured *The Drawn Blank Series*. As with his music, Dylan the visual artist has been prolific with four shows in London since *The Drawn Blank Series* in 2008: *Bob Dylan on Canvas* (2010), *Mood Swings* (2013), *The Beaten Path* (2016), and *Mondo Scripto* (2017). In New York, the Gagosian Gallery ran *Bob Dylan: The Asian Series* in 2011 and *Revisionist Art* in 2012. The latter was a particularly quirky exhibition that, as represented in the glossy catalogue, reverts to the kind of confrontational revisionism and satirical symbolism of mid-1960s Dylan songs.

---

[1] The Bob Dylan Archive [BDA] Box 42 F04.

Revisionist Art satirizes the pretenses of artistic syncretism while practicing a ludic, syncretic art. The Gagosian's website blurb ingenuously puts
it this way: "Dylan has long been a willful contextualizer of his own source
material. All personas are interchangeable. His diverse musical output
spans a wealth of genres. His Revisionist art provides a glimpse of an
artistic process that is equally maverick and elusive ... [his] visual art is
marked by the same constant drive for renewal that characterizes his
legendary music."[2] A "contextualizer" yes, but Dylan's artistic process in
music is manifestly transparent. Just as he expects his best listeners to
recognize his revisions and imitations of pre-existing music and lyrics, he
also asks the viewers of his art to understand his productions in the context
of a history of artistic expression.

Dylan's development as a visual artist furnishes proof of his relationship
with the past and, at the same time, underscores his engagement with other
media. From the 1974 painting lessons with Norman Raeben and *Writings
and Drawings* (1973) and his colossal artistic investments in the carnival-
esque, both in instigating the Rolling Thunder Revue and in making
Renaldo and Clara, to his exhibitions of painting and sculpture and
drawing in recent years, Dylan's multiple forays into the plastic arts are –
perhaps predictably – an aesthetic curiosity and a drive to challenge norms.
Not all his experiments have gone smoothly. While *Revisionist Art* flew
under the radar, *The Asia Series* attracted considerable attention, becoming
Dylan's most controversial exhibition to date. The show drew a large
crowd of fans less critical of the art than intent on appreciating a new
way to experience the artist. As later became clear, the paintings were in
fact copied from postcards and photographs depicting scenes redolent of
colonial-era East Asia, as Douglas Heselgrave put it, "the dusty postcards
you can still buy on Hong Kong's Hollywood Road of Chinese histories
that never existed."[3] These postcards, as Miwako Tezuka and Adriana Proser
explain, were themselves painted photographs.[4] Therefore, Dylan's paintings of photographs that are themselves paintings provoke new (and largely
overlooked) questions about imitation as an aesthetic practice.

[2] https://gagosian.com/exhibitions/2012/revisionist-art-thirty-works-by-bob-dylan/.
[3] Douglas Heselgrave, "Contents Under Pressure: Bob Dylan's Asia Series," *The Quarterly Journal of
     Roots Music* [Posted], September 30, 2011, https://restlessandreal.blogspot.com/2011/10/contents-
     under-pressure-bob-dylans-asia.html?q=asia+series
[4] Private conversation with Dr. Miwako Tezuka, former Director of the Japan Society, New York, and
     Dr. Adriana Proser, Mr. and Mrs. Quincy Scott Curator of Asian Art, The Walters Art Museum,
     New York. Tezuka notes that Dylan's painting *Mae Ling* is of a woman with a Chinese name dressed
     in ceremonial costume of the Ainu, an indigenous Japanese people.

Predictably, stories in the press brought out the best and the worst of Dylan criticism. Tony Norman summarized the controversy in the *Pittsburgh Post-Gazette*: "'The Asia Series' was originally billed by the gallery as 'firsthand depictions of people, street scenes, architecture and landscape.' From this description, one would assume that . . . the scenes he sketched or photographed while rambling around Asia provided the basis for his paintings."[5] Other reviewers cried foul and waved the plagiarism flag, expanding on a well-worn image of Dylan as imitator, this time focusing on the copying of three photographs by Cartier-Bresson, Leon Busy, and Dmitri Kessel. But the scandal over the photographs and postcards inevitably dovetailed with longstanding charges of plagiarism and theft leveled at Dylan regarding *Chronicles*, "*Love and Theft*," and even "Don't Think Twice" (see Chapter 17). As in his songwriting, Dylan the visual artist has the ambition to challenge the status quo of the *ars technica* with a calculated magpie approach to composition.

In the case of *The Asia Series*, as Heselgrave pointed out, "artists – like musicians – have always taken from life and worked with existing source material as a template to communicate their ideas and emotions."[6] Robert Morgan suggested "that the commercial news media is out of touch with issues of 'quotation' and 'appropriation' in contemporary art – as, for example, made explicit with Pop Art in the '60s – and that Dylan has done this with 'folk songs' since the outset of his career." To Morgan, Dylan's "deployment of photographs is not a criterion for negative judgment." Rather, scandalized critics exposed "how uninformed they are in relation to this widely-accepted practice in art today, including John Baldessari's exhibition at the Metropolitan Museum in New York (2010) and Gerhard Richter's exhibition earlier at MoMA in 2002."[7]

If anything, Dylan was emboldened by the firestorm his *Asia* series unleashed. His *New Orleans* paintings were exhibited in Milan in 2013, and curated by Francesco Bonami, while the National Portrait Gallery in London exhibited twelve "previously unseen and unpublished" pastels in an exhibition called *Bob Dylan: Face Value*. The frontal poses of these portraits forcibly bring to mind the *Self Portrait* album covers, but are somehow less amiable. In an interview for the exhibition catalog, John Elderfield asked whether the out-of-focus quality of the paintings implied something about the subjects. Dylan quickly denied this: "These are

[5] Tony Norman, *Pittsburgh Post-Gazette* (PA), September 30, 2011.
[6] Heselgrave, "Contents Under Pressure."
[7] Robert C. Morgan, "Can Bob Dylan Paint?", *The Brooklyn Rail: Critical Perspectives on Arts, Politics, and Culture*, November 2, 2011, https://brooklynrail.org/2011/11/artseen/can-bob-dylan-paint.

conventional people. One of the men is actually a member of the Sydney Yacht Club."[8] If the paintings seemed blurry, this was the fault of the kinds of pastels he had been using. In addition to quelling Elderfield's interpretive excitement, Dylan turns the conversation from subject matter to technique – a trick he learned early.

The year 2013 was something of an *annus mirabilis* in terms of Dylan's visual art. Along with the New York and Milan shows, the Halcyon Gallery in London exhibited his sculpture. *Mood Swings* reflects, or insists upon, Dylan's familiar recourse to gates and doors in such songs as "Gates of Eden" (1965), "Knockin' on Heaven's Door" (1973), or "Tryin' to Get to Heaven" (1997). The metal sculptures, all of them functioning gates, are made from "found" items: metal bars, florets, railings, wheels, pulleys, hooks, grinders, bicycle chainrings and bicycle chains, cogs, hooks, springs, and other iron fragments (even an old-fashioned steel roller-skate and what could be one of those stolen pump handles). Some of the objects have been deliberately distorted, like the bent wrench in *Untitled IV*. In some of these large gates, which incidentally are built to swing on hinges, Dylan nestles tantalizing musical shapes: a guitar, a prone bass clef, a treble clef. Other shapes suggest his more pseudo-Surrealist lyrics, such as crazy clocks that recall "Farewell Angelina" (1965). It's in these welded frames that we might hear the echo of

> I wait for them to interrupt
> Me drinkin' from my broken cup
> Askin me to open up
> The gate for you
> I want you
> I want you
> I want you so bad
> Honey, I want you.
>
> ("I Want You," 1966)

There is no broken cup, but the impact of twisted emotion and arbitrary fragmentation fills the gates, implying that it is through this sort of concatenation that we all must pass. The starkness of the *Mood Swings* exhibition – all white walls and gray gates – seems to aim at an otherworldly effect: whether it's the white expanse of heaven or the blankness of hell is for you to determine. Further, there is something uncanny about the narrowness of the gates framed in iron 2x2s as a reflection upon Dylan

---

[8] *Bob Dylan: Face Value*, National Portrait Gallery, London, August 24, 2013 to 5 January 2014 (London: National Portrait Gallery Publications, 2013), pp. 16–17.

the poet conforming to the strictures of meter and rhyme. These gates are not performances, of course, but permanent creations, impossible to improvise on: they are, inevitably, examples of "infinity on trial" ("Visions of Johanna," 1966). Yet he seems to give himself an escape hatch in these gates: they might hang statically while on exhibition, but, as gates, they resist the idea of stasis. These sculptures, while consummately decorative, seem determined to retain their functionality, as if infinity were not so much on trial as being asked to wait.

Four years later, in 2017, the Halcyon Gallery displayed *Mondo Scripto*, a fascinating return to line drawing which appears to turn the imitation question inward, on Dylan himself.[9] The show consisted of Dylan's autograph copies of some of his most memorable lyrics – expressly prepared for *Mondo Scripto* – set beside a series of line drawings. Many of the lyrics, however, were actually different from the petrified versions on the recordings, the published lyric collections, or Bobdylan.com. One of the most telling changes in the exhibition is the rewriting of "You're Gonna Make Me Lonesome When You Go" (1974). Tom Piazza supplied the critical blurbs in the exhibition catalogue:

> In their original recorded incarnation, the lyrics to this song are luminous with the sensuality of new love, intoxicated with its immediacy and worried that it won't last. In this almost wholly reimagined version, the poet is looking back at a distance from that love, with an older eye and a cagier relation to love's ups and downs. Dylan even throws in references to English poet John Milton, country music legends the Carter Family, and in the words "footprints in the snow", throws a wink at bluegrass music patriarch Bill Monroe for good measure.[10]

The unexpected allusion to Milton, replacing the usual French suspects, shifts the emphasis of the lines from Verlaine's twisted obsession with Rimbaud to Dylan's identification with a visionary English poet. Coming fast on the heels of his Nobel, this deliberate identification with Milton's "introverted" vision reflects how close to the surface Dylan's literary ambitions are, despite his self-deprecating denials to the contrary.

In fact, what Piazza calls an "almost wholly reimagined version" conveys a material instability. There are crossings-out in four verses, giving the exhibited sheets an impermanent feel. Instead of fair copy, Dylan inexplicably provided his viewers with what could be a notebook page (but isn't), as

---

[9] Halcyon Gallery, Bob Dylan – *Mondo Scripto*, October 9–November 30, www.halcyongallery.com /exhibitions/bob-dylan-mondo-scripto.
[10] *Mondo Scripto* (London: Halcyon Gallery, 2018), p. 227.

if to complicate and elevate the process of composition and throw the notion of a pure original into doubt. In contrast, while the written lyrics indicate fluidity and self-imitation, the line drawing set beside them is particularly static: a shaded country road running through tall trees. It seems fair to wonder what the material connection might be between the handwritten characters and meaning – not necessarily the meaning of the verses themselves but of the process of transcribing and transfiguring. Does the deliberately included corrected text reflect a change in Dylan's attitude to his literary and musical forebears, or are the corrections themselves the message?

Natural Artifice

In 1965 Andy Warhol invited Dylan to do a screen test that Warhol hoped would turn into a movie, perhaps with Edie Sedgwick. Dylan evidently asked for a painting in return for the test and Warhol somewhat reluctantly allowed him to take a painting known as the silver *Elvis*. Factory denizen Gerard Malanga has claimed it was well known that "Dylan kind of frowned on" Warhol's work. His attitude toward the painting, it must be said, seems to underscore Malanga's view: "Dylan's group obviously didn't take Andy that seriously, you know. They were out to walk all over Andy and walk away with something. And they did. Dylan walked away with a very expensive Elvis Presley painting."[11] Evidently, Dylan and Bob Neuwirth lashed the painting to "the roof of their station wagon." Malanga concludes: "Knowing Andy, and how possessive he was with his art, I suspect it must have irked him to give away the painting."[12] Legend has it that soon after this episode Dylan traded the silver *Elvis* for Albert Goldman's couch.

Did design govern in a thing so small? Malanga would say yes, and that the insouciant trade of the valuable painting for Goldman's old couch, even if that couch was immortalized on the cover of *Bringing It All Back Home*, would indicate a less than reverent attitude toward the painting, if not toward the medium itself. Yet the sudden flurry of exhibitions in the last fifteen years testifies to the surprising productivity of Dylan the visual artist, reflecting not only on recent decades of painting and sculpture, but also on a lifetime of working in the plastic arts. We now know that Dylan

[11] John Bauldie, ed., *Wanted Man: In Search of Bob Dylan* (New York: Citadel Underground Press, 1991), p. 68. Malanga accounts for the Dylan group's disdain as partly due to the clash between "heterosexual groupings" and "homosexual groupings."

[12] Ibid, p. 70.

began drawing and painting around the same time as these Factory events took place, and within ten years he had become a devoted painter. As Fabio Fantuzzi has shown, Dylan's contact with the artist and instructor Norman Raeben came through his wife's friend Robin Fertik in 1974 and extended to his embracing the "Ten commandments of art," a document affixed to the wall of Raeben's studio near Carnegie Hall. Dylan might have studied only for a few weeks with Raeben, but he has unfailingly traced a sea-change in his music to the encounter: "*Blood On The Tracks* did consciously what I used to do unconsciously . . . I knew how to do it because of the technique I learned – I actually had a teacher for it."[13]

Christopher Ricks has asserted that "there is in Dylan's songs a sense that competition between the sister-arts is as inevitable and (mostly) unproductive as any other sibling rivalry."[14] He is probably right if we think of this rivalry as a *paragone* (struggle of equals) between poetry and painting or the plastic arts. But Dylan has characteristically steered his audience in another direction. As early as "Mr. Tambourine Man" (1964), he sang, "I have no one to meet / And the ancient, empty street's too dead for dreamin' . . . ," in two short lines laying bare – precociously and maybe with puzzlement – recognition of his isolated, uncategorizable artistic status. The puzzlement didn't last, however. Dylan commandingly reframed the old *paragone* to accommodate – and validate – his incursion into the high-culture gallery of the other arts.

A postcard from Allen Ginsberg offers a reminder of how deeply saturated in ideas of the aesthetic Dylan's milieu could be. He jots a note, dated 10/18/88:

> The concert was exciting! . . . I get sublime feelings anonymous and powerful sound in the audience!
> Anyway – taking your picture is easy, while we're doing something else, I don't use flash, just window light or street or good bright library lamplite –
> A Capella would also be sublime Contact!
> Love, Allen[15]

The last line acknowledges (even at this late date in Dylan's career) that the sublimity of the music can be found in Dylan's voice alone. In Martin Scorsese's documentary *No Direction Home* (2005), Ginsberg describes the

---

[13] Bert Cartwright, "The Mysterious Norman Raeben," in *Wanted Man*, ed. Bauldie, p. 88.
[14] Christopher Ricks, *Dylan's Visions of Sin* (London: Ecco, 2003), p. 28.
[15] BDA Box 39 F02. There is no period between "sublime" and "Contact!"

young Dylan of the *Blonde on Blonde* period as "pure breath." His idea that Dylan "A Capella" would resonate sublimely seems to support that otherworldly description. But the postcard also contains a reference to Ginsberg's wish to photograph Dylan. To convince the apparently reluctant sitter, he emphasizes the naturalness of the session and the use of available light. While these remarks scribbled on the back of a postcard might not prove much, they are very suggestive when thinking about a visual art. After all, the postcard is written by one of the most famous American poets-of-the-page to *the* most famous American poet-of-the-stage. The subject isn't poetry, however. It is photography: lighting and posing, so-called "natural" art and an inevitably specious promise of a lack of artifice.

As even this short card suggests, Dylan was immersed in an intellectual and artistic milieu that complemented his musical life. He emerged from an unhomogenized Greenwich Village mélange of musicians, stand-up comics, poets, writers, and painters. At the center of it all, for the folksingers, stood Dave Van Ronk. Known locally as the Mayor of MacDougal Street, he acted as Dylan's cicerone around the Village folk scene. As Dylan writes in *Chronicles* when first describing the tiny club called the Gaslight: "Van Ronk played there. I'd heard Van Ronk back in the Midwest on records and thought he was pretty great, copied some of his recordings phrase for phrase . . . I loved his style. He was what the city was all about. In Greenwich Village, Van Ronk was king of the street, he reigned supreme."[16]

Van Ronk was probably the most artistically cosmopolitan of Dylan's early connections. He had a casual, familiar sense of parity with renowned figures from the other arts, if we can trust his responses in an interview Andy Friedman published after Van Ronk died:

> I'm a big fan of de Kooning's. "Women" started out as a joke. He had a funny comment to make, and he made it. And now the solemnity that surrounds these paintings – it does Bill and those paintings a disservice. I think those paintings are funny, and I think de Kooning thought they were funny, too. It's a very hawky[17] sense of humor, but he's a Dutchman. What's funny to an American is not necessarily funny to a Dutchman by association, generally. I don't think I'd like to be locked in a room with a Dutch comedian. Maybe better than a Swedish comedian. But de Kooning was, I believe, a very witty painter . . .

---

[16] Bob Dylan, *Chronicles, Volume One* (New York: Simon & Schuster, 2004), pp. 15–16.

[17] This is a misprint, according to Elijah Wald, Van Ronk's biographer/co-author. The word should be "hokey." (Wald, personal communication, July 2018.)

> I used to be around those artists at the Cedar, on University Place, the old one. I knew a lot of those artists to nod hello to and that kind of thing. When Jackson [Pollock] was around he was funny, his jokes were funny, but you didn't park your car nearby, because he would hot-wire it and take off. There was nothing you could do.[18]

The way Van Ronk speaks of rubbing shoulders with de Kooning and Pollock is emblematic of the kinds of encounters Dylan would have experienced even before he became famous. The "street" and Dylan's Caffe Reggio crowd were manifestly bohemian, replete with artists of all kinds. The daily reality of artistic cross-pollination became for the sponge-like songwriter from the Midwest a pattern reflected in his lyrics and his music from the 1960s to *Tempest* (2012).

A similar cross-pollination marks Dylan's "When I Paint My Masterpiece" (1971): "Someday everything's gonna be smooth like a rhapsody / When I paint my masterpiece." Music and painting merge into one force in this image, the artist's eventual masterpiece somehow producing a rhapsodic musical composition. Here again, in one of his most famous references to a visual art, Dylan demonstrates an instinct for syncretism. While I am inclined to support Tim Riley's description of the song as a "hilarious parable about the disorienting comedy of rock touring," painting is Dylan's metaphor of choice.[19] The parable of artistic perfection leads (though no one could guess it at the time) to a Never Ending Tour forty years later.

First Art

Art, for Dylan, has never been a panacea for social or personal ills. Within the framework of his general skepticism of the arts, however, it did enjoy a privileged place. In "Shot of Love" (1981) according to John Hinchey, Dylan builds a whole song out the conceit of the "fix that won't fix anything."[20] This is true of all but one fix in the song, all but one shot – the shot of love. In the Christian myth, this would be the love Jesus urged humankind to feel for each other and, concomitantly, the love his sacrifice represented and through which he redeemed anyone who believed in his authority. With this shot of love, past sins disappear and a believer can live forever. Compared to this, everything else, including the arts, constitutes useless equivalents to conventional habit-forming drugs:

---

[18] Andy Friedman, "A Long-Ago Interview with Dave Van Ronk About the Blues," *The New Yorker Magazine*, June 30, 2016.
[19] Tim Riley, *Hard Rain* (New York: Vintage Books, 1993), p. 209.
[20] John Hinchey, *Like a Complete Unknown* (Ann Arbor, MI: Stealing Home Press, 2002), p. 157.

Don't need a shot of heroin to kill my disease
[Don't] need a shot of turpentine, only bring me to my knees
Don't need a shot of codeine to help me to repent
Don't need a shot of whiskey, help me be president

The parallel verse structure aligns turpentine, the solvent that cleans brushes, with heroin and alcohol, effectively making painting, heroin addiction, and alcoholism parallel substance abuses. It's ironic, not to say ambiguous, that taking a metaphorical shot of turpentine would bring the speaker to his knees, because being brought to one's knees can either mean to suffer a humiliating defeat – as in "Tempest" (2012) describing the *Titanic* at "45 degrees / Comin' to her knees" – or, alternatively, might mean the speaker is being forced down into a praying position. Inasmuch as the speaker "don't need a shot of turpentine," he resists being brought to his knees. But the cause-and-effect of his shooting-up turpentine and then ending up on his knees implies a connection between art and religious conversion. As in the *imitatio Christi*, defeat and humility can be adjacent, contiguous experiences offering a possibility of spiritual salvation. Painting, the song suggests, can serve as a kind of trigger to conversion. Or at least it would be pretty to think so.

Unfortunately, the song dismisses the arts of film and literature without a redeeming ambiguity. Like "turpentine," they are consigned to the list of habit-forming fixes (in the third verse): "Don't show me no picture show or give me no book to read / It don't satisfy the hurt inside me nor that habit that it feed[s]." The song descries a full rejection of the arts as useless distractions from "love." Seen in broader, metaphorical terms, "Shot of Love" helps us recognize again how Dylan's work traverses the arts – and not simply as competition or unproductive sibling rivalry. Ultimately, however, the serial rejections of "Shot of Love" uncover the abiding irony found in any work of art that condemns works of art: an irony that redeems art itself, or at least exempts it from the condemnations of moral equivocation.

In his interview-conversation with Elderfield at the time of *The Asia Series* exhibition, Dylan casually consigns film to a lower level in the pantheon of the arts: "It's not comparable to a live musical performance. There really is no reason to equate the two mediums. They're vastly different. There's nothing tactile about film. You can't smell it or touch it. It's an illusion. A magic trick. A film is abstract. A great painting or musical performance is visceral."[21] The clear alignment of painting with musical performance

---

[21] Bob Dylan, *The Asia Series* catalogue, interview with John Elderfield (New York: Gagosian Gallery, 2011), p. 12.

inevitably calls for scrutiny of songs in which paintings and visual-art references occur. Such references are legion and include familiar ones in "Visions of Johanna," "She Belongs to Me" (1965), and "When I Paint My Masterpiece." Scores of other allusions, mini-narratives, and musical arrangements attest to his engagement with painting, sculpture, photography, and film. In Dylan's songs we can find prolific evidence of a poetics as well as of genuine syncretism, mixing and encompassing the modes and moods of the arts.

In his "Foreword" to the *Drawn Blank* exhibition catalogue, Dylan recalls a predecessor to Raeben:

> My drawing instructor in high school lectured and demonstrated continuously to "draw only what you can see" so that if you were at a loss for words, something could be explained, and even more importantly not misunderstood. Rather than fantasize, be real and draw it only if it is in front of you, and if it's not there, put it there and by making the lines connect, we can get at something other than the world we know.[22]

The paradoxical advice is playful and sublimely indicative of Dylan's poetics as much as of his graphic art: "draw it only if it is in front of you," he says, but "if it's not there, put it there." Rather than being confined to being "real," Dylan's artist connects the lines between what he sees and what he imagines so to make "something other than the world we know."

As a songwriter, Bob Dylan not only made something other than the world we know by transforming his models, he also *re*-formed the musical genres he worked in – if not the medium itself. His paintings, in contrast, don't have the same authority, despite being studiously accomplished. Nevertheless – and this is where uninitiated art critics falter – paintings such as those in the *Asia Series* deserve to be judged on their own merits. It is true that the emergence of so many, very different exhibitions in this recent decade does not compare to the staggering efflorescence of Dylan's musical creativity in the 1960s. Yet what in contemporary culture can compare to that? Even so, disproportionate comparisons would have been inevitable (see, for example, the criticism of *Writings and Drawings* in 1973), as Dylan no doubt knew. And, now that we have seen so much of his art, it is unfortunate that his painting and sculpture are so often judged against his musical production. His visual art not only provides uncomplicated distinctions between copying and transformative imitation, but also

---

[22] Bob Dylan, *The Drawn Blank Series* [Halcyon Gallery] (New York: Random House, 1994), np.

demonstrates the kind of interpretive originality Dylan applies to his music. His indefatigable work in the plastic arts reflects his ongoing commitment to refashioning past models – and more importantly, past styles – in producing new art.

Dylan's songs will always be his first art. They are the reason we study and thrill to his music. Yet as evidence of his dedication to the visual arts builds up, it probably behooves us as critics and listeners not to underestimate Dylan's singular, and closely observed, personal contributions to those arts. His gallery exhibitions and his publication of poetry and prose prove the obvious – that he engages in demonstrable and practical ways with the sister (or sibling) arts. In addition to being a poet, he is a painter, sculptor, sketch artist, and draftsman – not to mention filmmaker – and he has always sought to express himself in media other than song. It is no surprise, then, that his songs reflect on, joke about, vamp, parody, admire, and borrow from the arts he practices. Ultimately, there's no profit in trying to disentangle the threads of Dylan's creativity. Yet this much is clear: when he alludes to the other arts in his songs, they are often the same arts he himself practices and exhibits. To ignore this reality would be to miss the immediacy of Dylan's creative syncretism, like glancing too quickly into the kind of distorting mirror the songs hold up to nature.

CHAPTER 17

Borrowing

Kevin Dettmar

The term "plagiarism" (from the Latin for "kidnapping") is a pretty blunt instrument with which to try to comprehend the complex relationship of any artist to his or her source materials. It suggests a cartoonish model of artistic inspiration. The devil, named Plagiarism, sits on one shoulder, whispering to the musician, "Ah, go ahead. Lift that phrase (lyrical or musical): no one will ever know." On the other shoulder the angel, Originality, urges the virtues of inspiration over imitation. It's a picture of artistic creation as a straightforward struggle between genius and subterfuge, good and evil. No one who had ever struggled to create anything could have come up with it.

In his great polemic essay "Tradition and the Individual Talent," poet T.S. Eliot pushed back against the constraints of a certain Romantic conception of originality, arguing that "no poet, no artist of any art, has his complete meaning alone" – that "we shall often find that not only the best, but the most individual parts of [a poet's] work may be those in which the dead poets, his ancestors, assert their immortality most vigorously."[1] Rather than springing forth fully formed from the brow of Jove, Eliot argues, the work of art comes into being when the artist's mind plays the role of a catalyst – in Eliot's metaphor, "a bit of finely filiated platinum ... introduced into a chamber containing oxygen and sulphur dioxide" – allowing familiar elements to come together in unfamiliar combinations. Critics would later point out that this was an especially important argument for Eliot to make at the moment he was about to embark upon *The Waste Land* (1922), a poem patched together from "fragments" he had "shored against [his] ruin." As he suggested in a talk delivered in 1936, paraphrasing and expanding upon his unpaid literary agent Ezra Pound, "The perpetual task of poetry is to *make all things new*. Not necessarily to

---

[1] T.S. Eliot, "Tradition and the Individual Talent" (1919), in *Selected Prose of T. S. Eliot*, ed. Frank Kermode (New York: Harcourt Brace Jovanovich, 1975), p. 38.

make new things. . . . It is always partly a revolution, or a reaction, from the work of the previous generation."[2]

A half-century later, cultural theorist Roland Barthes took the argument a step further, suggesting that all writing is, whether or not the fact is acknowledged, ultimately a process of quotation: the text is "a multi-dimensional space in which a variety of writings, none of them original, blend and clash. The text is a tissue of quotations drawn from innumerable centres of culture."[3] For Barthes, then, plagiarism is simply the name we give to unacknowledged theft from a single source. The name for literary theft, writ large, is *writing*.

One might argue, then, that what's at stake when we talk of a writer's "originality" isn't really originality, per se, but intent: that phrase in the work of X sounds very much like this phrase in the work of Y. Was the echo intentional or not? If intentional, did the author mean for readers to recognize the source (hence artful terms like *quotation, echo, allusion*), or not (the blunt accusation of *plagiarism*)? Theft isn't quite theft if it's carried out in broad daylight, with the knowledge of all the involved parties: but we don't really have a better word for it. Unless, again, that word is *writing* – or perhaps James Joyce's neologism from *Finnegans Wake*, "stollentelling."[4]

The boundaries for all artists, then – if such there be – between quotation, plagiarism, piracy, echo, allusion, and creation are notoriously porous. In his move from the folk scene (where music is something of a shared resource, a public commons) to rock and its singer-songwriter emphasis on originality and virtuosity, Dylan systematically and strategic-ally muddied any clear distinctions between original and borrowed mater-ials. Like Eliot, he understood himself to be working within a tradition and signaled as much, long after the fact, by titling his 2001 album *"Love and Theft"* – with quotation marks – as if to cite Eric Lott's scholarly study of blackface minstrelsy.[5] (This title Lott has, in turn, acknowledged "riff[s] on" Leslie Fiedler's landmark study of American fiction, *Love and Death in the American Novel*.) And it's turtles all the way down.

Track 1, side 2 of *"Love and Theft"* is titled "High Water (for Charley Patton)." Good student of intellectual property law that he is, Dylan

---

[2] T.S. Eliot, "Tradition and the Practice of Poetry" (1936), ed. A. Walton Litz, *Southern Review* (October 1985), p. 883.

[3] Roland Barthes, "The Death of the Author" (1968), trans. Stephen Heath, in *Image, Music, Text* (New York: Noonday/Farrar, Straus and Giroux, 1977), p. 146.

[4] James Joyce, *Finnegans Wake* (New York: Viking, 1939), p. 423.

[5] Eric Lott, *Love and Theft: Blackface Minstrelsy and the American Working Class* (New York: Oxford University Press, 1993).

knows that titles, like those of Lott's monograph, cannot be copyrighted, and neither can common phrases like the title of Patton's own 1929 Paramount single "High Water Everywhere" – so Dylan's title certainly does not constitute piracy. The fact that he acknowledges the reference ("for Charley Patton") and frames his own song as an homage further means that this is not plagiarism. Instead, the parenthesis serves as a kind of informal footnote pointing us back into the complex history of the blues, which is built around floating lyrics, response songs, and sly references to other songs and performers. This is not piracy, not plagiarism: that leaves quotation, echo, and allusion. And as Bruce Springsteen might put it, "Mama, that's where the fun is."[6]

Although the release of *"Love and Theft"* perhaps represents the apex of Dylan's intertextual creative process, it also coincided with the burgeoning corpus of searchable online digital texts and the growing sophistication of the Google search engine, under whose scrutiny the songwriter's entire catalog has been revealed to be full of patches and duct tape. On the website www.dylanchords.com, Chris Johnson identifies a dozen different passages on the album lifted from Junichi Saga's *Confessions of a Yakuza*; 2006's *Modern Times* sports allusions to sources as disparate as Ovid's *Tristia* and the Civil-War poet Henry Timrod. Such accusations go back to the earliest days of Dylan's career; in 1963, *Newsweek* ran a story wrongly claiming that he had stolen his first big hit, "Blowin' in the Wind," from a high-school student named Lorre Wyatt. (Fifteen years later, Dylan responded that no, he'd developed the tune from the spiritual "No More Auction Block.")[7]

And not just his musical but also his literary catalog: *Chronicles, Volume One* "samples," for instance, long passages from Marcel Proust's *À la recherche du temps perdu* (alongside American worthies like Carl Sandburg, Mark Twain, and Jack London). It was Google, of course, that helped enterprising *Slate* reporter Andrea Pitzer discover that portions of Dylan's Nobel Prize acceptance speech were cribbed from that wellspring of cribbing, SparkNotes. Of course, Dylan has a complicated and well-publicized history with accepting accolades, and giving thanks for them: Princeton gave him an honorary degree and he wrote "Day of the Locusts":

> I put down my robe, picked up my diploma
> Took hold of my sweetheart and away we did drive

---

[6] Bruce Springsteen, "Blinded by the Light," *Greetings from Asbury Park, N.J.*, Columbia KC 31903.
[7] David Yaffe, *Bob Dylan: Like a Complete Unknown* (New Haven, CT: Yale University Press, 2011), p. 100.

Straight for the hills, the black hills of Dakota
Sure was glad to get out of there alive. . ..

Here, the only thing Dylan borrowed was his title, from Nathanael West's savage 1939 Hollywood satire, *The Day of the Locust*.

So much has been written by this point about Dylan and plagiarism that new work is hardly possible without extensive outright quotation – or a lot of plagiarism.[8] By now we can stop debating whether or not Bob Dylan has built some of his songs through a process of intertextual reference – it's an essential part of his technique and a fundamental part of creativity writ large. Thus we can turn to the much more interesting question: So what? Or to quote (not plagiarize) Morrissey: "What difference does it make?"[9]

Let's tackle these questions by drilling down into some actual tracks and thinking about how they work on and in a listener. The recent release in Columbia's Bootleg Series of the *Blood on the Tracks* materials provides a rich laboratory for such an inquiry. *More Blood, More Tracks* sent many back to the 1975 studio album with renewed interest and big ears. What has struck me most forcefully in my round of bootleg-informed re-listening is the second-hand nature of much of the emotion that's said to characterize this "break-up album" (a designation Dylan has always rejected). In his "Real Life Top Ten" for October 25, 2018, Greil Marcus called *Blood on the Tracks* "an album that has been overpraised and over-fetishized for more than 40 years"; in that piece for *Rolling Stone*, and in a seminar conversation with my students and faculty colleagues at Pomona College the previous month, he expressed a skeptically revisionist take on the album, describing the emotion of "Shelter from the Storm," for instance, as "phony."[10]

I'd like to dig into, and to some degree push back against and attempt to complicate, Marcus's description, "phony." He's not wrong: of course he's not. He's Greil Marcus, perhaps our most astute living cultural critic. But I do think that in his harsh October 2018 reassessment of *Blood on the Tracks*, there's a dimension that he's missing – one, in fact, that he alluded to in his keynote address at the World of Bob Dylan conference at the University of Tulsa in May 2019 (reproduced as Chapter 6).

In spite of Dylan's repeated protests, *Blood on the Tracks* has been understood since its release, by many of its listeners and critics – including

---

[8] For succinct accounts of the situation up until 2010, see David Yaffe's contribution to *The Cambridge Companion to Bob Dylan*, ed. Kevin J. H. Dettmar (Cambridge: Cambridge University Press, 2009), pp. 15–27; and chapter 4 of his *Like a Complete Unknown*, pp. 93–127.

[9] The Smiths, "What Difference Does It Make?," *The Smiths*. Rough Trade ROUGH 61.

[10] Greil Marcus, "Real Life Top Ten: All-Bob Dylan Edition," *Rolling Stone*, October 25, 2018, www.rollingstone.com/music/music-features/real-life-rock-top-ten-746600/.

me, I guess I need to say – as a breakup album. Some think that so designating it means that it's something less than art; but let's stipulate at the outset that there's no necessary contradiction in saying a work that grows out of an artist's own experience can be a consummate work of art. The highlights of *Blood on the Tracks* rank among Dylan's very strongest tracks ever – songs like "Tangled Up in Blue" and "Idiot Wind." But let's look for a minute at the track that Marcus calls a "stupid hoedown," "You're Gonna Make Me Lonesome When You Go."[11] In one sense, it's too easy a target; no one has ever argued that it's one of the album's heavyweights. Closing side 1, it feels like a bagatelle; it's a brisk and lightweight song that moves along at a clip seemingly incompatible with deep thought. Its title announces it as a breakup song, at least of sorts; but that conventional-sounding title, which makes up the tag line of every verse, just falls apart the longer you think about it.

"You're Gonna Make Me Lonesome When You Go": let's break that down. First, "You're": the song deploys a second-person address, like the middle song of side 1, "You're a Big Girl Now." "You're going to": this is a prophetic song – not Old Testament prophetic, but more like a prediction, like a bet – "I bet you're gonna . . ." Gonna what? Well, you're gonna go. You're gonna leave me. And when you do, I've got a further prediction: I'm gonna be *lonesome*. Not *lonely*, mind you, not *alone*: *lonesome*. (Can one person ever make another person lonesome? There seems to be a fair bit of what the vulgar call not owning one's shit going on here; lonesome's on you, buddy, not her – especially since you know in advance that eventually you'll be driving her away.)

In that "Real Life Top Ten" column, Marcus rightly questions the sincerity of this supposed breakup song: "yeah," he writes, "that's a real heartbreaker of a breakup song, especially if you can't remember the name of the person you're supposedly breaking up with."[12] But I want to argue that the song's more complicated than that – that it is, to use a hallmark Marcus word, much *weirder* than that. It's actually a proleptic breakup song, one that foresees the end of a relationship that's really only just begun. Indeed, the song forges the endgame narrative for an affair that's still relatively new: if biographical sources can be trusted, the unnamed about-to-be-ex lover is Ellen Bernstein, a Columbia Records executive, and the unnamed still-legally-married spouse, of course, is Sara Dylan, "Sweet virgin angel, sweet love of my life, / . . . / Radiant jewel, mystical wife."

---

[11] Greil Marcus, "Real Life Top Ten: All-Bob Dylan Edition," *Rolling Stone*, October 25, 2018.
[12] Ibid.

(Or in this case, perhaps, *mystified* wife.) Texts that use second-person address always hail us, always seem to be speaking to us: so imagine for a minute that you're actually being addressed by this song. It's being sung to you, on the eve of your new relationship, by your prospective lover – and he's telling you, in essence, "don't let the door hit you on your way out." And if you've got any brains at all, you realize as well that his wife could hear it speaking to her in exactly the same way. And that, I would suggest, is why the singer can't, in Marcus's words, "remember the name of the person [he's] supposedly breaking up with": it's not just one person. This is a mighty *efficient* breakup song.

Most interesting, though – and bearing on the question of quotation, allusion, echo, plagiarism, and piracy – is that signature word "lonesome." A quick peek into the *Corpus of Contemporary American English* (a database of 560 million word-usages) provides a bit of data: the word "lonely" occurs almost *nine times* as frequently as "lonesome," and the word "alone," nearly *eighty* times as frequently.[13] In American popular music, I want to suggest, "lonesome" is never just a word like any other – it's haunted. It's always enclosed in invisible quotation marks. For if other songs had given a voice to the lonely (for instance, Elvis's "Heartbreak Hotel" [1956] and Roy Orbison's "Only the Lonely" [1960]), after "I'm So Lonesome I Could Cry" (1949) Hank Williams had a virtual trademark on the word "lonesome." (In 1960, long after his death, his label MGM went so far as to issue a compilation called *The Lonesome Sound of Hank Williams*.)

Dylan was, of course, deeply aware of Williams's music. In his liner notes for *Joan Baez in Concert, Part 2*, he writes that Williams was his "first idol," and in *Chronicles* he says that he "listened to [Williams's songs] a lot and had them internalized":

> Even at a young age, I identified with him. I didn't have to experience anything that Hank did to know what he was singing about. I'd never heard a robin weep [an allusion to a line from "I'm So Lonesome I Could Cry"] but could imagine it and it made me sad.[14]

Among the Williams 78s that he owned, according to Robert Shelton, were "I'm So Lonesome I Could Cry" and "(I Heard That) Lonesome Whistle"; Scorsese's *No Direction Home* captures a bit of Dylan playing piano and singing "I'm So Lonesome I Could Cry," with a very wasted Johnny Cash, on May 11, 1966, backstage at the Capitol Theatre in Cardiff, Wales.

---

[13] www.english-corpora.org/coca/.
[14] Bob Dylan, *Chronicles: Volume One* (New York: Simon & Schuster, 2004), p. 96.

Let's return for a moment to that scenario invoked earlier: imagine that you are the "you" who is addressed in the song. The song's title starts to unnerve you as you let its various implications sink in. How much more so when you realize that it's the echo of another's expression, the articulation of someone else's relationship? Early in their relationship Nora Barnacle, James Joyce's lifelong companion, wrote him a love letter that Joyce discovered had been copied out of a book of models. Her letter has not survived, but it's not hard to imagine that such a forgery would come as a disappointment to a paramour looking for a somewhat more authentic expression of passion. (As for Joyce's own love letters to Nora, what they lack in originality, they make up for in . . . well, call it *candor*.)

Dylan's "You're Gonna Make Me Lonesome When You Go" is thus less about a breakup or two (never mind that one of them hasn't happened yet), than it is about breakup songs – and the echo/allusion/quotation (take your pick) to Hank Williams is the way he achieves this effect. Carrie Brownstein, in her essay for the *Cambridge Companion*, writes that "*Blood on the Tracks* is a self-elegy; it sings to itself, and breaks its own heart."[15] It's just this self-consciousness, and consciousness of its place in the larger tradition of American song, that makes *Blood on the Tracks* such a complicated, even duplicitous, breakup album.

In the postscript to his novel *The Name of the Rose*, Umberto Eco gives a quick and colloquial example of one aspect of postmodernism. Here's what he says:

> I think of the postmodern attitude as that of a man who loves a very cultivated woman and knows he cannot say to her, "I love you madly," because he knows that she knows (and that she knows that he knows) that these words have already been written by Barbara Cartland. Still, there is a solution. He can say, "As Barbara Cartland would put it, I love you madly." At this point, having avoided false innocence, having said clearly that it is no longer possible to speak innocently, he will nevertheless have said what he wanted to say to the woman: that he loves her, but he loves her in an age of lost innocence. If the woman goes along with this, she will have received a declaration of love all the same. Neither of the two speakers will feel innocent, both will have accepted the challenge of the past, of the already said, which cannot be eliminated; both will consciously and with pleasure play the game of irony . . . . But both will have succeeded, once again, in speaking of love.[16]

[15] Carrie Brownstein, "*Blood on the Tracks* (1975)," *The Cambridge Companion to Bob Dylan*, ed. Dettmar, p. 155.

[16] Umberto Eco, "'I Love You Madly,' He Said Self-Consciously," in *The Truth About the Truth: De-Confusing and Re-Constructing the Postmodern World*, ed. Walter Truett Anderson (New York: Jeremy P. Tarcher/Putnam, 1995), pp. 32–33.

If it makes things easier, imagine Dylan's title with a trademark symbol: to adopt Eco's formulation, it's as if Dylan is saying, to his lover (or lovers) and to us, "As Hank Williams might say, 'You're gonna make me "lonesome"™ when you go.'" It's not, first and foremost, a song that documents the demise of a relationship, or two – it's about the way in which such songs stealthily script such breakups, and about the way in which these songs can help us share these experiences vicariously.

Blood on the Tracks teaches us that there is nothing *but* plagiarized emotion. And it does so, not by flat-out plagiarism (a term poorly suited to nearly any kind of art), but through the non-judgmental catch-all term that post-structuralism bequeathed us to refer to all instances of textual influence: intertextuality. There's no real blood on these tracks, or in these tracks; and the bootleg release gives us more tracks, yes, but no more blood. For songs are never simply expressions of our feelings: they're the way we learn how to express our feelings; they're *how we learn how to feel*. Remember what Dylan wrote in *Chronicles*, "I didn't have to experience anything that Hank did to know what he was singing about. I'd never heard a robin weep but could imagine it and it made me sad."[17]

This can, of course, have serious real-world consequences. Though not a real-world example, Nick Hornby's narrator in *High Fidelity*, Rob Fleming, spells it all out quite memorably:

> Some of my favorite songs: "Only Love Can Break Your Heart" by Neil Young; "Last Night I Dreamed That Somebody Loved Me" by the Smiths; "Call Me" by Aretha Franklin; "I Don't Want to Talk About It" by anybody. And then there's "Love Hurts" and "When Love Breaks Down" and "How Can You Mend a Broken Heart" and "The Speed of the Sound of Loneliness" and "She's Gone" and "I Just Don't Know What to Do with Myself" and . . . some of these songs I have listened to around once a week, on average (three hundred times in the first month, every now and again thereafter), since I was sixteen or nineteen or twenty-one. How can that not leave you bruised somewhere? How can that not turn you into the sort of person liable to break into little bits when your first love goes all wrong? What came first – the music or the misery? Did I listen to music because I was miserable? Or was I miserable because I listened to music? Do all those records turn you into a melancholy person?
>
> People worry about kids playing with guns, and teenagers watching violent videos; we are scared that some sort of culture of violence will take them over. Nobody worries about kids listening to thousands – literally thousands – of songs about broken hearts and rejection and pain and misery

---

[17] Dylan, *Chronicles*, p. 96.

and loss. The unhappiest people I know, romantically speaking, are the ones who like pop music the most; and I don't know whether pop music has caused this unhappiness, but I do know that they've been listening to the sad songs longer than they've been living the unhappy lives.[18]

In his keynote address at the World of Bob Dylan, Marcus pointed out that in the blues tradition, "words came first from a common store of phrases" – could this be true, too, of heartbreak songs? He said that the challenge of the blues was to take a story from that common store and "present it as though it happened to you," which he called "a mandate to write fiction." Defending the 20-year-old Dylan's decision to record "See That My Grave Is Kept Clean" – how, one might protest, does a kid have the moral authority to take on such a song? – Marcus said, "maybe what he knew about death is what the songs taught him." So too, perhaps, what he knew about love and loneliness? Or to put it differently: "What's love," as Tina Turner taught us to ask, "but a second-hand emotion?"[19]

---

[18] Nick Hornby, *High Fidelity* (New York: Riverhead, 1995), pp. 24–25.
[19] Tina Turner, "What's Love Got to Do With It," *Private Dancer*, Capitol 1C 064 2401521.

CHAPTER 18

Judaism: Saturnine Melancholy and Dylan's Jewish Gnosis

Elliot R. Wolfson

For as wisdom grows, vexation grows;
To increase learning is to increase heartache.

Ecclesiastes 1:18

Always remain obscure in order to exist.

Babylonian Talmud, Sanhedrin 14a

I've paid the price of solitude, but at least I'm out of debt.

Bob Dylan, "Dirge"

Many have written about Bob Dylan's complex relationship to his Jewish upbringing. The scope and magnitude of the knowledge of Judaism that Dylan received as a child in Hibbing is debatable, but what is incontestable is that his lifelong quest for matters of the spirit was inspired by the priestly distinction between transgression and devotion, the prophetic demand for social justice, and the rabbinic propensity to resist systematic totalization in favor of interrogating issues incessantly – to answer a question with another question as a way of understanding multiple perspectives. One can safely assume that Jewish religious traditions informed Dylan's advocacy for the downtrodden and his restless search for integrity in a world of guile – searching for a gem, as he sings in "Dirge," "in this age of fiberglass" – was shaped, in part, by these dimensions of the Jewish tradition. Even the occasional refusal to undertake his mission – "It's never been my duty to remake the world at large / Nor is it my intention to sound the battle charge" from "Wedding Song" – is reminiscent of the prophets who reluctantly accepted their calling.

Dylan's relationship with Judaism is complicated. While on occasion he delved into the study of sacred Jewish texts and attempted to comply with ritual practices, his Christian period seemingly pulled him in other directions. I contend, however, that Dylan's flirtation with Christianity was a demonstration of rather than a departure from his Jewishness. Consider these stanzas from "Precious Angel" on *Slow Train Coming* (1979):

> We are covered in blood, girl, you know our forefathers were slaves
> Let us hope they've found mercy in their bone-filled graves
> . . .
> But there's violence in the eyes, girl, so let us not be enticed
> On the way out of Egypt, through Ethiopia, to the judgment hall of Christ.

Dylan forged a nexus between the experiences of Israelites in Egypt and the experience of black people, symbolized by Ethiopia, as one typically finds in Hebrew scripture. From their shared history as enslaved peoples emerges the possibility of salvation. The move from the somatic to the pneumatic echoes Dylan's acknowledgment that his precious angel is both the queen of his flesh and the lamp of his soul; the foundation of the erotic bond is not sensual delight – rendered in the biblical image of being enticed by the eyes – but the legacy of escape from bondage. The particular expression "judgment hall of Christ" is likely based on the King James translation of *praetorium* in John 18:28, which originally meant the place in the Roman camp where the general's tent stood but which, scripturally, denotes the residence that Pilate occupied in Jerusalem. Dylan has modified the literal sense by attributing the hall to Christ rather than to Pilate, and thus he alludes to the location where the final judgment of the righteous and the wicked will transpire, an eschatological motif that Christianity and later Islam appropriated from Judaism. For Dylan such a proposition is the fulfillment of rather than an assault on the Jewish narrative of liberation from servitude.

This chapter will focus on a facet of Dylan's Jewishness that has not been sufficiently appreciated: the link between Jews and melancholia. Since late antiquity, this juxtaposition has been based on the connection between melancholy and Saturn, and the further association of the Hebrew name of that planet, Shabbetai,[1] and the Jewish Sabbath. Judaism is commonly depicted as a life-affirming religion that promotes the obligation to make the mundane holy, an idea that is both enhanced and subverted by the kabbalists' emphasis on repairing the world by unfettering the sparks of godly light from their entrapment in the diabolical shells of materiality. The melancholic predisposition of Jews to view the world as a place of hostility and dissension has had important anthropological,

---

[1] It is apposite to note that Dylan's Hebrew name is Shabbetai Zissel.

cosmological, and theological repercussions. The unquenchable desire buttressing the messianic ideal peculiar to Judaism reveals the cadence of a temporal transcendence that comports the future as the distance that is distant by being proximate and proximate by being distant. The point is well captured in Gershom Scholem's celebrated remark that the messianic idea in Judaism "has compelled a *life lived in deferment*, in which nothing can be done definitively, nothing can be irrevocably accomplished."[2] In a similar vein, Franz Rosenzweig wrote that eternity is a today that is always conscious of being more than today,[3] that is, a tomorrow that is forever now in virtue of forever not being now. Relentlessly, the future is not yet there; it is coming eternally, and of that which comes eternally it can never be said that it has come.

The philosophic import of the melancholic nature of the asymptotic curvature of messianic time, and by extension of the finitude of temporality more generally, finds a deep resonance in Dylan's oeuvre. In particular, Dylan has been acutely attuned to the apocalyptic dimension of Judaism, which incarnates the infinite negativity of time; that is, the impossible possibility that makes it continually possible – indeed necessary – that the future that is coming threatens not to be the future that has been antici-pated. In the refrain from "I Shall Be Released" (1967), Dylan seemed more sanguine about the tenability of achieving redemption:

> I see my light come shining
> From the west unto the east
> Any day now, any day now
> I shall be released.

Sounding a similar note in his symbolic transference of the messianic ideal to the mythic image of Quinn the Eskimo, Dylan comments that everyone is getting ready by building ships, boats, and monuments, while others are jotting down notes, waiting for the arrival of the mighty Quinn, so that he would alleviate the despair of every girl and boy and terminate the insom-nia by inducing a pervasive longing to slumber. When one considers the totality of Dylan's work, however, it becomes clear that he does not view redemption as the consequence of historical development, the effect of a causal chain that links the retention of the past and the protention of the future, but rather as the metahistorical corollary of an expectation that is

---

[2] Gershom Scholem, *The Messianic Idea and Other Essays on Jewish Spirituality* (New York: Schocken, 1971), p. 35.
[3] Franz Rosenzweig, *The Star of Redemption*, trans. Barbara E. Galli (Madison: University of Wisconsin Press, 2000), p. 241.

realized as the expectation of what cannot be realized. Even in "Ye Shall Be Changed" (1979), a song that extols the inevitability of the bodily resurrection, Dylan insists on the acausality of the past and on the indeterminacy of the future, noting that the former does not control the person and that the latter is "like a roulette wheel spinning."

The hopelessness of hope proceeds, therefore, from the fact that the future we are awaiting can never transpire in time and the homeland we are coveting can never materialize in space. As Jesus reportedly said to the one who vowed to follow him wherever he might go, "Foxes have holes, and birds of the air have nests; but the son of man has nowhere to lay his head" (Matthew 8:20; Luke 9:58; Gospel of Thomas 86). In "Like a Rolling Stone" (1965), Dylan echoes this and expands it to the human condition:

> How does it feel
> To be without a home
> Like a complete unknown
> Like a rolling stone? . . . How does it feel
> To be on your own
> With no direction home?

The itinerant quality of being in the world is attested as well in "I Pity the Poor Immigrant" (1968), whose title character "wishes he would've stayed home / who uses all his power to do evil / but in the end is always left so alone," the one "who passionately hates his life / and likewise, fears his death." The immigrant serves as a paradigm for the soul that wavers between displeasure with existence and anxiety about non-existence. Dylan has taught us repeatedly that the homelessness of being at home converges with the homeliness of being banished. In the youthful "Mixed Up Confusion" (1962), he precociously sings, "I'm too old to lose, babe, I'm too young to win / And I feel like a stranger in the world I'm living in." The feeling of uprootedness is reiterated in "Nobody 'Cept You" (1973): "I'm a stranger here and no one sees me." In "Trouble in Mind" (1979), Dylan allocates this disaffection more specifically to Satan, who deadens the singer's conscience to the point that he worships the work of his own hands and serves "strangers in a strange, forsaken land." Analogously, he writes in "You Changed My Life" (1982), "There was someone in my body that I could hardly see ... Making me feel like a stranger in a strange land." Fifteen years later, he returns again to this theme in "Highlands" (1997): "Feel like a prisoner in a world of mystery / I wish someone would come / And push back the clock for me." Underlying the entreaty to revisit the past is the eagerness to unravel the mystery of the beginning that will shed light on the mystery of the end.

At the melancholic heart of human creativity is the challenge of conceptualizing truth and then falling silent in every effort to give it shape in speech or in writing. A writer is thus left with the too much that is too little, the surplus of meaning that resounds as inadequate. This sentiment, however, is prone to yield the grim realization that the future is ceaselessly arriving and therefore can never have arrived. As Dylan put it in "Night after Night" (1987):

> Night after night some new plan to blow up the world
> Night after night another old man kissing some young girl
> You look for salvation, you find none
> Just another broken heart, another barrel of a gun
> Just another stick of dynamite night after night.

In the nocturnality of exile, one rummages for salvation but comes up empty. Already in the final stanza of "Gates of Eden" (1965), Dylan gave us a preview of the saturnine melancholy of his worldview:

> At dawn my lover comes to me
> And tells me of her dreams
> With no attempts to shovel the glimpse
> Into the ditch of what each one means
> At times I think there are no words
> But these to tell what's true
> And there are no truths outside the Gates of Eden.

The poet tries to find truth in the dreams his lover retells to him, but alas, he does not succeed because there are no truths outside the Gates of Eden. Not even the intimacy of love has the capacity to release one from the shackle of deceit. As Dylan would sardonically write in "Million Miles" (1997), "You told yourself a lie, that's all right mama I told myself one too." Like Ophelia, our eyes may be fixed on Noah's great rainbow, but we spend our time peeking into desolation row. The covenantal sign of reconciliation is reassuring but the chaos of the world is too tantalizing to dismiss. Consider the beguiling words in "I and I" (1983):

> Took an untrodden path once, where the swift don't win the race
> It goes to the worthy, who can divide the word of truth
> Took a stranger to teach me, to look into justice's beautiful face
> And to see an eye for an eye and a tooth for a tooth.

The last line is a verbatim repetition of the *lex talionis* promulgated in the Pentateuch (Exodus 21:24, Leviticus 24:20, Deuteronomy 19:21). Dylan here embraces the idea of justice as the retaliatory measure for measure that was famously condemned by Jesus in the Sermon on the Mount. For centuries Jesus's words served as a watershed distinguishing the lawfulness of Judaism and the gracefulness of Christianity. Dylan apparently saw no conflict between the two, and in "Wedding Song" (1973) he even used this image to characterize the incisive passion between lovers, "Eye for eye and tooth for tooth, your love cuts like a knife." But what does Dylan wish to divulge in the first two lines by noting that the untrodden path goes to the worthy who divide the word of truth? The language is derived from the King James translation of *orthotomeo ton logon tes aletheias* in 2 Timothy 2:15 as "rightly dividing the word of truth." The literal meaning of *orthotomeo* is to cut straight, and thus the likely connotation is to dissect the word of truth in order to adduce an accurate interpretation. But what meaning does it assume for Dylan? Is there a hint here to a more radical explanation of this metaphor?

Conventionally, by the law of non-contradiction, truth is indivisible – if something is true, it cannot be false. However, Dylan may be alluding to a more paradoxical notion of a divisible truth, that is, a truth that cannot be true unless it is untrue. "The naked truth," he complains in "Dirge" (1973), "is still taboo whenever it can be seen." The naked truth cannot be seen because truth is rendered visible only through the veil of invisibility, which is to say, there is no truth denuded of the investiture of untruth. The disrobing of truth, consequently, will always disclose another layer of truth to be disrobed as untrue. In "Outlaw Blues" (1965), Dylan mockingly growled, "Don't ask me nothin' about nothin' / I just might tell you the truth." Truth is exposed in the veneer of the double negative – nothing about nothing, the something that is nothing. As the songwriter agonizingly proclaims in "Things Have Changed" (1999): "All the truth in the world adds up to one big lie." One is reminded of the words of the Psalmist, "I trust [in the Lord]; out of great suffering I spoke / and said rashly, 'All men are false'" (Psalms 116:10–11). Or in the searing exclamation of Ecclesiastes, "Utter futility! All is futile! / What real value is there for a man / In all the gains he makes beneath the sun?" (Ecclesiastes 1:2–3). Wisdom may be superior to folly as the light is superior to darkness, but ultimately mortality and oblivion await the wise man as well as the fool; hence there is no advantage of one over the other (Ecclesiastes 2:13–16). Although as moral agents we must discriminate righteousness from wickedness, closer scrutiny reveals that the human and the beast suffer the identical destiny – both amount to nothing as they come from and return to the dust (Ecclesiastes 3:16–20).

Dylan's despair over the human plight accords with these scriptural formulations: no person can be trusted and even if we were to add all the truths of the world together, they would amount to nothing but a lie. There is no sustainable benefit for our toils and tribulations; our endeavors, well intended as they may be, are as pointless as the pursuit of the wind (Ecclesiastes 2:17). We can hear a reverberation of this fatalism in the 1965 masterpiece "It's Alright, Ma (I'm Only Bleeding)," which insists that "not much is really sacred," and that "it's only people's games that you got to dodge" since "all is phony." Returning to this theme in "Abandoned Love" (1975), Dylan muses, "Everybody's wearing a disguise / To hide what they've got left behind their eyes." Differentiating himself from those who participate in the masquerade, Dylan insists he cannot cover who he is. Nevertheless, the travesty of detecting that every face is nothing but another mask hiding a face that is a mask leads to his resignation:

> I've given up the game, I've got to leave
> The pot of gold is only make-believe
> The treasure can't be found by men who search
> Whose gods are dead and whose queens are in the
>   church.

The dark vision is one of the enduring elements of Dylan's poetry, rooted in the longstanding Jewish penchant for melancholy and the related gnostic suspicion about the plausibility of finding redemption in a world where, as Dylan forthrightly expressed it in 1989, "everything is broken." In "Shelter from the Storm" (1974), he communicated the futility of life in this way: "Well, the deputy walks on hard nails and the preacher rides a mount / But nothing really matters much, it's doom alone that counts." To make matters worse, bargaining for salvation leads to being given a lethal dose, and the offering up of innocence to being repaid with scorn. The bleakness of the human lot is underscored in the conclusion of the enigmatic "Changing of the Guards" (1978):

> Peace will come
> With tranquility and splendor on the wheels of fire
> But will bring us no reward when her false idols fall
> And cruel death surrenders with its pale ghost
>   retreating
> Between the King and the Queen of Swords.

Ostensibly, Dylan endorses a more affirmative resolution: peace will come on the wheels of fire and the ghost of death will surrender to the King and Queen of Swords, the archetypes of the masculine and the feminine powers of intellect. There is, however, no recompense when the false idols fall.

Notably, in "What Can I Do for You?" (1980), Dylan cast the salvific faith in Jesus in gnostic-kabbalistic terms: "Soon as a man is born, you know the sparks begin to fly / He gets wise in his own eyes and he's made to believe a lie / Who would deliver him from the death he's bound to die?" This lyric is derived from 2 Thessalonians 2:11, where it refers to the delusion that God sends in the form of the lawless one imbued with the activity of Satan. It seems, however, that Dylan has utilized the phrase to convey the allure of the world, which amounts to nothing but death, the deliverance therefrom that can come only through the savior. Even in this moment of religious fervor, Dylan could not avoid preaching that hope rests on an acceptance of the inherently duplicitous nature of our being.

Pointedly, in *Infidels* (1983), the album that marks Dylan's turning from a blind faith in Jesus, he succumbs to the more gnostic viewpoint in "Jokerman":

> It's a shadowy world, skies are slippery grey
> A woman just gave birth to a prince today and dressed him in scarlet
> He'll put the priest in his pocket, put the blade to the heat
> Take the motherless children off the street
> And place them at the feet of a harlot.

The biblical reference (Ecclesiastes 11:1) in this song to the image of sending forth the bread upon the waters indicates that we are karmically responsible for our actions. The ominous implication is accentuated by the additional images of the glowing eyes of the idol with the iron head and the clutching of the serpent in both fists amidst the blowing hurricane of a storm. The imagery transmits the sense of impropriety and peril, the tension between faith and heresy, monotheism and idolatry. Freedom may be around the corner, but is of no avail when truth is unattainable in the shadowy world. Trying to hold on to the belief in Jesus – the prince dressed in scarlet[4] – Dylan complicates and repudiates his earlier evangelism by noting the inability of the Jokerman to respond. The challenge to faith is even more pronounced in the last stanza in "Man of Peace" (1983):

> Somewhere Mama's weeping for her blue-eyed boy
> She's holding them little white shoes and that little broken toy
> And he's following a star
> The same one them three men followed from the East
> I hear that sometimes Satan comes as a man of peace.

---

[4] It appears that Dylan's words are based on the description of the robe that Pontius Pilate's soldiers placed on Jesus as scarlet (*kokkinen*) according to Matthew 27:28. In the parallels from Mark 15:17, 20 and John 19:2, 5, the robe was purple (*porphuran*).

Sometimes Satan comes as a man of peace – an alluring statement that, evocative of William Blake's mysticism, undercuts the dichotomy between Christ and Antichrist, good and evil, light and dark, holy and profane. Dylan undermines such binaries in the striking first stanza of this song:

> Look out your window, baby, there's a scene you'd like to catch
> The band is playing "Dixie," a man got his hand outstretched
> Could be the Führer
> Could be the local priest
> You know sometimes Satan comes as a man of peace.

The insight that opposites are the same in virtue of their opposition resonates with a central idea that has influenced the kabbalistic perspective: the conviction that the deceptiveness of the demonic is an inherent aspect of the veracity of the divine. To the extent that evil is the other side and not the privation of good, that darkness is a manifestation and not the occlusion of light, it follows that there can be no truth that is not itself untruth. Enlightenment in the intrinsically unredeemable world consists of casting light on the shadow so that the shadow is illumined as light. Unlike the gnostics of old, however, Dylan rejects the feasibility of escaping the murky and transient domain of appearance by fleeing to a realm of radiant and everlasting truth. The only truth is that there is no truth to behold. What is dark is not dissolved in brightness; it remains concealed as it is manifest in the light. Dylan's poetic sensibility thus illumines the dark light by uncovering the shadow as shadow. One is thereby emancipated and reveals that in the showing of the unhidden, beings hide themselves; what is finally disclosed is the concealment that conceals itself in its disclosure.

This vision of luminal darkness has grown incrementally darker through the years. In "Tight Connection to My Heart (Has Anyone Seen My Love)" (1985), Dylan bluntly affirms the gnostic rejection of meaning in this life:

> I'll go along with the charade
> Until I can think my way out
> I know it was all a big joke
> Whatever it was about
> Someday maybe
> I'll remember to forget.

The depiction of everything as a big joke recalls the second stanza of "All Along the Watchtower" (1968), which declares that "life is but a joke / But you and I, we've been through that, and this is not our fate / So let us not talk falsely now, the hour is getting late." At this juncture, Dylan eschewed – temporarily at least – the cynical and derisive posture that life is nothing but the dissimulation of life. The urgency to overcome such skepticism is spurred by the apocalyptic sense that the hour is getting late, that the judgment is imminent. Years later, Dylan declares that, indeed, it is all a big joke, even if he cannot delineate the exact nature of the pretense of "this version of death called life," as he put it in "Huck's Tune" (2007). The only hope is that maybe one day he will remember to forget, a paradox that echoes the biblical command to Moses to inscribe in a book the mandate to wipe out the memory of Amalek from under heaven (Exodus 17:14). To remember to forget still holds out a shimmer of hopefulness – as the thirteenth-century kabbalist Abraham Abulafia observed "the end of forgetfulness is the beginning of remembrance"[5] – but to forget to remember to forget is to be thrust deeper into darkness, to be plunged deeper into the abyss of exile, the "hollow place where martyrs weep and angels play with sin" ("Dirge").

As Dylan writes in "Not Dark Yet" (1997), "I was born here and I'll die here against my will." One does not choose to be born and one does not choose to die, a mindset that likely reflects the words attributed to R. Eleazar ha-Qappar in the *Chapters of the Fathers*, "Against your will you were formed, against your will you were born, against your will you live, and against your will you die" (4:22). Dylan adds to the rabbinic dictum the observation that any sense of movement is an illusion because "I'm standing still." So vacuous and numbing is the experience of being alive in this world that the poet cannot even remember what it was that he wanted to forget. In this state of alienation, not even the murmur of a prayer provides hope. The claustrophobia communicated in this song is so extreme that there is "not even room enough to be anywhere," and it has become evident that "behind every beautiful thing there's some kind of pain." Notwithstanding his peregrinations to places as exquisite as London and Paris, Dylan bemoans the wretchedness of his burden that seems too heavy to bear, "I've been down on the bottom of a world full of lies / I ain't looking for nothing in anyone's eyes."[6]

So destitute is the human predicament that even the reviving of one's dreams during sleep is only a pretext to appreciate the vacuity of our wakefulness:

> Gonna sleep down in the parlor
> And relive my dreams
> I'll close my eyes and I wonder
> If everything is as hollow as it seems. ("Tryin' to Get to Heaven," 1997)

---

[5] Abraham Abulafia, *Or ha-Sekhel*, ed. Amnon Gross (Jerusalem, 2001), p. 94.
[6] Dylan, "Not Dark Ye" (1997).

The glimmer of light that this murkiness preserves – the luminescence of "the dark land of the sun" ("Standing in the Doorway," 1997) – is the realization that in the brokenness, we are unbroken; in the inability to find salvation, we are saved. In "Love Sick" (1997), Dylan captures poignantly this intractable hankering for love even as he doubts its existence: "I'm sick of love; I'm trying to forget you / Just don't know what to do / I'd give anything to be with you." His ongoing struggle with the ephemerality of relationships bespeaks a poetic impulse derived from the deferred messianism that has informed Judaism for centuries: the melancholic work of preparing for the savior who comes by not coming, foreseeing the ghost that appears by not appearing. This inescapable suspension of consummation, however, occasions the abundance of time: the voyage that returns interminably to the place whence one feels out of place. At the conclusion of "Oh Sister" (1975), a song infused with images drawn from the biblical Song of Songs, Dylan says to his bride/sister, "Time is an ocean but it ends at the shore / You may not see me tomorrow." The melancholy of Jewish messianism procures this certitude of endless doubt, the questioning that elicits no response but another question.

In "Ain't Talkin'" (2006), Dylan laments his being inconsolable and estranged in this world:

> They say prayer has the power to help
> So pray for me mother
> In the human heart an evil spirit can dwell
> I'm trying to love my neighbor and do good unto others
> But oh, mother, things ain't going well.

The poet appeals to walking as opposed to talking as the means by which he traverses through "the weary world of woe." The heart is still enflamed with craving even if no one seems to know. Once more, Dylan mentions prayer as a possible intervention to help. We must pray specifically from the mother – perhaps an allusion to the *Shekhinah*, the feminized persona of the divine presence according to the theosophic symbolism of the kabbalah – in spite of the fact that the evil spirit dwells in the human heart. Dylan tries to live up to the quintessential command to love one's neighbor as oneself (Leviticus 19:18, Matthew 22:39, Mark 12:31, Luke 10:27) and the golden rule of doing good unto others (Matthew 7:12, Luke 6:31), but confesses that things are not going well. Tellingly, even in his depiction of the mystic garden, he speaks of the wounded flowers dangling from the vines. In consonance with a well-entrenched Jewish inclination not only to bear affliction as a cross but also to transpose the torment into joy, Dylan's art and biography attest to his belief that one must keep walking the "long and lonesome road" that has no altars, practicing a "faith that's been long abandoned." And this is so even if one is doomed, as Dylan said of himself, to go barefoot while making shoes for everyone. In this avowal, one can envisage redemption as the event that cannot transpire in time but which is nonetheless constitutive of time.

Dylan invokes this obstinate will to keep on keeping on in the seemingly simplistic lyrics of "Buckets of Rain" (1974) and "Can't Wait" (1997). We venture to the future even though the future is always receding from us, and thus we move but are standing still. The dichotomy of inertia and mobility collapses in the face of time's inexorable coming to be in its incessant passing away. The poet embodies the discernment that, in its profoundest inflection, time is the arresting kinesis of the moment constantly shifting in its stasis. "Yesterday everything was going too fast / Today, it's moving too slow." The one who walks barefoot well knows that motion is the most vibrant stillness and stillness the most vigorous motion. As Dylan remarked at the beginning of his journey in the 1963 song "Long Time Gone":

> I know I ain't no prophet
> An' I ain't no prophet's son
> I'm just a long time a-comin'
> An' I'll be a long time gone.

CHAPTER 19

Christianity: An Exegesis of Modern Times

Andrew McCarron

On November 17, 1978, while Bob Dylan was playing a gig in San Diego, an audience member threw a small silver cross onto the stage. Dylan picked it up and put it into his pocket. He was exhausted and physically ill, worn down by an emotionally grueling divorce and demanding world tour. The following night, in Tucson, he was feeling even worse and reached into his pocket, pulled out the cross, and put it on. That night, while stuck inside a hotel room, he felt the overwhelming presence of Jesus. He described the experience a few years later to journalist Karen Hughes:

> Being born again is a hard thing. You ever seen a mother give birth to a child? Well it's painful. We don't like to lose those old attitudes and hang-ups . . . Jesus put his hand on me. It was a physical thing. I felt it. I felt it all over me. I felt my whole body tremble. The glory of the lord knocked me down and picked me up.[1]

Six days after the Tucson show, while performing in Fort Worth, Dylan was spotted wearing the same cross around his neck. Although he wouldn't go public with his conversion for a number of months, concertgoers present during the final weeks of the '78 tour noticed that he'd replaced the lyrics from "Tangled Up in Blue" that referenced the song's mysterious lady quoting lines from a thirteenth-century poet with lines from the Gospel according to Matthew, and then later from Jeremiah. By the time his next album, *Slow Train Coming*, was completed in the spring of 1979, stories of his conversion had trickled into the media.

Dylan's conversion inspired the recording of a trilogy of deeply inspired gospel albums: *Slow Train Coming* (1979), *Saved* (1980), and *Shot of Love* (1981). He began traveling around with a trio of black female backup singers (known as the Queens of Rhythm), and for a time refused to play any of his pre-Christian music. A previously shy Dylan openly preached to

---

[1] Jonathan Cott, ed., *Bob Dylan: The Essential Interviews* (New York: Wenner Books, 2006), p. 293.

audiences with mini-sermons between songs, saying things like "Anyway, we know this world's gonna be destroyed; we know that. Christ will set up His Kingdom in Jerusalem for a thousand years, where the lion will lie down with the lamb. Have you heard that before? I'm just curious enough to know, how many people believe that?"[2] Many fans never forgave him. But he evangelized nonetheless. The end of the world was nigh and the only option was to repent and be saved. The alternative was eternal damnation in the fiery pit of hell.

By the mid-1980s, however, Dylan had more or less stopped making overtly Christian statements in public. When asked about his religious feelings during interviews, his answers were opaque. He claimed the press had largely misunderstood his conversion and that he wasn't "Born Again," which was "a media term."[3] Had he lost his faith? Like so many things about the elusive songwriter, no one could say for sure. Then, in the early 1990s, he appeared on a few Chabad-Lubavitch telethons, and was spotted at various synagogues. Speculation deepened. Had he reconnected to the Judaism of his ancestors? Some said yes, others no.

The truth is that Bob Dylan has never stopped being Christian. Nor is his Christianity just one facet of a highly syncretic spirituality with tributaries into Judaism, New Age, and Greco-Roman mythology. In his book *Trouble in Mind: Bob Dylan's Gospel Years: What Really Happened*, Clinton Heylin claims, I think accurately, that Dylan has remained true to Christianity over the decades.[4] Heylin understands his subject's reluctance to discuss where he's at with religion as a consequence of the unforgiving scrutiny he was subjected to for the overtly religious music he wrote, recorded, and performed between 1978 and 1981. But the slow train has continued down the tracks.

Dylan has suggested that if people want to know what he believes, they should listen to his songs. And a careful examination of his later work reveals more than an abundance of New Testament quotations. Albums like *Modern Times* convey a theological worldview deeply influenced by Christianity, especially that faith's understandings of sin, apocalypse, and salvation. Furthermore, when compared to the zealousness of *Slow Train Coming* and *Saved* (recorded in Dylan's late-thirties), *Modern Times* (recorded in Dylan's mid-sixties) tells a story about how the faith of

[2] Andrew McCarron, *Light Come Shining: The Transformations of Bob Dylan* (Oxford: Oxford University Press, 2017), p. 18.

[3] Cott, *Essential Interviews*, p. 305.

[4] Clinton Heylin, *Trouble in Mind: Bob Dylan's Gospel Years: What Really Happened* (New York: Lesser Gods, 2017).

mystically inclined people may change over their lifetime. What can look like loss of faith from the outside might constitute a spiritual maturation in which doubt and ambiguity become aspects of religious faith.

Apocalypse

The lyrics of *Modern Times* resemble a collage of Bible verses, blues lines, and borrowed poetry. But the album isn't merely a random hodgepodge fused together by a master songwriter and well-rehearsed road band. Similar in ways to T.S. Eliot's poem *The Waste Land*, *Modern Times* builds something coherent from the wreckage of a crumbling world. Dylan, who characterized himself in a 2001 interview as "a person that feels like he's walking around in the ruins of Pompeii,"[5] is no stranger to a world gone wrong. A descendant of persecuted European Jews, he grew up in an over-mined, ecologically devastated region of Minnesota, came of age during the height of the Cold War, witnessed the social and political upheavals of the 1960s and 1970s, and embraced a fire and brimstone apocalyptic Christian worldview by the time he was middle-aged. As he put it in a 1984 interview, "I believe that ever since Adam and Eve got thrown out of the garden, that the whole nature of the planet has been heading in one direction – towards apocalypse."[6]

So many things on *Modern Times* are "out of whack,"[7] even the Good Book itself. Quotations and allusions from Genesis, Exodus, Isaiah, the Psalms, Gospels, Pauline Letters, and Revelation are reworded and out of order. The singer croons lines from the Jewish and Christian Bibles as he walks through an inhospitable land where few can be trusted, where danger awaits around every corner, and where he pines for the redemptive love of a good woman. But the world has gone to pieces, and his woman is lost, dead, indifferent, or adversarial (though in some songs she saves him).

The opening number, "Thunder on the Mountain," a rockabilly staple in Dylan's live shows since being premiered on stage in 2006, warns of "thunder on the mountain" and "fires on the moon." The imminence of the Second Coming is suggested by the second line – "There's a ruckus in the alley and the sun will be here soon" – provided that we accept the possibility that "sun" could be homophonic for "son" – a technique that Dylan also may employ elsewhere (e.g., in the line "I've still got the scars

---

[5] Cott, *Essential Interviews*, p. 452.
[6] Clinton Heylin, *Still On the Road: The Songs of Bob Dylan, 1974–2006* (Chicago: Chicago Review Press, 2010), p. 165.
[7] Bob Dylan, "Nettie Moore," Bob Dylan, 2006, www.bobdylan.com/songs/nettie-moore/.

that the sun didn't heal" from "Not Dark Yet" [1997]). The bad luck woman who's guilty of charming his brains away on the third track, the hard-driving "Rollin' and Tumblin'," a reworking of a Delta blues song recorded by Robert Johnson, Robert Estes, and Muddy Waters, is told by the singer that "Sooner or later, you *too* shall burn." The fires and floods are coming. Incidentally, this woman shares interesting parallels with the Whore of Babylon from Revelation 17–18: both beguile prominent men, both are associated with burning landscapes, and both die by fire. The apocalypse also reappears in the seventh verse with a Christological image from Revelation 10:3:

> The night's filled with shadows, the years are filled with early doom
> The night's filled with shadows, the years are filled with early doom
> I've been conjuring up all these long dead souls from their crumblin' tombs.

Modern Times is packed with other apocalyptic images as well: the poppin' pistols and power outages in "Thunder on the Mountain"; the crumbling levees of the Hurricane Katrina-inspired "The Levee's Gonna Break"; and "the cities of the plague" referenced in "Ain't Talkin'." In a 2007 interview with Jann Wenner promoting the album, Dylan explains the songs as an ongoing response to the annihilation anxiety he experienced growing up. He discusses how the Cold War created the social and psychological conditions from which early rock 'n' roll emerged. "If you look at all these early performers, they were atom-bomb-fueled," Dylan says. "Jerry Lee, Carl Perkins, Buddy Holly, Elvis, Gene Vincent, Eddie Cochran . . . They were fast and furious, their songs were all on the edge."[8] Wenner asks Dylan whether he's "still dealing with the cultural effects of the bomb" on *Modern Times*, to which Dylan responds: "I think so." Later in the interview he adds a theological dressing to his atomic anxiety: "We really don't know much about the great Judgment Day that's coming, because we've got nobody to come back and tell us about it. We can only assume certain things because of what we've been taught."[9]

The Christian theology that Bob Dylan was taught during several months of intensive post-conversion Bible study at the Vineyard Fellowship in Tarzana, California stressed an end times, apocalyptic message partially derived from Hal Lindsey's bestseller *The Late Great Planet Earth* (1970). The coming apocalypse was understood by Lindey as a response to human sinfulness and he advised that you fulfill your God-given destiny before it was too late. There was no time to lose. Events in the

---

[8] Cott, *Essential Interviews*, p. 486.   [9] Ibid.

world like the formation of Israel, the Soviet Union's ill-fated invasion of
Afghanistan, and the Iranian Revolution pointed to the cataclysmic even-
tuality predicted by John of Patmos in the first century CE. Dylan proclaimed this message night-in and night-out during the live shows he
played across 1979 and 1980 to support *Slow Train Coming* and *Saved*. At
one concert in the fall of 1979, he openly witnessed to his audience:

> You know we're living in the end times . . . The scriptures say, "In the last
> days, perilous times shall be at hand. Men shall become lovers of their own
> selves. Blasphemous, heavy, and high-minded." . . . Take a look at the
> Middle East. We're heading for a war . . . I told you "The Times They
> Are A-Changin'" and they did. I said the answer was "Blowin' in the Wind"
> and it was. I'm telling you now Jesus is coming back, and He is! And there is
> no other way of salvation . . . Jesus is coming back to set up His kingdom in
> Jerusalem for a thousand years.[10]

Twenty-seven years later, he predicted a similar calendar on "The
Levee's Gonna Break": "Put on your cat clothes, mama, put on your
evening dress / Few more years of hard work, then there'll be a thousand
years of happiness." Indeed, Dylan has never stopped worrying about the
causal relationship between sin and destruction. There's no shortage of
good old-fashioned Biblical sin on *Modern Times*. He openly wonders
"what's the matter with this cruel world today" and makes plans to raise an
army of "tough sons of bitches" recruited from orphanages in "Thunder on
the Mountain"; he's lamenting the exploitation of the proletariat in
"Workingman's Blues #2"; and getting hit from behind while walking
through a "weary world of woe" in "Ain't Talkin'." The subjects aren't
merely passive observers of lawlessness and strife. Their morally dubious
actions directly contribute to the macabre state of things. The singer
threatens to straighten out a woman's tongue in "Workingman's Blue's
#2"; he's blocked from entering paradise in "Spirit on the Water" for
killing a man, echoing the fratricidal slaying of Abel by Cain; and he's
making his way through a desolate landscape "Carrying a dead man's
shield" in "Ain't Talkin'." Like Oedipus, even the best of us end up living
out the darker fates we try our hardest to avoid. Despite being called
Modern Times, the world of heroes, villains, odysseys, and prophecies
depicted by the album feels more ancient than contemporary.

The album's images of sin and destruction have a markedly Christian
character. Jewish and Christian theologies share eschatological conceptions
of time as an irreversible progress from creation to apocalypse. But how the

---

[10] McCarron, *Light Come Shining*, pp. 152–153.

"end times" are imaged differs significantly. Whereas some Jewish theology conceptualizes a Godly era ushered in by a messiah who will deliver the faithful from suffering and tribulation, predictions about when this deliverance will take place and the form it will take (e.g., spiritual, political, cosmic) are left as mysteries by the majority of Jewish thinkers. Absent from Jewish eschatology is the intrinsic connection between the end of history and original sin. The founder of the Reconstructionist Movement in Judaism, Mordecai Kaplan (1881–1983) put it this way:

> The suffering and the tragedy have always been viewed [by Jews] merely as interruptions which have postponed the fulfillment of the blessing. They were never thought of as the fulfillment of some irrevocable doom. It is only Christianity, which has assimilated a great deal of the Greek spirit, that has made the doctrine of original sin a fundamental teaching.[11]

At a certain point in his journey, Dylan began to understand the sicknesses of the world through a theological lens rather than a sociopolitical one. The utopian social visions of leftist folkies and protest singers like Joan Baez and Phil Ochs failed to account for the enduring persistence of "power and greed and corruptible seed."[12] Dylan saw signs of decadence and wreckage everywhere he went, not least of all in the shadowy recesses of his own heart and mind. Such a worldview has long outlasted his so-called Christian period. As recently as 2015, he told *AARP Magazine*: "I've always been drawn to spiritual songs. In 'Amazing Grace' that line – 'that saved a wretch like me' – isn't that something we could all say if we were honest enough."[13]

Salvation

Bob Dylan's songs have been equally preoccupied with salvation, whether sociopolitical, personal, romantic, or spiritual in nature. In *Bob Dylan in America*, historian Sean Wilentz reports on how a young Bob Dylan abandoned the utopian political visions of the folk movement for a new vision of personal transcendence embodied by the Beat poets Allen Ginsberg, Jack Kerouac, and Neal Cassady.[14] Rejecting the protest-sensibilities of the lefties, the Beats favored a lifestyle of sexual liberation, open expression, and a derangement of the senses as a means of freeing their

---

[11] Mordecai M. Kaplan, *The Meaning of God in Modern Jewish Religion* (Detroit: Wayne State University Press, 1994), p. 79.

[12] Bob Dylan, "Blind Willie McTell," (1983).

[13] *AARP* Interview in J. Burger, ed., *Dylan on Dylan: Interviews and Encounters* (Chicago: Chicago Review Press, 2018).

[14] Sean Wilentz, *Bob Dylan in America* (New York City: Anchor Books, 2011).

trembling, mystical spirits from the crushing conformities of Moloch. But Cassady and Kerouac's tragic lives were proof that a diet of wine, women, and song could lead even the most brilliant souls to sad ends. Biographers have suggested that Dylan himself was barreling on a crash course of post-divorce confusion, overwork, and grief through the months leading up to his conversion to Christianity in 1978. Many of the things that had given him meaning and stability (songwriting, touring, women, various substances) were not working. This is precisely when Jesus entered his life.

Dylan's dogged search for salvation has continued over the decades, despite his report of no longer adhering to rabbis, preachers, or evangelists. But the search has been long and hard. There's an unmistakably Calvinistic quality to Dylan's religious worldview in recent decades. God's will is unknowable; the line separating good from evil is porous; and atonement is limited. Doubt and uncertainty notwithstanding, *Modern Times* explores forms of salvation that appear and reappear in various permutations across his discography: biblical virtue, Jesus/God, and romantic love. The ways that these sources interact within and across the album's ten songs may reveal a good deal about the nature of Dylan's religious worldview at the time of the album's recording in February 2006.

The moral universe of Dylan songs has always been contoured by biblical virtue, or what he has called "the original rule." Time and time again, his songs mine the depths of the Bible for moral truths. "I hate to keep hitting people over the head with the Bible," Dylan told Mikal Gilmore in 1986, "but that's the only instrument I know, the only thing that stays true."[15] Justice, prudence, temperance, fortitude, and love guide his world-weary heroes as they journey through an amoral world in search of shelter from the storm. Many of the most memorable subjects of his earlier protest songs – whether Hattie Carroll, Medgar Evers, Rubin Carter, or Dylan himself – are voices crying in the wilderness, men and women trying to preserve dignity in an undignified world of injustice, chaos, and danger. Dylan's inherited Judaism is nowhere more evident than in the jeremiads of his most impacting political songs, songs that don't sugarcoat the tribulations of the world. As he said to journalist Scott Cohen in 1985, when asked what it was in his words that went unheard: "The things I have to say about such things as ghetto bosses, salvation and sin, lust, murderers going free, and children without hope."[16]

---

[15] Cott, *Essential Interviews*, p. 367.
[16] Bob Dylan, "Don't Ask Me Nothin' About Nothin' I Might Just Tell You the Truth," interview by Scott Cohen, *Spin*, December 1985.

Proverbs 21 states: "Whoever pursues righteousness and love finds life, prosperity and honor."[17] Likewise, the songs on *Modern Times* equate righteous living with redemptive hope, no matter how faint the promise may be. The singer of "Thunder on the Mountain" resolves that he's "Gonna forget about myself for a while, gonna go out and see what others need," and extols the virtue of forgiveness on "When the Deal Goes Down," crooning, "We learn to live and then we forgive / O'er the road we're bound to go." But a life of good works is challenging, especially in an eye for an eye world in which survival necessitates moral compromise, not to mention the evil that dwells in every heart. These impediments, one situational and the other conditional, are named in the second stanza of "Ain't Talkin'":

> They say prayer has the power to help
> So pray for me mother
> In the human heart an evil spirit can dwell
> I'm trying to love my neighbor and do good unto others
> But oh, mother, things ain't going well.

Despite their attempts at rectitude, the characters who inhabit the album are far from saintly. They've lied, cheated, fornicated, hated, and killed in vengeance as well as in cold blood. Many are banished or barred from entering the promised land. For the singer of "Spirit on the Water," for instance, paradise is lost on account of the singer's Cain-like defilement: "I can't go to paradise no more / I killed a man back there."

The moral of the story is bleak: the longer one lives, the more defiled one gets. In the end, our fates lie in the hands of a mysterious and arbitrary God. As Dylan put it during a bizarre acceptance speech for a 1991 Lifetime Grammy Achievement Award, supposedly paraphrasing something his father once said: "it's possible to become so defiled in this world that your own father and mother will abandon you, and if that happens, God will always believe in your ability to mend your ways."[18] But the God of *Modern Times* isn't the personal deity that inspired Dylan's songs and concerts during the late 1970s and early 1980s. This father and this son are distant and elusive, as if on a receding horizon, perpetually out of reach. "Some sweet day I'll stand beside my king," the singer pines in "Thunder on the Mountain." Salvation isn't automatic, grace is scarce, and love is

---

[17] Prov. 21, New International Version.
[18] Michl Mayr, "Feb 20 '91 . . . Grammy Award Ceremony, acceptance speech. . . " YouTube Video, 1:42, June 1, 2019, www.youtube.com/watch?v=6h4QR_ZBPlk.

a fading memory. Still, the wayfarer yearns for the morsels of redemption that remain.

A number of the album's characters are on long arduous journeys, sometimes toward something or someone they love, but more often they're running from primordial wounds of fratricide, lost love, natural disaster, or displacement. By the album's concluding song, the narratively sprawling "Ain't Talkin'," the singer is wandering through a mystic garden, starved of fulfillment and forgiveness. In addition to being pursued for killing a sheriff, he's practicing "a faith that's long been abandoned," stranded "In the last outback, at the world's end." Jesus is remote and unresponsive. And there "[a]in't no altars on this long and lonesome road." The penultimate stanza of the song echoes the twentieth chapter of John's Gospel in which Mary Magdalen mistakes the risen Jesus for a gardener on the Friday after his crucifixion and entombment. "Excuse me, ma'am I beg your pardon," sings Dylan, "There's no one here, the gardener is gone."

As a 65-year-old, the brightness of God's presence had dimmed, especially when compared to the intensity of the Jesus that Dylan encountered in Tucson in 1978. Although I'm wary of drawing comparisons to Mother Teresa, it bears mentioning that her private letters and journals, made public in 2007, revealed that in later years she felt abandoned by a God whose presence she felt more profoundly and assuredly when she was younger. "In my heart, there is no faith," she wrote in one entry. "I want God with all the powers of my soul, yet between us there is terrible separation."[19] The pathos of many mystics is that their experiences of the divine are at best perennial, leaving them haunted by loneliness, longing, and doubt.

In God's absence, the more tangible source of salvation is romantic love. Dylan's love songs, which mellow the tone of *Modern Times* with shuffles and summery swings, are testament to the potency of desire and erotic memory. Dylan's holiest of holies have always been women. Even through the zealous period after his 1978 conversion, he was neither a Puritan nor a Promise Keeper, and went out of his way to distance himself from the Moral Majority movement. Many of the love songs on the gospel trilogy (1978–1981) exude erotic innuendo and anticipation. Sex is part of God's plan as well. Songs like "Precious Angel," "Covenant Woman," and "Caribbean Wind" combine spirituality with sexuality, infusing women with the Christ-like capacity to touch, comfort, and

---

[19] Mother Teresa, *Mother Teresa: Come be My Light: The Private Writings of the Saint of Calcutta*, ed. Brian Kolodiejchuk (New York: Crown Publishing, 2007), p. 193.

heal. The phenomenon of a man finding God through the love of a holy woman has a poignant history in Christianity: Aquila and Priscilla, Pelagia and Nonnus, Abelard and Heliöse, Dante and Beatrice, Petrarch and Laura, and Thomas Merton and Margie Smith, the young nurse who Merton fell in love with while convalescing from back surgery in 1966.

Alongside its apocalyptic preoccupations, *Modern Times* is an album of battle-scarred romance. The aging singer is pining for a woman he no longer sees but continues to think about; lusting after a young woman he'll likely never meet; expressing gratitude for the loyalty of a good woman; or cursing the ones who've wronged him. The album pulses with desire, but this isn't youthful desire. It's the persistent desire of a man whose body is diminishing, but whose hunger for sex and companionship remains. "You think I'm over the hill / You think I'm past my prime," the singer chides in the final verse of "Spirit on the Water," "Let me see what you got / We can have a whoppin' good time."[20] He finds his closest approximation to salvation in the love of a sexually powerful woman with whom to share the covenant of his faith:

> Each invisible prayer is like a cloud in the air
> Tomorrow keeps turning around
> We live and we die, we know not why
> But I'll be with you when the deal goes down,

he sings in the parlor ballad "When the Deal Goes Down." Performed in a waltz-like cadence, the song blesses the nostalgia and contented silences of a long marriage with Christian iconographic qualities:

> The midnight rain follows the train
> We all wear the same thorny crown
> Soul to soul, our shadows roll
> And I'll be with you when the deal goes down.

A couple – together through life.

Arguably the most powerful love song on the album is the eighth track, "Nettie Moore," a piece that Dylan himself singled out as a favorite. Written as a romantic lament, it is modeled on a heavily reworked nineteenth-century parlor song titled "The Little White Cottage, or Gentle Nettie Moore." The singer is paying for a life of sin, threatened by legal and divine judgment, and "beginning to believe what the scriptures tell." Vengeful ("Fore you call me any dirty names, you'd better

---

[20] Bob Dylan, "Spirit on the Water," 2006, www.bobdylan.com/songs/spirit-water/.

think twice") and lost ("The world has gone black before my eyes"), he can do little more than pine for his lost love, the gentle Nettie Moore, without whom salvation is impossible. "Got a pile of sins to pay for and I ain't got time to hide," Dylan sings. "I'd walk through a blazing fire, baby, if I knew you was on the other side." It's romantic redemption the singer is after: "When you're around me all my grief gives 'way / A lifetime with you is like some heavenly day." But when he realizes, yet again, that Nettie is only a memory and won't be returning, he resolves to live out the remaining days of his unhappy life by faith alone:

> Today I'll stand in faith and raise
> The voice of praise
> The sun is strong, I'm standing in the light
> I wish to God that it were night.

Dark Night of the Soul

The songs on *Modern Times* reveal the lifeworld of an artist who's doing more than merely drawing from the religious tropes of the Delta blues or weaving random biblical verses into his lyrics for aesthetic purposes. The songs instead reflect the heartache of a man whose connection to God has changed as he has aged. Themes of isolation and estrangement haunt the songs: estrangement from one's values, from others, and from God. Christian mystics have written about the struggles and terrors of separation from the ultimate. Saint John of the Cross called it the dark night of the soul in the sixteenth century, and the twentieth-century religious writer Evelyn Underhill called it "the dark ecstasy."[21] People who experience God's illuminative presence cannot remain in the divine light forever. During spiritually fallow periods, darkness sets in. The mystic may begin to believe that the divine presence has been extinguished and that he or she has been abandoned altogether. This is by no means an indication that one's faith has died, however. As one ages, faith must assume a form in which doubt and distance from God become aspects of one's experience of incarnation.

---

[21] Evelyn Underhill, *Essential Writings*, ed. Emilie Griffin (Ossining: Orbis Books, 2003), p. 83.

PART IV

Political Contexts

CHAPTER 20

The Civil Rights Movement

Will Kaufman

When Sean Wilentz watched Bob Dylan perform in Minneapolis on the night of Barack Obama's election in 2008, he noted how "the stubbornly reticent Dylan broke with habit" and spoke directly to his audience, telling them that, although he had "lived in a world of darkness," the election of America's first black president made it look like "things are gonna change now." Wilentz himself wasn't too sure, either about Dylan's prediction or, in fact, his sincerity: "Though I understood the symbolism and the emotive force, I was more skeptical at the time, and could imagine that Dylan was being ironic or at least ambiguous. But without betraying any kind of certainty let alone commitment, he sounded sincere and even excited."[1] The lack of certainty over Dylan's "commitment" to the civil rights movement (or to anything else, for that matter) is one of the defining aspects of the critical response to his work. At the grimmest end of the spectrum is Wayne Hampton, who has characterized the electric, post-folk Dylan in particular as "steeped in paranoid cynicism about politics, both radical and conventional," with "a highly pessimistic – even nihilistic – disposition toward the possibilities of social change . . . . Bob Dylan gave us the cult of chaos and non-involvement."[2]

Dylan himself didn't help to clarify things by telling Joan Baez – as she later related to one of Dylan's earliest biographers, Anthony Scaduto – "I knew people would buy that kind of shit, right? I never was into that stuff."[3] Yet other close friends and associates of Dylan assured the same biographer otherwise. Dylan's producer John Hammond was adamant: "Bobby really wanted to change things."[4] His fellow songwriter Phil Ochs also rejected the charge of cynical opportunism: "He definitely meant the

[1] Sean Wilentz, *Bob Dylan in America* (London: Vintage, 2011), p. 326.
[2] Wayne Hampton, *Guerrilla Minstrels: John Lennon, Joe Hill, Woody Guthrie, Bob Dylan* (Knoxville: University of Tennessee Press, 1986), p. 214.
[3] Anthony Scaduto, *Bob Dylan* (London: Abacus, 1972), p. 120.   [4] Ibid, p. 120.

protest ... and he meant every word he wrote. He was just going on to bigger things when he started denying it, that's all."[5]

In light of such contradictory impressions, any attempt to assess Dylan's place in the struggle for civil rights in America is freighted with the problem – but also, possibly, with the solution – of distinguishing between the man himself and the cultural work that his songs have performed and might still perform. Relying on Dylan's own utterances may indeed lead us nowhere, as Dave Van Ronk warned: "[H]is thinking is so convoluted that he simply does not know how to level, because he's always thinking of the effect that he's having on whoever he's talking to."[6] Still, Van Ronk was confident in telling Scaduto: "He was no opportunist. He really believed it all. I was there .... It's entirely possible he fell into the *Broadside* bag knowing what those songs could do [for his career], but he believed. He meant it."[7]

The "*Broadside* bag" was the repository of Dylan's earliest civil rights anthems – indeed, the bulk of them. As Jeff Place and Ronald D. Cohen describe it, *Broadside* was the "modest topical song magazine" that went on to stimulate "a national movement": "The first issue of *Broadside*, subtitled 'A handful of songs about our times,' appeared in February 1962; the run was 300 copies and the price 35 cents."[8] Dylan's association with *Broadside* began with the very first issue and its publication of his "Talking John Birch Society Blues."

Dylan's initial approaches to *Broadside* in 1962 were roughly coterminous with his introduction to two major civil rights organizations, the Congress of Racial Equality (CORE) and the Student Nonviolent Coordinating Committee (SNCC or "Snick"). It has been generally assumed that Dylan came to the civil rights movement through his first major romantic liaison in New York, Susan ("Suze") Rotolo, who was a CORE activist along with her sister and her mother. Rotolo herself downplayed her early influence on Dylan, telling Victoria Balfour in an interview that his interest in civil rights was simply down to "the climate of the times."[9] Still, it was the Rotolo women who encouraged Dylan to

---

[5] Ibid.

[6] Dave Van Ronk with Elijah Wald, *The Mayor of MacDougal Street: A Memoir* (New York: Da Capo, 2006), p. 159.

[7] Scaduto, *Bob Dylan*, pp. 120–121.

[8] Jeff Place and Ronald D. Cohen, *The Best of Broadside, 1962–1988: Anthems of the American Underground from the Pages of Broadside Magazine* (Washington, DC: Smithsonian Folkways Recordings, 2000), np.

[9] Susan Rotolo, "Bob Dylan" (interview with Victoria Balfour), in *The Dylan Companion*, ed. Elizabeth Thomson and David Gutman (New York: Da Capo, 2001), p. 76.

perform for a number of CORE benefits during his first two years in New York. Robert Shelton reports that Dylan quickly became disenchanted with the organization, telling a small Minneapolis audience as early as August 1962 that "CORE is a white organization for Negro people."[10] SNCC, on the other hand, captured Dylan's admiration and enthusiasm at the outset, largely due to their frontline organizing in the Jim Crow south. A leading SNCC activist, Bernice Johnson Reagon – one of the celebrated Freedom Singers and, later, a founder of the a cappella women's group Sweet Honey in the Rock – recalled that, even after Dylan had begun to withdraw from conspicuous civil rights activism around 1964 (to the predictable cry of "sell out" from many in the folk-protest movement), the black activists in SNCC were largely non-judgmental. She told Shelton:

> Some whites moved with us out of some special sort of love of blacks, while others were just loaded with guilt. Dylan wasn't the same. When he simply drifted away from the movement, it was the whites in Snick who were resentful. The blacks in Snick didn't think like that, or say that. We only heard the phrase "sellout" from whites, not from the blacks.[11]

If SNCC's black members were willing to give Dylan more of a pass than their white colleagues, it might partially be due to the respectful distance he chose to maintain between himself and any assumed black voice, in both a political and a musical sense. His deep knowledge and utilization of African American blues is, of course, a matter of record, beginning with his youthful determination to discover all that he could about black music. It was Dylan's first encounters with the songs of Lead Belly and Odetta – *not* Woody Guthrie – that drew him out of early rock 'n' roll and into folk music. Performing and recording associations with John Lee Hooker, Harry Belafonte, Big Joe Williams, and Victoria Spivey marked his first two years in New York. But Dylan never fell into the trap that had snared so many other white performers of black music – attempting to *be* black, at least in voice. As Spivey recalled for Scaduto:

> I told Bobby that Big Joe was gonna record for me and he said, "Moms, you want a little white boy on one of your records?" Bobby, you know, had no color denomination to him at all, everybody was people, not color, so I said, "What do you mean? You're just one of my sons," and he said, "You should

[10] Robert Shelton, *No Direction Home: The Life and Music of Bob Dylan*, revised and updated by Elizabeth Thomson and Patrick Humphries (London: Omnibus, 2011), p. 66.

[11] Ibid, p. 113.

have a white boy on some of your records," and I said, "You got some around?" and he said, "Yeah, me." So I told him we'd get together.[12]

None of this is to say that Dylan's early persona was never steeped in imitation or denial. His attempted mimicry of the "Okie bard" Woody Guthrie extended famously not only to his voice and repertoire, but also – to the horror of Guthrie's family – to his bodily tics and contortions, the outward signs of Guthrie's fatal Huntington's disease. There was also Dylan's apparent early need to deny his own Jewishness, not only in high school – where Echo Helstrom was warned by a friend, "Don't ever ask him that" after she had innocently asked, "Bobby, are you Jewish?" – but also at the University of Minnesota – where a girlfriend recalled, "Even after he knew that I knew he was Bob Zimmerman from up on the Range, he was not being Jewish. He was saying his mother wasn't."[13]

The point to be made here is that, however much imitation and ethnic denial may have been a part of Dylan's presentational strategies, they apparently did not extend to his engagements with African American culture, people, or voice. Indeed, as David Hajdu notes, Dylan came to feel "especially uncomfortable as a white man in the civil rights movement; he could never understand the black experience, he said, and his own sympathies extended beyond race." Hajdu quotes Dylan's exasperated outburst in an interview shortly following his appearance at the August 1963 March on Washington, where Martin Luther King, Jr., had delivered his "I Have a Dream" speech:

> What's a Negro? I don't know what a Negro is. What's a Negro – a black person? How black? What's a Negro? A person living in a two-room shack with 12 kids? A lot of white people live in a two-room shack with 12 kids. Does this make them Negro? What's a Negro – someone with African blood? A lot of white people have African blood. What's a Negro?[14]

Dylan's reluctance to identify with, or to presume to explain, black American experience is understandable, given some of the critical responses to his presence and performance at the March on Washington. As the African American comedian and activist Dick Gregory asked Hajdu: "What was a white boy like Bob Dylan there for? Or – who else? Joan Baez? To support the cause? Wonderful – support the cause. March. Stand behind us – but not in front of us." (To which Harry Belafonte responded:

---

[12] Scaduto, *Bob Dylan*, p. 96.   [13] Ibid, pp. 14–15.
[14] David Hajdu, *Positively 4th Street: The Lives and Times of Joan Baez, Bob Dylan, Mimi Baez Fariña and Richard Fariña* (New York: Farrar, Straus and Giroux, 2001), pp. 201–202.

"Joan and Bob demonstrated with their participation that freedom and justice are universal concerns of import to responsible people of all colors . . . . Were they taking advantage of the movement? Or was the movement taking advantage of them?"[15]) By all accounts Dylan would have recoiled at the suggestion that he was standing "in front" of African Americans in the civil rights struggle, or that he could presume to speak for them, either politically or musically. It is perhaps for this reason, as Michael Gray notes, that by 1963 Dylan had become highly circumspect over when or where he would choose to perform the blues:

> When Dylan performed specifically to black audiences, as in Greenwood, Mississippi in 1963 and at a women's penitentiary in New Jersey during the Rolling Thunder Revue of 1975, he didn't hesitate to sing about racial politics but chose to do so via his white "protest" songs – "Only a Pawn in Their Game" and "Hurricane" respectively – rather than via blues songs.[16]

Dylan's circumspection in assuming an identification with blackness is apparent in his earliest *Broadside* anthems. The distance between himself and the subjects of his songs manifests itself in a variety of ways: he affects the persona of a historian, a reporter, a casual observer, or an ironic commentator – but never a black victim of white racism himself. Thus, in his first major civil rights composition, "The Ballad of Emmett Till" (1962) – shortly retitled "The Death of Emmett Till," which Joan Baez maintained had turned her into "a political folksinger"[17] – Dylan reaches back seven years, to the notorious lynching in 1955 of a 14-year-old black child in Mississippi. In addition to the temporal distance, there is the spatial distance between the observed and the observer. Aldon Lynn Nielsen points out that in his recounting of the lynching and the travesty of justice that followed (with the acquittal of both of the killers), Dylan "does not presume to speak on behalf of black suffering, displacing black people from their own narrative, as still occurs in travesties like *Mississippi Burning* and very nearly occurs in *Amistad*." Rather, Nielsen writes, "Dylan's song is written from the point of view of an implicated witness."[18]

Dylan may have felt that he had good reason to refer to "The Death of Emmett Till" only two years after its composition as "a bullshit song." But his oft-quoted dismissal – brutal and disingenuous as it was – contains

[15] Ibid, p. 183.
[16] Michael Gray, *Song and Dance Man III: The Art of Bob Dylan* (London: Continuum, 2000), p. 272.
[17] Hajdu, *Positively 4th Street*, p. 147.
[18] Aldon Lynn Nielsen, "Crow Jane Approximately: Bob Dylan's Black Masque," in *Highway 61 Revisited: Bob Dylan's Road from Minnesota to the World*, ed. Colleen J. Sheehy and Thomas Swiss (Minneapolis: University of Minnesota Press, 2009), p. 188.

a simple nugget of truth about his wayward relationship to civil rights activism: "But when I wrote it, it wasn't a bullshit song to me." Indeed, at the time, as he told the folklorist Izzy Young, he thought it "the best thing I've ever written."[19] The song certainly has its structural problems, not least some noteworthy errors concerning "the facts of the case" – as Clinton Heylin notes, "a pattern he would repeat in two more Southern murder ballads: 'Only a Pawn in Their Game' and 'The Lonesome Death of Hattie Carroll.'"[20] This issue of factual error comes up frequently in Dylan criticism; but similar charges could be made against Woody Guthrie – and it gets to the heart of the cultural work that a song is capable of performing in spite of such errors. Hence "The Death of Emmett Till," which Howard Sounes notes is "the first original Dylan composition that could be called a protest song – a song speaking out against injustice"[21] – at least as important an objective as getting "the facts of the case" right. Nonetheless, even when granting such indulgence, Wilentz, for one, observes, "Dylan had never been consistently good at writing narrative songs out of the newspaper headlines"; consequently, "The Death of Emmett Till" appeared "forced and formulaic," concluding with "platitudes."[22]

Maybe so. But Dylan was, at only twenty-one, on a pretty steep learning curve. By the time he came to his next explicit civil rights anthem, "Oxford Town," toward the end of 1962, he had already written "Blowin' in the Wind," through which the cultural work was more a matter of influence than of enlightenment or explanation. In spite of the song's political vagueness, "Blowin' in the Wind" did the work – among other things – of lighting a flame beneath the black songwriter Sam Cooke, who marveled aloud about "a white boy writing a song like that."[23] Dylan's song, for all its "equivocation,"[24] led directly to Cooke writing his own signature anthem, "A Change Is Gonna Come." (Cooke told a friend that folksingers like Dylan "may not sound as good, but the people believe them more."[25]) Whether or not Cooke was aware that Dylan had drawn partly on the black spiritual "No More Auction Block" for the musical setting of "Blowin' in

[19] Clinton Heylin, *Revolution in the Air: The Songs of Bob Dylan, Vol. 1: 1957–73* (London: Constable, 2010), pp. 87–88.
[20] Ibid, pp. 88–89.
[21] Howard Sounes, *Down the Highway: The Life of Bob Dylan* (London: Doubleday, 2001), p. 109.
[22] Wilentz, *Bob Dylan in America*, p. 152.
[23] Jack Hamilton, *Just Around Midnight: Rock and Roll and the Racial Imagination* (Cambridge, MA: Harvard University Press, 2016), p. 27.
[24] Robert Christgau, "Tarantula," in *Dylan Companion*, ed. Thomson and Gutman, p. 140.
[25] Craig Werner, *A Change Is Gonna Come: Music, Race, and the Soul of America* (Edinburgh: Payback Press, 2000), p. 44.

the Wind," he could apparently enter into a dialogue with it. As Jack Hamilton argues, "'A Change Is Gonna Come' can be heard as an emphatic response to the questions of 'Blowin' in the Wind': 'A Change Is Gonna Come' asks no questions and instead is a series of declarative statements . . . [It] corrects the indeterminate ambiguity invoked by the 'Blowin' in the Wind' refrain, declaring that, in fact, a change *is* going to come."[26]

A distinct change *did* come in Dylan's own writing with the appearance of "Oxford Town" in *Broadside* in December 1962, a mere two months after the black student James Meredith had enrolled in the segregated University of Mississippi, backed up by the federalized National Guard and 500 federal marshals, in the midst of campus riots that had left two dead. Gone were any "platitudes," preaching, or hints of white-guilt breast-beating; in their place was the bewilderment – slightly comedic, at that – of a visiting narrator caught up in the midst of a raging storm. Meredith isn't mentioned by name, nor are the university or the state's segregationist governor, Ross Barnett. Dylan's calculated distance extended to an interview with the Chicago radio host Studs Terkel, to whom he said, "Yeah, it deals with the Meredith case . . . but then again it doesn't."[27]

Elijah Wald reminds us that, in such civil rights songs as "The Death of Emmett Till" and "The Lonesome Death of Hattie Carroll," both of which are aimed at conveying outrage over miscarriages of justice following racist killings, Dylan "was not writing 'We Shall Not Be Moved' or 'We Shall Overcome.' He was writing about individuals, and often difficult, complex individuals"[28] – whether they were victims or killers. But relatively early on, in such songs as "Who Killed Davey Moore?" and "Only a Pawn in Their Game" (both 1963), Dylan turns his sights on institutional or systemic racism, where individuals take a back seat to the structures that enable, encourage, and entrench racist practices. "Who Killed Davey Moore?" recounts, in the coy fashion of the old English ballad "Who Killed Cock Robin?," the death of the black boxer in March 1963. With the boxing ring being one of the few arenas in which a black man could excel in a racist society such as the USA in the mid-twentieth century, Dylan places "money at the center of boxing's ethical morass," as Mike Marqusee argues.[29] With his focus on system and structure rather than on

---

[26] Hamilton, *Just Around Midnight*, p. 52.
[27] Studs Terkel, *And They All Sang* (London: Granta, 2005), p. 211.
[28] Elijah Wald, *Dylan Goes Electric! Newport, Seeger, Dylan, and the Night that Split the Sixties* (New York: Dey Street, 2015), p. 107.
[29] Mike Marqusee, *Wicked Messenger: Bob Dylan and the 1960s* (New York: Seven Stories Press, 2011), p. 78.

individuals, there was a grain of truth to Dylan's dismissive introduction to the song in his Town Hall concert in 1963: "This is a song about a boxer. It's got nothing to do with boxing; it's just a song about a boxer really. And, uh, it's not even having to do with a boxer, really."[30]

In similar fashion, Dylan implied that the murdered civil rights activist Medgar Evers, as well as Byron De La Beckwith, his cowardly assassin, were – in a sense – both smaller than the system (the "game") that had pitted them against each other. In "Only a Pawn in Their Game," Evers is not without his earned stature; but nonetheless, in terms of agency, both he and his killer are positioned as chess pieces by a larger, unseen hand. It may be surprising that Dylan's song should have received such a warm reception from civil rights activists (white and black) as it appears to have done at his performance in Greenwood, Mississippi, in July 1963. NAACP and SNCC activist Howard Romaine recalled Dylan's performance as "an awakening prophetic cry which penetrated to the core," leading him, along with other workers, directly to the "Mississippi Freedom Summer, where we heard [the African American activist] Margaret Burnham singing the words as we came in."[31] For any of its questionable assertions of Beckwith's diminished responsibility (he was "*only* a pawn," after all), the song did more than inspire activism on the ground: it also articulated the concept of "institutional racism" four years before Stokely Carmichael and Charles V. Hamilton coined the term.[32]

For those who had been following the developing poetics of Dylan's civil rights songs, it should have come as no surprise when he confessed to Nat Hentoff in his *Playboy* interview of 1966, "I do believe in equality, but I also believe in distance."[33] Indeed, he had told Hentoff in a *New Yorker* interview two years previously: "I'm not part of no Movement. If I was, I wouldn't be able to do anything else but in 'the Movement.' I just can't have people sit around and make rules for me. I do a lot of things no Movement would allow."[34] This is not to say that his songs wouldn't continue impacting upon the civil rights movement (fractured as it was to become), doing their cultural work in spite of any denial, or indeed any

---

[30] Wilentz, *Bob Dylan in America*, p. 95.

[31] Charles Hughes, "Allowed to Be Free: Bob Dylan and the Civil Rights Movement," in *Highway 61 Revisited*, ed. Sheehy and Swiss, p. 50.

[32] Stokely Carmichael [Kwame Ture] and Charles V. Hamilton, *Black Power: The Politics of Liberation in America* (New York: Random House, 1967), *passim*.

[33] "Interview with Nat Hentoff," *Playboy*, March 1966, in Jonathan Cott, ed., *Bob Dylan: The Essential Interviews* (New York: Simon & Schuster, 2017), p. 111.

[34] Nat Hentoff, "The Crackin', Shakin', Breakin' Sounds," *New Yorker*, October 24, 1964, in Cott, ed., *Essential Interviews*, p. 28.

inscrutable intention, on the part of their composer. In *Seize the Time*, Black Panther founder Bobby Seale recalled how Dylan's musical puzzle, "Ballad of a Thin Man" (1965), had gripped his fellow co-founder Huey P. Newton, as well as Stokely Carmichael:

> Huey P. Newton made me recognize the lyrics. Not only the lyrics of the record, but what the lyrics meant in the record. What the lyrics meant in the history of racism that has perpetuated itself in this world. Huey would say: "Listen, listen – man, do you hear what he is saying?"

Seale concluded:

> Old Bobby did society a big favor when he made that particular sound. If there's any more he made that I don't understand, I'll just ask Huey P. Newton to interpret them for us and maybe we can get a hell of a lot more out of brother Bobby Dylan, because old Bobby, he did a good job on that set.[35]

Seale published *Seize the Time* in 1970, the same year that another young black militant, George Jackson, published his collection of prison letters under the title *Soledad Brother*. The following year, Jackson was killed in a shoot-out in San Quentin prison. Within three months, Dylan hastily wrote a ballad in Jackson's honor, which might well be considered the nadir of his writings on race in America. "George Jackson" was roundly condemned by critics such as Wilentz, who deplored the song's lyrical insincerity – particularly its assertion, "They killed a man I really loved."[36] (As Peter Doggett observed, "Dylan had only become aware of Jackson a matter of hours before writing the song."[37]) The song sparked a ludicrous spat between members of the so-called "Rock Liberation Front," which included, on one side, the self-proclaimed "Dylanologist" A.J. Weberman, who had been attacking Dylan for "deserting the movement," and, on the other side, David Peel, Yoko Ono, and John Lennon, who all felt that "George Jackson" was proof of Dylan's commitment to "the movement" that he had in fact "helped create."[38]

It is difficult to say precisely what cultural work "George Jackson" succeeded in performing, beyond Dylan's rehabilitation for a nearly forgotten, self-important faction in rock music history. The same can be said

---

[35] Bobby Seale, *Seize the Time: The Story of the Black Panther Party and Huey P. Newton* (Baltimore: Black Classic Press, 1991 [1970]), pp. 183, 186–187.

[36] Wilentz, *Bob Dylan in America*, p. 153.

[37] Peter Doggett, *There's a Riot Going On: Revolutionaries, Rock Stars, and the Rise and Fall of the 60s* (New York: Grove Atlantic, 2008), p. 459.

[38] Ibid, p. 462.

for what is, to date, Dylan's last explicit, targeted engagement (through composition) with civil rights and race in America: his 1975 ode to the wrongly convicted and jailed black boxer Rubin "Hurricane" Carter, co-written with Jacques Levy. Carter's ordeal had begun with the fatal shooting of three people in a Paterson, New Jersey, bar in 1966; it ended long after Dylan's involvement with his case – in 1985, when, following two convictions and appeals, a judge in the US District Court for New Jersey ruled that the prosecutions and convictions had been "predicated on an appeal to racism rather than reason, and concealment rather than disclosure."[39] Having been moved by Carter's prison memoir, *The Sixteenth Round* (1973), Dylan lent his energies to a massive campaign to free Carter, a campaign that included not only the writing of the single "Hurricane," but also a lengthy performance tour – the Rolling Thunder Revue – that culminated in two high-profile fund-raising concerts at New York's Madison Square Garden and Houston's Astrodome. Predictably, Dylan's motives were put under the microscope. Rock critic Lester Bangs sneered, "Dylan doesn't give a damn about Rubin Carter, and if he spent any more than ten minutes actually working on the composition of 'George Jackson' then Bryan Ferry is a member of The Eagles. Dylan merely used Civil Rights and the rest of the Movement to advance himself in the first place."[40] With comparable skepticism, the film critic Pauline Kael proposed that Dylan's aim was "to show us that Bob Dylan cares more about Black people than they do themselves."[41]

Nonetheless, Dylan and his fellow activists raised a great deal of money for Carter – 600,000 dollars (over 2.7 million dollars today). Never mind, as Carter recalled ruefully, that it had all "been swallowed up by lawyers."[42] The "Night of the Hurricane" concert at Madison Square Garden raised more than money: it helped to raise consciousness. The playwright Sam Shepard recalled the moment when Carter's telephone call from prison was broadcast to the thousands in the arena:

> The whole reality of his imprisonment and our freedom comes through loud and clear. "I'm sitting here in jail and I'm thinking that this is truly a revolutionary act when so many people in the outside world can come

---

[39] James S. Hirsch, *Hurricane: The Miraculous Journey of Rubin Carter* (Boston: Houghton Mifflin, 2000), p. 273.

[40] Lester Bangs, "Bob Dylan's Dalliance with Mafia Chic," in *Dylan Companion*, ed. Thomson and Gutman, pp. 210–211.

[41] Pauline Kael, "The Calvary Gig," *Dylan Companion*, ed. Thomson and Gutman, p. 228.

[42] Rubin Carter with Ken Klonsky, *Eye of the Hurricane: My Path from Darkness to Freedom* (Chicago: Chicago Review Press, 2011), p. 122.

together for someone in jail . . . . I'm speaking from deep down in the bowels of a New Jersey penitentiary."[43]

Dylan himself never again performed "Hurricane" live after the Houston Astrodome concert in January 1976, and the song's last high-profile use was as an ignominious musical backdrop to a *Family Guy* episode in which the megalomaniac baby Stewie struts away, boasting "I am who I am."[44]

One final project – the guitarist Steve Van Zandt's Sun City boycott – demonstrates that perhaps Dylan ultimately came to the conclusion that his mere celebrity might do more for the advancement of civil rights than his own songs could do. After all, the year 1985 had proven that just by showing up to sing someone else's lyrics, Dylan could be instrumental in raising 75 million dollars through his contribution to the charity single "We Are the World" (written by Michael Jackson and Lionel Richie on behalf of "United Support of Artists for Africa" – or "USA for Africa"). The same year had shown that even an offhand, ill-judged utterance of Dylan's could lead to a positive development: onstage at the Live Aid concert in Philadelphia in 1984, "the transcendent BOB DYLAN!" (as Jack Nicholson introduced him) had made the tone-deaf mistake of proposing that "some of the money that's raised for the people in Africa" could be siphoned off to "pay the mortgages on some of the farms . . . the farmers here owe to the banks."[45] Roundly deplored at the time, Dylan's gaffe led directly to the establishment of Farm Aid, an organization that still thrives to assist struggling farmers in the USA. Van Zandt had been outraged at musicians continuing to play at the lavish Sun City resort in the Bophuthatswana "black homeland" in then-apartheid South Africa, declaring: "To forcibly relocate people is bad enough, but to erect a $90-million showplace to celebrate their imprisonment is beyond all conscience."[46] Dylan thus became one of the Artists United Against Apartheid, whose "Sun City" video of 1985 was one of the many projects feeding into the global cultural boycott that helped bring down the apartheid government and usher in black-majority rule with Nelson Mandela at the helm.

Importantly, the "Sun City" video in which Dylan appears blends footage of the South African resistance struggle with that of the civil rights movement in the USA, with the township police batons matching Bull

---

[43] Sam Shepard, *Rolling Thunder Logbook* (New York: Viking, 1977), p. 172.
[44] *Family Guy*, season 6, episode 8: "McStroke." Original broadcast January 13, 2008.
[45] Sounes, *Down the Highway*, pp. 366–367.
[46] Dorian Lynskey, *33 Revolutions Per Minute: A History of Protest Songs* (London: Faber, 2010), pp. 501–502.

Connor's water hoses, and with Mandela harkening back to Martin Luther King and the March on Washington where Dylan had performed.[47] "Sun City" shows that the movement itself had moved on into more global territory, just as Dylan had – supposedly – "moved on" from the movement. However, as Dylan showed, to "move on" is not necessarily to leave. It might mean, rather, to transform, to morph, to change.

---

[47] Artists United Against Apartheid, "Sun City," www.youtube.com/watch?v=4BIvf-ZlJNc.

CHAPTER 21

The Counterculture

Michael J. Kramer

His songs and public role are guides to survival in the world of the image, the cool, and the high.

Ellen Willis[1]

One mask will not do
The mask has died
It is not the mask but you.

Bob Dylan[2]

If you squinted hard enough in early 1968, you just might be able to make out the faces of the Beatles. There they were, fans thought, in the tree behind Bob Dylan on the cover of his album *John Wesley Harding*. Dylan put them there, supposedly, as one of a number of clues for how to interpret the surprising, new LP. After all, didn't the hat in the foreground of the image hide a stash of marijuana? Dylan must be concealing "the psychedelic aroma so exposed and prominent on the Beatles' *Sgt. Pepper's* LP to which *John Wesley Harding* is a reaction," playfully claimed Columbia Records staff photographer John Berg, the man who had taken the photograph for the cover of the album. Years later, he still relished the scrutiny given to the image. "Maybe just folklore," Berg wryly admitted of the drug and Beatles references.[3]

But this sort of folklore matters. In the late 1960s, recordings by prominent musicians such as the Beatles and Dylan were important because they catalyzed shared inquiries into pressing questions of life in the modern world. Sure, these collective inquiries often assumed silly and

[1] Ellen Willis, "Dylan," in *Bob Dylan: A Retrospective*, ed. Craig McGregor (New York: William Morrow, 1972), p. 221, originally published in *Cheetah* (1967).
[2] Bob Dylan, Untitled, Series IV: Notebooks, Box 7, Folder 3, Bob Dylan Archive, The Helmerich Center for American Research at Gilcrease Museum (hereafter BDA).
[3] John Berg, quoted in *The Telegraph* 51 (Spring 1995), Mitch Blank Collection, BDA.

absurdist forms. Most fans probably knew that Dylan had not actually placed the Beatles on the cover of *John Wesley Harding*. Nonetheless, it felt pleasurable, maybe even important, to join the mysterious, almost conspiratorial fun. Imagining that secret messages about shared social life lurked in pop music became a way of pondering serious matters together. What did it mean that Dylan seemed to reject the psychedelic fantasies of the Beatles' *Sgt. Pepper* for the more stark, restrained, and somber sounds of *John Wesley Harding*? Did Dylan's album offer a different response to the times than the Beatles? What could one learn about how to live from his new style?

What came to be known as the counterculture emerged, in part, *from* the folklore Berg mentions. Pop music generated a countercultural milieu. The actual term, "counterculture," did not appear until well after the music, only applied to the amorphous phenomenon in 1969, when social critic Theodore Roszak published the best-selling book *The Making of a Counter Culture: Reflections on the Technocratic Society and Its Youthful Opposition.*[4] It was well underway by then, powered as much by interest in Dylan as anything else. Along with a puff of marijuana or an intense trip on LSD, maybe linked to participation in the civil rights or anti-Vietnam War movements, or serving as the soundtrack to a romantic relationship or a close friendship, Dylan's music contributed to the rise of a new kind of public sphere during the late 1960s: the counterculture as a "counter-public" or what sociologist Bruno Latour evocatively describes as an "atmosphere of democracy."[5] The music was commercial, to be sure, released by corporate labels such as Columbia, but when it circulated, its recipients introduced unexpected meanings, connections, puzzles, and ideas that, like unpredictable weather, went far beyond the neat transactions of commerce alone. The music became, as John Berg implies, folklore for the mass-mediated age. It fostered and sustained collective engagements suffused with shared hopes and fraught dilemmas.

For an album that accomplished such public work, *John Wesley Harding* was mysteriously private. Released at the end of 1967 with almost no publicity, named after an obscure old West outlaw, the LP was surprisingly

---

[4] Theodore Roszak, *The Making of a Counter Culture: Reflections on the Technocratic Society and Its Youthful Opposition* (1969; reprint, Berkeley: University of California Press, 1995).
[5] Michael Warner, *Publics and Counterpublics* (New York: Zone Books, 2005); Bruno Latour, "From Realpolitik to Dingpolitik or How to Make Things Public," in *Making Things Public: Atmospheres of Democracy*, ed. Bruno Latour and Peter Weibel (Cambridge, MA: MIT Press, 2005); much of this literature on the public sphere as a communicative and discursive formation draws upon Jürgen Habermas's classic study *The Structural Transformation of the Public Sphere: An Inquiry into a Category of Bourgeois Society*, trans. Thomas Burger (Cambridge, MA: MIT Press, 1989).

different from the popular sounds of its day. So too, it radically diverged from the music Dylan had been making just prior to his infamous motorcycle crash in late 1966. Amid a swirl of rumors, he had all but disappeared from view. When he re-emerged, gone were the Beat-inspired explosions of conscience, to paraphrase a line from the song "Visions of Johanna." No more of "that thin, that wild mercury sound," as Dylan had called it, that defined hit singles such as "Like a Rolling Stone" (1965) and albums such as *Blonde on Blonde* (1966). Instead, Dylan offered a stripped-down album of only acoustic guitar, electric bass, and drums, with a sprinkling of pedal steel guitar on a few songs. The lyrics were very different too, marked by short, taut, elliptical, and allegorical stories about bandits, immigrants, landlords, founding fathers, and religious figures. Dylan sang them in a more restrained vocal style. It was as if he had stepped back from his neon madman rantings of the mid-1960s, screamed at the roaring edge of the Jet Age, and disappeared into a rustic nineteenth-century frontier from the long-lost past. While his peers the Beatles seemed to embrace the decadent hallucinations of the hippie, Dylan retreated from them, offering instead a different vision.

Some took his new album to be an outright rejection of the contemporary psychedelic counterculture; however, closer attention to both the making of *John Wesley Harding* and the ways in which the LP was received suggests that Dylan's music was less a repudiation of the counterculture than an exploration of new directions in which it might move. The album raised the possibility that hippies need not only become futuristic star-children of the utopian Age of Aquarius, but could also acquire the wizened maturity and skepticism of a more rustic, pain-filled America.

Overall, albums such as *Sgt. Pepper* and *John Wesley Harding* were central to the counterculture in part because they seemed directly in dialogue with each other. The Beatles provided a vision of mass-mediated pop fellowship in their songs, performances, and films. They struck a pose of inclusivity; the world was chaotic, full of woozy disorientation, but all would "get by with a little help from my friends." Dylan offered a darker, tougher, more critical, and individualistic viewpoint. As he moralized in the song "The Ballad of Frankie Lee and Judas Priest": "Don't go mistaking paradise for that home across the road." On *John Wesley Harding*, the answers were still blowing in the wind, harder to catch hold of than on *Sgt. Pepper*.

Dylan later criticized the "indulgence" of *Sgt. Pepper*'s sounds, but the unease of *John Wesley Harding* was actually not entirely different from what the Beatles had put forward. Dylan's LP was also psychedelic in a way. The radical remixing of historical references resembled what the Beatles did with British music hall traditions. So too, while both albums sounded quite different on the surface, they shared the quality of creating musical spaces of mythical intensity in which elusive lyrics pointed to questions about how people should carry themselves. Most of all, as with the Beatles on *Sgt. Pepper*, Dylan on *John Wesley Harding* sought to dislodge listeners from solid foundations. The Beatles created carousel-like sounds that resolved into reassuring lyrics. Dylan insisted on staying in the uncertainty and difficulty of the world, with only domesticity ultimately offering a shelter from the storm.

No wonder so many wanted to spot the faces of the Fab Four on the cover of Dylan's new recording. Linking the musicians together helped to give some shape to the sense that something was happening by the late 1960s (even if you didn't quite know what it was, did you Mr. Jones?). *Sgt. Pepper* announced that a new world might be dawning. *John Wesley Harding* reminded many that they would need older resources to navigate the horizon. If we revisit the making of Dylan's album, using previously untapped sources from the Bob Dylan Archive®, and take stock of its reception, particularly among critics, we begin to glimpse how the album was not a rejection, but rather a contribution to the making of a counterculture.

"Nothing is Revealed": The Making of *John Wesley Harding*

"I'd hate to think I was speaking for a generation," Bob Dylan wrote on a scrap of paper sometime in the late 1960s, "I'd like to think I was speaking for myself too."[6] *John Wesley Harding* had the feeling of appearing out of nowhere, spectral and ghostly, yet also quite monumental and complete, a full statement in a brand-new style that also sounded ancient and wizened. Dylan seemed little concerned with the popular sounds of the day. This was auteur music. Yet by insisting on speaking for himself, he also wound up speaking if not *for*, then certainly *to* others. Arriving as if from what Dylan would call with a much later album title a "time out of mind," *John Wesley Harding* offered a fresh way for listeners to encounter themselves and their world through history-bending parables and allegories that cut through the contemporary world with potential parallels and lessons from the past.

Dylan's album evoked a different country than the extravagant electronic rock of its day, but it shared an interest in questions many were considering by the turn of 1968: how was one to lead a moral life in

[6] Notebooks, Series IV: Notebooks, Box 1 Folder 5, BDA.

a modern world that made both individual and collective being increasingly intolerable, even for those who enjoyed material abundance? With generational conflicts raging in many homes, continued problems of racial injustice unsolved, and the still escalating war in Vietnam, the USA was a troubling place. Yet if one threw off the existing mores and protocols, where did one turn for guidance to construct a set of alternative principles? Dylan seemed to register these concerns, and recast them into a set of moody parables on *John Wesley Harding*.

He begins working up to his new approach in notebooks from 1966 and into 1967. Although difficult to date precisely, the notebooks from this era are filled with purposeful attempts to write in shorter lines that suggested old folk songs yet also seemed allegorically relevant to modern times. As he said in an interview with *Rolling Stone* in 1968, "What I'm trying to do now is not use too many words. There's no line that you can stick your finger through, there's no hole in any of the stanzas. There's no blank filler. Each line has something."[7] Gone was the long, meandering, first-person verbiage of his earlier work, particularly the mid-60s electric albums. Even the playful lyrics of the Basement Tapes sessions during 1967 are fewer and farther between. Instead, as Dylan explained in another interview, he pursued a more "concise" style.[8]

Dylanologists speculate on when and how the songs for the album were written. Whereas in the past, Dylan developed lyrics in the studio, with the band waiting for him to experiment, the three sessions for *John Wesley Harding* in Nashville in October and November 1967 had Dylan arriving ready to record, with the lyrics almost entirely put down on paper.[9] According to Robbie Robertson, Dylan may have written the songs spontaneously on the two-day train ride from New York to his first recording session in Nashville. Another theory is that Allen Ginsberg delivered a trunk of classic literature to Dylan, who read intensely as he recovered from his motorcycle accident. Another is that the album came about from mourning the death of Woody Guthrie in October 1967. Another is that Dylan was simply fulfilling his contractural commitment to Columbia Records with a hastily assembled LP.[10]

[7] Dylan in a 1968 interview, quoted in Clinton Heylin, *Bob Dylan: Behind the Shades Revisited* (New York: HarperCollins, 2001), pp. 286–287.

[8] Quoted in John Cohen and Happy Traum, "Conversations with Bob Dylan," *Sing Out!*, October–November 1968, p. 10.

[9] Matt Damsker, "Rock & roll is all I listen to: Bob Dylan talks about his roots," *Circus Magazine*, December 19, 1978, p. 20.

[10] Heylin, *Behind the Shades*, p. 288.

It must be said, however, that the songs on *John Wesley Harding* are anything but hasty and one glimpses Dylan slowly laboring on the material in his notebooks, working with shorter lines and curious about traditional American country, folk, and blues songs as well as passages from the Bible. Like many in the emerging counterculture of 1966 and 1967, Dylan was searching for something new, but not quite defined yet.[11] Little snippets of the songs that would be on *John Wesley Harding* began to appear at that time. Almost all of "I am a Lonesome Hobo" shows up. Hints and then a full verse of "Dear Landlord" (as well as verses that are not included in the final version) are there. A very different take on what would become "As I Went Out One Morning" surfaces in the notebook. There is a quatrain that seems to have the same meter and cadence as "I Dreamed I Saw St. Augustine," but could have well been inspired by the nursery rhyme "Mary Had a Little Lamb":

> Mary went out and wept one day
> She wept for you and me
> And everywhere that Mary wept
> There grew a tall oak tree

A few pages later, something closer to the song's final form shows up:

> Oh I awoke in agony
> With no place to stand and hide
> I put my fingers against the glass
> And bowed – cried.[12]

Characters in the notebook preview the cast of the final album: "the invalid and the farmer," a "pilgrim," someone from a "beggar's kingdom," a "cabin boy" and a "captain" at sea, Benjamin Franklin (or maybe Dylan was just noting a planned visit to the local craft store!), a woman named Sweet Sally Brown and a man named Jeremiah Clyde.

Hinting at the pastoral approach of *John Wesley Harding*, there is an intriguing quote on one notebook page about using "Wordsworthian words." History, reworked, is present too: "how Abraham Lincoln was supposed to have looked," Dylan wrote down in one notebook. There are also verses and titles for various classic blues and country songs as well as intriguing titles of unrecorded Dylan originals. Among them one finds "Trouble on the Allegheny," "No Particular Length of Time," "It's Been

---

[11] Notebooks, Series IV: Notebooks, Box 1 Folder 5, BDA.
[12] Notebooks, Series IV: Notebooks, Box 1, Folders 4, 5, and 6, BDA.

a Long, Long Day," "Shine," and "Cash on the Barrelhead."[13] A newfound attention to biblical scripture certainly influenced Dylan, as commentators have often noted. In a much-quoted interview in 1968, Dylan's mother Beatty Zimmerman mentioned that "in his house in Woodstock . . . there's a huge Bible open on a stand in the middle of his study. Of all the books that crowd his house, overflow from his house, that Bible gets the most attention. He's continuously getting up and going over to refer to something."[14] The notebooks are filled with quotations from Ecclesiastes and Proverbs, which seem to be how at least one song on *John Wesley Harding*, "The Wicked Messenger," received its title.[15]

Full of sketches and fragments, the notebooks provide the background of *John Wesley Harding* as a deeply personal inquiry into religion, myth, and history. We might speculate that the notebooks could well have been in Dylan's shirt pocket or bag as he rode the train to Nashville in late 1967 to record the album. Or perhaps he was working on the shift in his sound and style earlier in 1967, developing ideas, lyrics, and concepts that rang true to his own ear and self. Whatever the case, the contents of the notebooks suggest Dylan's determination to discover a fresh approach to his music and songwriting in 1967. A deceptively simple rustic mode became an avenue to communicating far greater complexity, drama, and relevance to contemporary conditions. Going back became a way to push forward. These choices, stemming from Dylan's own individual artistic curiosity and intuition, wound up also speaking to a far broader audience of countercultural participants. They too were struggling, as members of a nascent mass assembly, with questions of how to relate tradition to the contemporary, allegorical wisdom to modern challenges. If the reception of the album among rock critics and other listeners is to be believed, *John Wesley Harding* spoke to them less as a straightforward rejection of the counterculture than as constitutive of it.

The final look of the album visually was as important in this respect as the songs that countercultural listeners took in with their ears. The impressionistic cover image of *John Wesley Harding*, with its black-and-white mystical frontier imagery (actually Dylan with two members of the Bauls of Bengal and a local stonemason in front of trees on the Catskills

---

[13] Notebooks, Series IV: Notebooks, Box 1, Folders 4, 5, and 6, BDA. "Shine" was written in 1910 by Cecil Mack and Lew Brown with music by Ford Dabney. "Cash on the Barrelhead" was written and performed by the Louvin Brothers in 1956.

[14] Beatty Zimmerman, quoted in Heylin, *Behind the Shades*, p. 285.

[15] Mike Marqusee, *Wicked Messenger: Bob Dylan and the 1960s* (New York: Seven Stories Press, 2005), pp. 248–249; Notebook, Box 1, Folder 4, BDA.

property of Dylan manager Albert Grossman close by an abandoned swimming pool), contributed to its ghostly quality, but the liner notes made intriguing connections to the present. They featured an elusive, shaggy-dog story about three kings and a man named Frank (possibly Frankie Lee of one of the songs). Consistent with Dylan's earlier liner notes, they seemed designed, maybe, to offer a map to the significance of the album. "Mr. Dylan has come out with a new record. This record of course features none but his own songs and we understand that you're the key," one of the kings says to Frank. While another character named Terry Shute exclaims, "There is a creeping consumption in the land. It begins with these three fellas and it travels outward," a reference that suddenly threads the oddly medieval tale of three kings to contemporary times in the abundant 1960s. It's all typically puzzling Dylan fun that, like a traditional song, seems to conceal relevance within its meandering nonsense, inscrutability, and mystery. The imagery and liner notes destabilize any hold on precise meaning and intention, but in doing so they let the listener in on a world of potential ideas, feelings, positionalities, postures, references, and implications.[16]

The music itself adds to this alluring sense of polysemy. Dylan worked again with producer Bob Johnston, but he chose to record the album with a far more restricted ensemble than on previous records. Only two ace studio musicians who had been part of the ensemble for *Blonde on Blonde* accompanied Dylan: drummer Kenny Buttrey and bassist Charlie McCoy. Dylan reportedly wanted them to help capture his version of the sound they generated for Gordon Lightfoot's *The Way I Feel* (1967).[17] Pete Drake, another renowned Nashville session player, added pedal steel to two songs. At one point, Dylan pondered bringing members of the Band to overdub more instrumentation, but Robbie Robertson supposedly told him he thought the songs were complete in their original takes.[18] The music itself was deceptively simple. Buttrey flutters on the drums, attuned to the narrative flow of Dylan's lyrics (listen, for instance, to his wonderful basstom flourishes during Dylan's harmonica solo at the end of the title track, or the way he slyly places a Motown beat below "All Along the Watchtower," or his entry into "Dear Landlord"). McCoy's bass becomes

---

[16] Liner notes, *John Wesley Harding*, 1967, Columbia Records CS 9604.
[17] Dylan is quoted to this effect in an interview with Jann S. Wenner, *Rolling Stone*, November 29, 1969, reprinted in Jonathan Cott, ed., *Bob Dylan: The Essential Interviews* (New York: Simon & Schuster, 2017), p. 157. Lightfoot was also managed by Albert Grossman, Dylan's manager of the time.
[18] Heylin, *Behind the Shades*, p. 288.

almost like another character on the album, a response to the call of Dylan's vocals. We hear this, for example, in the descending bass at the end of "I Dreamed I Saw St. Augustine," the signature riff between the lines of "As I Went Out this Morning," the syncopated lines dancing around the verses of "Dear Landlord," the R&B-esque pulse of "Drifter's Escape," and the wonderful chase after Dylan's descending guitar on "The Wicked Messenger." Overall, Buttrey and McCoy offer support and occasional musical commentary, while delivering a sense that Dylan's narrator on the record is not alone, but surrounded by a small community of like-minded fellow travelers: the congregation is assembled for his backwoods preaching. Then, on a mass-produced record, it leaps out of the rustic setting to speak to contemporary matters of self and society.

It is Dylan's own musical performance, however, that lends *John Wesley Harding* a full psychedelic quality. His sometimes ever-so-slightly out-of-tune acoustic guitar, piano, and harmonica work gives the songs an off-kilter quality, accomplishing as much in the way of expressive tension as the technical wizardry of electronic rock recordings from the period. There are far fewer addresses to the second person on the album than in previous Dylan songs. Along with the timbre of his voice – slightly more resonant and from the chest, not yet at the full crooner sound of *Nashville Skyline*, but getting there – the shift from second-person address contributes to the more allegorical mood of the lyrics. They become parables widely if ambiguously applicable to many situations rather than confessional tales of psychic fragmentation or accusatory songs of romantic persecution. The songs resound all along the telegraph; at the same time, one can never quite chain them down. *John Wesley Harding*, as an album, had nothing to hide; yet, as the famous line from the album's song "Frankie Lee and Judas Priest," put it, "nothing is revealed." This quality of being complex, elusive, available to multiple interpretations, while also sounding elemental allowed audiences, critics especially, to respond richly and heterogeneously to *John Wesley Harding* and the album became a particularly crucial artifact for those engaged with the state of the counterculture.

"Outside, the Crowd was Stirring": Responses to *John Wesley Harding*

Dylan himself knew he was linked to the counterculture, but by 1967 he had largely given up hope on the amorphous phenomenon. "It seemed to have something to do with me, this Woodstock Nation and everything it represented," he told Kurt Loder in 1984, referring to the 1969 festival that took place near his home in the Catskill Mountains of upstate New York.[19] As strangers showed up unannounced in his family's house and intruded endlessly into his private life, Dylan complained, "Whatever the counter-culture was, I'd seen enough of it."[20] Because it limited his freedom and threatened his family, Dylan explained, "I got very resentful about the whole thing."[21] Yet Dylan's own demand for artistic and personal freedom and space on *John Wesley Harding* helped, ironically, to redirect the counterculture itself to new places. In firmly rejecting the anything-goes anarchy that some thought the counterculture embodied, Dylan's album spoke to those displeased with this version of their efforts to imagine and enact a new society. The album sparked ideas, if not guidance, for how to act in the world not as reckless, footloose, and fancy-free youth, but rather as wiser and more responsible citizens aware of sin, yet still in search of salvation, and keen to imagine a stronger sense of mutual respect and obligation.

Writers and critics in particular did not decry the counterculture of the era when considering *John Wesley Harding*; rather, they sought out new and wiser potential pathways for it. For starters, in place of the over-wrought psychedelic rock from 1967, *John Wesley Harding* seemed to provide a model of a higher quality, wider-ranging musical artistry. Ellen Willis, in *Cheetah*, thought the recording "serves its purpose, which is to liberate Dylan – and the rest of us – from the *Sgt. Pepper* straightjacket." Dylan's album offered a "sudden removal of the mask – see, it's me, a songwriter, I just want to write nice songs," she contended, but "of course," she pointed out "being Bob Dylan, he has turned this reconciliation into rebellion." Dylan's turn away from the counterculture seemed to be an abandonment of the latest rock fads, but to Willis it was in fact as countercultural as one could get.[22]

If Willis heard *John Wesley Harding* as a personalist turn with public implications, rock critic Robert Christgau, writing in *Esquire*, interpreted the album in almost the opposite direction: "This is the most impersonal record Dylan has ever made," he decided. "Persona has always been important to his work," Christgau wrote, "but this time the 'I,' when it appears, is almost anonymous." Nonetheless, Christgau too heard the album as suggesting a more mature orientation for countercultural politics. "Almost alone among the pop stars, he no longer comes on like a questing

---

[19] Dylan quoted in "Interview with Kurt Loder, 1984," in Cott, ed., *The Essential Interviews*, p. 301.

[20] Bob Dylan, *Chronicles Vol. 1* (New York: Simon & Schuster, 2004), p. 115.

[21] "Interview with Kurt Loder, 1984," p. 301.   [22] Willis, "Dylan," pp. 238–239.

adolescent," Christgau argued of Dylan. "This is not a better record than *Sgt. Pepper*, but it should have better effect. It is mature work that still shows room for rich development."[23]

While they diverged in their interpretations, Willis and Christgau both focused on *John Wesley Harding* as an album that broke away from the Beatles and *Sgt. Pepper*, but did not dismiss the larger countercultural project of rethinking and altering both self and society in 1960s America. *John Wesley Harding* was, to their ears, at the leading edge of where counterculturalists might go if they took the necessary corrective measures in response to the decadence of high psychedelia.

For other critics, the ways the album resonated with contemporary events made it all the more relevant to the counterculture. To John Landau, writing in *Crawdaddy!* magazine, the album was most of all about "a profound awareness of the [Vietnam] war and how it is affecting all of us."[24] To Landau, who would one day manage Bruce Springsteen, it was not so much that "the particular songs are about the war or that any of the songs are protests over it," but instead that they "acknowledge it by attempting to be real, by attempting to not speak falsely, and by playing fewer games than ever before." For Landau, "the Dylan of *JWH* is profoundly moral," but it was not "pop moralizing" or melodrama so much as a fresh expression of "a prudential kind of wisdom." Landau believed that Dylan was "determined to search for authenticity" while also being "prepared to look at the pieces of reality, and let the miller tell his tale." Here was countercultural opposition to the dominant powers of modern America, but in a more mature register than adolescent rebellion.[25]

Other critics made similar points about how Dylan broke away from the overblown psychedelic norms established in 1967 by trimming the music back. As Christgau put it, "instead of plunging forward, Dylan looked back. Instead of grafting, he pruned."[26] Responding to this world of troubling mass culture and a counterculture whose style and message he was not convinced offered a satisfying response, Dylan turned to what some critics imagined as a new kind of pop pastoralism that would become quite central to the counterculture by the early 1970s.[27] Writing in

---

[23] Robert Christgau, "John Wesley Harding," in *Studio A: The Bob Dylan Reader*, ed. Benjamin Hedin (New York: W.W. Norton, 2004), p. 66.

[24] John Landau, "John Wesley Harding," in *Bob Dylan: A Retrospective*, ed. McGregor, p. 259.

[25] Ibid, p. 264.   [26] Christgau, "John Wesley Harding," p. 66.

[27] On countercultural pastoralism, among other works see Bennett M. Berger, "American Pastoralism and the Commune Movement," in *The Survival of a Counterculture: Ideological Work and Everyday Life Among Rural Communards* (Berkeley: University of California Press, 1981), pp. 91–126; Timothy Miller, *The Hippies and American Values* (Knoxville: University of Tennessee Press,

Commonweal, Jean Strouse called *John Wesley Harding* "gently anarchic." To her, "It is the anarchy of everyone doing his own thing, assuming that freedom can exist only outside the laws and layers of society. The outsiders – outlaw, hobo, immigrant, joker, thief, girl in chains, drifter, saint – form an existential community simply in reaction to 'them.'"[28] A few years later, in a more academic essay, Gregg M. Campbell located Dylan in a long-running "pastoral apocalyptic" tradition that was more dramatic and not so gentle in its critique of modernity, but was still deeply engaged with the questions of how counterculture related to dominant culture.[29]

What remains most noticeable about responses to *John Wesley Harding* is how, on the whole, critics interpreted the album less as a rejection of countercultural ideals than as a call to shift the counterculture in new directions. Some chose to hear Dylan on *John Wesley Harding* as providing promising new possibilities. Others were more hesitant. Maybe Dylan's pastoralism shifted all too easily into reactionary conservatism rather than countercultural transformation. All the critics used Dylan's own artistic and musical changes on *John Wesley Harding* to consider the larger 1960s counterculture as a whole. They drew upon his artistry to contribute to a robust counterpublic of discussion, an atmosphere of democracy in which theirs were but a few of the many ears listening and the manifold voices responding to Dylan.

"To Breathe the Air Around Tom Paine": Conclusion

After the release of *John Wesley Harding*, Dylan slid more fully into the pastoral mode some of his critics feared. On the country squire stylings of *Nashville Skyline*, the easy-going cover songs on *Self Portrait*, and the lord-of-the-manor feeling of *New Morning*, he seemed less capable of producing albums that harnessed his own personal creative intuitions for public issues. At the end of 1967, however, he was still in something of a report-

---

1991); Dominick Cavallo, *A Fiction of the Past: The Sixties in American History* (New York: St. Martin's Press, 1999); Timothy Miller, *The 60s Communes: Hippies and Beyond* (Syracuse, NY: Syracuse University Press, 1999); Andrew G. Kirk, *Counterculture Green: The Whole Earth Catalog and American Environmentalism* (Lawrence: University Press of Kansas, 2007); David Farber, "Building the Counterculture, Creating Right Livelihoods," *The Sixties: A Journal of History, Politics, and Culture* (May 2013), pp. 1–24.

[28] Jean Strouse, "Bob Dylan's Gentle Anarchy," *Commonweal*, 1968, in *The Bob Dylan Companion: Four Decades of Commentary*, ed. Carl Benson (New York: Schirmer, 1998), p. 89.

[29] Gregg M. Campbell, "Bob Dylan and the Pastoral Apocalypse," *Journal of Popular Culture*, 1975, in *The Bob Dylan Companion*, ed. Benson, pp. 99, 105.

from-the-underground mood. Far away from the Haight-Ashbury hippie hoopla in San Francisco or the Beatles' Abbey Road studio experiments in London, Dylan too was recalibrating what music might mean to the swirling social conditions of the late 1960s and its nascent counterculture.

His audience, from critics giving the album deep attention to fans squinting at the cover for clues, drew upon his music for inspiration about how to understand – and perhaps reshape – the counterculture. To listen to *John Wesley Harding* in context again, more than fifty years later, is to breathe in the counterculture's atmosphere of democracy – the "air around Tom Paine" – as its tempest shifted course from the Summer of Love to darker horizons at the start of 1968. With the Vietnam War turning even more sour with the Tet Offensive later that January, followed by political assassinations, urban riots, contested political conventions, and student protests throughout the rest of the year, *John Wesley Harding* became a fulcrum upon which the counterculture tilted in new directions. Its participants, like the joker and the thief in Dylan's most famous song from the album, listened intently and spoke with each other, poised on a precarious watchtower as the winds began to howl.

CHAPTER 22

Gender and Sexuality: Bob Dylan's Body

Ann Powers

The most iconic pictures of Bob Dylan depict him as a giant brain. The photograph on the cover of his first Greatest Hits album, released in 1967, shows the music legend onstage, his face in profile, partly buried in his harmonica-holding hands. He's backlit, so that his clumpy frizz seems to exude light. This Grammy Award-winning shot by Rowland Scherman relates to an even more famous portrait of Dylan: the one created by the pioneering graphic designer Milton Glaser for a poster insert in that same hits package, which quickly became one of the most ubiquitous illustrations of the late twentieth century. Inspired by both Dada and Pop Art, Glaser rendered Dylan's face as a solid black mass against a white background, his famous hair a wild tangle of colors, a magic garden sprouting from an overactive mind. By 1971, when Barry Feinstein's photograph repeated the electrically haloed look yet again for his *Greatest Hits Vol. II*, Dylan's head had become a defining image of the era.

But where was Dylan's body? Unlike most of his peers on the international rock stage – from the often-half naked Jim Morrison and Robert Plant to Janis Joplin in sheer gauze tops and Jagger in satin pants packed with bulge – Dylan rarely displayed much below his neck. Instead, he presented himself as a shape-shifter and a mask-wearer, "a creature void of form" serving as a conduit for America's moods and mythologies. Dylan has always written about his sensual attachments to women, though usually as a character longing for, fleeing, or eulogizing love; only occasionally would he write a line as carnal as his 1966 *cri di crotch*, "I want you *so bad*." Still, he's always been a sex symbol and has obviously enjoyed the power of his fame and charisma, coupling with beautiful women, and extolling their attractions in lyrics that namecheck Sara and Johanna, Isis and Ophelia, Brigitte Bardot and Erica Jong. Courting from across the room was Dylan's thing – he expressed desire as a one-way energy flow, emanating away from his own form. "How do you explain your attraction?" a reporter once asked him, meaning people's attraction to him.

"Attraction to what?" Dylan deflected. Locating his erotic energy along with the rest of his power, within his role as a visionary, Dylan gazed outward while all around him sought to seduce.

But Dylan does have a body. It is visible during performances and in the images that appear on his album covers, in promotional material and in the press. It's also audible, through his voice. The voice, as the philosopher and psychoanalyst Mladen Dolar has written, is what language and the body have in common: it is the bridge between the sensual and the symbolic, the idiosyncratic and the universal.[1] In performance and on record, Bob Dylan has used his voice to stage an ongoing exploration of his body's relationship to the stream of words he has generated. Throughout his career, Dylan has often referred to himself as intangible, disappearing, or simply not there in the first place. But it's the voice that expresses his relationship as a man to his own stories and to the world.

His most famous utterance, perhaps – the drawn hiss of him asking "How does *feeeeeel*" in "Like a Rolling Stone" – feels like a cry from the body to the mind, a call for recognition and for connection. As the chorus pours out over the rest of the song, thick and sticky, it seems elemental, somehow deeper in its directness and in the urgency of Dylan's utterance than the tangled verses. *How does it feel?* Dylan's been asking himself that from the beginning, in the midst of all the thinking and the envisioning. The body feels the mind's attachments.

The Soft Body

"We both had our baby fat," Joan Baez once said with a laugh when shown an early picture of herself and Dylan performing at the Newport Folk Festival.[2] Baez has been asked incessantly over the years to describe her relationship with Dylan, whom she ushered into the spotlight after they met in 1963, and who has remained a complicated presence in her life ever since. In David Hajdu's *Positively 4th Street*, the definitive account of their early relationship, Baez describes her love for the young Dylan as sweetly protective: "He was so shy and fragile. I wanted to mother him, and he seemed to want it and need it. He seemed so helpless."[3] Hajdu also quotes Dylan characterizing himself onstage with Baez, then the queen of the folk scene, as "baggy elephant me." To counteract his peers' understanding of

---

[1] Mladen Dolar, *A Voice and Nothing More* (Cambridge, MA: MIT Press, 2006).
[2] "In Bob We Trust," *The Times*, September 19, 2005.
[3] David Hajdu, *Positively 4th Street* (New York: Picador, 2001), p. 161.

him as Baez's precocious pet, Dylan would assert himself in zany ways, like carrying around a bullwhip or improvising surrealist poems, his words like a boxer's feinting punches.

But Dylan was a baggy elephant before he met Joan Baez. In a photograph of him with Suze Rotolo, his first serious New York girlfriend and the person who introduced him to many of the literary and art world sources that would inspire his early songs, the couple recline on a rumpled bed. Dylan, wearing Buddy Holly glasses, leans back into Rotolo, extending his arms overhead to wrap around her. Both are laughing. At first glance, they look like an adorable lesbian couple. They are comfortable, soft.

Writing in 2001, Hajdu described the Dylan of this period as "elementally desexualized and androgynous."[4] In 2020, however, with gender fluidity more visible in the culture, we can better see his softness as emblematic of shifting gender roles. It was clearly visible in the very young Bob Dylan's face – that baby fat, which caused his first champion at the *New York Times*, Robert Shelton, to call him "cherubic" – and audible in his voice.[5] Though listeners noticed his stern intonations on political ballads or his mimicry of black Southern or working-class vocalisms, what also distinguished Dylan was his vocal flexibility and playfulness. He was figuring out how to inhabit a soft body, one that would appeal to both young, progressive women and the men trying to figure out how to be with them.

The early songs Rotolo likely inspired showed Dylan's audience that he was not simply a brilliant synthesizer of folk idioms but also a man of his moment, in a personal as well as political way, which meant he was responding to the nascent sexual revolution. One of the most memorable is "Don't Think Twice, It's All Right," which introduced what Keith Negus calls Dylan's "intimate voice" and tapped into the informal cadences of country music in ways in which folk revivalists often did not. That song looks to country's take on folk forms to offer a melancholy version of a familiar tale, that of the wayfaring stranger, driven by fate and his lady's betrayal back onto the hard road. The two songs that bookend the 1964 album *Another Side*, however, confound this narrative, as does the way he uses his soft body's voice to relate them.

The first is "All I Really Want To Do," one of Dylan's funniest and most appealing come-ons. "I ain't lookin' to compete with you," Dylan begins, stretching into the top of his vocal range as he tells a flat-out lie – at this point he'd met his sister–lover–mother Baez, and their rivalry always generated heat at the core of their connection. Baez quickly became

[4] Ibid, p. x.   [5] Robert Shelton, *New York Times*, September 29, 1961.

besotted with Dylan, but he was still into playing games, which is what this song is. Its torrent of rhyming couplets enumerate the ways typical men interact with their would-be paramours – brutal behavior ("beat or cheat or mistreat you") but also totally normal moves ("analyze you, categorize you") and some that relate to the usual progression of a romance ("meet your kin," "knock you up"). Dylan doesn't want to be that guy. Instead, he yodels, shifting into a rare but strong falsetto, "All I really wanna do-ooooo is baby be friends with you."

What an idea. It's a line, of course, the kind some shifty character would say to any chick who catches his fancy. But as a hard turn away from the rest of the song's laundry list of dominant-male moves, it feels radical. Was he kidding? Humor is definitely part of Dylan's charm arsenal – at a couple of points in the song he almost succumbs to giggles. And then there's the chorus, centered on that yippy yodel, with none of the finesse of Hank Williams's high notes but a lot of the goofy allure of Buddy Holly's. The song feels like Dylan's idea of one Holly might have written. It's his answer to "Every Day" or "Maybe Baby," dreamily assertive come-ons that are just as much about the singer's thought process as about what he hopes will materialize. From Holly, Dylan learned that a comical affect can be a vehicle for new ideas – in this case that a man and a woman can be friends first and anything else they want to be in addition. This line of thinking recalled what certain women of the Beat generation, Dylan's biggest literary source, were seeking in relationships with men that shifted from camaraderie to romance, depending on the circumstances. "Myself I loved the mess of it, the murk of smoke and emotion, the quick, laughing flirtations, flattery from men I admired," wrote Hettie Jones of the pre-feminist free-for-all of the Beat era, though she also pointed out that such friendships with benefits often collapsed under the weight of old ideas about the disposability of a woman who wasn't a wife.[6]

Dylan didn't have a wife in 1963 and evidently wasn't looking for one. The final song on *Another Side* makes his refusal to be an old-school patriarch more clear. "It Ain't Me Babe" takes its first line from John Jacob Niles's 1907 composition "Go 'Way from My Window," itself supposedly inspired by a work chant that the white composer and song collector had overheard from an African American farm worker. Niles's often-covered song is pure knightly virtue imagined by a 16-year-old dreaming of, as he wrote, "a blue-eyed, blond girl who didn't think

---

[6] Hettie Jones, *How I Became Hettie Jones* (New York: Grove Press, 1990), np.

much of my efforts."[7] She has rejected him, and he's willing to wander off, but he promises to love her "as long as songbirds sing." Dylan turns that scene around by making himself the naysayer: the woman who begs him for commitment will only be left in tears. Critic Jonathan Gould has called this the first "anti-love" song, and there's no arguing that here Dylan falls prey to bohemian men's tendency to view women as dangerously conventional and worth ultimately avoiding.[8] Taken as a self-critique, however, "It Ain't Me, Babe" becomes something else – an examination of the singer's failure to conform to the standards of heroic maleness. He will be weak; he will be unfaithful; he will let his lover down.

Is it possible, perhaps, to see the soft Dylan, the Dylan who can't claim conventional masculinity, in a queer light? His early work was shaped, in part, by the influence of two gay men – the folksinger Paul Clayton, who mentored Dylan when he first arrived in Greenwich Village, and the poet Allen Ginsberg, his liaison to the Beat world and a lifelong friend. In both cases these mentors allegedly made sexual advances to Dylan, who said no, but maintained their friendship – not a given in early 1960s bohemia and certainly not in the disappointingly straight musical subcultures Dylan inhabited. Dylan and Ginsberg, in particular, became running buddies, serving each other's artistic and professional needs in what the historian Sean Wilentz has called a "mutual reinforcement pact."[9] As Wilentz describes, Ginsberg played a major role in helping Dylan become in popular music what he himself was in the literary world – an "antibourgeois seer" illuminating a path beyond the square world. In order to free men's minds from gendered expectations, Dylan needed to present a different kind of body: that soft body, extended by a voice that goofed and hiccupped as much as it declaimed. It would prove transitional for him, but it allowed him to make a crucial step.

The Mod Body

By 1966 the baggy elephant had sleekened his coat. He'd been shedding his baby fat for a while, looking alarmingly emaciated in his Woody Guthrie get-ups. Newly found London fashion offered him armor that better suited his frame. His look reflected the circular conversation happening between

[7] John Jacob Niles, www.hymnsandcarolsofchristmas.com/Hymns_and_Carols/Biographies/john_ja cob_niles.htm
[8] Jonathan Gould, *Can't Buy Me Love: The Beatles, Britain, and America* (New York: Harmony Books, 2007), p. 300.
[9] Sean Wilentz, *Bob Dylan in America* (New York: Anchor Books, 2001), p. 77.

white English and American musicians at the time: polka-dot shirts he'd found in American thrift shops under a tight suit jacket he'd had custom tailored on Carnaby Street; sleek zippered boots replacing his work shoes; his ruffian hair transformed into what the art historian Thomas Crow has called "a cloud of styled ringlets," part of an image, as Crow writes, "suspended somewhere between Swinging London and the Sunset Strip."[10] There's an apocryphal story of Brian Jones and Dylan making the party rounds in London with the American troubadour clutching a Temptations single in his hand all night long. As Dylan dove into British Invasion rock, he was also moving away from the civil rights activism that had justified both his earnestness and his borrowings from black blues and gospel. He needed to find another way to make it seem like his black affectations came from the inside.

Bands like the Stones were getting away with this by adopting the stance and the sounds of blues and R&B performers while still foregrounding their own identities as children of the white cosmopolitan middle class. In British invasion music, youth became the new blackness. It was both the wellspring of insight, if not wisdom, and the reason for oppression by the powers that were. In his folk days, Dylan had concocted a history of encounters with black bluesmen and Southwestern gamblers to justify his stance as a truth-teller, not to mention his put-on rural drawl and made-up hard luck stories. Brian Jones and his bandmates couldn't pull off that old minstrel move, so they figured out a new one, leaning into their callowness and their urbanity. They looked to Motown and Harlem instead of the rural South. There, loving groups like the Temptations and the Ronettes, they found dapper looks, choreographed dance moves and the newest recording studio technology – an engagement with the modern metropolis also being explored in the Pop Art movement, by the British invasion's art-school uncle Richard Hamilton and Dylan's rival for the title of New York It Boy, Andy Warhol. These sources took Dylan beyond the cultivated heat and wildness of the Beats and into his cool phase.

That cool manifested in his physical appearance and his performances. Absorbing black urban style, he adopted a white rock star's stance. Until this period, Dylan employed the harmonica as his detachable penis – a vehicle for accessing explosive libidinal energy. Now he also had an electric guitar, rock's classic phallic weapon. With other men onstage

---

[10] Thomas Crow, *The Long March of Pop: Art, Music, and Design, 1930–1995* (New Haven: Yale University Press, 2015).

playing with him, he could turn away from his audience, conjuring energy his fans could feel but did not necessarily directly inspire. The energy exchanges that happen in an all-male band can be read as homosocial or queer, but they are not a form of soft power. Early footage of Dylan performing with his electric bands show him relishing the prowess amplification provides, no longer seducing the audience but pillaging instead.

Amplification also required a new vocal approach. *Blonde on Blonde* (1966), the album that fully expresses Dylan's collision with modernity, solidified a new tone in Dylan's singing: the tight-lipped hiss that every Dylan imitator from then on would imitate. Expanding his musical palette to include Al Kooper's beefy gospelized keyboard parts and the varied contributions of an elite crew of Nashville and New York studio musicians, Dylan sharpened his own performances, using his voice to establish a new persona. Gone was the soft boy, the "little boy lost" he chides in "Visions of Johanna": "he's sure got a lot of gall to be so useless and all." In his stead comes a grown man, a stranger whose social position alights on some indeterminate point between street tough and dandyish aesthete.

In the rock scene Dylan was now joining, Mick Jagger embodied this voice most seductively, lacing his minstrel blues shouts with the clipped syllables of the upper crust, embodying the slippery mobility of decadence. Though his meeting with the Beatles has gone down as the world historical encounter, there's little doubt that Dylan heard himself much more in Jagger, Jones, and their band. I agree with Greil Marcus's assessment of this lynchpin moment in Dylan's career: that the song that made *Blonde on Blonde* and all that followed possible – "Like a Rolling Stone" – really is a song about that band first, as much as it can also be read for clues about the singer's hatred of Andy Warhol or his love for Edie Sedgwick or his unsettled views of Vietnam. Within the physical experience of making loud rock 'n' roll music, he has found himself anew. It was, after all, a magic act turning plenty of skinny white boys into massive new men.

The mod body that British Invasion rock and its offshoots presented offered men a way to channel the charisma of domination as the sexual revolution progressed. Women could choose soft boys now, ones who were in some ways more like themselves. The new sexual ideal that rock presented was meant to provide a target for that desire without compromising male entitlement. Jagger and other slender, girlish, unkempt but elegant pinups offered women a partial reflection of themselves. Yet young men remained loathe to surrender the authority conventional relationships gave them. That's why the sexiness of British Invasion rock is also so often spiteful and suspicious about women. On *Blonde on Blonde*,

Dylan fully picked up on this. The cruelty that runs up against the album's frank seductions can be read, perhaps too generously, as a defensive move – against the women who threaten to overpower such a slender man, and against the softer man he once was and now fears to remain.

"Not since Rimbaud said 'I is another' has an artist been so obsessed with escaping identity," Ellen Willis wrote in 1967.[11] In his songs of this period, Dylan rarely describes himself, but he incessantly describes his desire, his positioning in relationship to the women who inflame it, and his willingness to engage in what he seems to consider self. And he is building up that voice like a muscle. It is the sonic apotheosis of a style of masculinity that offers power to those who, to quote his friend Marlon Brando's key monologue in Sidney Lumet's 1960 movie *The Fugitive Kind*, are neither "the buyers or the ones who get bought," but inhabitants of a third space, birds who "sleep on the wind."[12] This is the new machismo of the countercultural refusenik – a man who has come to realize the limits of his gendered body, to doubt its position in the culture, even as he still deploys its power. Contempt bubbles at the core of this new man's self-expression, as it does throughout *Blonde on Blonde*. Though its open target is often a woman, the true battle is an inner one, a mortal struggle between self-preservation and a self-annihilation that seems like one way to deal.

The Star Body

Around 1975, Bob Dylan took his shirt off. Usually modest and buttoned up, and often clad in scarfy layers on his album covers rather than semi-nude like many of his peers, Dylan showed skin in the climactic (if you can call it that) scene from his rambling four-hour art film *Renaldo and Clara* (1978), made in complicated tandem with the Rolling Thunder Revue tours, the peak expression of his rapprochement with arena rock.

In the scene, Dylan and his wife Sara are making out on a twin mattress in what looks like a tour stop dressing room. Sara is fully clothed, in long sleeves and a fashionable vest; Dylan, too, wears a vest and jeans, but his chest remains bare. Baez enters the room as the Woman in White, shrouded in glamor – a flowing robe, a fur-like collar, a white turban befitting a Hollywood movie star. The two women tussle over their object of desire, and honestly it's pretty funny, especially when Sara flat-out tackles Dylan and pulls him back onto the bed. Joan loses herself in silent

---

[11] Ellen Willis, "The Sound of Bob Dylan," *Commentary*, November 1967, p. 71.
[12] *The Fugitive Kind*, dir. Sidney Lumet, United Artists, 1960.

giggles at the clumsiness of Dylan losing his balance and almost squashing Sara. Is this the best he can do, sex-symbol-wise, at the very moment when Robert Plant was vying for his crown with Freddie Mercury, David Bowie, and the young David Lee Roth? Dylan seems less like a golden god than a cuddly toy about to be torn apart by two willful girls. (Baez's laughter is a comfort to anyone concerned that she might have felt humiliated by her on-and-off-again lover's pure hubris in staging this battle scene between her and his soon-to-be ex-wife. At least someone realized how ridiculous this all was.)

Before we get to Rolling Thunder, though, let's to go back to 1967, when Dylan first turned toward the pop arena in a way he hadn't before. As usual, his vehicle was a new voice. This was the "country croon" he uncovered in Nashville, where he'd first gone to salvage the failing *Blonde on Blonde* sessions, and where he'd return to make two more albums, *John Wesley Harding* (1967) and *Nashville Skyline* (1969). The latter showed Dylan fully realizing his goal of absorbing the sounds Nashville offered; the apotheosis of this transformation is also one of his most erotically expressive songs. In her chapter on Dylan's gender politics in *The Cambridge Companion to Bob Dylan*, Barbara O'Dair writes of herself as a 12-year-old, fascinated by the "tenderly paternalistic" tone of "Lay Lady Lay," Dylan's successful entry into the soft-rock/soft-porn sweepstakes taking place on turn-of-the-1970s FM radio. "The man with dirty clothes and clean hands was, in my dreams, Bob Dylan," she recalls, noting that the song's descriptions of the ideal lover and love nest blended muscularity with gentleness in a way that had never been quite so clear before.[13]

If "Lay Lady Lay" is one of Dylan's most paradoxically impersonal, though intimately cast hits, its tone still lingered in the openly autobiographical work he would release in the mid-1970s. The 1975 *Blood on the Tracks* shows Dylan moving through most of his accumulated voices – the soft boyishness of "You're Gonna Make Me Lonesome When You Go," the hard chill of "Idiot Wind," the grown-man croon of "If You See Her, Say Hello" – and sharing lyrics that, if they still rarely speak of his own physical condition, communicate a willingness to invest in the internal in ways that belie his cultivated image as an escape artist. "People tell me it's a sin, / to know and feel too much within," he sings in "Simple Twist of Fate," an expression of heartache as relatable as the Glen Campbell and

---

[13] Barbara O'Dair, "Bob Dylan and Gender Politics," in *The Cambridge Companion to Bob Dylan*, ed. Kevin J.H. Dettmar (Cambridge: Cambridge University Press, 2009), p. 80.

Freddy Fender tearjerkers that were topping the charts when it was released. As remarkable as the song's lyric is the way Dylan sings it, always on the edge of the kind of declamatory tone that could turn this story into a legend, but then pulling back, choosing the murmur instead of the shout, keeping things personal.

If *Blood on the Tracks* represents one version of the naked Bob Dylan – a construction like all the rest, but one with more doorways in – *Desire* (1976), the studio album that followed, is its complementary opposite. Recorded by a version of the band that had realized Dylan's arena rock dreams on Rolling Thunder, it is collaborative in its composition and epic in its lyrical scope. Dylan seems to have mostly lost the personal thread that allowed him to craft such nuanced and novelistic songs on *Blood on the Tracks*, instead producing, along with playwright Jacques Levy, sweeping visions playing upon all of the most problematic archetypes common in his songwriting, from the mystical, treacherous fallen woman to the dark gypsy to the heroic criminal. What redeems *Desire* is the music, which is wild, overwrought, and glorious. It shows Dylan pushing himself into rock-god territory as he never would again, and notably, he did so inspired by women collaborators.

The violinist Scarlet Rivera and the singers Emmylou Harris and Ronee Blakely are Dylan's main interlocutors throughout the album, complicating the machismo of Levy and Dylan's narratives and daring Dylan to take the same improvisatory risks they did. As he and Levy composed these songs full of golden-skinned silver-clad women and rough men straight out of a spaghetti Western, Dylan's imagination ran rampant through the global South. Harris, Blakeley, and Rivera's musical performances don't suggest that they scoffed at Dylan's visions the way Baez would in *Renaldo and Clara*, but their presence as women – obvious in the case of the singers, and readable in the curves and swerves of Rivera's playing – lends palpability to Dylan's high flying tales. His decision to make the recording sessions improvisational threatened to push the band off the rails, but Rivera, Harris, and Blakely can be heard leading at every opportunity, the strength of their artistry setting the album's tone and pushing Dylan toward different kinds of emotional release than he had managed before.

The Mortal Body

When Bob Dylan partially disrobed in order to better understand his star body, he was in his mid-thirties. Nothing was quite as elastic as it was in his earlier years. Within a few years, he'd turn away from his explorations of muscular masculinity and begin the long desert wanderings of his forties, a period that would include repeated attempts to engage with the popular soundscapes of the 1980s, none very successful by the estimation of critics or the general public. Dylan entered his lost era after a brief but prolific and showily "found" one – his born-again Christian phase. In interviews, Dylan described his life-changing encounter with Jesus in visceral terms, comparing it to childbirth, an experience he never had but had likely witnessed several times as the biological father of four children. (He would soon conceive another with Carolyn Dennis, a gospel singer with whom he frequently collaborated.) He also described himself as being reborn and reduced to the vulnerable state of babyhood. "You have to learn to drink milk before you can eat meat," he told Karen Hughes in 1980.[14] The searching, inept, vulnerable way Dylan felt during this time of spiritual absorption comes through in his singing on *Slow Train Coming* (1979) and his other gospel-based works. Babies don't swagger, and neither did Dylan then. He reached for things beyond his grasp, and occasionally flailed.

During his marriage to Dennis, which ended in 1992, Dylan may have been committed to otherworldly goals, but he was also evidently enjoying his own fleshly existence. One journalistic account of this period noted that when he appeared onstage with Dennis and her mother, who had been part of Ray Charles's backing group the Raelettes, he wore "jangly jewelry and dangly earrings, as well as dressing in leather trousers, singlets, leather gloves with cut-off fingers and multicolored t-shirts." Dylan would refine this peacockery over the course of the next few decades, finally settling on a look borrowed from a Western movie: wide-brimmed hats, three-quarter frock coats, and satin scarves or turquoise-studded bolo ties, his face adorned with a pencil thin mustache. The mod Dylan was now presenting himself as an American version of timeless – eternally wandering at the nation's old New Frontier.

It was there that the showdown took place that would revitalize Dylan's reputation and his influence. In 1997, at age 56, he survived an attack of pericarditis, an inflammation of the membrane around his heart. Ultimately curable, the illness shook the pop world; not since his 1966 motorcycle accident had the possibility of musical life without Dylan seemed so real. *Time Out of Mind* was released just months after his hospital stay, and many listeners read songs like "Love Sick" and "Not

---

[14] Interview with Karen Hughes, *Dominion*, May 21, 1980. Reprinted in Jonathan Cott, ed., *Bob Dylan: The Essential Interviews* (New York: Wenner Media, 2006), pp. 275–278.

Dark Yet," with their direct, vivid descriptions of a man whose senses and inner stability are failing him, as inspired by his health struggles. When he recorded those songs, Dylan might have been suffering from some symptoms of the infection that would bring him within miles, if not inches, of death, though he was unaware then of its name. He'd written the songs at his Minnesota ranch, and his infection, possibly caused by inhaling bird or bat feces spores while cleaning away dead wood, may have manifest as a lingering flu. He certainly sounds under the weather on "Love Sick," croaking out lines like, "I'm sick of love, / I hear the clock tick" in the tone of someone who's not righteous or romantic but simply tired and perhaps a little nauseous.

"Mostly I was in a lot of pain. Pain that was intolerable. That's the only way I can put it," Dylan later told David Gates.[15] He may have still considered his identity intangible, but his flesh and organs could no longer be etherized by metaphor. *Time Out of Mind* is a landmark album for Dylan because its songs squarely confront how a man in the drooping middle of his life actually feels. As Grayson Haver Currin has commented, it comes closer than any of his other work to the genuine feeling of the Delta blues Dylan had fetishized and expanded on for thirty-odd years. By working through "the cobwebs of his beleaguered voice," Dylan accesses something intimate and as solid as flesh ever gets: "The blues become an emotional state of being."[16] As always, Dylan seeks to empower himself by shape-shifting, girding himself with talismans borrowed from others' battles, but his own body remains inconveniently immediate. He is too hot to sleep. Lights give him a migraine. He's cut up by the wind. All of these ill symptoms connect to the despondency he feels. He has been rejected by a woman. Trying to win her back, he appeals to her need for physical comfort – in one of the least romantic opening lines ever plopped down inside a great love ballad, he sings in "Make You Feel My Love": "When the wind is blowing in your face, / and the whole world is on your case, / I could offer you a warm embrace." Bob Dylan as North Face jacket. It's what he can muster at this point.

Perhaps the goal on *Time Out of Mind* was not grandiose, but practical: contemplating pain, both emotional and chronic, Dylan sought to present himself within a body he could maintain as he aged. He would still move forward, but more deliberately. He would be his age. Perhaps it is in this

---

[15] David Gates, "Dylan Revisited," in *Studio A: The Bob Dylan Reader*, ed. Benjamin Hedin (New York: Norton, 2004), p. 237.
[16] Grayson Haver Currin, "Bob Dylan: Time Out of Mind," *Pitchfork* (2018), https://pitchfork.com /reviews/albums/bob-dylan-time-out-of-mind/.

context that we can view one of the most controversial acts of Dylan's mid-
to late career – the 2004 Victoria's Secret ad for which he licensed "Love
Sick," and in which he appeared. Barbara O'Dair disapprovingly poked fun
at the ad, in which Dylan wanders into a mostly vacant palazzo, encounters
a very young woman clad in lingerie and angel's wings, and tosses her his hat.
O'Dair called this "a parody of Thomas Mann's *Death in Venice*" in which
"an aging hero confronts the allure of youth – and broods."[17] But if we're
feeling generous, it can also be read as another admission by Dylan that, at
this point, he needs some help to get his mojo working. After all, it's the hat,
not Dylan himself, that the ingénue suggestively rubs against her thighs.
There is no shame, the ad (which was directed by a woman, Dominique
Isserman) suggests, in using sexual aids when the need arises.

Conclusion

We have now reached a certain point in Bob Dylan's life and our own – not
the end point but getting there – when his mortal body may soon no longer
move among us. He's been moving it as much as possible since his heart
scare, which interrupted his tour schedule for a few months; beyond that
enforced respite, Dylan continues to keep the punishing schedule that he
describes as his job and his fans continue to welcome as modestly miraculous. "He looked like a small vigorous corpse," the late novelist Barry
Hannah wrote of a 1990 show in Oxford, Mississippi. "I feared for his
health, was dismayed by his frailty."[18] Dylan was then not even fifty.
Hannah did admire his "stamina," though "I wrote it off to cocaine."
These judgments read now as charmingly overwrought, perhaps responding to a certain disaffection from a star promoting recent material that was
good but not a landmark, in front of an audience that wanted to hear the
hits and not the twisted way he liked to deliver them.

A few years later, Alex Ross followed Dylan for 3,000 miles across the
country and discovered delight where Hannah had seen weakness, finding
humor and a puckish wisdom in the way Dylan made do with the "tatters
of his voice," and "the scatteredness of his inspiration."[19] Ross noted that
a major part of Dylan's act since 1997 has been a sly acknowledgment of
his elder status – and the infirmities that go with it. This is clear in his lyrics
from *Time Out of Mind* onward, and perhaps more subtle in his live

---

[17] O'Dair, "Bob Dylan and Gender Politics," p. 82.
[18] Barry Hannah, "Constant Time for Bob Dylan," in *Studio A*, ed. Hedin, p. 281.
[19] Alex Ross, *Listen to This* (New York: Farrar, Straus and Giroux, 2010), p. 285.

performances. For much of this century, Dylan turned away from playing guitar, reportedly because he suffers from arthritis in his hands. But at least one fan saw the old virility – or a commentary on it – in the rocker's stance at a 2016 show. "He looked like a badass gunslinger," the fan wrote in an online forum. "The way he stood, feet apart, left hand hovering around his hip, intense look in his eyes, I thought he was about to let his .44 go off a rooty-toot-toot."[20] In that moment Dylan joined other great actors playing aging gunslingers in this era of revisionist Westerns – Ian McShane as Al Swearingen in *Deadwood*, Sam Elliott as Avery Markham in *Justified.*

More than an outlaw, however, Dylan at 80 has returned to a self-presentation that echoes his earliest appearances in the common consciousness. Advertising his latest hobby, building giant wrought-iron gates, or his business pursuit, craft whiskey, Dylan occupies the role of artisan – of someone, as Carlo Rotello has described it, good with his hands. "Being good with your hands is a deceptively simple virtue," Rotello writes in his 2002 book of that title, which is mostly about boxers and bluesmen. "It involves technical skill and finesse, craft mated with strength ... but it implies much more. The hands express a larger competence."[21] Dylan also seems to be seeking a kind of competence on his most recent recordings, technically imperfect but meticulously assembled forays into the American songbook, which form alliances with interpretive singers often more lauded as masters of craft than as geniuses or rock gods (see Chapter 11). It may seem strange that an artist who has achieved the highest honors for the use of his mind – a Pulitzer and the Nobel Prize in Literature – would turn to the hands as his central source of power as he tends to his legacy, his body of work. But perhaps, for Dylan, there is a certain urgency now to show himself engaging in the physical world. The care and tending of Dylan's immortal body will one day be up to others. In the meantime, he will touch what he can.

---

[20] www.quora.com/Why-has-Bob-Dylan-not-played-guitar-at-his-concerts-in-over-ten-years.
[21] Carlo Rotello, *Good with Their Hands: Boxers, Bluesmen, and Other Characters from the Rust Belt* (Berkeley: University of California Press, 2002), p. 2.

CHAPTER 23

Justice

Lisa O'Neill-Sanders

Bob Dylan's interest in justice, injustice, and crime is evident throughout his entire body of work. Many of his song lyrics contain explicit questions pertaining to right and wrong conduct in the context of particular historical events, people, or situations. Others reference the subjects of crime, justice, and injustice indirectly. Dylan clearly grasps the outrageousness of humanitarian, political, economic, and legal injustice, while also questioning the guilt of agents or enterprises partaking in or bearing witness to those acts. His songs also identify when exploitation occurs, and when accountability should be questioned.

In noting or identifying injustice and crime, Dylan presupposes a notion of what justice is, but he does not always reveal its exact nature. Not all of the crimes he writes about, after all, are ethically ascribed to responsible agents. When a crime is committed, the question of what is just or unjust is not always easily answered and we are thus forced to consider the concept of moral agency and probe who is responsible and why. What is clear, however, is that, for Dylan, people have an ethical right to live free from exploitation. Crimes against humanity, crimes against people by the legal system, crimes pertaining to unjust laws are inherently exploitative, and matters of ethical concern. Dylan's music lays the framework for this perspective in the early albums and the ideas persist throughout his career. This chapter will chronologically trace the songwriter's treatment of crime, justice, and injustice to understand how they function as a source of artistic inspiration and commentary on American culture.

Dylan's 1962 debut album includes songs dealing with gambling, theft, gun violence, genocide, murder, and lynchings, themes that also made their way onto unreleased tracks. "Rambling, Gambling Willie," for example, features a poker player resembling Wild Bill Hickok, famous for being

Special thanks to Nicole Font for her assistance with formatting and Professor Kari Larsen for her guidance regarding crime statutes.

murdered while holding what's called the "dead man's hand" of cards. The "Ballad of Donald White" tells a tale from the perspective of a criminal (the narrator) convicted for a Christmas Eve killing in 1959 and sentenced to death by hanging. The narrator describes a poor, lonely, parentless upbringing that led to a wandering life and an adult ultimately more at home with inmates. The song's concluding lines: "Are they enemies or victims ... Of your society" compels us to consider the consequences to society of absent or poor education, parenting, and childhood environment. Dylan often appeals to a sort of Socratic approach when considering such lapses of justice and this appeal is evident in the other three unreleased songs from his first album.

The songs "Long Ago, Far Away", "Train-A-Travelin'," and "The Death of Emmett Till" handle horrific crimes and major violations against humanity. In "Long Ago, Far Away" Dylan traces moral and ethical atrocities, ultimately questioning whether humanity has seen much progress through the centuries. Verse one makes an explicit reference to Christ, who paid the ultimate price for preaching "of peace and brotherhood." Subsequent verses concern slavery in the USA, the lives lost in the Second World War, injustices of wealth inequality, and death by lynching. Regarding death by lynching, it is not clear exactly to whom Dylan refers. "One man died of a broken heart, / To see the lynchin' of his son," but the punch of injustice from this major crime against humanity is strong. The sixth verse references Roman times and gladiator fighting. Here Dylan notes people's obsession with bloodshed and death noting that the spectators' "eyes and minds went blind" while witnessing barbaric deaths. As he notes by returning in the final verse to the theme of the first verse, the cost of advocating for peace and brotherhood is high and we are still paying the price.

This cost of injustice to humanity frames "Train A-Travelin'" and "The Death of Emmett Till." In the first, images of Nazi Germany and the horrific realities of concentration camps confront the listener and the singer wonders "if the leaders of the nations understand, / This murder-minded world that they're leavin' in my hands." To be sure, the "firebox of hatred and a furnace full of fears" that the song describes has been rolling through history and took the life of the young African American boy Emmett Till, who was murdered in 1955. When Dylan performed his song about the event on Cynthia Gooding's radio show *Folksingers Choice* on March 11, 1962, and again at the Finjan Club in Montreal, Quebec on July 2, 1962, Till had been dead for nearly seven years. Yet Dylan reminds us "that this kind of thing still lives today in that ghost-robed Ku Klux Klan." The murder of Till and the fraudulent trial of his assailants is the worst form of injustice, a complete mockery of humanity, a loss of rational life which, in the Western moral tradition, renders us ethically useless. The cost of injustice is the loss of humanity.

The Freewheelin' Bob Dylan (1963) includes released and unreleased songs with themes similar to those from his first album. "Walls of Red Wing," for example, is sung from the perspective of a man who recalls spending time in a juvenile correctional facility in Saint Cloud, Minnesota. The song notes that the young inmates, aged 12–17, are societal castoffs who face a bleak and dismal reality behind bars and have to deal with corrupt guards. Although some hope is expressed at the end of the song that some young men will end up as lawyers, others face a future of prison life. The questions of juvenile delinquency, its cost to society, and the hopelessness some young people will inevitably face linger.

"Oxford Town," another song on *Freewheelin'*, draws on racial crimes and injustices prevalent in the USA at the time. The Supreme Court decision *Brown v. Board of Education of Topeka* (1954) ruled that racial segregation in public schools was unconstitutional. When federal marshals enforced desegregation orders by escorting James Meredith onto the campus of the University of Mississippi in September 1962, deadly violence erupted and two people lost their lives. The moral weightiness and ethical burden of racism is communicated throughout the song. Heads are down, the sun is not shining, weapons are everywhere, doors are closed, sorrowful songs are sung, "All because his face was brown / All because of the color of his skin." And in a typical Socratic fashion, we are asked "What do you think about that, my frien'?"

Officials from the University of Mississippi and the governor of Mississippi, Ross Barnett, committed crimes in an attempt to prevent Meredith from accessing education. Criminal violations by other officials turn up in other songs during this period. In "Seven Curses," Dylan tells the tale of an unjust and illegal punishment carried out by a corrupt judge. We are told in the song that a man named Reilly stole a horse and was sentenced to death. When his daughter learned of the sentence, she went to see the judge to plead her father's case. The judge agreed to free Reilly on the condition that she provide sexual favors to the judge. She reluctantly agreed despite her father's protest, but the judge carried out the death sentence anyway.

The theme of corrupt or questionable judges continues with Dylan's next album, *The Times They Are A-Changin'* (1964). "Percy's Song" was recorded for the album, but not released until 1985 on *Biograph*. The song tells a tale of a driver whose car spun off the road due to "rain" and "wind" before landing in a field and killing four people. At best the crime is reckless homicide, but it is essentially treated as murder with a sentence of ninety-nine years in Joliet prison. We get the sense that the victim was railroaded by the criminal justice system and that the judge upholds a conviction and punishment that does not seem to match the crime. This unjust punishment exacts another life and the system fails to deliver justice.

In "The Lonesome Death of Hattie Carroll," Dylan further reminds listeners of the exploitation and lack of justice African Americans face within the legal system. African American bartender Hattie Carroll was accidentally killed by a wealthy young white man, William Zantzinger on February 9, 1963 at a hotel in Baltimore. He was ultimately charged with and convicted of assault and manslaughter rather than murder, served six months in jail, and paid minor fines.

Listeners are called to wonder, not only about the failure or absence of the criminal justice system, but also about the criminality of killing in "Who Killed Davey Moore?" Featherweight boxer Davey Moore died in August 1963 as a result of a boxing match with Sugar Ramos. Dylan chronicles the landscape of potential responsibility in the song, and raises questions about justified or unjustified killing and moral conduct. It is not clear if a crime was technically committed, but we get much more than simply the sense that something is not right. The song probes moral responsibility: if the referee, the crowd, Davey Moore's manager, gamblers, sports writers, and Moore's opponent, Sugar Ramos, are not responsible, then who is? Should responsibility be ascribed? Moore was killed, and it is unreasonable that this sort of act should go unpunished. Even unintentional killings bring involuntary manslaughter charges. Outrage after Moore's death was strong. Various states sought to impose restrictions or bans on boxing due to its apparent barbarism; the Catholic Church vocally opposed it as did others. In an attempt to regulate the sport, Senator Estes Kefauver, then Democrat, of Tennessee noted "The death of Davey Moore . . . is another milestone in the boxing industry's history of mistreated human beings."[1] The song leaves us wondering whether what happened should be considered criminal.

Another Side of Bob Dylan (1964), despite featuring a number of personal songs, contains a few also related to crime. "Playboys and Playgirls" calls out those who are playing with humanity and trying to run the world. The playboys and playgirls are responsible for creating fallout shelters, permitting Jim Crow laws in some places and permitting lynchings that

---

[1] "From the archive, 26 March 1963: The Death of Boxer Davey Moore," *The Guardian*, March 25, 2014. www.theguardian.com/theguardian/2014/mar/25/davey-moore-boxer-death

are, according to the song, amusing to some. The role of the government in perpetuating the heinous crimes is clear in the song: only it created the fallout shelters and the reality requiring them.

"Bob Dylan's 115th Dream" from *Bringing It All Back Home* (1965) depicts a chaotic sense of lawlessness where there appears to be a minimal, and ineffective government, but law enforcement and jails nevertheless exist. Eleven verses long, the song chronicles a surreal journey beginning with the Mayflower's discovery of America. Its major themes include unjust imprisonment by corrupt law enforcement (the cop who is "Crazy as a loon"), lack of legal order, and a fruitless search for the USA and its values. Although there is a US flag on display in the strange community that straddles the early colonies and the contemporary USA, its founding values are absent.

"Desolation Row," from *Highway 61 Revisited* (1965) is arguably Dylan's most surreal song and also quite long at ten verses. It similarly depicts a chaotic scene of lawlessness, lifelessness, and despair. The opening line, "They're selling postcards of the hanging," is a clear reference to the lynching postcards commonly produced and sold in the USA at the end of the nineteenth and early twentieth centuries. The practice of creating, selling, and sharing these despicable artifacts renders society ethically and morally bankrupt and Dylan captures that loss as the song evolves. Riots, medical emergencies, and other forms of violence are metaphorically represented and suggested, and the title of the song characterizes the desolate quality of life that pervades the album. Although people are represented as characters in the song, humanity is completely absent. Authentic human communities, after all, are impossible when the crime of lynching is routinely memorialized.

John Wesley Harding (1967) contains twelve songs, five of which pertain to crime and justice in some way. The album's title is a reference to infamous nineteenth-century American outlaw John Wesley Hardin whose lawlessness and brutality are legendary. The character in the song, "John Wesley Harding," however, is portrayed as the exact opposite of this historical figure. Dylan's Harding befriended the poor, never hurt honest folks, helped people whenever he could, and was falsely charged by authorities who were unable to make the charges stick. He was a victim of the system. There's a thief in the song "All Along the Watchtower" who consoles the victimized and exploited joker. The thief sympathizes but urges the joker to "not talk falsely." "The Ballad of Frankie Lee and Judas Priest" chronicles a tale of two friends one of whom, a gambler named Frankie Lee, is led to his death by the other, Judas Priest, and dies of thirst after seventeen days in a "home" with twenty-four women each occupying one room. Friends don't let friends die in a house of prostitution.

"Oh, help me in my weakness" begins "Drifter's Escape," a song about a vagabond who is seemingly victimized by an out of control jury that resembles a mob. But in a twist, Dylan's judge feels sorrow and compassion for the drifter, as do a nurse and attendant. Ultimately, fate weighs in with a lightning strike, giving the drifter an opportunity to flee. The escape is justified, thus pointing again to the idea that the punishment does not fit the crime. The drifter has something in common with the title character in "I Am a Lonesome Hobo." He too is a societal outcast who has no friends or family and has led a life of crime. He urges listeners to develop a sense of character, be true to themselves, and thus potentially avoid his sad fate. Again, the causes of criminal behavior are suggested, but the lines of responsibility are blurred.

Nellie Stone Johnson is a figure in Dylan's song "Wanted Man," recorded for *Nashville Skyline* (1969), his last album from the 1960s. She was an African American born in Minnesota in 1905 who became a civil rights activist, pro-union advocate, and the first black to hold public office in Minneapolis. While on the surface we may infer that the song refers to a lover who has skipped town leaving the women behind, it takes on a new meaning in the context of Nellie's life. The wanted man is wanted everywhere; perhaps all men are wanted men, "Wherever you might look tonight, you might see this wanted man." In the context of Nellie, and her fight for fair employment practices, the interpretation of the song turns on unfair and illegal treatment of labor. Workers are exploited everywhere, and so every boss is a wanted man.

In 1971, Dylan released the song "George Jackson" as a single. Jackson was an activist, a member of the Black Panthers, an author, and a prisoner who was murdered while serving time in 1971. The circumstances surrounding his death are controversial, but many argue that he was a victim of a corrupt criminal justice system and systemic racism. The song starts with the narrator's confession of grief at Jackson's killing. His unjust imprisonment is noted in the second verse, his strength of character in the third where Dylan explains that the "authorities, they hated him / Because he was just too real." The song concludes with an explanation of Jackson being slain by the prison guards who were afraid of his power and the narrator surmising that the world "Is one big prison yard," where some people are prisoners and some people are guards.

Dylan wrote "I Shall Be Released," in 1967 and it was recorded by the Band for their 1968 album, *Music from Big Pink*. His version appeared on

Bob Dylan's Greatest Hits, Volume II (1971), where it continues to explore the corruption of the criminal justice system. The motif of light in the song serves to illuminate the need to pay attention to those who are victims of the system. In a crowd of lonely people, we hear the cries of a man "who swears he's not to blame / Crying out that he was framed." The song "Billy" from the 1973 album *Pat Garrett and Billy the Kid* comments on the young outlaw's run from the law and slaying by Pat Garrett. "Lily, Rosemary and the Jack of Hearts" from *Blood on the Tracks* (1975) is sixteen verses long and tells a carnival-like story about a love triangle, robbery, and murder, a drunk "hangin' judge" and an execution.

His 1976 album *Desire* pays tribute to two notorious crimes: the unjust imprisonment of boxer Rubin "Hurricane" Carter and the story of organized crime figure Joey Gallo's murder in 1972. Jacques Levy collaborated on both songs. Carter served nineteen years before the charges were dismissed and he was released. Dylan tells "the story of the Hurricane / The man the authorities came to blame," a story about Carter's wrongful homicide conviction due to racial bias. Dylan details the barroom scene of the three murders in the first two verses of the song. Carter's name appears in verse three where Dylan notes at the end "If you're black you might as well not show up on the street, / Less you wanna draw the heat." "Joey" portrays a one-time mobster as a reformed criminal. After having served time in a New York state prison, Gallo refused to carry a gun, "'I'm around too many children,' he'd say, 'they should never know of one.'" Here Dylan presents the idea of the possibility of criminal reform, concluding the song with a line toward the end: "I know the men that shot him down will get what they deserve."

Four of nine songs on *Street Legal* (1978) deal with the idea of crime in some way. "Baby Stop Crying" mentions a man who is on the verge of firing a pistol and is unable to distinguish right from wrong. "Señor (Tales of Yankee Power)" is about being on the run, and "Where Are You Tonight? (Journey Through Dark Heat)" notes ineffective laws and criminal acts. "No Time to Think" points to useless laws and lawmakers: "Fools making laws for the breaking of jaws / And the sound of the keys when they clink."

"Slow Train," "Do Right to Me Baby (Do Unto Others)," and "When You Gonna Wake Up?" from *Slow Train Coming* (1979) deal with law. In the first, Dylan notes that man-made laws no longer work. In the second, the Golden Rule is the subject. The singer repeatedly expresses a desire to live in the right kind of society, one where the act of judging does not occur, people are not harmed, no one shoots or gets shot, people do not cheat, and no one is exploited. The song "When You Gonna Wake Up?" challenges listeners to consider the influence of Karl Marx and Henry Kissinger on society, an intellectual contrast to the bloated, too powerful state on the one hand, and the retreat of the state on the other. The song asks listeners to consider when they will wake up and realize that innocent people are incarcerated, physicians are not healing us with their prescriptions, and that society is crumbling. The answer is an appeal to divine law: "Do you ever wonder just what God requires?"

Dylan released several songs in the 1980s dealing with crime, law, and injustice. The song "Lenny Bruce" from *Shot of Love* (1981) is about the stand-up comedian famous for being vulgar and for pushing the boundaries of tolerance. He was frequently arrested for obscenity and, in the song, Dylan questions the criminality of such performances. Plain, truthful humor is what Bruce gave us, according to the song and thus in no way is he an outlaw. He never committed any crimes, the song claims, never robbed a church, or harmed the innocent. Instead, at least in Dylan's view, he fought for the right to freedom of speech, free expression, and transparent authority.

"Dead Man, Dead Man," also from *Shot of Love*, offers a metaphorical challenge to what it means to live. The dead man in the song is urged to recognize the lifelessness of living without faith, with the absence of love, being seduced by "the politics of sin." The song is not overwhelmingly oriented toward the theme of crime, but the second-to-last verse raises a poignant question: "What are you tryin' to overpower me with, the doctrine or the gun?" That a weapon is raised forces us to consider its context: is it military, is it the culture of violence? Perhaps it is both.

Infidels (1983) reflected deteriorating international affairs in the aftermath of the Soviet invasion of Afghanistan, the US boycott of the 1980 Olympics, and the rise of the Polish Solidarity movement. The theme of war permeates the song "Jokerman" and its cascade of images include a rifleman exploiting the weak, Molotov cocktails, and judges. But the judges, those normally responsible for upholding the rule of law and principles of justice are "false-hearted." "Molotov cocktails and rocks behind every curtain" is a clear reference to crude weapons, the Soviet's iron curtain, and Vyacheslav Mikhailovich Molotov, a Stalinist whose role in the exploitation of Poland is well documented. The natural law according to the song "I and I" is just the rule of "an eye for an eye and a tooth for a tooth." Perhaps we are living in a state of nature on the brink of complete lawlessness.

The album *Oh Mercy* (1989) is Dylan's last of the 1980s and the song "Political World" deals directly with the topic of crime and its consequences.

The first verse notes that crime is without a face and characteristic, along with the absence of love, of a world that is purely political. As a consequence, there is no wisdom – "it's in jail" –an obvious reference to unjust imprisonment. We thus become governed by images of ourselves; virtues are nonexistent; and people are fearful. The political world is criminal because politics too often result in the miscarriage of justice and the exploitation of the innocent and weak.

Dylan seems to have turned away from themes of crime and justice in the first decade of the 2000s.[2] Three songs from *Tempest* (2012) return to the earlier themes of crime, justice, and corruption. "Pay in Blood" describes a struggle of an individual trying to live life who repeatedly confronts corruption. "Another politician pumping out his piss" captures the song's sentiment. References to being chained, being exploited, lack of justice, and absence of virtues persist in the song. The sprawling narrative of "Tin Angel" (it's twenty-seven verses long), tells the story of a wealthy couple's demise due to a love triangle. All three end up dead: the lover kills the husband, the wife kills the lover and then kills herself.

"Early Roman Kings," the third song of note from the album, serves as a fitting conclusion. The Roman kings described in the song are timeless. Their clothing is not typical of clothing worn in ancient times, but their actions are typically exploitative. The last verse of the song begins "I was up on Black Mountain the day Detroit fell / They killed them all off and they sent them to hell." The reference to Detroit falling is twofold. On the one hand, the 1967 riots in Detroit come to mind, on the other the economic decline of the city partially due to the loss of US manufacturing jobs. The two are not unrelated. Without economic opportunity, fair laws upheld by an impartial judicial system, and equal treatment under the law, people cannot flourish, especially those who are in a position to be exploited due to historical and other factors. If individuals do not have the opportunity to flourish, we all pay a price.

---

[2] According to Pew Research Center, crime rates in the USA have declined steadily since the early 1990s. It is possible that this fact could be expressed in Dylan's art given that it is relatively absent compared with the preceding three decades.

PART V

Reception and Legacy

CHAPTER 24

The Bob Dylan Brand

Devon Powers

The purpose of this chapter is to explore the relationship between Bob Dylan and branding, a task that requires disentangling three powerful myths. Myth one is the colossus of Bob Dylan himself, a musician whose ascent to legendary status happened almost simultaneously with his debut and who casts the longest shadow over everything, especially himself. Myth two concerns the 1960s, times that continue to possess and occupy Dylan as both hostage and host. And myth three: the brand in all its power and plasticity, capable of restructuring businesses and rewriting history, of refashioning the world in its image.

The three myths share a capacity to define the parameters of discussion, to act almost as arguments in and of themselves. For example, when it comes to Bob Dylan, sober assessments are scarce. Take *The Cambridge Companion to Bob Dylan*, a book whose unassuming title fails to prepare the reader for the excited proclamations contained within. "No rock performer's shows are more cherished by his fans than are Dylan's (only Bruce Springsteen really comes close)," explains Kevin Dettmar in the introduction, in one of many rhapsodic statements.[1] Other chroniclers have called Dylan "the first real Rock Star,"[2] "not only a genius but a misunderstood one,"[3] and an artist whose work is "unprecedented and unmatched."[4] Alan Light, in the *Rolling Stone Illustrated History of Rock & Roll* muses that "[it] is impossible to imagine the Sixties protest movement, the Seventies singer-songwriters or even the outspoken politics of rap without him."[5] Bob Dylan

---

[1] Kevin Dettmar, "Introduction," in *The Cambridge Companion to Bob Dylan*, ed. Kevin J.H. Dettmar (New York: Cambridge University Press, 2009), p. 6.

[2] Lee Marshall, *Bob Dylan: The Never Ending Star* (Cambridge: Polity, 2008), p. 93.

[3] David Yaffe, *Bob Dylan: Like a Complete Unknown* (New Haven, CT: Yale University Press, 2011), p. 42.

[4] Donald Brown, *Bob Dylan: American Troubadour* (New York: Rowman & Littlefield Publishers, 2014), p. xxxvi.

[5] Alan Light, "Bob Dylan," in *The Rolling Stone Illustrated History of Rock & Roll*, ed. Anthony DeCurtis, James Henke, and Holly George-Warren (New York: Straight Arrow Press, 1992), p. 299.

may or may not be America's greatest songsmith, but he is among the most worshipped – at least for those of a certain critical disposition and cultural station, who feel at ease seeing their own taste and experience as reflective of all.

It is from that vantage that "branding" might seem too vulgar a lens for thinking about Dylan. After all, cultural icons hardly have a need for branding. Moreover, there is a common lament that using the music of the 1960s for something as debased as advertising is offensive, an affront to an entire generation's sense of self. For example, in a *New York Times* piece from 1989, critic Jon Pareles laments how "[m]usic from a time that was often ambivalent about materialism, and about its own commercial success, now urges fans to consume for fun and status" – in his view a blatant emblem of the selling out of 1960s radicalism.[6] In 2005, Albert Brooks issued an even stronger rebuke in *Newsweek*, accusing "Madison Avenue" of "taking the very things we were born to change and are now shoving them down our throats, with our own music as the lubricant."[7] To go even further and comprehend one of those revolutionary musicians as himself a brand could easily be interpreted as adding insult to injury.

Reading Dylan through branding is a tad ahistorical. Brands, defined by Liz Moor as an "integrated approach to marketing and business strategy" that coalesces "product design, retail design, point-of-purchase marketing" and more, took on its contemporary form during the 1990s.[8] Only then did it begin its wholesale shift from a descriptor of products to a general term for identity, reputation, and image that has utility well beyond traditional consumer goods. Despite this anachronism, I argue here that Dylan offers one way to comprehend how and why branding emerged as a strategic response to commercial and cultural changes within the recording industry and the wider world in which it operates. Despite the longstanding rhetoric, especially fervent in the 1960s, that commerce should not contaminate music, musicians like Dylan came not only to take up branding as their primary business platform but also to represent how other kinds of goods and services could communicate personality, longevity, and meaning for their consumers. The 1960s matter, therefore, not just because they are the backdrop against which the transformation of Dylan from singer to icon to brand began to take shape, but also because they are the repository from which his cultural meaning – and in turn, his brand value – continues to be drawn.

---

[6] Jon Pareles, "The 60s Reinvented: Only the Beat Goes On," *New York Times*, February 5, 1989.

[7] Albert Brooks, "The Times They are A-Changin'," *Newsweek*, November 13, 2005.

[8] Liz Moor, *Rise of Brands* (Oxford: Berg, 2007), p. 3.

Narrative, Myth, and Brand Value

So much reflection about Bob Dylan begins the same way – with a tale about a young man named Robert Zimmerman from Hibbing, Minnesota. He arrived in New York City in January 1961 and, having renamed himself Bob Dylan, began a rapid ascent to celebrity within the local folk scene and beyond. Little was known about the singer when that ascent began. As Robert Shelton wrote in his career-making 1961 *New York Times* review, "Mr. Dylan is vague about his antecedents and birthplace, but it matters less where he has been than where he is going, and that would seem to be straight up."[9]

Even as the rather plain details of Dylan's origin emerged, they melded with the fantastical liberties he regularly took with his story to result in a beguiling celebrity persona (and, later, a brandable asset). "Dylan not only changed his name but persistently reinvented himself, fabricating tall tales of a bohemian past that had been far more conventionally bourgeois than he let on" explain R. Clifton Spargo and Anne Ream in a commentary on the singer's ties to religion.[10] Religion too formed a central, if ambiguous, aspect of his reinvention; adoption of the Dylan moniker masked his Jewishness and presaged a lifelong back and forth about whether and on what terms faith and ethnicity defined him.[11] In addition to the license he took with these biographical details, Dylan was a musical chameleon who subverted listener attempts to draw a straight line between the songs and the man who sang them. "Dylan is the very definition of hidden in plain sight," writes Anthony DeCurtis in an essay on Dylan's songwriting. "He has perfected a version of himself that permits his being available virtually everywhere while letting very little of himself be known."[12]

Yet if there was any one factor that contributed the most to Dylan's heightened mystique – bolstering his narrative, inspiring debate, and ever burnishing his star – it was his interactions with the press. Notoriously wary of reporters, Dylan manipulated journalists seeking to define or pigeonhole him. One minute he could be straightforward and cooperative,

---

[9] Robert Shelton, "20-Year-Old Singer Is Bright New Face at Gerde's Folk City," *New York Times*, September 29, 1961.

[10] R. Clifton Spargo and Anne K. Ream, "Bob Dylan and Religion," in *The Cambridge Companion to Bob Dylan*, ed. Dettmar, p. 90.

[11] Ibid; David Yaffe, "Bob Dylan and the Anglo-American Tradition," in *The Cambridge Companion to Bob Dylan*, ed. Dettmar, pp. 16–17.

[12] Anthony DeCurtis, "Bob Dylan as Songwriter," in *The Cambridge Companion to Bob Dylan*, ed. Dettmar, p. 43.

the next off-topic, inappropriate or hostile. Take, for example, the following exchange from a 1965 press conference in Berkeley, California:

QUESTION: Josh Dunson in his new book implies that you have sold out to
            commercial interests and the topical song movement. Do you have any
            comment sir?
DYLAN: Well, no comments, no arguments. No, I sincerely don't feel guilty.
QUESTION: If you were going to sell out to a commercial interest, which one
            would you choose?
DYLAN: Ladies garments.[13]

What are we to make of the Dylan who showed up to answer questions
that day? Though his responses show a sense of humor, they also reveal
his penchant for insolence and sabotage. Over time, an increasingly
mercurial Dylan would regularly indulge in such feral impulses. "[H]e
is . . . at once obviously reluctant, self-protecting, and self-concealing but
equally often a stunningly direct, heartfelt, epiphanic, poetic, and, most
important, *playful* expositor of his munificent and inspiring thought-
dreams," explained Jonathan Cott in his edited collection of Dylan
interviews.[14] Cott further recounts how Dylan's interviewers could feel
intimidated and off-balance around him; the fact that he was a difficult
interview doubtlessly shaped his coverage and the reputation he held
both within and outside of journalistic circles. If the goal of journalists
was to "get the story" about Dylan, they were also part of constructing
that story in many ways.

   While Dylan confused the press in general, he seduced the emergent
rock press in particular. Beginning in the mid-1960s, rock inspired a
younger generation of writers to approach the music as a serious artform
and a medium for cultural and social commentary. Stylistically, rock
writers leaned toward the intellectual and literary, but by turns could be
spectacular, excitable, even hyperbolic – especially considering journalistic
norms of the time. "Bob Dylan is worshipped by legions of pubescent
'teeny-boppers' and, at the same time, considered a major American poet
by many serious students," noted Richard Goldstein in the July 14, 1966
edition of his *Village Voice* column, Pop Eye.[15] Later that summer, in the
pages of *Crawdaddy!*, Paul Williams took part in what he called "the

---

[13] Ralph J. Gleason, "Bob Dylan Gives Press Conference in San Francisco," *Rolling Stone*,
      December 14, 1967.
[14] Jonathan Cott, ed., *Bob Dylan: The Essential Interviews* (New York: Simon & Schuster, 2017), p. xv.
[15] Devon Powers, *Writing the Record: The* Village Voice *and the Birth of Rock Criticism* (Amherst, MA:
      University of Massachusetts Press, 2013), p. 67.

favorite sport in America ... discussing, worshiping, disparaging, and above all interpreting Bob Dylan"[16] when he reviewed Dylan's latest effort *Blonde on Blonde.* Williams called the record "a cache of emotion, a well-handled package of excellent music and better poetry, blended and meshed and ready to become a part of your reality."[17] Statements such as these celebrated the spirit of the music as they also desired to persuade and arouse – a far cry from objective reportage or the tempered accounts one might expect of so-called high art. In this sense, Dylan "belonged" to the rock press; writers wanted to "get" him and to turn their readers on.

Hunger to read, decipher, and amplify Dylan was not just about his music, however. It likewise reflected and reinforced his celebrity, and the idea of music celebrity more generally. Famous musicians existed long before the 1960s, as did ample commercial opportunities of which those musicians might take advantage. However, the 1960s was the decade in which "a new generation was portrayed as exhibiting a new and radical social consciousness and popular music stars came to be seen as embodying that radical consciousness,"[18] as Lee Marshall has phrased it. In turn, many believed that Dylan "virtually single-handedly [was] providing popular music with political awareness."[19] Because one effect of celebrity is to stand in for social complexities, Dylan would stand up as one of the most significant flash points for generational sentiment and attachment. Even as he receded from public life following a motorcycle accident in 1966, he continued to be canonized in this fashion. The more he came to epitomize the 1960s, the more other aspects of the period receded from view.

Dylan has spent most of his career contending with the monumentalism of his first few years – a task even he has admitted is limiting and frustrating. "'[Y]ou can't achieve greatness under media scrutiny,'" Dylan has said. "'You're never allowed to be less than your legend.'"[20] That he was so revered so quickly highlights the distance between "Bob Dylan" the brand and the actual human being. It is useful, then, to think about "Bob Dylan" as referencing not so much a person as a meaningful symbol, or an ongoing story, co-constructed by many complicit storytellers. As confining as it might be, it is that story that has since become valuable in both a literal and a figurative sense.

---

[16] Paul Williams, *The* Crawdaddy! *Book: Writings (and Images) from the Magazine of Rock* (Milwaukee, WI: Hal Leonard, 2002), p. 30.
[17] Ibid, p. 36.   [18] Marshall, *Bob Dylan*, p. 55.   [19] Ibid.   [20] Ibid, p. 227.

From Recording to Rights: Music Industries in Transition

Dylan's rise and subsequent career transpired amid major changes the music business operated. Observers have noted, for instance, that Dylan's success relied heavily upon Albert Grossman, a savvy manager whose innovative practices transformed the field in both style and substance. "Grossman's relationship with Dylan was . . . a partnership of visionaries," explains Fred Goodman. "While Dylan created songs whose content, form and imagery challenged the limits of pop music, Grossman set about to extend the boundaries of the business."[21] In addition to cultivating a cult of personality and exclusivity around Dylan, Grossman played an instrumental role in developing contracts that gave musicians creative control as well as hefty advances.

The maturation of artist management took place alongside horizontal and vertical integration that restructured the music industries. The trend toward concentration and conglomeration has continued through to the present day, ensnaring not just record labels but also radio stations, live venues and concert promotion, and music publishing. At each stage, the remaining players have increased their hold on power. Equally significant, what has happened to music companies has been replicated among musicians themselves. "[P]rofessional musicianship changed from a career in which many, though never all who aspired, could make a respectable living through live performance into one in which an elite few did extremely well, a few more created middle class lives, and most were unable to make ends meet," notes Nancy Baym in her study of the changing relationship between musicians and the audience.[22] Earning the lion's share of profits and reflecting widespread cultural beliefs about individualism and artistry, stars – the musical elite – became the spindle around which the industry increasingly revolved.

Stardom served several economic purposes for a recording industry beset by concentration and conglomeration. Stars helped labels manage the risks associated with record production; they were also strategies for anticipating consumer demand. Additionally, as the labels turned their attention from manufacturing records to managing rights, stars emerged as an effective interface through which to exploit those rights, attached not just to repertoires of songs or performances but also to personalities, likenesses,

---

[21] Fred Goodman, *The Mansion on the Hill: Dylan, Young, Geffen, Springsteen, and the Head-on Collision of Rock and Commerce* (New York: Vintage, 1997), p. 92.
[22] Nancy Baym, *Playing to the Crowd: Musicians, Audiences, and the Intimate Work of Connection* (New York: NYU Press, 2018), p. 63.

and merchandise. When record labels experienced a recession in the 1980s, for example, stars remained a reliable pathway toward profit, as gargantuan artists like Madonna, Whitney Houston, Michael Jackson, and Prince dominated the charts, earned hefty sales, and became cultural icons through plentiful media coverage. The decade also saw these stars commonly extending their reach into both emerging and expanding music sectors such as videos, commercials, toys, and apparel.

Bob Dylan has never been a star of the order of a Michael Jackson or Madonna. His heyday predated MTV by a generation and never adjusted to it; only ever a modest seller, "synergistic stardom" did not play to his strengths.[23] Nonetheless, because "stardom is the means through which music's noncommodity status is asserted, and it is ultimately the thing that creates the value of the popular music commodity itself,"[24] Dylan remained an important artist during this shifting era. His legend, cultural clout, and dedicated fanbase were priceless assets that remained profitable even if he did not release high-selling new albums. Creatively and culturally, Bob Dylan was also a lodestar for other musicians – an object lesson in how to stay relevant.

Since the 1980s, Dylan and Columbia, his label, have pursued business strategies that would make the most of his longevity and legendary status. The release of more than three dozen live albums, box sets, rarities, and compilations since the mid-1980s has given fans ample opportunities to consume Dylan's music or update their collections to later musical formats – as happened, for example, after the appearance of the compact disc (CD) in 1982. The 1980s also mark the beginning of Dylan's so-called "Never Ending Tour," a period during which Dylan only rarely takes breaks from the road. Prior to 1988, he had been an infrequent and erratic live performer, often taking several years off in between tours. Yet in light of the influence of the Grateful Dead, Dylan has used constant touring as a way to reinterpret his songbook. The tour, which continues to the present, also signifies a canny business strategy, allowing him to connect with audiences, extend his reputation, and capitalize on new revenue streams. Seen from this vantage, Dylan is a trailblazer. In the years since the Never Ending Tour began, live performance has become an important way to make money in an age of waning sales for recording.

[23] Marshall, *Bob Dylan,* pp. 117, 171.
[24] Lee Marshall, "The Structural Functions of Stardom in the Recording Industry," *Popular Music and Society* 36, no. 5 (2013), pp. 588–589.

In another example of both innovativeness and business acumen, Dylan has not shied away from licensing his music. This practice began early in his career and included movies like *Easy Rider* (1969) and TV shows such as *Mission Impossible* (1970). Despite steady licenses since then, the frequency in narrative television and film exploded in the last two decades. For instance, of the nearly 800 licensing occurrences listed with the Internet Movie Database, more than 65% of them have occurred since the year 2000. Especially significant is the 2017 PBS television documentary *The Vietnam War*. Dylan's music appears in most episodes of the ten-part series, with songs such as "A Hard Rain's A-Gonna Fall" playing a prominent and symbolic role.

On top of a growing use of his music in TV and film, Dylan has slowly but surely embraced the use of his music in commercials – a practice that often evokes consternation. The earliest advertising use I was able to find took place in 1994, when Richie Havens performed a cover of "The Times They Are A-Changin'" in a commercial for Coopers & Lybrand, a British firm. Perhaps anticipating a backlash, Dylan disallowed the company from using his name, even in discussing the spot. Yet whatever shame or worry about fallout slowly eroded as the number of usages ticked upwards; like film and television syncs, placement of Dylan's music in advertising exploded after 2000. In 2004, he even made good on his promise to "sell out" to "ladies garments" when he appeared in a Victoria's Secret commercial with his song "Love Sick" as soundtrack. Over the next decade, his music appeared in commercials for many companies, including Apple, Cadillac, Pepsi, Budweiser, Kaiser Permanente, IBM, Chobani Yogurt, and Google; some of those spots even aired during the Super Bowl. Licensing expanded well beyond advertisements, too: he allowed one of his songs to appear on the video game *Rock Band 2*; Starbucks issued an exclusive CD release in 2005; Twyla Tharp produced two Broadway dance shows based on his songs; and in 2016, he has licensed his repertoire for development into an Amazon series. Though he found opportunities for his more recent fare, many of these opportunities relied upon his earlier songs.

More recently, Dylan has tried his hand at cross-promotion and product licensing. In 2015, he trademarked the phrase "bootleg whiskey," in anticipation of developing Heaven's Door Spirits, a line of boutique spirits released in 2018. "Dylan has these qualities that actually work well for a whiskey," noted Mark Bushala, his business partner, in an interview with the *New York Times*. Mr. Bushala continued by noting that Dylan has "great authenticity" and is "a quintessential American" whose unpredictability is "very much on brand."[25]

There are several ways one might interpret Dylan's prominence in commercial endeavors. On the one hand, they simply indicate his extraordinary cultural station. That it is easy to call up myriad examples of his marketization simply acknowledges that we live in a thoroughly commercialized culture where it is hard to escape capitalism's grip. Perhaps, too, Dylan is somehow a victim of this fact. Some of the writers quoted early on in this chapter might certainly think so, and so he should hardly take the blame for being co-opted as he has. Yet I find those answers to be unsatisfying at best, dishonest at worst. Not only do they fail to give Dylan and his affiliates any agency over how he has managed his career, but they also neglect the demands increasingly placed upon musicians of all kinds to navigate the changing expectations of and opportunities within music and its companion industries. To be a successful musician has long required business sense. Whether we like it or not, a critical way in which Dylan has remained salient is through very good business sense, which has among other skills demanded thoughtful stewardship of his brand.

Brand Music

What makes Dylan a brand? In the past, we might point to "Bob Dylan" as a shorthand – for instance, if we note how other musicians have been compared to Bob Dylan as a way to generate buzz. Yet a brand encompasses much more than simply a catchphrase or a selling tool. Over the course of the 1990s and 2000s, *brand* ascended into the popular lexicon as "a symbolic shorthand for market savvy, business acumen, and global competitiveness";[26] brands stood for personality, reputation, and image all rolled into one. New technologies, modes of socializing, and greater acceptance of corporate sponsorship coincided with the application of branding to areas far beyond the corporate and product space where it originated. Now, it hardly raises an eyebrow to think about a movement, a city, a sound, a flavor, a politician, or even a regular person as a brand.

We also exist during an era of "artist-brands" being a signature element of the contemporary business of recording. As Leslie Meier notes, "artist-brands" implies musicians who use licensing, touring, merchandising, and

---

[25] Ben Sisario, "Bob Dylan's Latest Gig: Making Whiskey," *New York Times*, April 28, 2018.

[26] Melissa Aronczyk and Devon Powers, *Blowing Up the Brand: Critical Perspectives on Promotional Culture* (New York: Peter Lang, 2010), p. 2.

cross-market partnerships to build a career and earn revenue.[27] Artist-brands are the avatars of what's known as the "360" or "multi-rights" deals, a type of contract that came into existence in the mid-2000s to give music companies a greater share of a wider variety of musicians' revenue streams. The concept of an artist-brand also reflects a contemporary landscape in which musicians – especially those building a career – must utilize social media, streaming services, and multiple other kinds of digital platforms in order to maintain their visibility.

It is also critical to consider how music serves as both a source of value and a role model for other kinds of products and services seeking to connect emotionally and resonate authentically with their consumers. Mark Knight, Strategy Director for the British marketing firm MEC Access, explained in *The Guardian* that music "provides a much richer narrative to which brands can align" due to its enthusiastic fandom and high levels of engagement.[28] Put another way, brands want to matter to people like music does; brands also "extract value from musicians' creative ability to facilitate the circulation of meaning, identity and social relations."[29] When a whiskey company partners with Dylan to give soul to its spirit or when Apple or IBM use Dylan in their commercials, Dylan is borrowing that platform while the brand is simultaneously borrowing his significance and his story.

As uncomfortable as it may be for some of his fans to admit, "brand" is one of the few media concepts that can fully encapsulate Bob Dylan. He became a brand because the music business, and everyone around it, figured out how to mine repositories of emotion, turn songs into lucrative intellectual property, and capture the universe of cultural associations within a wide-ranging, flexible business system. Rather than be antithetical to these processes, Dylan was the perfect subject for them: mythic and capricious, well-worn and true, he was an icon to those who loved him and an exemplar for those who came in his wake. Indeed, Bob Dylan became a brand because brands – artist or otherwise – aspired to be more like him: to matter, to delight, to enrapture, and above all, to last.

---

[27] Leslie Meier, *Popular Music as Promotion: Music and Branding in the Digital Age* (Cambridge: Polity, 2017).

[28] Mark Knight, "When Bands Meet Brands: The Mutual Benefits of Music Partnerships," *The Guardian*, October 14, 2015.

[29] Nicholas Carah, "Brand Value: How Affective Labour Helps Create Brands," *Consumption, Markets & Culture*, 17 (2014), p. 347.

CHAPTER 25

The Nobel Prize: The Dramaturgy of Consecration

James F. English

If you search the web for "Bob Dylan Nobel Prize," Google returns three million items.[1] That is not a huge result for a Google search, but it's a hell of a lot for a literary award. Consider that the same month Dylan was announced as laureate, Britain's Man Booker Prize was awarded to an American author for the first time ever. The Booker has generally been a more reliable publicity-generating machine than the Nobel, and Paul Beatty's win for *The Sellout* was a major milestone in its history, marking a recalibration of the transatlantic literary relationship that had been anxiously anticipated and hotly debated for years. But a search for "Paul Beatty Booker Prize" returns barely a tenth as many relevant pages as the Dylan Nobel search. We shouldn't infer too much from these crude search counts, but this much seems clear: Dylan's consecration by the Swedish Academy and Nobel Foundation as one of the world's greatest literary artists was sufficiently disruptive of established norms to generate an outsized volume of commentary. What I wish to argue here, however, is that this unsettling impact was superficial, and the episode was on the whole a positive one for the judges, the recipient, and the institution of the prize. The scandals of corruption and abuse that emerged soon after in Stockholm, paralyzing the Academy and forcing a reboot of the entire administrative operation, should not blind us to the fact that in 2016 the Nobel enjoyed a very good year.

When the Nobel Committee began deliberations that spring, it had been twenty-three years since an American was selected as laureate. Even allowing for normal ebbs and flows and the somewhat more global distribution of Nobel medals in recent decades, that is a long stretch. From 1930, when Sinclair Lewis became the country's first laureate, until 1993, when Toni Morrison was crowned, the average interval between American recipients was just seven years. When twice that many years passed without

---

[1] Search results discussed here are in response to a four-word sequence, not an exact phrase.

another American winner after Morrison, observers began to suspect an anti-American bias among members of the Swedish Academy. Horace Engdahl, then Permanent Secretary, inflamed these suspicions in 2008, when he made a point of denigrating US literary culture across the board, calling it "too isolated, too insular" to be of much consequence in "the big dialogue of literature." American authors, he said, are trapped in the bubble of "their own mass culture," and this "ignorance" of the wider world "constrain[s]" their literary achievements.[2] Engdahl's outburst was not as far off the mark as indignant responses in the USA suggested; compared with elsewhere, reading in America is indeed a domestic affair in which foreign, and especially translated work plays a minimal role. In literature, as in other cultural domains, the USA is all about the export trade. But Engdahl's sweeping dismissal of American writers, which he attributed to "more than 10 years of assiduous labor" evaluating their work, was hard to credit. The leading American contender throughout the period was Philip Roth, who was not too parochial for the judges of other major international awards; he won the *Prix du Meilleur Livre Étranger*, the *Prix Médicis Étranger*, the Prince of Asturias Award, and the Man Booker International Prize, and was named a Commander of the French Legion of Honor for his "contributions to global literature and his decades-long relationship with France." However one might rate Roth's accomplishments, the essays, interviews, and thirty novels he published over the six-decade span of his career were scarcely limited by ignorance of the world.

Nevertheless, the Swedish Academy, or at least some faction around the Permanent Secretary, remained firm in its plot against America. It seemed to have settled into the role assigned to it in Pascale Casanova's model of the world-literary system, as the principal symbolic counterweight to America's commercially driven, homogenizing power.[3] The problem was that this binary conception of literary production was becoming increasingly anachronistic in the twenty-first century. European literary institutions could not credibly claim to represent the interests of the "world" against the USA at a time when rising social forces were reshaping the literary sphere around more transregional and diasporic networks of production and reception and the whole infrastructure of literary power was shifting from a system of geographic centers and peripheries to one of

---

[2] Suzanne Godenberg, "No Nobel Prizes for American Writers: They're too Parochial," *The Guardian*, October 2, 2008, www.theguardian.com/books/2008/oct/02/nobelprize.usa.

[3] Pascale Casanova, *The World Republic of Letters* (Cambridge, MA: Harvard University Press, 2005), pp. 166–172.

digital platform "stacks."[4] Alongside these literary developments, the general cultural rift between the USA and Europe that had opened during the Bush era was largely healed in the years of Obama's presidency, undermining the Franco-Scandinavian view of America as Europe's cultural enemy. By persisting in its refusal to acknowledge any American voices in the "big dialogue of literature," the Academy seemed mainly to be risking its own marginalization.

In selecting Bob Dylan, the Academy contrived a balletic escape from the corner they'd painted themselves into. Dylan, of course, was not in any sense a product of America's literary establishment, had never won a National Book Award or a Pulitzer Prize for Poetry or taught classes in literature or creative writing at an elite university; well-positioned writers and critics in the USA had never expressed the least outrage that the Academy was overlooking him.[5] Naming Dylan as laureate was thus a way to end the nearly quarter-century-long freeze on American winners while remaining conspicuously aloof from the received map of American literature and reaffirming the autonomy of the judges in Stockholm.

That autonomy, however, is a tricky thing. It expresses itself through selections, occurring every decade or so, which are aberrant enough to elicit a hue and cry, yet manage to stay just within the outer range of possibilities. If the Academy's judgments remain too comfortably and for too long inside the horizon of normative expectations, its consecrating power is reduced to that of mere ratification and the Nobel risks fading into the crowded field of book awards, becoming almost just one prize among others. But if the Academy allows itself to go truly rogue, with selections for which there is no adequate precedent or rationale, it may be subject to no less a diminishment, its accumulated symbolic authority reduced in the public mind to the level of pure whimsy.

The selection of the Italian playwright and comic performer Dario Fo in 1997 is an example of how the Academy periodically tests this boundary between independence and illegitimacy. No one had seen Fo's selection coming, and it was greeted with a mixture of outrage and bewilderment. While admirers hailed Fo as an elder statesman of the cultural opposition,

---

[4] For recent discussions along these lines, see Benjamin Bratton, *The Stack: On Software and Sovereignty* (Cambridge, MA: MIT Press, 2016), and Nick Srnicek, *Platform Capitalism* (New York: Polity, 2016).

[5] I should note that Dylan did receive a "Pulitzer Prize Special Citation" in 2008 that gestured toward poetic as well as musical achievements. The commendation reads: "For his profound impact on popular music and American culture, marked by lyrical compositions of extraordinary poetic power." www.pulitzer.org/winners/bob-dylan.

an uncompromising political artist with a vital role to play in the age of Berlusconi, many critics regarded him as more of a public jester and nose-tweaker than a serious man of letters. The resulting critiques and counter-critiques were never completely resolved; they stand even today as a memorable "storm of controversy" in the history of the Nobel. That, indeed, is the point. Such storms are part of the regular rhythm of exchange between a prestigious cultural award and its public. Every iteration of the prize meets with some measure of doubt and derision, which rises to a high pitch in certain years before subsiding back to usual levels.[6] The role of the Swedish Academy is to manage the whole cadence of consecration and credulity, not simply to minimize the vicissitudes.

As compared with the case of Fo, the controversy surrounding Dylan's Nobel was more focused on the broad questions of eligibility, less on the caliber of specific achievements. There were some commentators prepared to dismiss all popular culture as de facto lightweight and unworthy of symbolic reward. Tim Stanley in *The Telegraph* objected to the selection of Dylan as a "pandering" to popular tastes that threatened to turn the Nobel Prize into "Sweden's Got Talent."[7] The Lebanese-American novelist Rabih Alameddine compared the decision to "Mrs. Fields being awarded 3 Michelin stars."[8] Others complained that Dylan was too much a throwback to the 1960s, a musical icon for the octogenarian Academy members but scarcely relevant in the fourth decade of hip hop. In choosing him, said the music critic Everett True, the Swedish Academy was "like your third-rate English teacher at school, trying to look 'cool.'"[9] The award was "fundamentally kinda nostalgic," wrote cultural studies scholar Jenn Webb, expressing a sentiment put more strongly by Irvine Welsh, who tweeted: "I'm a Dylan fan, but this is an ill-conceived nostalgia award wrenched from the rancid prostates of senile, gibbering hippies."[10] These jibes notwithstanding, neither the scale of Dylan's artistic accomplishments nor his present-day stature was ever really the salient issue. No other contender for the 2016 prize (not even Philip Roth) was as richly

---

[6] The outcry was notably loud in 1974 when Swedish authors Eyvind Johnson and Harry Martinson were selected to share the award; between Fo in 1997 and Dylan in 2016 the greatest controversy was in 2004, when Elfriede Jelinek received the prize.

[7] Tim Stanley, "A World That Gives Bob Dylan a Nobel Prize Is a World That Nominates Trump for President," *The Telegraph*, October 13, 2019.

[8] @Rabihalameddine on Twitter, October 13, 2016.

[9] Everett True, "Bob Dylan Wins the Nobel Prize for Literature: Some Facts," blog post, https://everetttrue.wordpress.com/2016/10/13/.

[10] Jenn Webb, "In Honoring Bob Dylan, the Nobel Prize Judges Have Made a Category Error," *The Conversation*, October 14, 2016, theconversation.com; @IrvineWelsh on Twitter, October 13, 2016.

decorated with national and international awards as Dylan. On top of his ten Grammy Awards, his Oscar and Golden Globe and Pulitzer Prize certificate, his National Medal of Honor, Presidential Medal of Freedom, and membership of the American Academy of Arts and Letters, Dylan held honorary doctorates from St. Andrews and Princeton, a Prince of Asturias Award from Spain, Sweden's own Polar Prize (the "Nobel Prize of Music"), and the rank of Commander in France's Order of Arts and Letters as well as its Legion of Honor. When presenting him with America's highest civilian award, President Obama said, "there is not a bigger giant in the history of American music," and even those who denounced his Nobel selection as a mistake tended to accept that view. What sustained the controversy was, of course, the question of Dylan's suitability, as a singer-songwriter, even to be considered for the premier prize in literature. Dylan might be a giant in the world of music, but his selection as the laureate in literature was, according to Ryu Spaeth in *The New Republic*, a "basic . . . category error," a "farcical screw-up" on the part of the Swedish Academy.[11] As such, it opened the door to a thousand wise-cracks on the theme of apples winning prizes for orangeness. "I'm happy for Dylan," tweeted the novelist Jodi Picoult, "but #DoesThisMeanICanWinAGrammy?"[12]

The Academy was fully expecting this outcry. The Permanent Secretary, Sara Danius, could not suppress a mischievous smile when she delivered the announcement to a room full of stunned reporters, and she was well prepared for the skeptical questions in the press interview that followed.[13] Asked if, in making such a "radical" selection, the Academy was deliberately "widening the horizons" of the literary field, Danius acknowledged that "it might look that way," but insisted the judges were actually keeping faith with the past. "If you look back far enough," said Danius, "you discover Homer and Sappho," two of the greatest figures in literary history, who "wrote poetic texts that were meant to be listened to, were meant to be performed, often together with [musical] instruments. And it's the same way with Bob Dylan." Asked whether Dylan's lyrics really lend themselves to reading as *The Odyssey* does, she said he absolutely "can and should be read; he is a great poet in the English tradition, in the grand English poetic tradition." Pressed on his specifically literary skills and accomplishments,

---

[11] Ryu Spaeth and Alex Shephard, "Bob Dylan Won the Nobel Prize in Literature?! A Conversation," *New Republic*, October 13, 2016.

[12] @Jodipicoult on Twitter, October 13, 2016.

[13] According to the Nobelprize.org website, the interviewer was freelance journalist Sven Hugo Persson. The live stream of the announcement and interview (from which all quotes in this paragraph are taken) can be viewed on the Nobel Prize YouTube channel.

she called him an ingenious "sampler" who "embodies the tradition" while repurposing its elements and "constantly reinventing" it and himself, moving the tradition forward in original ways.

These points, placing heavy emphasis on the "traditional" literary character of Dylan's work, were echoed by some who approved of his selection, including prominent writers like Salman Rushdie, who called Dylan a "brilliant inheritor of the bardic tradition," and Billy Collins, who agreed that, unlike most modern song lyrics, "his words do hold up on the page" as works of poetry.[14] Detractors responded with passages from Dylan's messiest, most nonsensical lyrics, or quoted the *New Yorker*'s first popular music critic, Ellen Willis, who wrote in a famous 1967 essay that great song lyrics are not great poetry: "poetry requires economy, coherence, and discrimination, and Dylan has perpetrated prolix verse, horrendous grammar, tangled phrases, silly metaphors, embarrassing clichés, muddled thought."[15] The two sides thus fell into the classic point/counterpoint format of journalism, and within a couple of days of the announcement hundreds of culture sites and media outlets had run debate-style pieces or war-of-quotation lineups.

Since forums of this kind tend toward escalation, with remarks like Welsh's "rancid prostates of senile, gibbering hippies" getting more play than thoughtfully considered statements, the prevailing temper seemed to be outrage. In fact, however, if one pages through all the storm-of-controversy documents, what surprises is the extent of support for the Academy's selection. Nearly all the distinguished poets, novelists, and critics who weighed in expressed a favorable view, and not because they fully shared the idea of Dylan as a "traditional" poet, but because they embraced a wider, less traditional conception of literature and were happy to leave the strict defense of its limits to conservative culture-warrior columnists and social media trolls. As Rushdie put it, "the frontiers of literature keep widening, and it's exciting that the Nobel prize recognizes that."[16]

The quarreling over categories, however, was only the first phase of the consecration process. What most sharply distinguishes prizes from other

[14] "Nobel Prize in Literature Won by Bob Dylan – As it Happened," *The Guardian*, October 13, 2016; Jay Lustig, "Billy Collins, Former US Poet Laureate, Says Dylan Deserves Nobel Prize," NJ Arts online, October 20, 2016.
[15] Ellen Willis, "Dylan," *Cheetah* (1967), quoted in Bijan Stephen, "Nobel Failure: Bob Dylan is a Legend but Doesn't Deserve this Award," *Vice*, October 13, 2016.
[16] "Dylan Towers Over Everyone: Salman Rushdie, Kate Tempest, and More Pay Tribute to Bob Dylan," *The Guardian*, October 13, 2016.

mechanisms of literary recognition is their dramaturgical interest. As rituals of presentation and acceptance, prizes involve nuanced social performances in which highly conventionalized displays of mutual gratitude and humility are always liable to betray signs of reluctance, condescension, or just plain bad manners. The potential for lapses of etiquette, for public embarrassment or scandal, for exposure of the petty underside of literary society, is indeed one of the main attractions of awards and a leading reason why, for all their supposed redundancy, they continue to proliferate.

In the case of Dylan's Nobel Prize, this dramaturgical aspect held particular fascination. Asked at the announcement ceremony whether she had actually spoken to Dylan, Darius admitted that she had not. That official exchange – the proverbial early morning phone call from Sweden – had yet to take place. Still ahead were the official presentation and acceptance of the gold medal at the Nobel Day ceremony in December and the laureate's official Nobel Lecture, normally delivered a few days before the banquet but allowable up to six months after it. Given Dylan's record of discomfort with prizes and their sponsoring institutions, not to mention his mercurial behavior more generally, there was no guarantee that any of these further steps in the process would be taken without major embarrassments for the Nobel Foundation. Some Dylan fans, including the British novelist Will Self, were openly rooting for him to refuse the prize, something that had not happened since Sartre's selection in 1964. Inverting the argument that Dylan, as a popular music celebrity, was unworthy of the world's most prestigious literary award, critics like Self took the view that an honor decided by elderly Scandinavian academics, and funded by the estate of a munitions manufacturer and arms merchant, was unworthy of the world's greatest songwriter.[17] As they saw it, the value proposition was lacking: the Foundation stood to gain more from an association with Bob Dylan than he ever could from an association with Alfred J. Nobel.

This was not a frivolous argument. Though wrapped in the rhetoric of the pure gift, the prize is a form of exchange, a transaction from which the presenter as well as the recipient hopes to realize a symbolic profit. In leaving virtually the whole of his fortune as "a gift to mankind," Alfred Nobel was indeed arranging to offset the stigma he had acquired as Europe's "merchant of death" through annual conversions of munitions

---

[17] "It cheapens Dylan to be associated at all with a prize founded on an explosives and armaments fortune." Will Self, quoted in "Bob Dylan Removes Mention of Nobel Prize from Website," *The Guardian*, October 21, 2016.

wealth into reputational capital.[18] Year after year, each prize ceremony would burnish his name via close commerce with a heroic champion of peace and renowned geniuses of science and literature.[19] Would Bob Dylan participate in this ceremony of cultural money-laundering? Though he was at least as much of an irritant to 1960s anti-war activists as an inspiration, he continues in the public mind to be strongly associated with the protest movement. The possibility that he might protest the Nobel Foundation by refusing its gift seemed real, especially when, a week after the announcement, he continued to be unavailable for phone calls from the Swedish Academy and his website silently deleted its one line acknowledging their decision. But as a second tense week unfolded without any word from the designated laureate, the Academy dispatched Per Wastberg, a longtime member, to apply some pressure. Speaking to Sweden's leading newspaper, *Dagens Nyheter*, Wastberg denounced Dylan for his extraordinarily "impolite and arrogant" behavior.[20]

A week after Wastberg delivered this reprimand, Dylan finally contacted the Academy, tersely expressing his "appreciation" for the honor. Presumably he realized that the Academy's spokesman was right, the Academy held the winning position: refusing the award would make him look more arrogant than principled. Sartre, after all, had made it a consistent policy to refuse all honors and sponsorships, whether Soviet or Western; he was guarding his hard-won position as an independent intellectual. Nowadays, such a stance of purity would be impossible to maintain. The gesture of refusing a major award cannot be distinguished from a bid for public attention, a gambit to promote one's brand. Such would be the case in italics for Dylan, an artist who besides having accepted Grammys, Oscars, and all manner of state honors, has done TV commercials for Chrysler, Cadillac, Pepsi, and *Victoria's Secret*. For a corporate-sponsored celebrity like Dylan to place himself above a prize that was graciously accepted by William Faulkner and Toni Morrison would be to render himself ridiculous.

Or rather, Dylan could certainly place himself above the prize – the true artist is expected to represent a higher plane of value than that of the awards

---

[18] Legend has it that Nobel was inspired to create the prizes when a Parisian newspaper mistook the death of his brother Ludvig in 1888 as his own, and headlined the obituary, "The Merchant of Death is Dead." Though the story is likely invented, there is ample evidence of Nobel's desire to shed the association with bombs and killing and link himself in collective memory with those who "have conferred the greatest benefit to mankind."

[19] James F. English, *The Economy of Prestige: Prizes, Awards, and the Circulation of Cultural Value* (Cambridge, MA: Harvard University Press, 2005), p. 55.

[20] "Bob Dylan Criticized as Impolite and Arrogant," *Agence France-Presse*, October 22, 2016.

circuit – but his superiority would need to be signaled indirectly, not by outright refusal but through the kind of performative duplexity that Pierre Bourdieu calls a "strategy of condescension."[21] This Dylan understood very well. Asked by an interviewer at *The Telegraph* whether his acknowledgment of the prize meant he would actually attend the December ceremony to receive his medal from the Swedish king, he said he "absolutely" wanted to be there "if it's at all possible."[22] Apparently slow to check his calendar, he then waited until just a few days before the ceremony to announce that "other commitments . . . made it unfortunately impossible." By that point, however, the Nobel administrators, no doubt braced for the worst, had come up with a Plan B involving his musical peer Patti Smith. Smith's participation at the ceremony had nothing originally to do with Dylan. She had been scheduled to perform as a featured musician months before a laureate was selected. When Dylan's name was announced, the program was adjusted to have her perform his "A Hard Rain's A-Gonna Fall" rather than one of her own songs. And when Dylan confirmed himself as a no-show, offering his late and vague excuses, it was arranged that Smith would serve as a kind of emissary or symbolic substitute.

It was a strange deformation of the usual ritualized proceedings in the Stockholm Concert Hall, another irregularity in a wild year for the prize in literature. Though it assured that the show would at least go on – and the presentation ceremony is nothing if not a form of theatre – the arrangement was far from ideal. Smith could appear on the stage and sing a Dylan song, but she could not actually accept the award on Dylan's behalf. He had not authorized any acceptance of his certificate and gold medal from the hand of King Carl XVI Gustaf, nor had he delivered the requisite Nobel Lecture, on which depends the roughly million-dollar cash award. Watching the live stream, waiting through the dignified pageantry of prizes in science and medicine, one felt that the recipientless, musical non-presentation of a prize in literature, though intended to save face, might rather play out as a humiliation: a shambolic contrivance that merely amplified the awkwardness already created by Dylan's haughty and fickle behavior.

But far from collapsing into bathos, the ceremony was elevated by these deviations from normal routine. Dylan's absence drew attention to the sheer power of his songwriting, embodied by Smith as she delivered a nervous and halting but ultimately intense performance of "Hard Rain."

---

[21] Pierre Bourdieu, *Language and Symbolic Power* (Cambridge: Polity, 2002), p. 68.

[22] Edna Gundersen, "World Exclusive: Bob Dylan – I'll Be at the Nobel Prize Ceremony . . . If I Can," *The Telegraph*, October 26, 2016.

With its sad forests and dead oceans and pellets of poison flooding the waters, the giant waves that could drown the whole world, the hidden executioners and the masses of people with their hands all empty, it is a song whose urgent words have gained further urgency since Dylan wrote them more than a half century ago, in the midst of his first furious storm of creativity. When even the veteran performer Smith was so overcome by the song and the occasion that she jumbled a verse, muffed the recovery, and had to start over ("I'm sorry," she said, "I apologize. I'm so nervous"), the hall erupted with applause of an entirely different character, warmer and more genuine, than at any other time in the proceedings. As she built the song up to full strength for the fifth and final verse and delivered its great culminating sextet ("where ... where ... where ..."), much of the audience was in tears.

Yet even here the Dylan affair had not achieved closure, for there remained room after the ceremony for further scandalous breaches of etiquette. Though he allowed the American Ambassador to Sweden to read out a brief thank-you speech at the celebration banquet in Stockholm's Blue Hall, Dylan let the sun go down on Nobel Day with his certificate and gold medal conspicuously unclaimed. And there was still the matter of his lecture, which would need to be presented by June 10, 2017 in order for him to collect the monetary award. Failure to claim the medal and/or to do a lecture would not remove him from the list of laureates. As far as the Nobel Foundation is concerned, while the material tokens and monetary award are for laureates to accept or decline or to pass on in a further act of philanthropy, as they may see fit, the symbolic honor is bindingly conferred and inalienable. Still, to leave any part of the prize unclaimed would be universally recognized as a snub, a way of maintaining the posture of refusal despite official expressions of gratitude. Dylan seemed to encourage speculation along these lines, offering just a few vague and non-committal remarks about a possible arrangement in the new year. And even when, during a European concert tour in April, he did in fact stop in at the Swedish Academy to receive the medal and certificate at a small, unpublicized ceremony, he offered no lecture and made no pledge to deliver one at a later date. It seemed likely that he would follow the example of George Bernard Shaw, a highly reluctant laureate in 1925, who was prevailed upon to accept the honor, but refused to have any part of the money. For those who still embraced Dylan as a figure of protest, or the much larger contingent who merely enjoy opportunities to mock the pretensions of cultural elites and to expose the fraudulence of their prestige, a backdoor refusal of this kind was an enticing prospect. And once again Dylan kept the speculation alive as long as possible, holding off until just five days before the deadline, when he abruptly recorded a lecture in Los Angeles and sent in the audio file.

Dylan begins the lecture by promising a "roundabout" reflection on "how my songs relate to literature," and proceeds to trace his artistic roots to both musical and literary influences during his adolescence. Musically, he was inspired by Buddy Holly and Leadbelly to immerse himself deeply in the blues and folk traditions, listening to all the songs he could get his hands on, gradually "pick[ing] up the vernacular ... internaliz[ing] it," becoming a master of the "folk lingo." At the same time, he says, he developed his broader "principles and sensibilities," his "view of the world," from the literary classics he read at Hibbing High School. Most of the lecture consists of his descriptions of three of those English curriculum staples – *Moby Dick*, *All Quiet on the Western Front*, and *The Odyssey*. Sketching the major themes of these works, Dylan says they "were fundamental" to his ambitions when he started writing his own lyrics, providing him with "a way of looking at life, an understanding of human nature, and a standard to measure things by." But when he comes to conclude this attempt to show "where the connection is" between his songwriting and the literary tradition, he suddenly makes a contrary gesture, stressing their disjunction: "Songs are unlike literature," he abruptly declares. "They're meant to be sung, not read."

It is a quirky performance, Dylan's sing-songy voice backed by the jazz-lounge piano playing of Alan Pasqua, the "roundabout" discussion veering in characteristic Dylan fashion between humility and boastfulness, craft and cliché, clarity of purpose and self-contradiction. But it was a lecture perfectly on point for the occasion, a solid fulfillment of the laureate's final assignment, and one which we might have expected to bring some quiet at last to the unusually prolonged period of debate and disruption in Stockholm. In fact it had the opposite effect. For it soon emerged that in his discussion of the literary texts, Dylan relied heavily on phrases lifted from *CliffsNotes* and *SparkNotes*, those venerable cheat sheets for students short on time or just too lazy to read. Dylan incorporated many chunks of language from these websites into his own prose, and the borrowings spilled over into his attempts at direct quotation as well, with words that appear on the *SparkNotes* site, but nowhere in *Moby Dick*, attributed to Herman Melville.[23] Literary journalists were naturally quick to jump on

---

[23] As first pointed out by Ben Greenman on his blog *Occasional Things*, June 6, 2017, http://occasional-things.blogspot.com/2017/06/a-whale-of-tale.html and followed by a thorough accounting of the

this latest embarrassment for the Swedish Academy, whose choice for a great writer of ideal tendency might now be called out as a plagiarist. "It's Alright Ma, I'm Only Cheating," read the headline in *The Guardian*, over a photo of Dylan labeled "It weren't me, babe."[24] True to the storm-of-controversy template, the media lined up writers and critics in point/counterpoint formation. *Slate* quoted English professors who took a lenient view of the situation, saying "no alarm bells went off" when they looked at Dylan's use of secondary source material, versus stricter ones, like Northwestern's Juan Martinez, who said, "If Dylan was in my class and he submitted an essay with these plagiarized bits, I'd fail him."[25] As with the earlier controversy over the relationship between poetry and popular music, the debate hinged on whether Dylan represented something aberrant, a violation of the established rules of literary authorship, or rather belonged to a deeper tradition, what Andrea Pitzer called the "ancient tradition of theft in the name of art."[26] And once again, many authors and critics favored the liberal view of a broad and flexible tradition over the strident defense of narrow rules and norms. Writing for the *New York Times*, Ben Sisario pointed out that for a folk artist like Dylan, making use of other people's material is a first principle.[27] From his song lyrics for the 1985 LP *Empire Burlesque* to the 2001 album *"Love and Theft,"* to his 2004 memoir *Chronicles*, to the "Asia Series" paintings he exhibited in Manhattan in 2011, his artistic practice had always involved helping himself to words and images originally produced by others. Indeed, Dylan thematizes this magpie disposition in the Nobel Lecture itself when he boasts of his mastery over the full range of folk vernaculars, his ability to "pick up" and combine bits of "lingo" from the back catalog of American songwriting. Since he locates his most vital points of connection to literature in the demotic space of the high school English class, where the vernacular includes the resonant clichés of *SparkNotes*, we might expect that his rhetoric for discussing literature would feature plenty of lingo drawn from that quarter. This at any rate would align with the stance of the Swedish Academy, for whom the compositional method behind the lecture was just Dylan being Dylan. As Sara Danius had said

---

lifted phrases by Andrea Pitzer, "The Freewheelin' Bob Dylan: Did the Singer-Songwriter Take Portions of his Nobel lecture from SparkNotes?" *Slate*, June 13, 2017, https://slate.com/culture/2017/06/did-bob-dylan-take-from-sparknotes-for-his-nobel-lecture.html.

[24] "It's Alright Ma, I'm Only Cheating," *The Guardian*, June 7, 2017.

[25] Pitzer, "The Freewheelin' Bob Dylan."   [26] Ibid.

[27] Ben Sisario, "Accusations About Bob Dylan's Nobel Prize Lecture Rekindle an Old Debate," *New York Times*, June 14, 2017.

when first announcing his selection, he is a "wonderful sampler ... a very original sampler," a writer who so fully embodies the work that precedes him that repetition and recycling are the essence of his creativity. With his delivery of this "exceptional," lecture, she remarked, "the Dylan adventure is coming to a close."[28]

To which we might respond, yes and no. The Nobel Committee was by that point well along in its deliberations over the 2017 prize, which, in going to the widely loved and uncontroversially literary Kazuo Ishiguro, was a marked de-escalation from the previous year's excitements. And before the gold medal was even hung on Ishiguro's neck, the Academy would find itself embroiled in the scandals of sexual harassment, abuse of funds, and conspiring to place illegal wagers that tore its membership apart and forced a hiatus of the prize in 2018.[29] So yes, they were moving on from the "Dylan adventure." And Dylan himself, having squeezed more drama out of the Nobel, over a longer span of months, than any laureate before him, was already immersed in a dozen new projects. But it is not in the nature of award controversies to resolve and disappear. They tend rather to repeat and to accumulate, to join with other instances of alleged imbecility or inappropriateness. Prizes are serial rituals of belief and disbelief; our collective skepticism regarding the authority of the judges and the soundness of their judgments is predicated on our collective faith in some higher and non-negotiable scale of aesthetic value. Every opportunity to denounce the judges of a prize for their prejudice, corruption, or caprice – or, what amounts to the same thing, to denounce the recipient as unworthy – is a chance to invoke the magical standard of Art itself, the timeless qualities of beauty and genius that supposedly lie just beyond reach of our actual human mechanisms of assessment and distinction. By debating and deprecating prizes we put ourselves in their service, sustaining the magic that sustains them.[30] This is the paradoxical framework in which we should read the bumper crop of commentary around Dylan's Nobel. Partly due to the Academy's strategically outlandish escape from its anti-American stance, partly to Dylan's teasing,

[28] "Bob Dylan Delivers 'Extraordinary' Nobel Lecture – In the Nick of Time," *The Guardian*, June 5, 2017.
[29] The scandal broke when the investigative reporting of Matilda Gustavsson appeared in "Man with Swedish Academy Ties Accused of Sexual Assault," *Dagens Nyheter*, November 22, 2017, www.dn.se /kultur-noje/man-with-swedish-academy-ties-accused-of-sexual-assault.
[30] The argument is elaborated in my 2002 essay "Winning the Culture Game: Prizes, Awards, and the Rules of Art," *New Literary History*, 33 no. 1 (Winter 2002), pp. 109–135.

idiosyncratic way with the dramaturgy of prize acceptance, the 2016 prize lives on as a particularly vivid and well elaborated "storm of controversy." Perennially invoked as evidence against the legitimacy of the Nobel Prize in Literature, it will supply perennial fuel for the prize's further flourishing.

CHAPTER 26

Dylan: Stardom and Fandom

David R. Shumway

Bob Dylan was both a creature of the postwar explosion of celebrity culture and someone who played a major role in transforming it. From his earliest incarnations as a folksinger, Dylan showed an uncanny ability to manipulate the apparatus of publicity and fame. He continually transformed his persona as his songwriting and recording developed, and by the end of the 1960s, had become a star defined by his changes rather than the consistency of his persona. Yet, this did not mean that his fans or the large culture lacked a clear sense of him. Rather, as I argue in *Rock Star*, Dylan's stardom remained the voice of youth in rebellion despite the fact that he had explicitly rejected protest songs as early as 1964.[1] This disjunction between his variable personas and his relatively durable iconic significance belies a third level of concern: Dylan's own identity. His fans and the larger public have consistently conflated identity and persona, one of the things that has fueled the seemingly unquenchable thirst for biographies and fanzines. How many other stars have their own "ologists"? We tend to assume that artists are trying to tell us who they really are. But Michel Foucault has suggested otherwise in speaking of his own work as a writer, "I am no doubt not the only one who writes in order to have no face. Do not ask who I am and do not ask me to remain the same: leave it to our bureaucrats and our police to see that our papers are in order."[2]

The first commentator to recognize that there was something unusual about Dylan's relationship to celebrity was Ellen Willis in her 1967 essay, "The Sound of Bob Dylan," originally published in *Commentary*, an intellectual magazine clearly not aimed at fans. There she asserts that he "has self-consciously explored the possibilities of mass communication just as pop artists explored the possibilities of mass production. In the same

---

[1] David R. Shumway, *Rock Star: The Making of Musical Icons from Elvis to Springsteen* (Baltimore: Johns Hopkins University Press), pp. 94–96.
[2] Michel Foucault, *The Archaeology of Knowledge*, trans. A.M. Sheridan Smith (New York: Pantheon, 1972), p. 17.

sense that pop art is about commodities, Dylan's art is about celebrity."[3] Willis is concerned mainly with the ways in which the artist had resisted a public identity. Writing during Dylan's disappearance from public view after his motorcycle accident in 1966, Willis sees Dylan as refusing the norms of stardom. She observes, "Not since Rimbaud said 'I is another,' has an artist been so obsessed with escaping identity."[4] It is not clear whether Willis thinks this attempt to "escape identity" is a psychic state or a public stance. I will argue that it is best understood as the latter. Dylan's life, on the contrary, is better understood as a quest for identity (rather than an escape from it) and his career as a conscious engagement with the star system, including a rejection of many of its demands.

First, it is necessary to establish some keywords. In *Rock Star*, I argue that Dylan was a cultural *icon*.[5] An icon is a public sign, and Dylan's iconic status is rooted in how he presented himself and what he produced, but it emerges out of what other people – the press, his fans, biographers, etc. – have said about Dylan. An icon has broad cultural significance that extends beyond the realm of fandom. Dylan was also a *star*, which is also a condition that is produced out of the relationship of others – in this case, predominantly fans – to the celebrity. All stars are celebrities, but not all celebrities are stars, because stardom entails, among other things, achievement in a skilled field or profession. A star is experienced by his or her fans as a *persona*, which the star creates with the help of what Joni Mitchell called "the star-maker machinery."[6] Fans want to know the person behind the persona, but that person is always unavailable to them. For movie stars as actors, there are three levels: the role, the persona, and the person. Role and persona may sometimes be very similar, as for example in many of John Wayne's Westerns, but they are always formally separate. For rock stars, in most cases, there is no role, just a persona, though David Bowie, Madonna, and others have played different roles on stage or on particular albums. Understanding the merging of role and persona is vital in Dylan's case, since most emphatically he was not understood to play roles. Finally, celebrities, like the rest of us, have *identities*, which are an element of an individual's psychic world. Identities are social in the sense that they develop out of identification with others, but they are not public the way personas are.

---

[3] Ellen Willis, "The Sound of Bob Dylan," *Commentary*, November 1967, p. 72.   [4] Ibid, p. 71.
[5] Shumway, *Rock Star*, pp. 70–96.
[6] Joni Mitchell, "Free Man in Paris," *Court and Spark*, Asylum.

In the early 1960s when Dylan emerged as a star of the folk scene, the idea of celebrity was beginning to be publicly interrogated in a new way. The most important contribution to this was Daniel Boorstin's book *The Image: A Guide to Pseudo-Events in America* published in 1961, wherein the idea that "the Celebrity is a person who is well known for his well-knownness" was articulated and popularized.[7] Boorstin regards celebrities as artificially manufactured entities without any inherent or redeeming value. He likens them to commodities sold under brand names: "The qualities which now commonly make a man or woman into a 'nationally advertised' brand are in fact a new category of human emptiness."[8] What is entailed in this conception of celebrity is consistency, and Boorstin is not wrong in emphasizing its importance. Indeed, one of the earliest instances of explicit "star-making" was Carl Laemmle's attempt to convince the public that an actor – King Baggot in 1912 – was the sort of person he played on the screen by planting (false) news stories about his off-screen heroic exploits. The movie star was still paradigmatic in the early 1960s, and movie stars were typified by consistent personas that persisted through role after role. Dylan's rejection of this pattern is what Willis noticed in 1967.

One might think, given Willis's reading, that Dylan was from the start a critic of celebrity culture. His memoir, *Chronicles, Volume One*, however, suggests otherwise by seeming to embrace the phenomenon. Indeed, one might accuse Dylan of name dropping, so often does he mention the famous people he knew or who influenced him. He begins the book by asserting that when he arrived in New York at the end of 1960, "the 50s culture was like a judge in his last days on the bench. It was about to go." But, he claims, "Folk songs transcended the immediate culture," justifying his own artistic choices.[9] Dylan laments that Elvis Presley had stopped making great records, and expresses his interest in making an album rather than recording 45 rpm singles that then were dominant in popular music (*C* 34): "it wasn't that I was anti-popular culture or anything and I had no ambitions to stir things up. I just thought mainstream culture as lame as hell and a big trick" (*C* 35). There is ample evidence from Dylan's songs that he did think much of mainstream culture was lame (or worse), but *Chronicles* also reveals Dylan's immersion in it, especially in the culture of

---

[7] Daniel J. Boorstin, *The Image: A Guide to Pseudo-Events in America* (New York: Random House, 1961), p. 57.

[8] Ibid, p. 49.

[9] Bob Dylan, *Chronicles, Volume One* (New York: Simon & Schuster, 2004), p. 27. Subsequent references will be cited parenthetically in the text with the abbreviation *C*.

celebrity: "Up until this time I'd been raised in a cultural spectrum that had left my mind black with soot. Brando. James Dean. Milton Berle. Marilyn Monroe. Lucy. Earl Warren and Khrushchev. Castro. Little Rock and Peyton Place. Tennessee Williams and Joe DiMaggio. J. Edgar Hoover and Westinghouse. The Nelsons. Holiday Inn and hot rod Chevys. Mickey Spillane and Joe McCarthy. Levittown" (*C* 35–36). Some of these things are clearly intended to represent lameness, but others are actually things Dylan values. In context, the list seems intended to reveal his education before he arrived in New York, where he began to learn new things, such as "novels by Gogol and Balzac, Maupassant, Hugo and Dickens" (*C* 36). *Chronicles* is thus about Dylan's education, which seems to be learning about famous people with whom he had previously been unfamiliar.

This memoir is also about Dylan's success at entering the world of celebrity and of reaching the goals he had set for himself. He mentions many instances where he has had a connection to other celebrities: "Mae West would later record a song of mine" (*C* 65); "There was a letter from Archibald MacLeish waiting for me on the table" (*C* 107); "One night, Bono, the singer from U2, was over for dinner with some friends" (*C* 174). *Chronicles* strongly suggests, in other words, that far from rejecting celebrity, Dylan had ambitions to become one. He transformed our understanding of rock music by presenting himself as an artist.[10] After Dylan, rock could no longer be dismissed as a mere distraction for teenagers, as it had been right up through the first years of the British invasion. Dylan managed this not only by writing songs that dealt with serious matters in aesthetically interesting forms, but also by consciously fashioning different personas. *Chronicles* shows that it was no accident that Dylan became identified as an artist. In the first chapter, focused on his earliest days in New York, Dylan recalls, "In the world news, Picasso at seventy-nine years old had just married his thirty-five-year-old model. Wow. Picasso wasn't just loafing about on crowded sidewalks. Life hadn't flowed past him yet. Picasso had fractured the art world and cracked it wide open. He was revolutionary. I wanted to be like that" (*C* 55). This is an overt statement of identification.

Dylan's becoming a rock star helped to transform the idea of stardom. Along with Elvis, the Beatles, and the Rolling Stones, he changed the public's conception of a star from the one established during Hollywood's classic era. By the end of the 1960s, the rock star had replaced the movie star at the top of the celebrity pantheon. Rock stars differed from movie stars in

---

[10] Shumway, *Rock Star*, p. 71.

a number of important ways. Where the movie studios had done their best to protect their stars from scandal and controversy, for example, rock stars became identified with transgressions of social norms. Movie stars had been primarily understood as personalities who were amplified in the roles they played; but rock stars identified with forces of social transformation so that they became political even when they did not endorse or advocate any particular positions.[11] And, while movie stars were sometimes recognized for their artistic achievement as actors, they were not regarded as artists in the strong sense of that term since they were, after all, merely speaking the lines someone else had written, lines uttered in movies that most people regarded as mere entertainment. Rock stars, unlike previous generations of popular singers, wrote their own material, and their songs were understood to be more than pleasant ditties. Dylan more than any other rock star would lead people to see rock stars in general as artists.

Dylan's aspiration to be an artist would be fulfilled, but it was initially beyond his grasp. In discussing that "freezing winter" he first spent in New York, he says he was "lucky" he "had places to stay," but then laments "There's a lot of things I didn't have, didn't have too much of a concrete identity, either. 'I'm a rambler – I'm a gambler. I'm a long way from home.' That pretty much summed it up" (*C* 55). The admission that he lacked an identity suggests that he wanted one, rather than, as Willis suggested, he was trying to avoid one. Dylan quotes Rimbaud's statement toward the end of *Chronicles*, translating it as "I is someone else," and asserting "When I read those words the bells went off. It made perfect sense. I wished someone would have mentioned that to me earlier. It went right along with [Robert] Johnson's dark night of the soul and Woody's hopped-up union meeting sermons and the 'Pirate Jenny' framework" (*C* 288). We never learn why those things went together, except that Dylan seems to have encountered them around the same time. *Chronicles* itself may illustrate the point since it disperses Dylan's identity among the myriad influences he mentions. In traditional autobiography, there is a developmental narrative that produces an autobiographical self largely absent from Dylan's book, if by that one means what Paul John Eakin has called "narrative identity."[12] *Chronicles* works because we already know the voice articulating this discourse, even if we are not always sure what to make of the person who produces the voice. Hence the volume depends on

---

[11] Ibid, pp. 1–19.
[12] Paul John Eakin, *Living Autobiographically: How We Create Identity in Narrative* (Ithaca: Cornell University Press, 2008), pp. ix–xii.

the paradox that Bob Dylan's persona depends precisely on not having a single, fixed identity. He is an iconic rock star, Nobel laureate in literature, and author of a best-selling memoir, yet he can still be the subject of a film titled *I'm Not There* (dir. Todd Haynes, 2007) in which he is played by six different actors as six different characters. It seems that everyone has heard of Bob Dylan, but no one knows who he is. Indeed, one might even wonder if he knows who he is.

Public questions about Dylan's identity and persona go back at least to some of his earliest press coverage. *Time*, giving Dylan his first notice in a national magazine, opened with the question, "There he stands, and who can believe him?"[13] While the article on the whole is fairly positive, it focuses on the disjunction between his self-presentation ("his accent belongs to a jive Nebraskan, or maybe a Brooklyn hillbilly") and his current milieu, the folk-scene of Greenwich Village. "There is something faintly ridiculous about such a citybilly, yet Dylan is the newest hero of an art that has made a fetish out of authenticity."[14] The article later seems to be criticizing the scene as much as Dylan when it asserts, "An atmosphere of the ersatz surrounds him."[15] A few months later, *Newsweek*, in what has been called a "hatchet job," revealed that Dylan had lied about his ordinary, middle-class background, and questioned "why Dylan ... should bother to deny his past is a mystery. Perhaps he feels it would spoil the image he works so hard to cultivate – with his dress, with his talk, with the deliberately atrocious grammar and pronunciation in his songs."[16]

The news magazines observe somewhat differently the relationship between person and persona, with *Time* suggesting that Dylan was not what he seemed and *Newsweek* wondering why he worked so hard to make the persona appear to be the person. Dylan later admitted to Robert Shelton, "I shucked everybody when I came to New York."[17] This suggests another angle on Dylan's shifting persona: that it was an elaborate joke. Understood in this way, his shape shifting becomes an end in itself, and he becomes a trickster figure. Dylan's lyrics might provide support for this view in songs such as "Outlaw Blues," "Jokerman," and "I and I," and he has often made allusions to his own deceptions. In the recent film *Rolling Thunder Revue: A Bob Dylan Story by Martin Scorsese*, Dylan says "If someone's wearing a mask, he's gonna tell you the truth" (2019). But he is not wearing a mask when he says this, and the film itself includes

[13] "Let Us Now Praise Little Men," *Time*, May 31, 1963, p. 40.   [14] Ibid.   [15] Ibid.
[16] "I Am My Words," *Newsweek*, November 4, 1963, p. 95.
[17] Bob Dylan, quoted in Robert Shelton, *No Direction Home: The Life and Music of Bob Dylan* (New York: Da Capo, 1997), p. 90.

a mixture of performance footage and fictional elements that are presented in documentary style. One might classify as "shucking" the discoveries that Dylan "borrowed" numerous passages of *Chronicles* from well-known literary works; that his paintings "from life" were really very careful copies of other people's photographs; and that some of the lyrics on *Modern Times* (2006) were plagiarized.

Still "shucking" does not account very well for many of the changes in Dylan's persona, since it would reduce not just his image but also his work to an elaborate hoax. Rather, his career suggests a serious concern with persona making that began with his carefully managed entry into the folk scene. On his first album, *Bob Dylan* (1962), we see him in his cap and shearling jacket, looking the part of the folksinger. The clothes evoke work but from some other time and place from where folk music supposedly came. The cover photo on *The Freewheelin' Bob Dylan* (1963) depicts him without the cap and with a woman on his arm walking down a snowy urban street. His hair is tousled, but otherwise he looks remarkably ordinary. On the next record, *The Times They Are A-Changin'* (1964), he appears in a black-and-white photo frowning, wearing an open-collared work shirt and relatively short hair. Here Dylan adopts a more obvious identification with contemporary American workers and the political Left. All of these self-presentations can be understood as part of the culture of celebrity in that they are a collaboration between the artist and the record company to market both the artist and his albums.

Dylan's persona shifts repeatedly over the course of the 1960s, with a new one invented almost with each new album. But these changes need to be understood against the larger shifts in his career, the most important of which was his leaving folk music for rock & roll. His decision to go electric at the 1965 Newport Folk Festival is the legendary driver of this change, but it had been in the making since *Another Side of Bob Dylan* in 1964.[18] And yet it is important to insist that this shift was seen as a radical change only by some of Dylan's fans, the rest seeming to understand it as a kind of natural progression. The fact that Dylan continued to be regarded as the voice of New Left politics despite his explicit rejection of protest songs suggests that his fans saw consistency even where Dylan sought to reject it. Moreover, this political invocation of him confirms that his iconic status was not imperiled by becoming a rock star, but was rather a result of it. As

---

[18] For an exhaustive study of Dylan at Newport in 1965 and its contexts, see Elijah Wald, *Dylan Goes Electric: Newport, Seeger, Dylan, and the Night that Split the Sixties* (New York: Dey St., 2013).

an icon, Dylan's significance extended well beyond the adoration of fans, as he became a broadly recognized figure in the culture at large.

The reaction to his electric performance at Newport in 1965, in fact, tells us more about his original fan base than about the performer. Clearly this group was intensely invested in Dylan, otherwise they would not have been so disappointed in what they regarded as his apostasy. In 1964, Irwin Silber, editor of the folk-music magazine *Sing Out!*, had published an open letter to Dylan in response to the changes in his songs that began with *Another Side*: "I saw . . . how you had lost contact with people. It seemed to me that some of the paraphernalia of fame were getting in your way . . . Your new songs seem to be all inner-directed now." Silber here expresses that strong sense of ownership the folk community felt toward Dylan, and its deep suspicion of celebrity. The open letter continues:

> The American Success Machinery chews up geniuses at a rate of one a day and still hungers for more. Unable to produce real art on its own, the Establishment breaks creativity in protest against and nonconformity to the System. And then, through notoriety, fast money, and status, it makes it almost impossible for the artist to function and grow. It is a process that must be constantly guarded against and fought.[19]

Silber's critique is very close to Boorstin's, but its tone seems to come out of an Old Left that had long warned adherents not to stand out and make themselves more important than the party or the cause.

Dylan, however, rejected the claims people like Silber and his folk fans made on him. In *Chronicles*, he recalls another moment from Newport: "Ronnie Gilbert, one of the Weavers, had introduced me at one of the Newport Folk Festivals saying, 'And here he is . . . take him, you know him, he's yours.' I had failed to sense the ominous forebodings in that introduction. Elvis had never been introduced like that. 'Take him, he's yours!' What a crazy thing to say! Screw that. As far as I knew, I didn't belong to anybody then or now" (*C* 115). Here, Dylan refuses the demands of the particular fan culture that had made him a star. Elsewhere in his memoir, Dylan complains, "The actor Tony Curtis once told me that fame is an occupation in itself, that it is a separate thing. And Tony couldn't be more right" (*C* 123). A star is made by his or her fans, but an artist produces without regard for whether what he or she makes will be popular. In the face of this contradiction, Dylan embodied a newly redefined stardom that allowed the two to coexist in him.

---

[19] Irwin Silber, "An Open Letter to Bob Dylan," *Sing Out*, November 1964, quoted in Mike Marqusee, *Wicked Messenger: Bob Dylan and the 1960s* (New York: Seven Stories, 2005), pp. 103–104.

The song that most clearly explains these concerns is neither "Positively 4th Street" nor "My Back Pages," both of which are addressed to the folk community, but "It's Alright, Ma (I'm Only Bleeding)" on *Bringing It All Back Home* (1965). According to Nick Bromell, the songs on this album are rooted in "the perception of *oneself* as unfree, as oppressed."[20] The singer now understands himself and by implication all of us to be unfree, but also that something like the "culture industry" conspires to keep us from recognizing this fact:

> Advertising signs that con you
> Into thinking you're the one
> That can do what's never been done
> That can win what's never been won.

Here Dylan offers a critique of celebrity similar to the one Silber had used against him. Both men oppose the artist to the celebrity, but where Silber makes the opposition absolute, Dylan seems to see stardom as a field for the artist to exploit. It makes sense, then, that the song also proclaims what might be called the artist's own creed, "That he not busy being born / Is busy dying." Dylan articulated this creed more clearly in the 2005 documentary *No Direction Home*, where he says, "An artist has to be careful never really to arrive at a place where he thinks he's somewhere. You always have to realize that you are constantly in a state of becoming."[21] The song also proclaims the artist's freedom, "That it is not he or she or them or it / That you belong to." These last lines seem like a direct response to the demands of fans and of the "job" of celebrity.

The perception that Dylan is trying to avoid identity lies in his reaction to celebrity itself, his attempt to both use it and at the same time escape its demands. But there is evidence from the early years of his career that there was more going on. Anthony Scaduto's *Bob Dylan*, the first substantive biography of the artist, uses interviews from those who knew him during his brief period as a student at the University of Minnesota to suggest that Dylan was seeking an identity and not merely a way to present himself as performer. "He so absolutely became Woody Guthrie in the months I knew him ... 'We're going to see Woody,' he used to tell me all the time. He was painfully sincere in his feelings."[22] To Shelton, Dylan

[20] Nick Bromell, *Tomorrow Never Knows: Rock and Psychedelics in the 1960s* (Chicago: University of Chicago Press, 2000), p. 131, quoting Greg Calvert, national secretary of Students for a Democratic Society.
[21] *No Direction Home*, dir. Martin Scorsese (Paramount Home Video, 2005), DVD.
[22] Ellen Baker quoted in Anthony Scaduto, *Bob Dylan* (London: Helter Skelter, 1996 [1971]), p. 45.

"admitted that the change ... grew out of a genuine need for a new identity: He simply wasn't pleased with his former bland, directionless self."[23] Dylan's sudden interest in and intense devotion to Woody Guthrie is clearly an instance of fandom, one that might have been creepy had the older singer not been hospitalized and in need of the attention. If Dylan's successful attempt to claim Guthrie's mantle seems like an inspired career move, the details of his experience suggest that his motives were much more complicated. It is another clear example of identification, in this case one that seems to have immediately produced an identity.

To recall Rimbaud's words, in Dylan's case, "I is [or was] Woody Guthrie." To assert that "I is an another," is different from saying, as the movie star did, "Everybody wants to be Cary Grant. Even I want to be Cary Grant."[24] That represents an awareness of the difference between identity and persona, but what Dylan struggled with was who he was when he was at home. People often speak as if identity were an inherent quality, but Erik Erikson, a highly influential theorist of identity in the 1960s, argued that identity is an achievement and identification is the root process by which identity is achieved.[25] If we discover who we are only by identifying with others, then Rimbaud's assertion seems less like a denial of identity than an explanation of it. Still, "I is another" also might be read as evidence of what Erikson called an identity crisis. For Erikson, an identity crisis is a predictable event of late adolescence, when a young person must decide whether to become what his or her upbringing had intended or to strike out in some new direction. Dylan, all evidence suggests, had clearly chosen the latter, and so had to reinvent himself, initiating a prolonged struggle with identity, one which perhaps only came to end when he began the "never ending tour" in the 1990s.

The strongest evidence that Dylan's changes reflect a prolonged identity crisis is his evangelical phase in the early 1980s, when he was just turning forty, an age when we might be inclined to call such a major change a midlife crisis. Dylan didn't become an evangelical like David Bowie became Ziggy Stardust to make a more interesting album. We must assume that his conversion was deeply felt, as authentic as such experiences can be, despite the fact that it did not necessarily last (see Chapter 19). Here, Dylan's identity shifts – at least temporarily – and one might imagine that had he written an autobiography at this point in his life, the conversion

[23] Bob Dylan quoted in Shelton, *No Direction Home*, p. 90.
[24] Cary Grant, quoted in *Newsweek*, March 12, 1990.
[25] Erik H. Erikson, *Childhood and Society* (New York: Norton, 1950).

experience would be its turning point, the beginning of a new self. Dylan was not the only rock star to have flirted with evangelical Christianity. Paul Simon's "Bridge Over Troubled Waters," for example, was first written as a hymn, and was only slightly modified to become a love song. But Simon never publicly identified himself with a particular religious mission, as Dylan did on the gospel albums and at concerts during that period. It is because we cannot easily write off all Dylan's changes as mere conscious manipulation – as performance or "poses" – that his persona continues to embody authenticity despite our awareness that his identity is one cobbled together from various disparate sources.

During the gospel period, as Lee Marshall puts it, "Dylan's stardom is marked by ambiguity and uncertainty."[26] That's because his public conversion to and advocacy of evangelical Christianity was much more at odds with his established persona than any previous change had been. If album sales and critical reception are any measure, many fans abandoned him during this period, though certainly a significant number stuck with him. And, all evidence suggests that his fans returned, beginning perhaps with the critical success of *Oh Mercy* (1989), and then in larger numbers (if album sales are any indication) with *Time Out of Mind* (1997). After 1989, Dylan's persona becomes more or less static as he morphs into what Sean Wilentz calls "the wizened cultural elder statesman, an icon of musical America who still has plenty left to say, do, and sing, before it is too late."[27] Dylan seems here to have settled on an identity as a touring musician, as this period coincides with the "never ending tour."

Dylan's fan base always differed from that typical of other popular music stars. For example, Dylan sold far fewer recordings than Elvis, the Beatles, the Rolling Stones, Michael Jackson, or Madonna. While his influence deserves to ranked with this group of performers, it is less because of size of his audience than their position and devotion. This peculiar devotion is demonstrated not only by their continued interested in him even after the perceived decline of the 1980s, but also by the fan conferences and fanzines devoted to him. The first Dylan fanzine appeared in 1964, but lasted for two issues. The second one was first published in 1975, and thereafter many more were created. Dylan conventions were held in Manchester, England in 1979 and 1980, at a time when such events devoted to pop stars were uncommon. Both phenomena suggest that Dylan's fans are more cerebral in their interests, with the fanzines containing a lower proportion of gossip

---

[26] Lee Marshall, *Bob Dylan: The Never Ending Star* (Cambridge: Polity, 2007), p. 153.
[27] Sean Wilentz, *Bob Dylan in America* (New York: Doubleday, 2010), p. 288.

than is typical.[28] The fanzines and conferences, however, are evidence of the intensity of Dylan's fans, something that might make what he called "the job of celebrity" seem all the more difficult.

I have argued that fans can't know the private person behind a star's persona, but as a critic I have offered an analysis that supports a particular understanding of that person. My reading of Dylan's quest for an identity is an informed speculation. It assumes that the continual changes in persona are not all there is to be said about Dylan's private identity. Indeed, his iconicity depends upon the faith that there is more there than meets the public eye. As an icon, Dylan was an *artist*, an inventor of new forms and a creator of new meanings. As a star, he was a great performer beloved by fans who understood his changes as part of the persona they adored. We cannot know but we have good reasons to assume that Dylan's quest for identity lies behind these public perceptions.

---

[28] James Adams, "'Get in on the Action and Scribble' – The Fugitive World of Bob Dylan Fanzines," a paper delivered at "The World of Bob Dylan 2019," a conference sponsored by the Bob Dylan Center, the University of Tulsa, on June 1, 2019. James Adams kindly provided me with a copy of his paper. Adams has been working on a database of Dylan fanzines, a project that could greatly enrich Dylan studies.

CHAPTER 27

The Bob Dylan Archive®

Mark A. Davidson

Blood in the Stacks: On the Nature of Archives in the Twenty-First Century

On June 11, 2019, music journalist Jody Rosen published a bombshell report in the *New York Times Magazine* about a devastating fire on the Hollywood backlot of Universal Studios.[1] The fire itself wasn't "news" per se, or at least it shouldn't have been; it had happened eleven years earlier, in June 2008, and had been reported in the media. Initial reports estimated the damage to Universal's video vault assets to be extensive, but in the end, relatively inconsequential. Chief Operating Officer of Universal, Ron Meyer, told reporters that "Fortunately, nothing irreplaceable was lost. The video library was affected and damaged, but our main vault of our motion picture negatives was not."[2] But what went unreported were the massive losses to their audio archives. The biggest of the "Big Three" record labels (valued at $33 billion, ahead of Sony Music and Warner Music), Universal Music Group rose to prominence through acquiring dozens of other record labels, including classic and legacy imprints such as ABC, A&M, Decca, Chess, Geffen, Impulse, Interscope, and MCA. All told, the fire destroyed the master tapes of more than eight hundred artists spanning decades of musical history across numerous genres – approximately 175,000 assets and a half-billion song titles. The list of artists whose work was destroyed in the fire reads like a who's who of popular music, folk, blues, and jazz, and the work included not only commercially released recordings, but also recordings that have never seen proper release. The effect on the history of recorded music is immeasurable.

---

[1] Jody Rosen, "The Day the Music Burned," *New York Times Magazine*, June 11, 2019, www.nytimes.com/2019/06/11/magazine/universal-fire-master-recordings.html.

[2] Brad Brevet, "Universal Studios Suffers from Major Fire," *Comingsoon.net*, June 1, 2008, www.comingsoon.net/movies/news/527674-universal_studios_suffers_from_major_fire.

While poring over articles about the fire and its cultural casualties, I came across a statement that stuck with me by Benmont Tench, the former keyboardist for Tom Petty and the Heartbreakers:

> There is nothing like the original master. The master recording is like a painting. When you stand in front of the original, you are standing there in the presence of the artist. You can take a photo of the painting, but no photo – regardless of how high the resolution might be – can truly capture what's in the original canvas.[3]

Leaving aside the fact that a recording session is itself a mediated experience, a snapshot of a moment, oftentimes constructed through overdubs and careful take selection to make an idealized performance – and in this sense is somewhat of a conflation of what Walter Benjamin spoke of in the mid-1930s when he described the "aura" as regards photography and original paintings – Tench's statement gets at the crux of the archival moment we're in: the myth of permanence, the fetishization of cultural objects, the sense of loss when calamity strikes, and the push to preserve everything.[4]

This anxiety over cultural loss and fears of impermanence have only increased in the age of digital plethora. In fact, the use of the term "archive" has taken on a life of its own in the twenty-first century. Like "artisanal," or "curate," the term "archive" has become a buzzword, a branded experience. As a trained archivist I find myself homing in on the use of the term "archive" in its various contexts to see what people *mean* when they use it.[5] Not surprisingly, most of these uses of "archive" emerge from online sources or social media interactions. Newspapers, online magazines, and radio programs routinely recycle content in "from the archive" stories. A Facebook user reposts an old photo or video from years past as "dipping back into my archive." A Twitter user posts a tweet "archiving" a story – that is, relaying information into a social media forum in order to give it some public legitimacy and seeming permanence. An Instagram user "archives" a post so that it is no longer publicly visible, but remains undeleted on the platform. I can "archive" my emails, chats, photos, and

---

[3] Randy Lewis, "Lawsuits Against Universal Music Group Expected Next Week in Response to 2008 Fire," *Los Angeles Times*, June 14, 2019, www.latimes.com/entertainment/music/la-et-ms-umg-fire-recordings-lawsuits-universal-studios-20190613-story.html.

[4] Walter Benjamin, "The Work of Art in the Age of Mechanical Reproduction," (1935), in *Illuminations*, ed. Hannah Arendt (New York: Schocken Books, 1969), pp. 217–251.

[5] Trevor Owens, "What Do You Mean by Archive? Genres of Usage for Digital Preservers," *The Signal* (blog), Library of Congress, February 27, 2014, https://blogs.loc.gov/thesignal/2014/02/what-do-you-mean-by-archive-genres-of-usage-for-digital-preservers/.

videos so that they are out of the way and can be read or otherwise dealt with at a later time (usually the penultimate step before permanent deletion).

"Archive," then is multivalent, personal, a reckoning with the notion of "the past," however distant, fleeting, or uncomfortable. And many, if not all, of these uses of the term "archive" revolve around dealing with the aftereffects of living in the age of digital plethora. In fact, the amount of new data created annually is staggering. According to one study, 1.2 trillion digital images were to be created in the year 2017 alone, due in no small part to the prevalence of smartphones.[6] From an archival and historical standpoint, the effects on history, memory, and culture of such massive data generation are manifold. The internet is not an archive – at least in the traditional sense of the term – and digitization does not promise permanence. In fact, accessibility online and the overwhelming push for digitization places the internet in a position of being a one-stop-shop for the entirety of the world's information. With this push comes a sort of digital blindness, a false impression that everything is available online, resulting in a sort of re-canonization of culture and history. This is akin in many respects to the notion of "cultural grey-out" that Alan Lomax warned of in the early 1970s:

> A grey-out is in progress which, if it continues unchecked, will fill our human skies with the smog of the phoney and cut the families of men off from a vision of their own cultural constellations. A mismanaged, over-centralized electronic communication system is imposing a few standardized, mass-produced and cheapened cultures everywhere.[7]

One wonders what Lomax, as an archivist and documentarian who worked tirelessly in the twentieth century to preserve quickly disappearing world music subcultures, would have thought about the glut of musical content in the twenty-first century. Certainly he would have struggled with how quickly even documented music disappears or is forgotten in the digital realm. This phenomenon of forgetting underscores significant questions that remain for archivists today: Is everything worth saving, and if not, what makes the cut? Who deserves to have the responsibility for deciding? And what does it really mean to save, preserve, conserve, and keep things forever?

---

[6] Stephen Heyman, "Photos, Photos Everywhere," *New York Times*, July 29, 2015, www.nytimes.com /2015/07/23/arts/international/photos-photos-everywhere.html.

[7] Alan Lomax, "Appeal for Cultural Equity," *World of Music*, 14, no. 2 (1972), pp. 3–17; revised in *Journal of Communication*, 27 (1977), pp. 125–138, in *Alan Lomax: Selected Writings, 1934–1997*, ed. Ronald D. Cohen (New York: Routledge), p. 285.

Here it is necessary to pause and consider what an archivist does, who they are, and why they have been given such an awesome responsibility. For many people, archivists and librarians are supposed to be invisible, objective, and dispassionate, and are often depicted as caricatures such as the schoolmarm, the prison guard, the file clerk, the accomplished "shusher," or the bespectacled, cardiganed keeper of secrets. And some of the blame for these assumptions has to do with the view of the work itself, and who is qualified to do it. As noted British archivist Hilary Jenkinson described the vocation in 1922:

> The Archivist's career is one of service. He exists in order to make other people's work possible. . . . His Creed, the Sanctity of Evidence; his Task, the Conservation of every scrap of Evidence attaching to the Documents committed to his charge; his aim, to provide, without prejudice or after-thought for all who wish to know the Means of Knowledge. . . . The good Archivist is perhaps the most selfless devotee of Truth the modern world produces.[8]

To be sure, the life of an archivist can be quotidian, filled with policies, procedures, and best practices, but the discipline, like so many others in academic and public life, has shifted with the times. Archivists have naturally followed their own radical, theoretical turn toward inclusivity, access, openness, and ethical approaches to service in the broadest sense. "Evidence," "Truth," and "Knowledge" – those pillars of nineteenth-century positivism – have given way to subjectivity, interpretation, and an understanding that archives – colonial in their nature and history – can be sites of power and inequality, barriers to, and boundaries around, the creation and discovery of evidence, truth, or knowledge. They are subject-ive, constructed, and contested spaces. Part of the archivist's charge, then, is to understand and upend these power structures and to rectify the many false and fetishized assumptions underlying the work with which they are tasked. As an archivist, I take these questions seriously, while understand-ing the complexities and contradictions inherent in such work.

The Origins of the Archive and How It Landed in Tulsa

What, then, of The Bob Dylan Archive® and why is it significant in this particular cultural, historical, and archival moment? Quite simply, the archive is one of the most important collections ever constructed, and

---

[8] Hilary Jenkinson, quoted in Elisabeth Kaplan, "Many Paths to Partial Truths: Archives, Anthropology, and the Power of Representation," *Archival Science*, 2 (2002), p. 215.

although I'll surely be accused of engaging in hyperbole or of inherent bias, I assure the reader that I have considered this statement carefully. I would go as far as to say that the collection is not merely important because of the materials it contains, or even because of the person behind the materials themselves – in fact, readers of this volume may be shocked by how many people I encounter on a regular basis in Tulsa and elsewhere who *have no idea who Bob Dylan is*. Putting aside for the moment Dylan's influence, or his six-decade-long career, or his Nobel Prize in Literature, one could look merely at the sheer size and scope of the collection. For much of his creative career, Dylan existed in a largely analog world – from audiotape reels to typewriters to handwritten letters to thousands of feet of film stock, the physical evidence of Dylan's life and career is well documented within the collection. This era is over and it will never come again: digital recording and email have supplanted these modes of creation and communication, and archives of future artists will never have a comparable physical presence.

The real importance of the Dylan collection begins with the people behind its construction: Bob Dylan and his management team. Credit must be given Dylan for having the foresight to hang on to so many materials at a time when archives, especially of popular musicians, were not the cultural assets they are today. Dylan and his team were at the forefront of the reissue and "from the archives" release market dating back to at least 1984, when they released the *Biograph* compilation. Since that time the Dylan team has continued to mine the artist's back catalog and manuscript collection, with releases such as the ongoing *Bootleg Series* (1991–present) and projects like the *Bob Dylan Scrapbook* (2005). They've also played a major role in the success of Martin Scorsese's two Dylan documentaries, *No Direction Home* (2005), and *Rolling Thunder Revue: A Bob Dylan Story* (2019). Over the course of the past decade, they hired a trained archivist to help contend with the materials both physical and digital that they had been amassing, and partnered with Starchive to create a robust digital asset management system that is now at the forefront of archival technologies, particularly with regard to media collections. Thus, when the Dylan materials came up for sale, a large portion of it had been previously arranged and digitized.

The other critical part of the story of the Dylan collection lies with its purchaser: the George Kaiser Family Foundation (GKFF) of Tulsa, Oklahoma. Although the news that the Dylan materials would be heading to Tulsa was a surprise to many, GKFF's decision to purchase the collection for a reported $15 to $20 million in collaboration with the University

of Tulsa was carefully considered, as it dovetailed with billionaire philan-
thropist George Kaiser's larger goals of building the city into a cultural
destination point.⁹ Moreover, GKFF had a proven model on which to
build: in 2011 they purchased Woody Guthrie's archives and built the
Woody Guthrie Center around the collection as a way to highlight social
justice issues and Oklahoma's early populist leanings.¹⁰ (Early in his career,
Dylan, of course, admired and emulated Guthrie, even calling himself "a
Woody Guthrie jukebox."¹¹) The Woody Guthrie Center, which opened
in 2013, has been the cornerstone of the Tulsa Arts District, a revitalized
area north of downtown which features other GKFF projects including the
Tulsa Artist Fellowship, Duet jazz club, and Guthrie Green, a free concert
and community space in the heart of the District. Viewed together with
GKFF's early childhood education, parental engagement, and community
health and social services initiatives; its Tulsa Remote program, which
provides stipends to remote workers who relocate to the city; and its
$465 million, sixty-six-acre free public park (Gathering Place), located on
the Arkansas River in midtown, the archival/museum projects of GKFF fit
neatly alongside the Foundation's overall mission.¹²

Exploring the Archive: What it Reveals, Reinforces, and Reflects

Describing the size and the scope of the Dylan materials is no small task, in
part because it is so multifaceted and three-dimensional. Included in the
career-spanning collection are thousands of leaves of manuscripts, both
published and unpublished, dozens of notebooks and sketchbooks, some
40,000 photographic elements, hundreds of hours of footage, and thousands of hours of audio. Dozens of individuals have visited the archive
to pore over the materials – biographers, journalists, "Dylanologists,"

---

⁹ Ben Sisario, "Bob Dylan's Secret Archive," *New York Times*, March 2, 2016, www.nytimes.com/2
016/03/06/arts/music/bob-dylans-secret-archive.html; Andy Greene, "Exclusive: A Look Inside
Bob Dylan's Secret Archives," *Rolling Stone*, June 27, 2017, www.rollingstone.com/music/music-
features/exclusive-a-look-inside-bob-dylans-secret-archives-199434/.
¹⁰ Patricia Cohen, "Bound for Local Glory at Last," *New York Times*, December 27, 2011, www
.nytimes.com/2011/12/28/arts/music/woody-guthrie-gets-a-belated-honor-in-oklahoma.html?_r=1
&scp=3&sq=patricia%20cohen&st=cse.
¹¹ Bob Dylan, quoted in Martin Scorsese, dir., *No Direction Home: Bob Dylan, A Martin Scorsese Film*
(Paramount Pictures, 2005).
¹² Patricia Leigh Brown, "Transforming Tulsa, Starting with a Park," *New York Times*, August 10, 2010,
www.nytimes.com/2018/08/10/arts/design/tulsa-park-gathering-place.html; Karen Heller, "A
Billionaire's Quirky Quest to Create a Mecca for Bob Dylan Fans in Tulsa, Oklahoma,"
Washington Post, October 12, 2017, www.washingtonpost.com/lifestyle/style/a-billionaires-quirky-
quest-to-create-a-mecca-for-bob-dylan-fans-in-tulsa-oklahoma/2017/10/11/6e7f4754–93f9–11e7–89fa-
bb822a46da5b_story.html.

classicists, literature scholars, poets, folklorists, musicologists, and many others – and I would venture a guess that not one of them would come to the same conclusions about Dylan's life and career. A passage from Arlette Farge's 1989 monograph, *The Allure of the Archives*, speaks to the phenomenological experience of working in archives, which is worth considering in light of the present collection:

> [The archive] forces the reader to engage with it. It captivates you, producing the sensation of having finally caught hold of the real, instead of looking through a "narrative of" or "discourse on" the real.
>
> This gives rise to the naïve but profound feeling of tearing away a veil, of crossing through the opaqueness of knowledge and, as if after a long and uncertain voyage, finally gaining access to the essence of beings and things. The archive lays things bare, and in a few crowded lines you can find not only the inaccessible but also the living. Scraps of lives dredged up from the depths wash up on shore before your eyes. Their clarity and credibility are blinding. Archival discoveries are a manna that fully justify their name: sources, as refreshing as wellsprings.[13]

Dylan's collection, however doesn't offer "access to the essence," nor does it "lay things bare." And most scholars who have worked in the collection will agree that it certainly doesn't provide either "clarity" or "credibility." The Bob Dylan Archive – like its namesake – is difficult, sometimes inscrutable, open ended, and subject to interpretation. But this very multiplicity of interpretations makes the collection the rich resource it is. More sphinx than oracle, the archive demands to be explored, digested, interpreted, then reinterpreted anew.

What is immediately evident in exploring the collection is that he was, and continues to be, a tireless worker, almost obsessive in his attention to his craft. The materials from 1965 and 1966 alone are voluminous: Dylan's manuscripts for three of his classic albums – *Bringing It All Back Home*, *Highway 61 Revisited*, and *Blonde on Blonde*; the liner notes for the first two; multiple full drafts of his prose novel *Tarantula*; the footage from D.A. Pennebaker's *Dont Look Back*, and the footage and editing notes for Dylan's 1966 project *Eat the Document*; as well as stacks of leaves of typewritten poetry, unfinished lyrics, and other musings. In the case of a song like "Jokerman," from his 1983 album *Infidels*, Dylan wrote and revised the song over the course of nineteen pages. The two previously

---

[13] Arlette Farge, *The Allure of the Archives*, trans. Thomas Scott-Railton, foreword by Natalie Zemon Davis (New Haven, CT: Yale University Press, 2013), pp. 7–8. Originally published as *Le Goût de l'archive*, Editions du Seuil, 1989.

unknown *Blood on the Tracks* notebooks, written in Dylan's microscopic handwriting, shows the author's seemingly frenzied, yet determined and hyper-focused working methodology as he labored over songs like "Idiot Wind," "Tangled Up in Blue," and "Simple Twist of Fate."

Archives are seldom, if ever, complete, and the Dylan collection is no exception. One of the reasons that our manuscripts essentially begin with "Chimes of Freedom" (1964) is that Dylan was largely nomadic prior to buying his first house in Woodstock, and many manuscripts from his first few years in New York City have been spread out among private collectors, purchased from people who knew, or housed, the fledgling folkie. Another example is the cache of manuscripts that Dylan had with him at Newport 1965, when he famously "went electric." That we know about them at all is somewhat surprising, as Dylan left both the guitar and the lyrics (which were in the guitar's case) on a chartered plane. For decades the guitar and manuscripts sat in the pilot's home until they went up for auction in 2013.[14] Audiovisual elements have also gone missing over the years, including the original camera negatives for *Renaldo and Clara*, some of the session tapes for *John Wesley Harding* (1967), *Nashville Skyline* (1969), and *Desire* (1976), the session tapes for the Minneapolis *Blood on the Tracks* recording session.

The collectors' market is also worth exploring as we discuss building the collection, and auction houses in particular have been rich sources for Dylan manuscripts and other ephemera in recent decades. Other manuscripts that have appeared at auction in recent years include copies of "Like a Rolling Stone," "A Hard Rain's A-Gonna Fall," and a previously unknown draft lyric manuscript about Wisconsin, which Trapper Schoepp recorded in 2017.[15] In almost every case, each of these items commanded tremendous sums of money on the collectors' market, which has led, perhaps not surprisingly, to accusations and lawsuits surrounding alleged forgeries of Dylan manuscripts. The fallout from cases such as these is obvious and the consequences manifold: not only do potential bad actors taint the Dylan manuscript market, but they also directly impact the

---

[14] "Investigations: Bob Dylan Guitar," PBS *History Detectives*, season 10, episode 1, www.pbs.org/opb/historydetectives/investigation/bob-dylan-guitar/; and Ryan Reed, "Bob Dylan's Newport Guitar Sells for Nearly a Million Bucks," *Rolling Stone*, December 6, 2013, www.rollingstone.com/music/music-news/bob-dylans-newport-guitar-sells-for-nearly-a-million-bucks-244351/.

[15] Althea Legaspi, "Bob Dylan's 'Like a Rolling Stone' Handwritten, Signed Lyrics Up for Auction," *Rolling Stone*, September 27, 2017, www.rollingstone.com/music/music-news/bob-dylans-like-a-rolling-stone-handwritten-signed-lyrics-up-for-auction-198124/; Daniel Kreps, "Bob Dylan's Handwritten Lyrics to 'Wisconsin' Song Head to Auction," *Rolling Stone*, March 29, 2017; Andy Greene, "How a Wisconsin Singer Got a Bob Dylan Co-Writing Credit for New Song 'On, Wisconsin,'" *Rolling Stone*, November 13, 2018.

historical record, altering what we might believe to be true or not, and thus affecting Dylan studies going forward. Identifying what's out there, and verifying its provenance becomes paramount. As such it is necessary to scour auction blocks, follow leads, and work with people who "know where the bodies are buried." Putting together a union catalog of all extant Dylan collections in institutions and private hands – which Todd Harvey, of the American Folklife Center at the Library of Congress, has long advocated creating – is a critical first step in attempting to fill out our knowledge of what the Tulsa archive is currently and what it could become.

Thus far my discussion of the Dylan collection has been focused solely on the songwriter's creative output through his writings and recordings. But if the goal of the Dylan Center is to illuminate Dylan's life and work, we must contend with all of the materials, authorized or otherwise, that have been generated because of his life and work, including newspaper and magazine articles, fanzines, bootleg and pirate recordings, audience-generated recordings and videos, and ephemera. These items would themselves fill an entire archive, but they are critical for putting Dylan into context, for understanding Dylan's creativity as existing as performance and outside of its own canonical history of studio albums and official releases. And what about the lives and efforts of collectors and fanatics, the kinds of Dylan lifers detailed in David Kinney's monograph *The Dylanologists*, such as the Mitch Blanks, the Bill Pagels, and the Chris Coopers?[16] Surely their stories and collections add to our understanding of Dylan and his impact upon popular culture.

Conclusion: The World of Bob Dylan and Beyond

If, as Andy Greene noted in his 2016 *Rolling Stone* article, Tulsa has indeed become "the center of the Bob Dylan universe," then we have been tasked with an enormous responsibility.[17] As we have been preparing for the opening of the Bob Dylan Center in 2021 with our Seattle-based design firm Olson Kundig, we have attempted to be holistic in our vision of what such a museum might or should look like in the twenty-first century. How do we go about creating a space where everyone feels welcome, where both

[16] David Kinney, *The Dylanologists: Adventures in the Land of Bob* (New York: Simon & Schuster, 2014).

[17] Andy Greene, "Inside Bob Dylan's Historic New Tulsa Archive: 'It's an Endless Ocean,'" *Rolling Stone*, March 3, 2016, www.rollingstone.com/music/music-news/inside-bob-dylans-historic-new-tulsa-archive-its-an-endless-ocean-223265/.

the Dylan tyro and the Dylan fanatic will come away surprised and inspired, and where the themes that undergird Dylan's life and career – individuality, restless creativity, and perseverance – are presented in such a way as to be universal to all visitors? Interactivity and modularity are both key, as is exploring what archives mean in the twenty-first century and how they can be activated in the public realm. Although creating the Dylan Center will be a major undertaking, with the help of our partners in Bob Dylan's management team and the Institute for Bob Dylan Studies at TU we can work to make sure that the "Bob Dylan universe" is expansive enough to encompass not only the world of Bob Dylan, but also the overarching vision that is at the core of what the George Kaiser Family Foundation is building in Tulsa, Oklahoma.

Further Reading

Works about Dylan

Barretta, Scott, ed. *The Conscience of the Folk Revival: The Writings of Israel "Izzy" Young*. Lanham, MD: Scarecrow Press, 2013.

Bauldie, John, ed. *Wanted Man: In Search of Bob Dylan*. New York: Citadel Underground Press, 1991.

Bell, Ian. *Once Upon a Time: The Lives of Bob Dylan*. Edinburgh: Mainstream, 2013.

Time Out of Mind: The Lives of Bob Dylan. Edinburgh: Mainstream, 2013.

Benson, Carl, ed. *The Bob Dylan Companion: Four Decades of Commentary*. New York: Schirmer, 1998.

Bob Dylan: Dont Look Back. Directed by D. A. Pennebaker. Leacock-Pennebaker, 1967. DVD.

Bowden, Betsy. *Performed Literature, Words and Music by Bob Dylan*. Lanham, MD: University Press of America, 2001.

Brown, Donald. *Bob Dylan: American Troubadour*. New York: Rowman & Littlefield, 2014.

Browne, David. "Clydie King, Unsung Backup Singer for Ray Charles and Bob Dylan, Dead at 75," *Rolling Stone*, January 10, 2019.

Burger, Jeff, ed. *Dylan on Dylan: Interviews and Encounters*. Chicago: Chicago Review Press, 2018.

Campbell, Gregg M. "Bob Dylan and the Pastoral Apocalypse." *Journal of Popular Culture* 8, no. 4 (1975), pp. 696–707.

Charters, Ann, ed. *The Beats: Literary Bohemians in Postwar America*, vol. 1. Detroit: Gale Press, 1983.

Cott, Jonathan, ed. *Bob Dylan: The Essential Interviews*. New York: Wenner Books, 2006.

Dalton, David. *Who is That Man? In Search of the Real Bob Dylan*. New York: Hachette, 2012.

Dettmar, Kevin J.H., ed. *The Cambridge Companion to Bob Dylan*. Cambridge: Cambridge University Press, 2009.

Dylan, Bob. *Biograph*, Columbia, 1985. CD.

Chronicles: Volume I. New York: Simon & Schuster, 2004.

Lyrics, 1962–1985. New York: Alfred A. Knopf, 1985.

Lyrics, 1962–2001. New York: Simon & Schuster, 2004.

Mondo Scripto. London: Halcyon Gallery, 2018.

Tarantula. London: MacGibbon & Kee, 1971; New York: St. Martin's, 1994.

The Lyrics, 1961–2012. New York: Simon & Schuster, 2016.

The Nobel Lecture. New York: Simon & Schuster, 2017.

Ellison, J., ed. *Younger Than That Now: The Collected Interviews with Bob Dylan*. New York: Thunder's Mouth Press, 2004.

Francis, Richard. *Why Bob Dylan Matters*. New York: HarperCollins, 2017.

Gates, David. "Dylan Revisited," *Newsweek*, October 5, 1997. www .newsweek.com/dylan-revisited-174056.

Gilmore, Mikal. "Bob Dylan Unleashed," *Rolling Stone*, September 27, 2012.

Goldman, Albert. *Elvis*. New York: Viking, 1981.

The Lives of John Lennon. New York: William Morrow and Co., 1988.

Goodman, Fred. *The Mansion on the Hill: Dylan, Young, Geffen, Springsteen, and the Head-on Collision of Rock and Commerce*. New York: Vintage, 1997.

Gray, Michael, ed. *The Bob Dylan Encyclopedia*. New York: Continuum, 2006.

Song and Dance Man III: The Art of Bob Dylan. London: Continuum, 2000.

Griffin, Sid. *Shelter from the Storm: Bob Dylan's Rolling Thunder Years*. London: Jawbone, 2010.

Hajdu, David. *Positively Fourth Street: The Life and Times of Joan Baez, Bob Dylan, Mimi Fariña, and Richard Fariña*. New York: Picador, 2011.

Hampton, Timothy. *Bob Dylan's Poetics: How the Songs Work*. New York: Zone Books, 2019.

Hampton, Wayne. *Guerrilla Minstrels: John Lennon, Joe Hill, Woody Guthrie, Bob Dylan*. Knoxville: University of Tennessee Press, 1986.

Harcourt, Esther and Jane Quin. "Bertolt Brecht and Bob Dylan: Influence and Identity." PhD diss., Victoria University of Wellington, 2006.

Harvey, Todd. *The Formative Dylan: Transmission and Stylistic Influences, 1961–1963*. Lanham, MD: Scarecrow Press, 2001.

Hedin, Benjamin, ed. *Studio A: The Bob Dylan Reader*. New York: W.W. Norton, 2004.

Heylin, Clinton. *Behind the Shades*. London: Viking, 1991.

Behind the Shades: Take Two. London: Viking, 2001.

Behind the Shades: The 20th Anniversary Edition. London: Faber & Faber, 2011.

Bob Dylan: Behind the Shades: The Biography – Take Two. New York: Viking, 2000.

Bob Dylan: Behind the Shades Revisited. New York: Harper Collins, 2001.

A Life in Stolen Moments: Bob Dylan Day by Day: 1941–1995. New York: Simon & Schuster, 1996.

Revolution in the Air: The Songs of Bob Dylan, 1957–1973. Chicago: Chicago Review Press, 2009.

Still on the Road: The Songs of Bob Dylan, 1974–2006. Chicago: Chicago Review Press, 2010.

Trouble in Mind: Bob Dylan's Gospel Years: What Really Happened. New York: Lesser Gods, 2017.

Hinchey, John. *Like a Complete Unknown: The Poetry of Bob Dylan's Songs, 1961–1969*. Ann Arbor, MI: Stealing Home Press, 2002.

Hishmeh, Richard E. "Marketing Genius: The Friendship of Allen Ginsberg and Bob Dylan." *Journal of American Culture* 29, no. 4 (December 2006), pp. 395–404.

Kinney, David. *The Dylanologists: Adventures in the Land of Bob*. New York: Simon & Schuster, 2014.

Klein, Bethany, Leslie Meier, and Devon Powers. "Selling Out: Musicians, Autonomy and Compromise in the Digital Age." *Popular Music and Society* 40, no. 2 (2017), pp. 222–238.

LeBeau, Jennifer, dir. *Trouble No More: A Musical Film*. 2017.

Mai, Anne-Marie. *Bob Dylan. The Poet*. Odense: University Press of Southern Denmark, 2018.

Marcus, Greil. *Bob Dylan: Writings, 1968–2010*. New York: Public Affairs, 2010.
Invisible Republic, Bob Dylan's Basement Tapes. New York: Henry Holt, 1997.
Like a Rolling Stone: Bob Dylan at the Crossroads. New York: Public Affairs, 2005.
The Old, Weird America: The World of Bob Dylan's Basement Tapes. New York: Picador, 2011.
"A Trip to Hibbing High." *Daedalus* 136, no. 2 (Spring 2007), pp. 116–124.

Margotin, Philippe and Jean-Michel Guesdon. *Bob Dylan: All the Songs*. New York: Black Dog & Leventhal, 2015.

Marqusee, Mike. *Chimes of Freedom: The Politics of Bob Dylan's Art*. New York: New Press, 2003.
Wicked Messenger: Bob Dylan and the 1960s. New York: Seven Stories Press, 2011.

Marshall, Lee. *Bob Dylan: The Never Ending Star*. Cambridge: Polity, 2007.

Marshall, Scott M. *Bob Dylan: A Spiritual Life*. Washington, DC: BP Books, 2017.

McCarron, Andrew. *Light Come Shining: The Transformations of Bob Dylan*. New York: Oxford University Press, 2017.

McDougal, Dennis. *Dylan: The Biography*. New York: Turner, 2014.

McGregor, Craig, ed. *Bob Dylan: A Retrospective*. New York: William Morrow, 1972.

McPherson, Conor. *Girl from the North Country*. New York: TCG Books, 2017.

Meier, Leslie. *Popular Music as Promotion: Music and Branding in the Digital Age*. Cambridge: Polity, 2017.

Mellers, Wilfred. *A Darker Shade of Pale: A Backdrop to Bob Dylan*. New York: Oxford University Press, 1984.

Negus, Keith. *Bob Dylan*. Bloomington: Indiana University Press, 2008.
"Bob Dylan's Phonographic Imagination." *Popular Music* 29, no. 2 (May 2010), pp. 213–228.

O'Brien, James. "Bob Dylan's Fugitive Writings: Selected Poetry, Prose, and Playscript 1963–64." PhD diss., Boston University, 2012.

Orr, Jay, ed. *Dylan, Cash, and the Nashville Cats: A New Music City*. Nashville: Country Music Foundation Press, 2015.

Powers, Devon. *Writing the Record: The* Village Voice *and the Birth of Rock Criticism.* Amherst, MA: University of Massachusetts Press, 2013.

Ricks, Christopher. *Dylan's Visions of Sin.* New York: ECCO, 2003.

Rigovoy, Seth. *Bob Dylan: Prophet, Mystic, Poet.* New York: Scribner, 2009.

Riley, Tim. *Hard Rain: A Dylan Commentary.* New York: Vintage Books, 1993.

Robertson, Robbie. *Testimony.* New York: Three River Press, 2016.

Robertson, Robbie, Jim Guerinot, Sebastian Robertson, and Jared Levine. *Legends, Icons and Rebels: Music That Changed the World.* Plattsburgh, NY: Tundra Books, 2013.

Rosenbaum, Roy. "Bob Dylan: The Playboy Interview." *Playboy*, November 1978.

Rotolo, Suze. *A Freewheelin' Time: A Memoir of Greenwich Village in the Sixties.* New York: Broadway Books, 2008.

Russell, Melinda. "Dinkytown Before Dylan: Gene Bluestein and the Minneapolis Folk Music Revival of the 1950s." *Minnesota History* 65, no. 8 (Winter 2017–2018), pp. 289–301.

Scaduto, Anthony. *Bob Dylan.* London: Helter Skelter Publishing, 1996.
   Bob Dylan: An Intimate Biography. New York: Grosset and Dunlap, 1971.

Scorsese, Martin, dir. *No Direction Home: Bob Dylan, A Martin Scorsese Film.* Paramount Pictures, 2005.

Shank, Barry. "'That Wild Mercury Sound': Bob Dylan and the Illusion of American Culture." *boundary 2* 29, no. 1 (2002), pp. 97–123.

Sheehy, Colleen J. and Thomas Swiss, eds. *Highway 61 Revisited: Bob Dylan's Road from Minnesota to the World.* Minneapolis: University of Minnesota Press, 2009.

Shelton, Robert. *No Direction Home.* New York: Beech Tree Books, 1986.
   No Direction Home: The Life and Music of Bob Dylan, ed. Elizabeth Thomson and Patrick Humphries. Milwaukee: Backbeat Books, 2011.

Shepard, Sam. *Rolling Thunder Logbook.* New York: Penguin, 1997.

Sloman, Larry. *On the Road with Bob Dylan.* New York: Three Rivers Press, 2002.

Sounes, Howard. *Down the Highway: The Life of Bob Dylan.* New York: Grove Press, 2001.

Spitz, Bob. *Dylan: A Biography.* New York: McGraw-Hill, 1988.

Thomas, Richard F. *Why Bob Dylan Matters.* New York: Dey Street Books, 2017.

Thomson, Elizabeth and David Gutman, eds. *The Dylan Companion.* New York: Da Capo, 2001.

Trager, Oliver. *Keys to the Rain: The Definitive Bob Dylan Encyclopedia.* New York: Billboard Books, 2004.

Van Ronk, Dave and Elijah Wald. *The Mayor of MacDougal Street: A Memoir.* Cambridge, MA: DaCapo Press, 2005.

Wald, Elijah. *Dylan Goes Electric: Newport, Seeger, Dylan, and the Night that Split the Sixties.* New York: Dey St. Press, 2015.

Wilentz, Sean. *Bob Dylan in America.* New York: Anchor, 2011.
   "Woody Guthrie and Bob Dylan Hit Manhattan." *American Music Review* 42, no. 1 (Fall 2012), pp. 1–5.

Williams, Paul. *Bob Dylan, Performing Artist 1960–1973.* London: Xanadu, 1990.

Wolff, Daniel. *Grown-Up Anger: The Connected Mysteries of Bob Dylan, Woody Guthrie, and the Calumet Massacre of 1913*. New York: Harper, 2017.

Yaffe, David. *Bob Dylan: Like a Complete Unknown*. New Haven: Yale University Press, 2001.

"Tangled Up in Keys: Why Does Bob Dylan Namecheck Alicia Keys in His New Song?" Slate.com August 11, 2006.

Secondary Works

Baym, Nancy. *Playing to the Crowd: Musicians, Audiences, and the Intimate Work of Connection*. New York: NYU Press, 2018.

Bennett, Andy and Steve Waksman, eds. *The Sage Handbook of Popular Music*. Thousand Oaks, CA: Sage, 2015.

Boyer, Horace Clarence. *The Golden Age of Gospel*. Champaign, IL: University of Illinois Press, 2000.

Brackett, David, ed. *The Pop, Rock, and Soul Reader: Histories and Debates*, 3rd edn. New York: Oxford University Press, 2014.

Chapple, Steve and Reebee Garofalo. *Rock 'n' Roll is Here to Pay: The History and Politics of the Music Industry*. Chicago: Nelson Hall, 1977.

Ching, Barbara. *Wrong's What I Do Best: Hard Country Music and Contemporary Culture*. New York: Oxford University Press, 2001.

Cohen, Ronald D. *Folk Music: The Basics*. New York: Routledge, 2006.

 Work and Sing: A History of Occupational and Labor Union Songs in the United States. Crockett, CA: Carquinez Press, 2010.

 ed. *"Wasn't That a Time!" Firsthand Accounts of the Folk Music Revival*. Metuchen, NJ: Scarecrow Press, 1995.

Cohen, Ronald D. and Rachel Donaldson. *Roots of the Revival: American & British Folk Music in the 1960s*. Urbana: University of Illinois Press, 2014.

Cohen, Ronald D. and Will Kaufman. *Singing For Peace: Antiwar Songs in American History*. Boulder, CO: Paradigm, 2015.

DeCurtis, Anthony, James Henke, and Holly George-Warren, eds. *The Rolling Stone Illustrated History of Rock & Roll*. New York: Random House.

Doggett, Peter. *Are You Ready for the Country: Elvis, Dylan, Parsons and the Roots of Country Rock*. New York: Penguin, 2000.

 There's a Riot Going On: Revolutionaries, Rock Stars, and the Rise and Fall of the 60s. New York: Grove Atlantic, 2008.

Dolar, Mladen. *A Voice and Nothing More*. Cambridge, MA: MIT Press, 2006.

Frith, Simon, Will Straw, and John Street, eds. *The Cambridge Companion to Pop and Rock*. Cambridge: Cambridge University Press, 2001.

Hamilton, Jack. *Just around Midnight: Rock and Roll and the Racial Imagination*. Cambridge, MA: Harvard University Press, 2016.

Heilbut, Anthony. *The Gospel Sound: Good News and Bad Times*. New York: Simon & Schuster, 1971.

Jackson, Mark Allan, ed. *The Honky Tonk on the Left: Progressive Thought in Country Music*. Amherst: University of Massachusetts Press, 2018.

Kot, Greg. *I'll Take You There: Mavis Staples, the Staple Singers, and the Music that Shaped the Civil Rights Era*. New York: Simon & Schuster, 2014.

Levitan, Stuart D. *Madison in the Sixties*. Madison: Wisconsin Historical Society Press, 2018.

Lipsitz, George. *Time Passages: Collective Memory and American Popular Culture*. Minneapolis: University of Minnesota Press, 1990.

Lott, Eric. *Love and Theft: Blackface Minstrelsy and the American Working Class*. Oxford: Oxford University Press, 1993.

Lynskey, Dorian. *33 Revolutions Per Minute: A History of Protest Songs*. London: Faber & Faber, 2010.

Malone, Bill C. *Singing Cowboys and Musical Mountaineers: Southern Culture and the Roots of Country Music*, 2nd edn. Athens: University of Georgia Press, 2003.

Marcus, Greil. *Mystery Train: Images of America in Rock 'n' Roll Music*, 6th edn. New York: Plume, 2015.

Mellers, Wilfred. *Music in a New Found Land: Themes and Developments in the History of American Music*. New York: Oxford, 1987.

Pecknold, Diane. *The Selling Sound: The Rise of the Country Music Industry*. Durham: Duke University Press, 2007.

Petrus, Stephen and Ronald D. Cohen. *Folk City: New York and the American Folk Music Revival*. New York City: Oxford University Press, 2015.

Reuss, Richard A. and Joanne C. Reuss. *American Folk Music and Left-Wing Politics, 1927–1957*. Lanham, MD: Scarecrow Press, 2000.

Shumway, David R. *Rock Star: The Making of Musical Icons from Elvis to Springsteen*. Baltimore: Johns Hopkins University Press, 2014.

Sullivan, James. *Which Side Are You On? 20th Century American History in 100 Protest Songs*. New York: Oxford University Press, 2019.

Terkel, Studs. *And They All Sang*. London: Granta Books, 2005.

Warner, Simon. *Text and Drugs and Rock 'n' Roll: The Beats and Rock Culture*. New York: Bloomsbury, 2015.

Werner, Craig. *A Change is Gonna Come: Music, Race, and the Soul of America*. Edinburgh: Payback Press, 2000.

Williams, Paul. *The* Crawdaddy! *Book: Writings (and Images) from the Magazine of Rock*. Milwaukee, WI: Hal Leonard, 2002.

Index